The History Of The Alison Or Allison Family In Europe And America, 1135 To 1893: Giving An Account Of The Family In Scotland, England, Ireland

Leonard Allison Morrison

THE HISTORY

OF THE

ALISON OR ALLISON FAMILY

IN EUROPE AND AMERICA,

A. D. 1135 TO 1893;

GIVING AN ACCOUNT OF THE FAMILY IN SCOTLAND,
ENGLAND, IRELAND, AUSTRALIA, CANADA,
AND THE UNITED STATES.

With Twenty-five Illustrated Pages, Embracing Engravings of Forty-five
Faces and Two Residences.

By LEONARD ALLISON MORRISON, A. M.,

Author of "History of the Morison or Morrison Family;" "History of Windham
in New Hampshire;" "Rambles in Europe: with Historical Facts relating to
Scotch-American Families; Gathered in Scotland and in the North of Ireland;" "Among the Scotch-Irish; A Tour in Seven Countries;" "Lineage and
Biographies of the Norris Family;" "Supplement to the History of Windham in New Hampshire;" and "History and Proceedings of the Celebration
of the 150th Anniversary of the Incorporation of (the Scotch settlement of)
Windham, New Hampshire, Held June 9, 1892."

"ET PATRIBUS ET POSTERITATI."

BOSTON, MASS.:
PUBLISHED BY DAMRELL & UPHAM,
THE OLD CORNER BOOK-STORE.
1893.

Leonard A. Morrison

Dedication.

—

To my Kindred and Clansmen,

and to the

Members of the Scotch Race, Under All Skies and in Every Clime,

This History of

An Ancient and Honorable Scotch Family

Is Dedicated by

Leonard Allison Morrison.

My task is done!
From these harvest sheaves,
Garnered with infinite pains,
Others can take the golden grain,
And cast the chaff away.

LIST OF ILLUSTRATIONS.

TABLE OF CONTENTS.

HERALDRY.

THE ALLISON ARMS, CRESTS, AND MOTTOES.

From FAIRBAIRN'S BOOK OF CRESTS OF THE FAMILIES OF GREAT BRITAIN AND IRELAND. A new edition, revised and brought down to 1892. (This book contains illustrations of crests here described.)

Alison, Scotland, a tree ppr., with a bell hung on the branches on each side. *Crescit sub pondere virtus,*

Alison, Scotland, an oak tree ppr., with a weight hanging on each side. *Crescit sub pondere virtus.*

Alison, Scotland, an eagle's head erased ppr. *Vincit veritas.*

Alison, Rev. A., Scotland, an eagle's head erased ppr. *Vincit veritas.*

Alison, Major-General Sir Archibald, K. C. B. 2nd Bart., same crest and motto.

Alison and Allison, a falcon's head erased ppr. *Vincit veritas.*

Allison, Scotland, a falcon's head erased. *Vincit veritas.*

Allison, a pheasant holding in the dexter claw a key, and in the beak an ear of barley ppr.

Allison, Scotland, an eagle's head erased ppr. *Vincit veritas.*

Allison, Colonel James John, D. L., J. P., of "Beaufront," Roker, Sunderland, uses a peacock in pride ppr. *Vincit veritas.*

FROM BURKE'S GENERAL ARMORY.

Allison, Sa., a fesse engr. betw. three talbots pass. ar. Crest—An eagle's head erased ppr. Motto: *Vincit veritas.*

Allison, Ar., an inescutcheon gu. Crest—A pheasant holding in the dexter foot a key, and in his beak an ear of barley ppr.

Allison, Sa., a fesse engr. betw. three talbots pass. ar. surmounted by a bend sinister.

Allison (described in the Visitations as having been settled for five generations at Yardsley Hall, co. Cambridge). Ar., a fesse gu. betw. three blackbirds within a bordure of the second. Crest— A peacock ppr.

Allison (Roker Sunderland, co. Durham; Col. John James Allison, commanding 2nd Durham militia, J. P., D. L., eldest son of James Allison, esquire of Undercliff, same co.). Ar., a fesse gu. betw. three blackbirds ppr. a bordure of the second. Crest—A peacock in his pride ppr. Motto—*Vincit veritas.*

The motto *Vincit veritas* means "Truth prevails."
Crescit sub pondere virtus means "Virtue thrives under oppression."

In addition to what is here given relating to *Arms*, see p. 5.

THE ELLISON ARMS, CRESTS, AND MOTTOES.

From FAIRBAIRN'S BOOK OF CRESTS. '

Ellison, a griffin's head erased ppr., collared or.
Ellison, Scotland, a cross crosslet fitched gu.
Ellison, a lion passant gardant, holding in his dexter paw an anchor.
Ellison, a greyhound sa.
Ellison—Macartney, John William, Esq., Barrister-at-Law, J. P. of the Palace, Clogher co., Tyrone, Ireland: (1) A cubit arm erect, the hand grasping a rose-branch in flower all ppr. (for Macartney); (2) A buck's head erased ppr., charged on the neck with a trefoil slipped vert (for Ellison) *Stimulat, sed ornat,—Spe gaudeo.*
Ellison, Durh., an eagle's head erased or.
Ellison, an eagle's head erased per fess or and gu., murally gorged az.
Ellison, Carr,—Ralph, Esquire of Hedgeley, Northumb., and Dunstanhill, Durh.: (1) An eagle's head erased or, gorged with a collar vair, holding in the beak a branch of three roses gu., leaved and slipped ppr. (for Ellison); (2) A lion's head erased or, in front thereof a demi-Catherine wheel az. (for Carr.) *Nec te quaesiveris extra.*

From BURKE'S GENERAL ARMORY.

Ellison, per pale gu. and vert an eagle displ. or. Crest, An eagle's head erased per fesse or and gu. gorged with a mural coronet az.
Ellison, Ar., a chev. gu. betw. three griffins' heads; erased sa. Crest, a greyhound sa.
Ellison (Boultham Hall, co. Lincoln). Gu. a chev. or betw. three griffins' heads ar. Crest, a griffin's head erased ppr. collared or. Motto: *Spem sequimur.*

Ellison (Scotland).   Per bend gu. and or a fleur-de-lis in bend sinister counterchanged.

Ellison (Hebburn, co. Durham).   Gu. a chev. or betw. three eagles' heads erased ar.   Crest, an eagle's head erased or.

Ellison (Rotherham, co. York.) Gu. a chev. betw. three eagles' heads erased or.

Ellison (Carr-Ellison, exemplified to Ralph Carr, Esq., of Hedgeley, co. Northumberland and Dunstanhill, co. pal. Durham, upon his assuming the additional name of Ellison by royal license, 1871). Quarterly, 1st and 4th, gu. a chev. vair cottised or betw. three eagles' heads erased of the last, for Ellison 2nd and 3d ar. within two bendlets az. an estoile betw. two lions' heads sa. the whole betw. three Cornish Choughs ppr. for Carr, Crests, Ellison.   An eagle's head erased or gorged with a collar vair, holding in the beak a branch of three roses gu. leaved and slipped ppr.   Carr: A lion's head erased or, in front thereof a demi-Catherine wheel az.   Motto: *Nec te quaesiveris extra.*

TRANSLATION OF MOTTOES.

Stimulat, sed ornat.   "It stimulates, but it adorns."

Spe gaudeo.   "I rejoice in hope."

Nec te quaesiveris extra.   "Do not seek thyself outside of thyself."

Spem sequimur.   "We follow hope."

In addition to what is printed here relating to the Ellisons, see pp. 5, 39–42, 120–122, 242–252.

INTRODUCTION.

This work is vastly more comprehensive in its scope than was intended at the commencement of its preparation. The stream has been traced to its fountain, the river to its source, and the Allisons to their homes in Scotland of many centuries ago. There, among its moors, its mountains, and its glens, they have lived till the present, while collateral lines of this ancient stock, about whom lingers the love of the freedom of Scotland's mountains, struck out into other lands, have enlarged and become strong, numerous, prosperous, and vigorous. The Allisons have won homes and reputations not only in Scotland, but in England, Ireland, Australia, South America, Canada, and in nearly every state of the great American commonwealth, the United States.

A fascination, deep and abiding, clings to the ancient home of the family at Loupe, Argyleshire, and at Cairnduff, Avondale, Lanarkshire, Scotland. The matter relating to those homes and to those lines of the family are of preëminent value and absorbing interest. By the publication of this volume all of this information and history is permanently preserved.

The Allison family, taken as a whole, is strong and intellectual. In the Fatherland some of its members were martyrs for the "Solemn League and Covenant," and elsewhere contended, even unto death, for religious freedom, while others continued the struggle in Ireland, and later crossed the ocean and maintained the finally successful battle on American soil.

This family has loved church and state and learning. They helped found a government of, and for, and by the people. There have been many college graduates. The name Allison is found frequently in the catalogues of both European and American universities. Lawyers, physicians, ministers of the Gospel, senators, and other men high in the civil or military service of the state are among those of this stock.

This is mentioned, not in a spirit of unwise laudation of a family but as a historical fact, and that in the future, when those of other generations shall read this and see that their predecessors and relatives, who will then belong to "a buried generation," loved the school, the church, the state, it may stimulate them to higher deeds, influence them to nobler lives.

This work was undertaken to gratify my own curiosity to know all the accessible facts relating to the origin, history, and life and death of my ancestor, Charter Samuel Allison, of Scotch blood, of Londonderry, New Hampshire, together with that of his widely scattered descendants. The place selected for his abode in the New World became widely noted as the home of a stalwart people.

There is no locality, in New Hampshire, whose early local history has so deep an interest, or about which clings so much of fascination, as that of the *original* township of Londonderry, embracing the present towns of Windham, Derry, Londonderry, and a part of Hudson and Salem. Not that its soil was fertile, or that dormant riches lay in ground, forest, rock, or waters, for in none of these was the secret of its strong hold on the minds and in the hearts of antiquarians, scholars, and the general public. It was in a higher source, in an element of greater value, power, and influence, than in any or in all of these combined. It was in the inhabitants themselves. The first settlers were a peculiar people, and they, or their fathers, were *twice* exiles; first, from Scotland, their Fatherland, to the "green fields of Erin," which at Londonderry and the Boyne water they helped to save to King William and Protestantism in 1688–'89; second, to the wilderness wilds of Londonderry, N. H., in 1719. They were of Scotch blood, some of them were of Scotch birth, some were "accidentally born" in Ireland. Strong and rugged in their mental characteristics, having great courage and tenacity of purpose, they were valiant colonists of a frontier, capable of subduing a wilderness, of founding and building a state, and leaving the impress of their willing hands, strong minds, and valiant deeds, in the settlement they founded, the state they benefited, and in illustrious descendants who have worthily filled the higher positions in the community, the state, and the nation. Sixteen men with their families composed the advance guard of the infant colony. In 1718 they came from the north of Ireland, part if not all from the parish of Aghadowey, county of Londonderry, some eight miles from Coleraine, and forty miles from the city of Londonderry. Samuel Allison, previously mentioned, was one of that stalwart company.

This work, as such labor always does, fascinated me. It expanded greatly. In my investigations other important, equally large, and equally respectable branches of Alisons or Allisons were found, their history and genealogy procured. This includes the lines of Allisons in Orange and Rockland counties, New York, with those numerous ones in

Pennsylvania and in the southern states, together with those of Nova Scotia, Ireland, and Scotland. In fact, I have included in the pages of this book *all* branches of this Scotch family, wherever scattered, of which I could obtain information. The record is as full as the facts given to me could make it.

In the preparation of this work all known sources of information have been laid under contribution. Libraries have yielded their treasures; the offices of register of deeds and the offices of probate in many states have given of their rich stores; tombstones and family registers, church records, and town records, and many other sources have answered to demands upon them.

The gathering of the records of the family, with other facts collected in Scotland, England, Ireland, Australia, and the British Provinces in America, has been attended with much effort, expense, and delay, but it is of great historical value and will be of interest to the family and general reader in the present and future. These records link in one harmonious whole the various branches of the Allison family. Many of the long diverging lines converge once more and form a union. Each Allison can clasp the hand of every other Allison as that of a friend, or relative, or clansman.

ARRANGEMENT.

The arrangement is simple, and similar to that usually adopted in genealogical works.

The pedigree of each head of a family goes back to the emigrating or first known ancestor. The latter is indicated by the numeral 1, meaning the *first* known generation, and so following down the line, with the ancestor's name marked by a numeral figure denoting the generation in which the person stands.

On the left margins of the pages consecutive numbers are used. Heads of families, as a rule, appear with *two* numbers, first as a child, with number on the left, while on the right in brackets is the number where the person will be found as the head of a family. Turning to that number will be found the person with numbers reversed. At the right of the name in parentheses will be the number of the person as a child. By looking at the numbers back and forth the plan will be apparent.

ACKNOWLEDGMENTS.

I am indebted to Judge Nathaniel Holmes of Cambridge, Mass., for information of the Holmes family; to the late B. B. Whittemore,

Esq., of Nashua, N. H., for valuable records and facts; to William W. Moore, Esq., of Scranton, Penn., for furnishing records of the Moore, Shepard, McAfee, and Atwood families. The record of the descendants of Lieutenant Samuel Morrison and his wife, Martha Allison, are with slight changes taken from my published works, the "History of the Morison or Morrison Family," and "History of Windham in New Hampshire."

Rev. Charles E. Allison of Yonkers, N. Y., and his brother, Howard Allison, Esq., an attorney in New York, N. Y., have aided me greatly in collecting history of the Allisons of Orange county, N. Y., and by securing engravings of them for this work.

William O. Allison, Esq., of Englewood, N. J., of the Rockland county, N. Y., Allisons, has manifested his interest in many ways and by financial aid of this undertaking. George F. Allison, Esq., of New York, N. Y., has also aided materially in the publication of this work, and by furnishing valuable memoranda.

Rev. David Allison, D. D., President of Allison college, Sackville, New Brunswick, has furnished most valuable and interesting facts of the Nova Scotia Allisons.

Rev. Archibald Alison of Prestwick, Scotland, has given me valuable records.

To all these, and to others who have furnished information or portraits of themselves or others, I give my warmest thanks.

My love for literary work, and my strong desire to develop and perpetuate family, local, and general history have been potent factors in prompting me to prepare and send this work forth to the world. It is largely a labor of love. The widely scattered copies of this book will eventually be in all prominent parts of the English speaking world, will be in the larger public libraries, and will thus perpetuate this "History of the Alison or Allison Family in Europe and America."

This volume is now committed to my relatives of the Allison family, to its allied families, to all lovers of historical and genealogical lore, and to the general public. I trust that it will be of worth to them and that it will inspire them all with higher aims in life and a more loyal appreciation of the virtues of those whose lives are recorded herein, and that the fleeting years will not detract but add to the value of this historical record.

LEONARD ALLISON MORRISON.

WINDHAM, N. H. (Canobie Lake, N. H., P. O.)
    October 10, 1893.

HISTORY OF THE ALISONS.

CHAPTER I.

Various Theories.—True Origin of the Name of the Scotch Allisons.—Its Orthography.—Most Frequent Scottish Names. Old Divisions of Scotland and England.—Thomas Carlyle's Statement.

ORIGIN OF THE NAME OF ALLISON.

Robert Ferguson, M. P., F. S. A., and F. S. A. Scotland, in his "Surnames as a Science," London: 1883, pp. 204–206, is Women's Names, "Alice, Alicia, Eliza, Adeliza, Alison. Alice properly a man's name, and Eliza its proper feminine."

He derives these names from Anglo-Saxon Adelgis (masculine) and Adelgisa (feminine), whence come Aliza, Eliza, but not Eizabeth (the Latin form), the Hebrew form being Elischeba.

He cites for this the *Liber Vitæ* of Durham, "in which we can trace the changes that have taken place in Adelgisa since the first noble lady of that name laid her gift upon the altar. First we find it contracted into Adeliza, and then, from about the twelfth century, into Aaliza and Aliza, the latter name being henceforward rather a common one. The former of these two contracted forms, Adeliza, though not a name in common use, is one still given to the daughters of certain of our noble families ; the latter form, Aliza, I take to be the origin of our Eliza. (The initial vowel is of no account, the ancient name beginning indifferently with A or E, and Alice in some families appearing as Ellice)."

"About the beginning of the fifteenth century another Christian name for women, Alison, begins to make its appearance in the *Liber Vitæ*. This name, however, I take to be from an entirely different origin. There is an old Frankish woman's name, Alesinda, Elesind, Alesint, of the eighth century, from which, dropping the final *d*, it would naturally come, and which is derived from Grimm from Gothic *Alja*, Alius (in the probable sense of stranger or foreigner), and *Sind* in the sense of companion or attendant."

From the foregoing, if the theories of Mr. Ferguson are correct, it cannot but strike the reader with what exceeding ease (the initial vowel being of "no account") the same name could be written Alison, Elison, Allison, Ellison.

Charles W. Bardsley, M. A., in his choice work, "Our English Surnames, their Sources and Significations," London, cites these instances:

Alan (v. Allen) Alan fil.   Warin.
Alanson (v. Allinson), William Alynson, Thomas Allason.
Alison, Ric. fil. Alise, *A*.   Goselin fil.   Alice, *A*.
Alisceon de Tuxforth, W. 2.   Alison Gelyot, H.

These with other instances are cited.

In the text he says,—"Out of many forms to be found in every early roll, those of 'Ellis,' 'Elys,' 'Elice,' 'Ellice,' 'Elyas,' 'Helyas,' and the diminutive 'Eliot,' or 'Elliot,' seem to have been the most familiar. Numberless are the surnames sprung from it. It is thus that we get our 'Ellises' and 'Ellices,' our 'Ellsons' and 'Ellisons,' our 'Elkins' and 'Elkinsons,' our 'Elcocks' and 'Ellcocks,' and our 'Ellicots,' 'Elliots,' and 'Elliotsons.' In the North 'Alis' seems to have gained the supremacy. Thus it is we have our many 'Allisons' or 'Alisons.'" In a note he says,—"We cannot but believe, however, that in many instances these two are but the offspring of 'Alice,' at this period one of the most popular of female names. Nor must we forget that Allison was itself used as a personal name, that being the Norman-French pet name of Alise, after the fashion of Marion, Louison, Beaton," &c.

We are all acquainted with the "Alison" of the "Canterbury Tales,"—

> "This Alison answered; Who is there
> That knocketh so? I warrant him a thefe."

And again he says,—"With regard to 'Alis' and 'Elis,' and Alison and Elison recorded in the text, I may remind the reader that A and E were all but convertible names with the Normans."

Judge Nathaniel Holmes, of Cambridge, Mass., who has given the subject attention, says,—"I have little doubt that this use of A and E is a mere variation in the spelling consequent upon a difference of pronunciation. Further, I am inclined to think that the two names 'Allan,' 'Allenson,' Allinson, Allison, 'Ellis,' 'Alice,' Ellison,' 'Elison,' and perhaps 'Alison,' arose in two or more different places, among distinct and unrelated families, though originating as surnames in the same manner, viz., by adding *son* to the former Christian or 'personal' name, as Allen'son, Alan'son, and Alice's or Ellis'son. This is shown in the instances cited by Mr. Bardsley, Ric-fil. Alise, Goselin fil. Alice. So, also, in Alanson (v. Allinson) we have Brien fil. Alan, as also Allen'sson, perhaps, whence probably Alanson, Allinson, Alynson, Allason, Allison."

Henry Brougham Guppy, M. B., Edinburgh, F. R. S. E., F. R., Scottish Geographical Soc., &c., London, 1890, says in his " Homes of Family Names in Great Britain," that "Allen, —from Alan, a common personal name at the time of the Norman Conquest. Widely distributed, but excepting Northumberland, rare in the Northern counties beyond the Humber and the Mersey, and infrequent also in the four south-western counties of England; and the principal centres of the name seem at present to be in Derbyshire, Hants, Leicestershire, Rutlandshire, Lincolnshire, and Suffolk. Allan is a frequent form across the Scottish borders, and is especially characteristic of the south of Scotland; it extends into Northumberland, where Allen also occurs." Page 23.

The derivation of the name might be thus: Allen, Allenson, Allinson, Allison. He says,—" Allinson was a name well known in York (county) in the 17th century. William Allenson, draper, who received the honor of knighthood and represented that city in Parliament, was Lord Mayor of York in 1633 and 1655."

Rev. Archibald Alison writes, Oct. 23, 1892: " In a 'History of the Norman People and their Descendants in the British Dominions and the United States of America,' published in London, 1874, the writer derives the Allisons from Bernard de Alencon, who held several Lordships from Hervey de Bourges, Suffolk, in England. He alludes to a castle of this name, viz., Castle Alencon, which belonged to one of the sons of Alan, Duke of Brittany of the 8th century, a castle which is still to be seen, although now in ruins. The origin of these Allisons shows that they are *Allansons*, or sons of Alan. These Allisons are quite different from those of Avondale, Scotland, for the Allisons there were originally Allisters or Alexanders of Loupe, Scotland."

THE TRUE ORIGIN OF THE NAME OF THE SCOTCH ALISONS OR ALLISONS.

The studied and plausible theories of different and able writers, as expressed in the preceding pages, in relation to the origin of the name Alison, are interesting and instructive to the student and general reader. But while fascinating, they fail utterly in giving the correct origin of the Scotch Alison name, as will be shown at length in a following chapter on the Allisons of Scotland. It is a fact beyond doubt that *Alison* comes from *Alister*, or *Alexander*, and that the Alisons are off-shoots of the famous clan of MacAlister. (See chapter III.)

The following is from Rev. Archibald Alison, of Prestwick, Scotland :

MEANING AND ORIGIN OF THE NAME ALISON.

" There are some who maintain that almost all the roots of the Celtic and Saxon Languages are from the Hebrew. These are inclined to believe that this is the case with the name Alison. Deriving it from the Hebrew, then it signifies ' Son of my God.' But there are others who take a different view, and maintain that the name merely signifies ' Son of Alex.' Among the Highlanders of Scotland it has been common from very ancient times to denominate the descendants of any noted chief by the prefix ' Mac,' a prefix which signifies ' Son.' Hence we read of the McDonalds or descendants of Donald, the McArthurs or descendants of Arthur, and McAlisters or descendants of Alister. On the other hand, amid the Lowlanders of Scotland, it has been common to use an affix instead of a prefix to denominate the descendants of any chief. Hence we have the Donaldsons or descendants of Donald, the Williamsons or descendants of William, and the Cuthbertsons or descendants of Cuthbert.

This we think is the origin of the Alisons or descendants of Alister.

In ancient times, among the Scotch Highlanders, it was customary to have only one name. We read, for example, of Somerled, the king of the isles, of Dugald of Lorn, and of Alexander of Loupe. And who was Dugald but the chief of the Macdougalds, and who was Alexander but the chief of the McAlisters? Here it may be mentioned that Alister is the same with Alexander; and in the history of the Highland clans the one name is often given in the room of the other. Indeed, the name of Alexander is frequently mentioned as Ales, Aless, Alles, Alex, Alick, Alister, Alistaer, and even the Scotch Elshender is the same. Hales in Germany is the same also. Alison, therefore, signifies Alleeson or Alexson, in the same way as Allanson signifies the son of Allan, a name which is of Norman origin, and sometimes found in England, but not much in Scotland."

ORTHOGRAPHY OF THE NAME ALISON, ALLISON.

The names Alison, Allison, Alinson, Allinson, and of Elison, Ellison, Elissen, Ellissen, Ellysen, are found thus spelled in the early history of some branches of the present Allison family. They are interchangeably mixed. The name was often spelled Ellison, and Allison, when referring to the same individual. Allison seems to have been more acceptable, and the descendants of some of the early Ellisons now write their name Allison.

In ancient records names were often spelled phonetically, or according to their sound, and also, according to the taste, knowledge, or *lack* of knowledge of the writer. It has been found spelled Allison, Alison, Aleson, Alleson, Alason, Allason, Allisone, besides in the manner previously given. Alison seems to be the earlier form adopted, and the more correct orthography.

In a letter from Rev. Archibald Alison, of Prestwick, Scotland, dated August 11, 1892, he says,—"The spelling of Alison differs in various families that are nearly related. We have it Alison, Allison, Ellison, Allason, and even Allanson, but the last among none of our relatives."

EARLY PROMINENT ALLISONS.

Robert Allison was member of Parliament from Jedburgh, Scotland, in 1585, and his supposed father, William Allison, was a representative in Parliament in 1542.

THE ARMS.

The armorial bearings, as given by William Allison, of Bowmanville, Can. (for which I will not vouch), are a demigod with a drawn sword on the crest, with the words encircled, "Ready aye Ready."

MOST FREQUENT SCOTTISH NAMES.

In the list of homes of English and Welsh names is the following, given by Henry B. Guppy: "Allinson, Allison, Durham, 20; Yorkshire, North and East Riding, 25."

"Ellison, Lancashire, 13; Wiltshire, 22; Yorkshire, West Riding, 10."

In his list of most frequent Scottish names, "Allan 82, most characteristic of Southern Scotland." The foregoing numbers represent the frequency of occurrence in every ten thousand of the population in all Scotland; in England the numbers represent the relative frequency of occurrence in the *several counties* in each ten thousand of the population.

OLD DIVISIONS OF SCOTLAND AND ENGLAND.

"Up to the 10th century, Scotland, as we know it, was divided into three parts: North of the Forth and the Clyde lay a hostile and foreign land, the abode of the Picts and Scots under an independent prince. South of these boundaries were the kingdoms of Cumbria and Northumbria, the former including a part of the ancient kingdom of Strath-Clyde, extending from the Clyde to the Morecombe Bay, and including the whole south-west of the present Scotland, with Cumberland and Westmoreland, the latter extending from the Forth to the Humber, and including the south-east quarter of the present Scotland, with Northumberland, Durham, Yorkshire (Eng.). We observe, therefore, that in these early times there was a middle or neutral region between the English and the Scots, a region which was for the most part claimed by the Southern king, more particularly Northumbria, which was English in its speech and laws. In the 10th or 11th century Scotland acknowledged the English supremacy, and in return received Cumbria in fief as well as Lothian, that part of Northumbria between the Forth and the Tweed, though it is said by some that this last was held by right of conquest. But Lothian remained English in laws, language, and manners. And the result of the cession was the great extension of the English influence. The strength of the Scottish kings lay in the English part of their dominions. Lothian, once on the border land, now became the centre of Scotland, and Edinburgh, its capital, became the northern focus of the Anglo-Norman civilization.

"In the latter part of the 12th century Cumbria was divided, England receiving the present shires of Cumberland and

Westmoreland. Since that time the boundary between the kingdoms has experienced but little change."

THE TRUE SCOTLAND.

Again, Mr. Guppy says,—"But the broad fact we have to deal with is this, that *true* Scotland, as indicated by the names, begins at the Forth and the Clyde. South of these limits, and extending across the English border as far as Yorkshire and Lancashire, lies a 'middle land,' neither ·purely English nor purely Scottish, and possessing its characteristic names, of which the most frequent are those terminating in *son*, and the names of the border tribes. In this 'middle land,' throng the Wilsons, the Thompsons and Thomsons, the Johnsons and Johnstons, the Gibsons, the Bells, the Grahams, the Elliots and Elliotts, the Turnbulls, the Robsons, the Richardsons, the Blairs, the Crawfords, the Dunlaps, the Douglases, the Armstrongs, the Findlays, and many others. The explanation of the origin of this middle or neutral region between England and Scotland is to be found in the history of the changes which have affected the boundaries between these two nations."

Upon this matter Judge Nathaniel Holmes, of Cambridge, Mass., says,—"Dr. Guppy does not notice that the earlier history of the races shows that this region of Scotland was occupied by the Anglo-Saxons and Danish invasions as far north as the Forth and the Clyde, at about the same dates as the north, east, and south-east parts of England were. This history, beginning with the 10th century, does indeed explain much, but it is not all, nor quite enough. First, the Roman dominion of the time of Agricola, in Britain, extended to the Forth and the Clyde, or, at least, the conquest of Roman armies; and, second, the Anglo-Saxon and Danish invasions and settlements in their time, about the 5th or 6th century, occupied that region, as they did the north of England. This fact, of course, and the succession of descent, may help to explain the identity of names in some measure, as well as the identity of race, with Anglo-Saxon England. But it is true that surnames did not come much into use anywhere in Great Britain till about the year A. D. 1000. It helps to explain how it was that, prior to the 10th century, English rule or English claim reached to the Forth and the Clyde. The Lowland people are, of course, in the main, Anglo-Saxon and Norman in race as well as in language. They are not Celtic."

THOMAS CARLYLE'S STATEMENT.

A letter of Thomas Carlyle, on July 19, 1841, in Reid's Life of Milnes (Lord Houghton), London, 1891, Vol. I, page 265, to R. M. Milnes, gives an account of his visit to Tynemouth, and says that he "admired the rugged energy of that population, and how completely Annandale Scotch they are. From the Humber to the Forth, still more from the Tyne to the Forth, I find no real distinction at all, except what John Knox introduced; it is all Scotch—Scotch in features and face, in character, in dialect and speech. You, too, if yon behave yourselves, shall be accounted Scotch! They are all Danes, these people; stalwart Normans, terrible sea-kings; are now terrible drainers of morasses, terrible spinners of yarn, coal borers, removers of mountains; a people terrible from the beginning. The windy Celts of Galloway, you see, not many miles from this, in the edge of Nithesdale."

The foregoing in relation to the derivation, significance, and orthography of the Allison name, together with the copious extracts from the admirable work of Henry Brougham Guppy, and quotations from other able writers, taken in connection with the following chapter—"The Scotch-Irish: Who Were They?"—shows conclusively the blood to which the Scotch Allisons belonged who lived in Scotland, then in Ireland and England, and later in America. They were Scotch always, and of the Anglo-Saxon-Norman race.

So many of these Allisons originated in Scotland, then emigrated to the province of Ulster in Ireland, and removed later to the United States and Canada, that it is appropriate that a fuller account of their origin, blood, and race should be given in order to correct misapprehension in relation to the term Scotch-Irish. It is applied to a people wholly of Scotch blood. Important facts are included in the following chapter, "The Scotch-Irish: Who Were They?"

CHAPTER II.

THE SCOTCH-IRISH—WHO WERE THEY?[1]

Many centuries had passed in the building of the Scottish as in the building of the English nation; in each, different peoples helped to make the completed nation, and in blood they were substantially the same. The blending of these races in Scotland, and the sharp stamping of religious and political ideas, had developed and made the Scotch race a distinctive and sharply defined people; in their intellectual, mental, and moral characteristics different from all others a century before, and as we find them at the time of their settlement in the Emerald Isle. Thus they have still remained since their settlement in Ireland. They were Scotch in all their characteristics, though dwelling upon Irish soil. This fact has given rise to the supposition by some and the assertion by others—to whom the wish was father to the statement—that in the veins of the Scotch-Irish flowed commingled the blood of the stalwart Scotch and the blood of the Celtic-Irish. Never was mistake greater.

Hon. Charles H. Bell, ex-governor of New Hampshire, in his eloquent address at the celebration of the one hundred and fiftieth anniversary of the settlement of the Londonderry (N. H.) Colony, in 1869, said of the term "Scotch-Irish": "It is not inappropriate, as descriptive of their origin and prior abode, though it has given rise to not a little misapprehension. It has been supposed by some writers that the name denotes a mixed nationality of Scotch and Irish descent; and in order to adapt the facts to their theory, they have fancied that they could detect in the Londonderry settlers the traits derived from each ancestry. But history fails to bear out the ingenious hypothesis; for it is certain that there was no mixture of blood in the little band who cast their fortunes here; they were of Scottish lineage, pure and simple."

[1] From Among the Scotch-Irish; and A Tour in Seven Countries, with History of Dinsmoor Family, by Leonard Allison Morrison, A. M. Published 1891: Damrell, Upham & Co., Boston, Mass.

The Scotch-Irish were people of Scottish lineage who dwelt upon Irish soil.

The locality about Coleraine, Aghadowey, and Crockendolge, and in fact in many places in the province of Ulster, Ireland, is inhabited by people almost wholly of Scotch origin. They are the "Scotch-Irish," *i. e.*, Scotch people living upon or born upon Irish soil, but not mixed with the native people. Their ancestors, some of them, came to Ireland nearly two hundred and fifty years ago. They came in a body, they kept in a body, and they remain in a body, or class by themselves, largely to-day. The Scotch are called clannish, and *were* clannish; and the Scotch who settled in Ireland, and their descendants, were clannish. They stuck together, and kept aloof from the native Celtic-Irish. They were sundered by the sharp dividing lines of religious faith and by keen differences of race.

Macaulay says: "They sprang from different stocks. They spoke different languages. They had different national characters, as strongly opposed as any two national characters in Europe. They were in widely different stages of civilization. Between two such populations there could be little sympathy, and centuries of calamities and wrongs had generated a strong antipathy. The relation in which the minority stood to the majority resembled the relation in which the followers of William the Conqueror stood to the Saxon churls, or the relation in which the followers of Cortez stood to the Indians of Mexico. The appellation of Irish was then given exclusively to the Celts, and to those families which, though not of Celtic origin, had in the course of ages degenerated into Celtic manners. These people, probably about a million in number, had, with few exceptions, adhered to the Church of Rome. Among them resided about two hundred thousand colonists, proud of their Saxon blood and of their Protestant faith."[1]

And again, in speaking of the early Scotch and English settlers, he says: "One half of the settlers belonged to the Established Church and the other half were Dissenters. But in Ireland Scot and Southron were strongly bound together by their common Saxon origin; Churchman and Presbyterian were strongly bound together by their common Protestantism. All the colonists had a common language and a common pecuniary interest. They were surrounded by common enemies, and could be safe only by means of common precautions and exertions."[1]

[1] Macaulay's History of England.

In speaking of the differences between the races, he says: "Much, however, must still have been left to the healing influence of time. The native race would still have had to learn from the colonists industry and forethought, the arts of civilized life, and the language of England. There could not be equality between men who lived in houses and men who lived in sties; between men who were fed on bread and men who were fed on potatoes; between men who spoke the noble tongue of great philosophers and poets and men who, with perverted pride, boasted that they could not writhe their mouths into chattering such a jargon as that in which the 'Advancement of Learning' and the 'Paradise Lost' were written." [1]

And again, speaking of Scotland, from which the Scotch of Ireland came, he says: "The population of Scotland, with the exception of the Celtic tribes, which were thinly scattered over the Hebrides and over the mountainous shires, was of the same blood with the population of England, and spoke a tongue which did not differ from the purest English more than the dialects of Somersetshire and Lancastershire differ from each other." [1]

Such being the relative condition of the two classes, as eloquently described by the great English historian, it is the height of absurdity to claim that the blood of the distinct races was commingled except in isolated cases. *They did not commingle.* The Scotch, planted upon Irish soil, were Scotch still, and the Irish were Irish still. The Scotch took their language with them, and the dialect of the Lowlands fell upon the startled air and disturbed the mists arising from the peat-fields of the Emerald Isle. Their dialect *lived* in Ireland, was transplanted to American shores, and in all the New Hampshire and American settlements was understood and spoken for more than a hundred years after their settlement upon American soil. Letters were written in it; and many poems by Robert Dinsmoor, "The Rustic Bard," in a printed volume, are written in the Lowland-Scotch dialect.

Though it has now almost entirely disappeared, being supplanted by the purer English tongue, yet I have heard the rich brogue in the Scotch settlement in New Hampshire, and in the older Scotch settlements in Ireland, and know numerous families in New Hampshire, of Scotch blood, who since their coming to these shores one hundred and seventy-five years ago have not intermarried save with people of the same race, and they are of as pure Scotch blood and descent as

[1] Macaulay's History of England.

can be found in the Fatherland. The sterling traits of character of the Scotch in Ireland, their frugality, tenacity of purpose, indomitable will, must ever be an honor to their character. Their glorious achievements upon American soil will ever add lustre to their name, and the mighty men produced of this race in all parts of the American Union will give enduring fame to that Scotch race, pure and unmixed, which, through great tribulation, passed in mighty phalanxes from Scotland to Ireland, there recruited its strength, and then swept across the stormy Atlantic into the American wilderness, subdued forests, founded mighty states, and has been foremost in the onward march of civilization. They are proud to stand alone. Scotch in blood, living or born upon Ireland's soil, the honor is theirs, and theirs alone, and none can deprive them of their glorious fame!

Rev. John S. MacIntosh, D. D., in an eloquent historical address at the Scotch-Irish Congress, at Columbia, Tenn.,[1] in 1889, says of the Scotch and the Scotch-Irish:

"Peculiar and royal race; yes, that indeed is our race! I shrink not from magnifying my house and blood with a deep thanksgiving to that Almighty God who himself made us to differ, and sent His great messenger to fit us for our earth-task,—task as peculiar and royal as is the race itself. I shame me not because of the Lowland thistle and the Ulster gorse, of the Covenanter's banner or the Ulsterman's pike. If we be not *the* very peculiar people, we Scotch-Irish are *a* most peculiar people, who have ever left our own broad, dis-

---

[1] Lovers of the Scotch race, whether living in Scotland, Australia, Ireland, the United States, or Canada, will find much of interest on "The Scotch-Irish in America," and in Europe, in the published "Proceedings of the Scotch-Irish Congresses,"—4 vols. The first two were published by Robert Clarke & Co., Cincinnati, O. All can be obtained of Hon. A. C. Floyd, secretary, Columbia, Tenn. A large amount of facts, and family history not to be found anywhere else, is included in the published histories of the towns of Londonderry, N. H., by Rev. E. L. Parker; of Antrim, N. H., by Rev. Warren R. Cochrane; of Bedford, N. H., of Acworth and Gilmanton, N. H., of Peterborough, N. H., by Dr. Albert Smith; of Windham, N. H.; and "Supplement to the History of Windham in New Hampshire;" in "Rambles in Europe, with Historical Facts Relating to Scotch-American Families, gathered in Scotland and the North of Ireland;" in "Among the Scotch-Irish, a Tour in Seven Countries, with History of the Dinsmoor Family;" in "History and Proceedings of the Celebration of the One Hundred and Fiftieth Anniversary of the Incorporation of the Scotch Settlement of Windham in New Hampshire, held June 9, 1892;" and in "History of the Morison or Morrison Family." The last six books are by Leonard A. Morrison, A. M., Windham. N. H. P. O.; Canobie Lake, N. H., and all except the "History of Windham" can be obtained of him. "The Exercises at the Celebration of the One Hundred and Fiftieth Anniversary of the Settlement of Londonderry, N. H., held June 10, 1869," by Robert C. Mack, Esq., Londonderry, N. H.

tinct mark wherever we have come, and have it in us still to do the same, even our critics being judges. To-day we stand out sharply distinguished in a score of points from English, Dutch, German, and Swede. We have our distinctive marks, and, like ourselves, they are strong and stubborn. Years change them not, seas wash them not out, varying hopes alter them not, clash and contact with new forms of life and fresh forces of society blur them not. Every one knows the almost laughably dogged persistency of the family likeness in us Scotch-Irish all the world over. Go where you may, know it once, then you know it—aye, feel it—forever. The typal face, the typal modes of thought, the typal habits of work, tough faiths, unyielding grit, granitic hardness, close-mouthed self-repression, clear, firm speech when the truth is to be told, God-fearing honesty, loyalty to friendship, defiant of death, conscience and knee-bending only to God—these are our marks. And they meet and greet you on the hills of Tennessee and Georgia; you may trace them down the valleys of Virginia and Pennsylvania; cross the prairies of the West and the savannahs of the South, you may plow the seas to refind them in the western bays of Sligo, and beneath the beetling rocks of Donegal; thence you may follow them to the maiden walls of Derry, and among the winding banks of the silvery Bann; onward you may trace them to the rolling hills of Down, and the busy shores of Antrim; and sailing over the narrow lough, you will face them in our forefathers' collier homes and gray keeps of Galloway and Dumfries, of the Ayrshire hills and the Grampian slopes.

"These racial marks are birth-marks, and birth-marks are indelible. And well for us and the world is it that they are indelible. They are great soul-features, these marks. They are principles. The principles are the same everywhere; and these principles are of four classes,—religious, moral, intellectual, and political."

The Rev. John S. MacIntosh says again, in his eloquent, and almost classical, address on "The Making of the Ulsterman," at the second congress of "The Scotch-Irish in America," held in Pittsburg, Penn., in May and June, 1890:

"In this study I have drawn very largely upon the labors of two friends of former years,—Dr. William D. Killen of the Assembly's college, one of the most learned and accurate of historians, and the Rev. George Hill, once librarian of Queen's college, Belfast, Ireland, than whom never was there more ardent student of old annals and reliable antiquarians; but more largely still have I drawn on my own personal watch and study of this Ulster-folk in their homes, their markets, and their churches. From Derry to Down I have lived with them. Every town, village, and hamlet from the Causeway to Carlingford is familiar to me. Knowing the Lowlander and the Scotch-Irish of this land, I have studied the Ulsterman, and his story of rights and wrongs, and that eagerly, for years. I speak that which I have seen, and testify what I have heard from their own lips, read from old family books, church records, and many a tombstone in Kirkyards."

The Scotch settlers in Ulster were a picked class, as he proves from official and state papers. In a letter of Sir Arthur Chichester, deputy for Ireland, he says: "The Scottishmen came with better *port* (*i. e.*, manifest character), they are better accompanied and attended than even the English settlers. Just as to these western shores came the stronger souls, the more daring and select, so to Ulster from the best parts of Lower Scotland came the picked men to be Britain's favored colonists."

Speaking of the race conflicts between the Scotch and native Irish, he says: "But these proud and haughty strangers, with their high heads and new ways, were held as aliens and harried from the beginning by 'the wild Irish.' The scorn of the Scot was met by the curse of the Celt."

And again: "It has been said that the Ulster settlers mingled and married with the Irish Celt. The Ulsterman did *not* mingle with the Celt." Great care was taken by the government that the Ulster colonists should be so settled that they "may not mix nor intermarry" with the native Celts.

Dr. MacIntosh says again; "The Ulster settlers mingled freely with the English Puritans and with the refugee Huguenots; but so far as my search of state papers, old manuscripts, examination of old parish registers, and years of personal talk with, and study of, Ulster-folk, the Scots did not mingle to any appreciable extent with the natives. . . . With all its dark sides, as well as light, the fact remains that Ulsterman and Celt were aliens and foes. . . . It is useless for Prendergast, Gilbert, and others to deny the massacres of 1641. Reid and Hickson and Froude, the evidence sworn to before the Long Parliament, and the memories of the people, prove the dark facts. . . . In both Lowlander and Ulsterman is the same strong racial pride, the same hauteur and self-assertion, the same self-reliance, the same close mouth, and the same firm will,—'The stiff heart for the steek brae.' They are both of the very Scotch,

Scotch. To this very hour, in the remoter and more un-
changed parts of Antrim and Down, the country-folk will
tell you: 'We're no Eerish, but Scoatch.' All their folk-
lore, all their tales, their traditions, their songs, their poetry,
their heroes and heroines, and their home-speech, is of the
oldest Lowland types and times."

In continuation of this subject, I will say, that in the
Scotch settlements of New Hampshire, after a residence of
one hundred and seventy-five years, there are families of as
pure Scotch lineage as can be found in the Scotch settlements of Ireland or in the interior of the Scottish Lowlands.
In no instance since their coming to America have they intermarried with any save those of Scottish blood.

They retain in a marked degree the mental characteristics
of the race; there are the same lofty adherence to principle,
the same pride of race, the same tenacity of purpose, the
same manifestations of unbending and inflexible will-power
and devotion to duty, as were shown by their forefathers at
the "Siege of Derry," or by their Covenanting ancestors,
who, among the moors, the glens, and the cold mountains of
Scotland, amid sufferings numberless, upheld loftily the banner of the Cross, while some sealed their deathless devotion
to the faith of their souls by sacrificing the bright red blood
of their hearts.

In my veins flows, equally commingled, the blood of
Scot and Puritan; but I speak what I do know, and
declare, with all the force and emphasis which language is
capable of expressing, that after many years of careful historical and genealogical research, relating to Scotch-American
families; after tracing them from America to the Emerald
Isle, thence across the narrow belt of sea to the Fatherland,
Scotland; that only in exceptional cases has there been an
intermixture by marriage of the Scot with the Irish Celt.

I am somewhat familiar with the Scotch settlements in
Ulster, have met and talked and am acquainted with many
of her people of Scotch descent, and *they* declare with particular emphasis that the mixture of Scot and Irish Celt has
been of the slightest kind.

The love of Scotchmen, and the descendants of Scotchmen, in Ulster and elsewhere for the Fatherland and its history is phenomenal, and in America has existed for generations. It is as sweet, as strong, and enduring as that of
Burns for the object of his affections as expressed in the following lines, and which all of our race can apply to Scotland:

" An' I will love thee still, my dear,
   Till a' the seas gang dry.

" Till a' the seas gang dry, my dear,
   And the rocks melt wi' the sun;
I will love thee still, my dear,
   While the sands of life shall run."

CHAPTER III.

THE ALISONS OF SCOTLAND AND AUSTRALIA.

The family of Alison is of very old date (588 years) in the parish of Avondale, county of Lanark, Scotland, where they live in 1898.

" Macalister, the name of a clan that inhabited the South of Knapdale and the North of Kintyre in Argyleshire. They are traced to Alister or Alexander, a son of Angus Mor, of the clan Donald. Exposed to the encroachments of the Campbells, their principal possessions became, ere long, absorbed by different branches of that powerful clan ; clan badge, the five-leafed heather. The chief of this sept of the Macdonalds is Somerville Macalester of Loupe in Kintyre and Kennox in Ayrshire. In 1805, Charles Somervillé Macalester, Esq., of Loupe, assumed the name and arms of Somerville in addition to his own, in right of his wife, Janet Somerville, inheritrix of the entailed estate of Kennox, whom he had married in 1792." [1]

The Highland name of the Alisons was Alester, or McAlester, and was changed into the Lowland name Alison when this branch of the family was driven from Loupe, near Oban, in Argyleshire by the followers of King Robert the Bruce.

" From their descent from Alexander (Macalester), eldest son of Angus Mor, Lord of the Isles and Kintyre in 1284, the grandson of Somerled, the thane of Argyle, the Macalesters claim to be the representatives, after MacDonell, of Glengarry, of the ancient lords of the Isles, as heirs male of Donald, grandson of Somerled." [1]

Alexander MacAlister, of Loupe, last mentioned, took the side of Baliol, the competitor for the Scottish throne, and was attacked by King Robert the Bruce in his chief Castle Sweyn in Knapdale. This was not a great distance from Oban. He was overcome, compelled to flee, was taken prisoner on his way to Ayrshire, was confined in the Dundonald Castle, where he died in 1309. This castle is in parish of Dundonald, Ayrshire, four miles from Prestwick, four miles

---

[1] Anderson's Scottish Nation, Vol. 2, p. 708.

2

from Kilmarnock, and seven from Ayr. His two sons and a few of their followers escaped to Sir Winter de Hamelton, the ancestor of the dukes of this name, who also at first took the side of Baliol. To preserve them from the wrath of the followers of Bruce, Sir Winter de Hamelton placed them in a moorish district in the parish of Avondale, in Lanarkshire, with Cairnduff as their central home, and changed their name from the Highland Alister to the Lowland Alison. This was in 1310, or the Allisons were in Cairnduff in that year. The estate of Cairnduff was then the property of John Hamilton, a relative of the Hamilton family; so that the MacAlesters, or Alisons, were placed on that portion of the estate that required to be reclaimed from the moors and waste lands around. There they have continued for 583 years, and at the present day a great many of the farms or small estates in that neighborhood are owned by Alisons, and the wilderness has now become to a great extent a fruitful field.

The original estate of Loupe, near Oban, was confiscated and given to the crown, but was later conferred upon Alexander MacAlister's younger brother, Angus Oig, who remained faithful to Bruce. There the clan has retained the ancient name of McAlester to the present day, and the chief of the clan is now Lieutenant-colonel Charles Somerville McAlister, of Kennox, in Ayrshire. Some of the descendants of Alexander McAlister, of Loupe, who died in Dundonald Castle in 1309, are still to be found in Ayrshire.

When King Robert the Bruce landed in Ayrshire he drank of a well in Prestwick, which is called "Prince's Well" at the present day, and was greatly recovered of a cutaneous disease like to leprosy, of which, however, he ultimately died. The very ruins of the Prestwick hospital for lepers are still to be seen. In consequence of his betterness, he conferred freedoms on all the families that were in Prestwick. Freedoms which originally consisted of sixteen acres of land. Hence, in the old charter conferred by King Robert the Bruce, various of the thirty-six freemen were of the name of Alison, doubtless followers of their master, who died in Dundonald Castle, which is nigh at hand.

It is even maintained that a large portion of the lands in the south of Ayr was given to this clan; but in consequence of the commotions of those eventful times, those lands have long since passed into the possession of the well-known family of Kennedy, of whom the Marquis of Ailsa is chief.

It was John MacAlister, the second son of Alexander MacAlister, of Loupe, that was placed with a few of his followers in the estate of Cairnduff in Avondale. For a considerable time there we have no authentic history on which to depend to continue our account of the Alisons of Cairnduff; but, according to the traditions of the family, the estate was owned by a John Alison and an Alexander Alison almost alternately; the Johns being named after the Johns of the Isles, their ancestors, and the Alexanders after their great progenitor, Alexander MacAlister of Loupe. But, although history is silent for a little, yet again during the eventful times of Charles the First, the Alisons of Cairnduff gradually came into historical notice.

THE PARISH OF AVONDALE OR STRATHAVEN—THE ORIGINAL HOME OF THE ALISONS IN 1310.

My informant says,—"The parish of Avondale is situated in the Middle Ward of Lanarkshire. Its greatest length is fourteen miles and its greatest breadth is eight miles. It is nearly sixty-four square miles in extent, and contains about 32,000 acres. It is bounded by the following parishes, viz.: Kilbride, Glassford, Stonehouse, Lesmahagow, Muirkirk, London, Galston, and Sorn."

In the days of Bruce and Baliol the Bairds were the most powerful family in Avondale, but, taking the side of Baliol, they were rooted out by the followers of Bruce.

After the Bairds, several ancient families succeeded in holding important positions in the parish, such as the Crawfords, the Sinclairs, the Stewarts, the Murrays, and the Douglasses; but gradually these have disappeared, and now the Hamilton family are the largest proprietors in the parish. There is perhaps, however, no district in Scotland where the land is divided more abundantly among its farmers, and these are called Lairds in Scotland.

During these early times of commotion, Avondale could boast of three lords called by this name. The first Lord Avondale was an Andrew Stewart, who married into the Hamelton family and became the Lord Chancellor of Scotland. The second Lord Avondale was his nephew, Sir Andrew Stewart, and the third Lord Avondale was his son Andrew. With him the title ceased, till it was revived in the name of the late heir to the British throne who was called the "Duke of Clarence and Avondale."

THE ALISONS IN NEWTON OF AYR.

Near to Prestwick, is Newton, although it is now a part of
Ayr Town, yet, in the day of Bruce and of Baliol it was a
village containing forty-eight families. The well still known
as Bruces well was at that time very much in the centre
between Prestwick and Newton, so that Newton shared of the
same privileges which Bruce conferred upon Prestwick. At
the present day there are still forty-eight freedoms that were
conferred upon the forty-eight families then resident in
Newton. At that time there were several Alisons in this
place, as well as in Prestwick, who had freedoms conferred
upon them, evidently the followers also of Alexander of
Loupe, who died in Dundonald Castle in 1309, a castle which
is nigh at hand. But such are the changes that are con-
stantly occurring in human society, that none are now left
remaining; the only remembrance of the fact is the same
name given to a street, a quarry, and a park in the village.
The present inhabitants still remember Alison's Park and
Alison's Quarry, although the park and the quarry have
been gradually absorbed by that street which is still called
by the name of Alison.

A recapitulation in tabular form is as follows:

Somerled (which is the same as the Gallic name Somhairle
and the Hebrew name Samuel), Thane of Argyle and Lord
of the Isles, married in 1135 a daughter of the King of Man,
and had three sons; namely:

Dugald, who obtained possession of the islands of Mull, Coll, and Jura.
   From him are the McDugalds of Lorn or Argyle. He had a son Ewen,
   or John, but he died, and his isles went to his brother Ronald, or
   Reginald, the second son of Somerled.
Ronald, or Reginald, got Isla and Cantyre. He had two sons,—
      Donald.
      Roderic.
AngusMore got Bute and Arran. For his descendants, see the *History of
   the Lords of the Isles.*
Donald, son of Ronald or Reginald, and grandson of Somerled. From
   him are the McDonalds. He had a son,—
      AngusMore.
Roderick, son of Ronald or Reginald, and grandson of Somerled. From
   him are the McCroyes of Scottish history.
AngusMore, son of Donald, son of Ronald or Reginald, son of Somer-
   led, had two sons,—
      Alexander or Alister, (see below.)
      Angus. The latter in those troublous times remained faithful to
         Robert the Bruce, and on him were conferred the lands of his
         brother which were confiscated. He became the head of the
         MacAlisters, and his descendants are often mentioned in Scottish
         history.

¹ Allison and Alison are often employed by families nearly related as
synonomous. In the Martyr's roll, Edinburgh, the name is spelled Alisone.

And to elaborate this subject more fully I will say,—

Alister, or Alexander of Loupe, the elder of the two sons of AngusMore (Donald, Ronald or Reginald, Somerled), married a daughter of John or Ewen of Lorn, but joined the Lord of Lorn against Robert the Bruce. He surrendered to the king, and died a prisoner in Dundonald Castle, Ayrshire, in 1809. He had several sons. His second son, John MacAlister, with a few followers, fled to Sir Winter de Hamilton of Hamilton. He and they were placed in Cairnduff, Avondale, where his name was changed from the Highland Alister to the Lowland name Alison. He was settled in Cairnduff, Avondale, in 1810. Upon this estate one could have walked for five miles. From 1310 to 1630, or thereabouts, there is but little reliable information. But in the Covenanting times we find from published documents that there were Alisons on the farms previously mentioned, and the Alisons of Cairnduff gradually came into historical prominence. About 1630 these Alisons became greatly dispersed, caused by the persecutions of Charles the First, the intolerance of Archbishop Laud, the introduction of the English Liturgy into the Scottish Church, and the formation of the Solemn League and Covenant, with the attending consequences.

After James VI of Scotland fell heir to the English throne and was accepted as king under the title of James I, the Presbyterian Church became unpopular with the Royal Court. During his reign and that of the Charleses that succeeded him, the great design of Parliament was to abolish Presbyterianism in Scotland and establish Prelacy in its stead. By making the religions of England and Scotland the same they imagined that they would unite the two countries more closely together. So oppressively did they push this measure that a revolution took place and Cromwell seized the reins of government, and so conquered the Royalists that he was crowned as Protector of Great Britain. During the reign of the Charleses the whole Scottish nation was greatly moved, and was often on the brink of revolution. This was more especially the case in Avondale and many of the surrounding parishes. It was about 1630 that the Alisons of Cairnduff in Avondale were disturbed in their homes. It was then that the threatenings of Archbishop Laud and his coadjutors began to be realized. It was then that William and Michael Alison escaped to England and found their way to America, the land of the Pilgrim Fathers It was then that Thomas Alison, when a mere youth, went to the sea as a sailor, and in 1645 sailed to America in the ship called

Adventure.[1] It was then that Cairnduff, the original seat of
the Alisons, passed from them to the Cochranes, Mungo
Cochrane having married an Alison, the owner of the
estate.

After the death of Cromwell, his son Richard succeeded,
but soon after he was compelled to abdicate, and Charles II,
who had fled to the continent, returned again in 1660. Then,
if persecution existed before, it was increased ten fold now.
The acts he soon after passed testify to the severity of his
reign. By the Corporation act every individual who did not
conform to the religion of the state was dismissed from his
office, whether civil or sacred. By the Uniformity act 2,000
ministers in England and 400 in Scotland were ejected from
their churches and condemned as rebels to the state. By the
Conventicle act the Puritans of England and the Covenanters of Scotland were forbidden to assemble in the house or
in the field under the penalty of death. Then it was that
Claverhouse scoured the moors and mountains of Scotland,
slaying with his sword or shooting with his gun all who
refused to abjure the Covenant and take the oath of alle-
giance. These acts awakened a painful commotion in Avondale and surrounding parishes, where the adherents of the
Solemn League and Covenant were numerous and powerful.
It was in 1664 that a considerable number in Avondale, Kilbride, and Carmunock were banished from their parishes.
Among these were James Alison and Archibald Alison, previously of Cairnduff. They refused to attend the Prelatic
Church and otherwise aroused the indignation of the curates,
hence they were expelled from the parish of Avondale. James
Alison escaped to Renfrewshire, and became proprietor of a
farm called Kerrs, in the parish of Lochwinnoch. This James
Alison remained faithful to the Covenant in his new home.
In reading Crookshank's "History of the Church of Scotland," we find this James Alison, along with forty others,
compelled to walk through wind and snow to Stirling, where
they were imprisoned. We find the very same parties sent
to the Canongate prison, in Edinburgh, and after a mock

[1] Michael Alison and William Alison went to England to escape to
America, that was then described as the "Land of Freedom."
    The other brother that followed in 1645 was Thomas Alison. He was
born about the time the others left Scotland; but he left America, went
to Archangel, and there under the government of Russia commenced a
voyage to explore the North Pole. His journal of every day was published in 1699. He describes his visit to the Northern seas, but ultimately he reached the 71st degree of north latitude. He had numerous
Scotchmen for companions, and his voyage was finished in 1697. He
was then an old man, and for thirty-eight years had followed the seas.

trial condemned and consigned to the prison in Dunottar
Castle. After remaining there for a time, this James Alison
returned to his home and farm in Kerrs of Lochwinnoch.
He is supposed to be the ancestor of a considerable number
of Alisons that still reside in Paisley, Langbank, and Mearns,
in the county of Renfrew.

"The other Alison alluded to, and brother of James, was
Archibald Alison. He, along with a few others, was banished
to Elgin, whilst others were sent to Inverness and other
northern counties. This Archibald Alison and his exiled
companions did not cease to adhere to their adopted principles, for we find in Crookshank's 'History of the Church of
Scotland' that Bishop Ross, in whose diocese they lived,
wrote Archbishop Sharpe of St. Andrews to the effect ". that
these Covenanting exiles expelled from the south were
doing more harm in the north than they could possibly do
in their own homes, and begged of him to recall them that
they might spread the contagion no further." It was a
daughter of the same Archibald Alison, one Isabel Alison,
that was seized at Perth, when residing at St. Johnston's
there, and was condemned and executed in the Grass Market
of Edinburgh merely for conversing with rebels such as Donald Cargil and Hackston of Rathillet, and for adhering to the
Solemn League and Covenant. Hence Archibald Alison of
Windyedge, who was taken prisoner at Airsmoss and suffered
martyrdom the same year, was a cousin of Isabel Alison.
And it is not a little remarkable to notice that in the Roll of
Martyrs still kept in Edinburgh there are only four or five
names between them. They were separated from each other
in life because of their faithful adherence to Christ's crown
and covenant, but in death they were not separate, for they
died at the same place, for the same cause, and in the same
year; and now through union to the same Redeemer they
are together before the throne, where there are neither curses
nor crosses, sins nor sorrows, griefs nor graves, but where
they have met to part no more."

From Elgin, Archibald Alison is supposed to have come
southward to Perth and afterward settled in Forfairshire.

But although there was a scattering of the Alisons of
Cairnduff during these persecuting times, yet there was a
gradual extension of them in the neighborhood around. For
in the days of the Covenanters that soon followed, we
find in historical reminiscences one in Goslington in the
Parish of Lesmahagow, another in Muirhead, a farm in Avondale, County Lanark; a third in Crewburn, in Avondale; a

fourth in Bent in Avondale; a fifth in Allarstocks, in Avondale; and some as far west as Cessnock, Cumnock, and Ochiltree, in Ayrshire; all of whom are mentioned as sufferers for their faithfulness to the Covenanting cause.

Even Cairnduff itself passed from Alison to Cochrane, because the female proprietor of the estate from 1620 to 1680 married Mungo Cochrane, a son of Cochrane of the Craig.[1] Cairnduff was then and is now divided into a great many farms, and in 1898 a Cochrane lives on one of them. The Cochrans of Cray and Brownside claim to be the oldest family in Avondale, and the name is still very common. The Cochranes and the Alisons of Avondale are well known to each other still, and have been for three hundred years.[2]

The history of the Alisons now becomes transferred from Cairnduff to Windyedge, which was one of the farms belonging to the original estate of Cairnduff. Windyedge, in Avondale. County Lanark included then the farms of Windyedge, Couplaw, Heuk, and Heuklaw, all of which in 1898 belong to Alisons, together with the farms of Muirhead, Letham, and Blackmoss. It was there that Sir Robert Hamilton, Balfour of Burleigh, Hackstone of Rathellet, Brownlee of Torfoot, and several others met after the victory of Drumcloy, to consult as to their future procedure. It was then that they resolved to continue the fortunes of war which ended in their sad discomfiture at the battle of Both-

---

[1] That same Mungo Cochrane is frequently mentioned in these persecuting times as a zealous Covenanter.

[2] In tracing the history of the Alisons of Cairnduff, it is an interesting fact to notice their allied families. The Alisons came from the McAllisters, and are united by marriage with the Cochranes, the Morrisons, the Steeles, the Jamiesons: most of these families are reproduced in the Scotch settlement of Aghadowey, county of Londonderry, Ireland, and *all* are duplicated in the Scotch settlements of Londonderry, and Windham, New Hampshire, United States. We have seen that Michael Alison fled to Londonderry, Ireland, after the fight at Airsmoss, Scotland, where he remained many years, and left several children. The family of McKeen, the Morrisons, and the Alisons, and others of Agadowey and adjacent parishes, settled there about the same time, and for the same cause, and later came to Londonderry, and Windham, N. H. In the latter settlements are the McAlisters with their kinsmen, the Alisons, with the Morrisons, the Cochranes, the Steeles, the Jamesons, and the Wilsons, with many of the Scotch families with the same christian names which are found in the Scotch settlements of Pennsylvania and in the states farther south, found also in the Scotch settlements in Ireland, and tracing them again across the narrow belt of sea to the fatherland, Scotland, we find them there in the *old* homes. All are of the same blood, with the same characteristics, and all are Scotch still. They are not yet weaned from "the land of brown heath and shaggy wood," although more than two centuries have passed since their ancestors fled from persecution there.

well Bridge. Annie Swan in one of her novels called "Adam Hepburn's Vow," alludes to Windyedge as their place of meeting, and in "Old Mortality," by Sir Walter Scott, we find that it was there that Graham of Claverhouse obtained refreshments as he fled from his defeat at Drumcloy, and received them, too, from a widow who had three sons engaged in the battle. In the account given of the engagement at Drumcloy, Archibald Alison is mentioned by name, the same that was seized as a prisoner at Airsmoss, and suffered martyrdom at the Grass Market in Edinburgh, and whose dying testimony is recorded at great length in the volume called "The Cloud of Witnesses."

In a letter, dated Oct. 8, 1892, my informant says,—" I think almost all the Alisons of Scotland and Ireland are descendants of Cairnduff Alisons planted there in 1310."

In Scott, it is Lord Evandale who is mentioned as the person who received refreshments, yet the traditions of the Alisons say it was Claverhouse, and although two of her sons are only said to have been at Drumcloy, yet three were with the Covenanters at the time, namely, John Alison banished to Virginia, Michael Alison of Londonderry, Ire., and Archibald Alison, the martyr.

On the farm of Kilwakening, owned by Matthew Alison, 1898, occurred some incidents connected with the Covenanting times, which are worthy of notice. On this farm was killed the horse of the notorious Claverhouse, and where he narrowly escaped. At the head of Capernaum Park there is a bush planted on the spot where a small cottage once stood called by this name. It is about a mile from the battlefield of Drumcloy, where Claverhouse retreated with his men. He was passing this little cottage where several of the Covenanters were standing, who, seeing Claverhouse, wounded his horse with a scythe, hoping thereby to capture the defeated persecutor, but the horse continued to run for two hundred yards, and fell at the garden of Kilwakening. Claverhouse instantly dismounted his trumpeter, and mounted his horse and continued his flight.

By Sir Walter Scott, the trumpeter is described as fleeing away on foot through the Gill and Beemoss, marshy places where cavalry could not go, but localities now drained and made fertile, though still known by these names. In endeavoring to join the retreating army of Claverhouse he came upon the Covenanting victors returning from the pursuit, and there near the house of Joseph Alison of Hillhead, in Avondale, Lanarkshire, he was killed and buried, while over his remains a heap of stones is still to be seen, and nigh to the grave there is a rich spring of water which is well known at the present day as " the Trumpeter's well." [1]

ARCHIBALD ALISON. It is believed by many that this Archibald Alison was the grandfather of another Alison who became a successful merchant in Edinburgh, and was elected Lord Provost of the city. From him an illustrious race of Alisons are descended, viz., the Rev. Dr. Alison, of Edinburgh, author of the well known treatise on "Taste;" and from the reverend author of "Taste" have sprung Dr. Alison, of Edinburgh, of medical fame, and Sheriff Alison, of Glasgow, the historian, whose son is the present General Sir Archibald Alison of Crimean renown. Although we cannot vouch for the correctness of this connection, yet here we add the following extract of that branch of the Alisons from the volume called the "Scottish Nation."

Alison is the name of a family possessing a baronetcy of the United Kingdom, conferred in 1852 on Sir Archibald Alison, LL. D., D. C. L., F. R. S. He was born at Kinley, Salop, on the 29th of December, 1792. His father, the Rev. Archibald Alison, author of "Essays on Taste," was a scion of the family of Alison of Newhall, in the parish of Kettens, in Forfarshire.

By the mother's side, he is descended lineally from Edward I and Robert the Bruce. Sir Archibald Alison was educated at the University of Edinburgh, and admitted an advocate in 1814. He was advocate depute from 1828 to 1830. He was appointed Sheriff of Lanarkshire in 1835. The following works issued from his pen:

Principles of the Criminal Law of Scotland, 1832.
Practice of the Criminal Law.
History of Europe, 20 voumes, published in 1833.
Essays Contributed to *Blackwood's Magazine*.
Principles of Population, 1840.
England in 1815 and 1845, or a Sufficient and Contracted Currency.
Life of the Duke of Marlborough, 1847.

Sir Archibald Alison married, in 1825, Elizabeth Glencairn, youngest daughter of Lieut. Col. Patrick Tytler, second son of William Tytler, Esq., of Woodhouselee.

Issue: Archibald Alison, born January 21, 1826. Lieutenant-colonel in the army; military secretary to Lord Clyde when commander-in-chief in India. Lost an arm at Lucknow, and has a medal and clasps for his services in the Crimea. (He is now General Sir Archibald Alison.)

Frederick Montague Alison, the second son of Sir Archibald Alison, was born May 11, 1835; is a captain in the army and aid-de-camp to the same commander.

His only daughter is Ellen Frances Catherine, married to Cutlar Ferguson of Craigdarroch.

Sir Archibald Alison's brother, William Pulteney Alison, M. D., LL. D., F. R. S., was professor of practice of physic in the University of Edinburgh and first physician to the Queen in Scotland. He retired from his chair in 1855 and died in 1859.

---

[1] " Man has sometimes been described as a child of circumstances. We see this truth verified very strikingly in the history of the McAllisters of Loupe, from whom the Alisons are descended. The estate of Loupe was confiscated by the crown, but was afterward restored to the younger brother. His descendants long continued to be chiefs of the McAllister clan, and some of them instead of espousing the Covenanting cause, fought on the side of Claverhouse at Killiecrankie and finally fell at the battle of the Boyne."

The following is also an extract from the "Scottish Nation," upon the Rev. Archibald Alison, D. D.:

The reverend author of "Essays on the Nature and Principles of Taste" was the second son of a magistrate of Edinburgh, and sometime lord provost of the city, where he was born in 1757.

In 1772 he went to the University of Glasgow, and afterwards became an exhibitioner at Baliol college, Oxford, where he took the degrees of A. M. and LL. B. Entering into Holy Orders, he obtained the curacy of Brancepeth, county of Durham, and was subsequently made prebendary of Sarum. Having acquired the friendship of the late Sir William Pulteney, he was indebted to him for preferment in the church.

In 1784 he married, at Edinburgh, the eldest daughter of the celebrated Dr. John Gregory, by whom he had six children.

In 1800, on the invitation of Sir William Forbes, baronet, and the vestry of the Episcopal chapel, Cowgate, Edinburgh, he became senior minister of that place of worship. The congregation having removed to St. Paul's church, York place, in the same city, he continued to officiate there until a severe illness in 1831 compelled him to relinquish all public duties. He was one of the early Fellows of the Royal Society of Edinburgh, and the intimate friend of many of its most distinguished members. He was also a Fellow of the Royal Society of London. His principal work, the "Essays on the Nature and Principles of Taste," published in 1790, has passed through several editions, and was translated into French. He died on the 17th of May, 1839. His works are,—

Essay on the Nature and Principles of Taste, 1790.
A Discourse on the Fast Day, 1809.
A Thanksgiving Sermon, 1814.
Sermons, chiefly on particular occasions, 1814.
Life and Writings of the Hon. Alexander Fraser Tytler, Lord Woodhouselee, 1818.

Rev. Alexander Alison, formerly of Philadelphia, Pa., now (1893) of Seattle, Wash., was from Fife, Scotland, where some of the Alisons of Cairnduff or vicinity went about 1630.

Rev. Dr. Alison, of Edinburgh, Scotland, and his brother, Arthur Alison, the advocate, are from Eagles Law, next parish to Avondale, and probable descendants of an early Alison who went to Paisley.

ALISONS OF AVONDALE, SCOTLAND.

1. James Alison[1] is the first ancestor of this immediate branch of the Alisons at Cairnduff, Avondale. county of Lanark, Scotland, whose Christian name is definitely known, after the family again emerged into historic prominence. The name of his father is not known, but it was probably John or Alexander Alison, as those Christian names seemed to alternately prevail during the long historical obscurity in which the Alisons rested.

James Alison was born at Cairnduff in 1621, and resided on the farm at Windyedge, where he died about 1670. He married Jean, daughter of Samuel Wilson, of Rigfoot, East Kilbride. She survived her husband, and it was from his cottage at Windyedge that the notorious Claverhouse, the persecutor of the Covenanters, received refreshments while on his flight, after his defeat at the battle of Drumcloy, in 1679. The date of his death is unknown.

2. Jean Alison [2], m. James Torrance. Res. at Deadwaters, parish of Les-
      mahagow, county of Lanark, Scotland.
3. John Alison [2] (7), b. 1652. He was one of the 1,200 prisoners taken at
      Bothwell Bridge, and was banished to Virginia. His sword is
      still in possession of relatives.
4. Michael Alison [2] (8), b. 1654, a sturdy Covenanter, was at the siege of
      Londonderry, Ireland.
5. Archibald Alison [2], b. 1656, and suffered martyrdom at the Grassmar-
      ket, Edinburgh, Scotland, in 1680. He was in the battles of Drum-
      cloy, Bothwell Bridge, and at Airsmoss battle was taken pris-
      oner. His dying testimony is published at great length in "A
      Cloud of Witnesses," a book formerly, and now greatly, read in
      Scotland.
6. Margaret Alison [2], m. James Steele. Res. Lesmahagow, county of
      Lanark, Scotland.

7.   John Alison [2] [3] (James [1]). He was born, in 1652, at
Windyedge, which was one of the farms belonging to the
original estate of Cairnduff, in Avondale, county of Lanark,
Scotland. With his two brothers, Michael and Archibald
Alison, he was a stiff and zealous Covenanter, and fought at
Bothwell Bridge, where the Covenanters were sorely defeated.
He was one of the 1,200 prisoners taken; was tried at Edinburgh, and banished to Virginia in America. His name is
recorded in the well known Porteous Roll, a roll which contained the names of the criminals who were imprisoned in
those days, most of whom were pious Covenanters. After
his term of exile came to an end, he joined the settlement of
the Pilgrim Fathers in Massachusetts, and there was considerable communication between him and his friends in Avondale, for they were accustomed to hear that the heat in Virginia was so great that people could boil an egg upon the
sand, and how, in New England, they had to climb trees to
escape from the wild beasts; how they were caught in gin
set for deer; how the Indians formed their houses by bend-
ing branches and matting them over like an arbor; how their
graves were filled with bows and arrows and other instru-
ments of warfare; and how they caused the forests to reëcho
by the discharge of their muskets. These and many such
reminiscences have been handed down from father to son
among the relatives who remained in Scotland, to the present
time. His sword is still in the possession of his relative,
William Allison, of Hawbank, East Kilbride, near Strathavon,
county of Lanark, Scotland.
   If Mr. Alison left any descendants in America, they are
unknown to the relatives in Scotland.
   8.   Michael Alison [2] [4] (James [1]). He was born at Win-

dyedge, Scotland, in 1654. This was a part of the original estate of Cairnduff, in Avondale, Lanarkshire, Scotland. Like his brothers and family, he was a zealous and enthusiastic Covenanter, and battled bravely for his religious faith. With his brothers, Archibald and John Alison, he was in the battles at Drumcloy, Bothwell Bridge, and at the skirmish at Airsmoss, and participated in the siege of Londonderry, Ireland, in 1688–'89. At the skirmish at Airsmoss, where his brother, Archibald Alison, was taken prisoner, he fled so quickly that he reached Port Patrick and crossed over to Ireland before the news of the disaster to the Covenanters reached the Irish shore. Although he was questioned severely by their enemies, yet he escaped suspicion, and resided many years in the neighborhood of Londonderry, and was present at the famous siege in 1688–'89.

He either leased or bought a farm near Londonderry, for there he married and had a large family. From 1681 to the Restoration in 1690, the lands of Windyedge, his old home, and many others, were forfeited in consequence of their proprietors joining in so-called treasonable rising of Bothwell Bridge. So long as this decree of the Lords of Justiciary remained, Michael Alison could not return to Windyedge, where his widowed mother was still living. At the Restoration, after the battle of the Boyne, he returned to Windyedge with four members of his family, and the other members of his large family of children remained in or near Londonderry. He seems to have gone back and forth considerably between his two homes, living a part of the time at Windyedge and sometimes in Londonderry. He died at Windyedge and was buried in the burying-place of the family in Strathavon church-yard, leaving his eldest son, James Alison, the laird of the farm. Michael Alison's wife was Elizabeth Cooper, and the initials of her name, E. C., were engraved into the lintel of the old house at Windyedge. Mr. Alison married his own cousin for his second wife, and had a large family.

The sword of Michael Alison, with which he fought at Drumcloy, Bothwell Bridge, Airsmoss, and the siege of Londonderry, is still in existence, a precious memento, and is in the possession of Rev. George Alison, of Kilbarchan.

CHILDREN BY FIRST WIFE, ELIZABETH (COOPER) ALISON.

9. James Alison[2] (13), b. Londonderry, Ireland, in 1690; returned with his father to Windyedge, Scotland, where he resided. He m. Margaret Semple. He was called "Cooper" Alison and was well known in Avondale.

10. Alexander Alison[3] (18), b. near Londonderry, Ireland. He became
      laird of Letham, near Windyedge, Scotland.
11. John Alison[3] (23), b. at Windyedge, Scotland, in 1708; went to Foul-
      popple, London, Ayrshire, Scotland, in 1789.
12. William Alison[3] (27), b. at Windyedge, Scotland, in 1710; res. Dyke-
      head, East Kilbride, county Lanark, Scotland. The latter
      place is near Cairnduff, Avondale, county Lanark, Scotland.

13. James Alison[3] [9], (Michael,[2] James[1]).   He was
born near Londonderry, Ireland, in 1689. He returned to
Windyedge, Scotland, with his father, and married, in 1720,
Margaret, daughter of William Semple, of Nethershields,
Glassford Parish, Braehead, and Nettlyhole, and became heir
to these two last farms. The two latter places are names of
farms in Avondale, county Lanark.

CHILDREN.

14.   John Alison[4] (29), born at Windyedge, Scotland, in
1760; married Helen, daughter of Matthew Lawson, of Kilwakening, county of Lanark.
15.   Margaret Alison[4], born, 1762, at Windyedge; married
William Torrance, of Glasgow, and died in Glasgow.

CHILDREN.

1. Jane Torrance[5], m. Malcolm McLaren, of Glasgow, and her children
      were,—
      Margaret McLaren,[6] b. 1817; d. without children. William Mc-
      Laren,[6] b. 1819; d. without children. Jane McLaren,[6] b. 1820; m.
      James Dodds. Child: Jane Dodds.[7] Marrion McLaren,[6] m. Will-
      iam Cross, of South Lodgeayr, a merchant in Glasgow. He, with
      his brother, David Cross, constituted the well known firm of Alex-
      ander Cross & Sons, seed, grain, and chemical merchants.
      Children: Alexander Cross,[7] is member of parliament for Glasgow,
      Scotland. He m. Jessie, daughter of Sir Peter Coats, of Auchen-
      drane, so deservedly known as a thread manufacturer in Paisley
      and the United States, but still more honorably known for his lib-
      erality to every religious and benevolent cause, and whose mem-
      ory will never be forgotten so long as Paisley lasts and the United
      Presbyterian church continues. Alexander Cross owns a large
      tract of land in one of the states of the United States. Jane. T.
      Cross,[7] m. John R. Cassells, of Motherwell, Ironworks, in 1872,
      in Motherwell, county of Lanark. William Cross,[7] m. Jean Mar-
      shall, of London, in 1880. Marion Cross,[7] m. Robert Cassells, of
      Motherwell Ironworks. Jessie Low Cross.[7] Malcolm Cross,[7] m.
      daughter of Archibald Walker, of Vauxhall Distillery. Helen
      Cross,[7] m. Walter McFarlane, of the Saracon Foundry, Glasgow,
      Scotland. John Cross.[7] Maggie Ferguson Cross.[7] Agnes Cross.[7]
2. William Torrance,[5] went to Australia, and d. childless.
3. Margaret Torrance,[5] m. Charles Porteous, of Glasgow.   Children:
      Charles Porteous,[6] d. childless. William Porteous,[6] d. childless.
      Margaret Porteous,[6] m. Peter Ferguson, of Glasgow, Scotland.
      No children.

16.   Catharine Alison,[4] born at Windyedge, Scotland, in
1764.   She married Alexander Morrison, of Corneygroats, in
Avondale, county of Lanark.

CHILD.

16 a.   Alexander Morrison,[5] born at Corneygroats in
Avondale in 1785; m., in 1806, Jean, daughter of John Alison, of Windyedge.   His grandson in 1893 is proprietor of
that place.

CHILDREN.

1.   Helen Lawson Morrison,[6] b. at Corneygroats in 1808; m. James Stru-
     thers.   Children: Jennie Struthers,[7] b. 1830.   James Struthers,[7]
     b. 1833.   Annie Struthers,[7] b. 1838.   Helen Struthers,[7] b. 1841.
     Jennie Struthers,[7] b. 1849.
2.   James Morrison,[6] b. at Corneygroats in 1810; m. Annie, daughter of
     John Lombie, of Hallburn, Avondale, Scotland.   Children:
     Alexander Morrison,[7] b. 1836; d. young.   Katherine Morrison,[7] b.
     1838.   Jane Morrison,[7] b. 1840.   Alexander Morrison,[7] b. 1842.
     In 1893 he was proprietor of Corneygroats, and had a son, James
     Morrison.[8]   Anne Morrison,[7] b. 1845.   John Lambie Morrison,[7] b.
     1849.   Helen Morrison,[7] b. 1852.   Mary Morrison,[7] b. 1855.   Mar-
     garet Morrison,[7] b. 1859.
3.   Eliza Morrison,[6] b. at Corneygroats, and is deceased.
4.   Katherine Morrison,[6] b. Corneygroats; m. Robert Letham, of Glas-
     gow, Scotland.   Children: Robert Letham.[7]   Jeanie Letham.[7]
     Isabella Letham.[7]
5.   Jean Morrison,[6] b. at Corneygroats, 1821; m. William Kirkland, of
     Glasgow.   Children: William Kirkland,[7] res. Brisbane, Austra-
     lia.   Alexander Kirkland,[7] res. Canada.   James Kirkland,[7] d.
     aged 21 years.   John Kirkland,[7] d. aged 19 years.
6.   John Morrison,[6] b. at Corneygroats in 1824, and died, aged about 16
     years.
7.   Margaret Morrison,[6] b. at Corneygroats in 1825; m. John Donald, of
     Coulton.   Children: Gavin Donald.[7]   Jeanie Donald.[7]   Alexan-
     der Donald.[7]   Catherine Donald.[7]   Margaret Donald,[7] is deceased.
     Margaret Donald.[7]   Helen Donald.[7]   John Donald.[7]

17.   Margaret Morrison,[5] born at Corneygroats in 1787;
married James Turnbull, of Boghall, a farm near the town of
Tollcross in the Barony Parish, Glasgow, Scotland.

CHILDREN.

1.   Catherine Turnbull,[6] m. John French, of Tollcross, Barony Parish,
     of Glasgow.
2.   John Turnbull,[6] m. J. Buchanan; res. Boghall.
3.   Jennie Turnbull,[6] m. David Spencer, merchant; res. London, Eng-
     land.
4.   Janet Turnbull,[6] m. John Bogle, of Tollcross.

18.   Alexander Alison[3] [10] (Michael,[2] James[1]).   He was
born near Londonderry, Ireland; returned to Windyedge,
Scotland, with his father, and became laird of Letham, near

Windyedge. Letham is composed of three farms—Couplaw, Hookhead, and Letham. According to my informant, Rev. Archibald Alison, of Prestwick, he had the following children:

CHILDREN.

17.   Alexander Alison[4] (34), b. at Letham, Avondale, county of Lanark, Scotland.
18.   Thomas Alison[4] (39), b. at Letham, Scotland, and became laird of Calderbank.
19.   ———— Alison,[4] b. at Letham; m. Mr. Currie, of Frynlaw, near Strathavon. It has been the home of the Curries for two centuries.
20.   ———— Alison,[4] b. at Letham; m. Mr. Tennant, of Strathavon, Scotland.
21.   John Alison[4] went to Fyfeshire, or Forfarshire—the probable ancestor of Rev. Alexander Alison, D.D., of Seattle, Washington.
22.   ———— Alison,[4] a daughter, who died young.

23.   John Alison[3] [11] (Michael,[2] James[1]). He was born at Windyedge, Scotland, in 1708; went to Foulpopple, London, Ayrshire, Scotland, in 1789, and had three sons and several daughters.

CHILDREN.

24.   John Alison,[4] b. at Foulpopple. Children: 1, John Alison,[5] b. Hungryhill, Salston. Is m., but no children. 2, James Alison,[5] b. at Foulpopple in 1804; went to Harperscroft, Dundonald; m. Annie Cray, of Galston, Ayrshire. Children: William Alison,[6] b. at Harperscroft, Parish of Dundonald, Ayrshire, Scotland; m. Mary Smith. Child: Annie Cray Alison.[1] John Alison[6] went to Canada. Isabella Alison,[6] m. Reginald Bruce; res. Langholm, Scotland. Annie Alison.[6] Eliza Alison.[6] 3, William Alison,[5] res. Fairfield, Galston, Ayrshire, Scotland; is m. but has no family.
25.   James Alison,[4] born at Muirhead, Avondale. His descendants are still in Muirhead.
26.   Andrew Alison,[4] of Goslington. His descendants are still there.

27.   William Alison[3] [12] (Michael,[2] James[1]). He was born at Windyedge, Scotland, in 1710; went to Dykehead, East Kilbride, Lanarkshire. and had only one son that had children. East Kilbride is some two miles from Cairnduff and Windyedge.

CHILD.

28.   William Alison.[4] b. at Dykehead, East Kilbride, near Cairnduff, Avondale, in 1747. He resided in Hawbank, East Kilbride, Lanarkshire, Scotland, and d. there, aged 93 years. He m. Elizabeth Reed, of Castleton, East Kilbride, Lanarkshire, and had children: 1, William Alison,[5] m. Janet Findlay, and res. in Windlaw, parish of Carmunnock, Lanarkshire. Two sons: William Alison,[6] m. Isabella Dick; res. Turnlaw, parish of East Kilbride, and is factor for James Campbell, of Strathcarthro. Thomas Alison[6] died unmarried. 2, Janet Alison,[5] m. John

Spiers, of Glasgow, Scotland. 3, Elizabeth Alison,[5] m. Alexander Leggot, of Glasgow. 4, David Alison,[5] m. Margaret Reid, and res. in Hawbank. Children: Margaret Alison,[6] m. R. Steven; res. Newlands, East Kilbride. William Alison,[6] Lanarkshire, m. Janet Gilmour, of Fieldhead. Rev. James Alison,[6] m. Catherine McIntosh, of Glasgow.[1] John Alison,[6] m. Eliza Ballantine. Hugh Alison,[6] d. at Hawbank. Alexander Alison,[6] d. in infancy. Elizabeth Alison,[6] m. Alexander Warnock, of Glasgow.

29. **John Alison**[4] **[14]** (James,[3] Michael,[2] James[1]). He was born at Windyedge, Scotland, in 1760. He married Helen, daughter of Matthew Lawson, of Kilwakening, and became heir to that estate, and which in 1893 was owned by his grandson, Matthew Alison.

CHILDREN.

30. Margaret Alison,[5] b. at Windyedge in 1783; m. Archibald Thomson, of Strathavon, Scotland, in 1810. Children born at Strathavon, Scotland: 1, Helen Thomson,[6] b. 1810: m. William Wiseman, of Strathavon. No children living. 2, Margaret Thomson,[6] b. 1812; m. William Houston; res. in Australia. 3, Robert Thomson,[6] b. 1814. 4, John Thomson,[6] b. 1816. 5, Jean Thomson,[6] b. 1819; res. Otayo, New Zealand.
31. Jean Alison,[5] born at Windyedge in 1785; m. Alexander Morrison, of Corneygroats, in Avondale, in 1806. His grandson was proprietor of the place in 1893. He was an own cousin. (See *Catherine Alison's record, No. 16.*)
32. James Alison[5] **[44]**, born at Windyedge in 1791; d. in Fieldhead cottage in Strathavon, Scotland, in 1861.
33. Matthew Alison,[5] born at Windyedge in 1793; ordained at Kilbarchan in Renfrewshire, Scotland, in 1818; installed at Mufflington, Juniata county, Penn., in 1842, and d. when minister there. He married Agnes, daughter of William Gemmell, of Frankville, Ayr. His only surviving son is William M. Alison,[6] who is the editor and proprietor of the paper in that town where his father was minister.

34. **Alexander Alison**[4] **[17]** (Alexander,[3] Michael,[2] James[1]). He was born at Letham, Avondale, Lanarkshire, Scotland. He had the estate at Letham, comprising three farms, which originally belonged to Cairnduff.

[1] Rev. James Allison,[6] of Alexandria, Dumbartonshire, was educated in the University of Glasgow. After being licensed by the Hamilton Presbytery, he received calls from the congregations of Newburgh, Wolverhampton, and Oxenden Presbyterian church, London. In 1866 he was ordained as minister of Oxenden Chapel, London, a church which had as his predecessors several eminent men, such as the Rev. Dr. Jerment, the Rev. Dr. Broadfoot, and the Rev. Dr. Archer. There, in consequence of his health breaking down, he resigned his charge. After a few months' recreation, he was inducted minister of the Boston United Presbyterian church, Cupar-Fife. From Cupar he was translated to the United Presbyterian church, Alexandria, in the vale of Leven, county of Dumbarton. There he still ministers to a large and prosperous congregation.

CHILDREN.

35. Alexander Alison,[5] b. at Letham, Avondale, Lanarkshire, and res.
there; m. Marrion Hamilton, daughter of William Hamilton,
of Greathill. Children: Alexander Alison,[6] who died young.
James Alison,[6] M. D., went to New Zealand. Joseph Alison[6],
went to New Zealand. Thomas Alison,[6] d. at Letham, without
children.

36. Joseph Alison,[5] of Hillhead, b. at Letham; m. Ann, daughter of
David Paterson, of Strathavon, Scotland. Children: Margaret
Alison.[6] Joseph Alison.[6] James Alison.[6] David Alison.[6] Ann
Alison.[6] Jane Alison.[6] Matthew Alison.[6] Alexander Ali-
son.[6]

37. Margaret Alison,[5] b. at Letham; m. Mungo Cochran, of Strathavon,
Scotland.

38. James Alison,[5] of Tardoes, parish of Muirkirk, Ayrshire, and is a
J. P.; was b. at Letham; m. Elizabeth, daughter of Andrew
Hamilton, of Longridge. Children: James Alison,[6] of Tardoes; Elizabeth Alison,[6] m. Mr. Pearson, of Muirkirk. Andrew Alison[6] is a farmer; res. in the Isle of Man.

39. Thomas Alison[4] [18] (Alexander,[3] Michael,[2] James[1])
was b. at Letham, Avondale, Scotland, and became Laird of
Calderbank.

CHILDREN.

40. Thomas Alison,[5] b. at Calderbank; m. Mary, daughter of William
Hamilton, of Crummach. He m. second, Margaret, daughter
of John Flemming, of Hawkwood, and had eight children.

41. James Alison,[5] of the Grange, a farm in Avondale, Lanarkshire, and
near Strathavon; m. Janet Hamilton, of Halls. James Alison's[5] children: 1, Alexander Alison,[6] res. Melbourne, Australia.
2, Thomas Alison,[6] is a prosperous business man; res. Bridge of
Allan, near Sterling, Scotland. 3, James Alison,[6] res. South
America. 4, John Alison,[6] res. Glasgow, Scotland. 5, George
Alison,[6] res. Glasgow, Scotland. 6, Marion Alison,[6] d. young.

42. Marion Alison,[5] m. William Scott, of Breconrig, a farm in Avondale,
and afterwards of Netherton, Carnwath Parish.

43. Alexander Alison.[5] He is ancestor of the Letham Alisons.

44. James Alison[5] [82] (John,[4] James,[3] Michael,[2]
James[1]). He was born at Windyedge, Scotland, in 1791;
married Jean, daughter of William Jamieson, of Middlecroft,
Avondale, who was born at Auchenbart, Galston, Ayrshire,
Scotland, July, 1788. Mr. Alison died in Fieldhead Cottage,
Strathavon, in 1861.

CHILDREN.

45. John Alison,[6] b. at Windyedge, Scotland, August, 1814, and was
laird of that farm, and d. there in 1849. He m. Ann, daughter
of William Young, of Ryland, Avondale, Scotland. Children:
1, James Alison,[7] d. without children. 2, Janet Alison,[7] d.
without children. 3, Jean Alison,[7] b. at Windyedge in 1841;
m. in 1870 John Hamilton, of Colinhill, Avondale, Strathavon,
county of Lanark, Scotland. He is the eldest son of the late
James Hamilton, of Colinhill, the founder of the town known
as "Hamilton Brothers," Strathavon. On the death of his

father he became the proprietor of Colinhill farm, and through his marriage, the farm of Windyedge, which has been in the hands of the Alisons for nearly 600 years, will now pass into the name of Hamilton.

James Hamilton[8] d. young. John Hamilton[8] d. young. Anne Hamilton[8] b. 1873. Helen Fleming Hamilton[8] b. 1875. Jeanie Hamilton[8] b. 1876. James Hamilton[8] b. 1879. Janet Hamilton[8] b. 1881. Maggie Hamilton[8] b. 1883. John Hamilton[8] b. 1885.

46. William Alison[6] (55), b. at Windyedge, Scotland, in 1815; m. Eliza Thomson; res. Dunavon, Scotland.

47. Matthew Alison[6] (64), b. at Kilwakening, Avondale, county of Lanark, Scotland, in 1817; res. Sydney Villa, Strathavon, Scotland; unm.

48. George Alison[6] (65), b. at Kilwakening in 1819; m. Agnes Jamieson; clergyman; res. Kilbarchan, Scotland.

49. James Alison,[6] b. Kilwakening in 1821; d. there in 1835.

50. Alexander Alison[6] (68), b. at Kilwakening in 1822; m. Helen Hamilton, and, second, Isabella Murray; res. Blackmoss, Strathavon, county of Lanark, Scotland.

51. Archibald Alison[6] (76), b. at Kilwakening in 1825; m. Mary Robertson; clergyman; res. Prestwick, Scotland.

52. Christina Alison,[6] b. at Kilwakening in 1827; m. Hugh Wyllie, of Brigland, Mauchline, in 1849; res. Cessnock, Prestwick, Ayrshire, Scotland. Children: William Wyllie,[7] b. at Brigland in 1853; d. 1870. James Wyllie,[7] b. at Brigland in 1853; res. Braehead, Shieldhill, Dumfrieshire, Scotland. Jane Jamieson Richmond Wyllie,[7] b. at Brigland in 1855; d. 1862. ——— Wyllie.[7] ——— Wyllie.[7] John Wyllie,[7] b. at Brigland in 1858; res. Park, Mayfield, Sussex. Matthew Alison Wyllie,[7] b. at Brigland in 1861; d. 1862. Christina Wyllie,[7] b. at Brigland in 1864; res. Prestwick, Scotland. Jane Wyllie,[7] b. at Brigland in 1873; res. Prestwick, Scotland.

53. Robert Alison,[6] b. at Kilwakening in 1829; m. Margaret, daughter of Thomas Scoular, of Strathavon, Scotland; res. Kilwakening, Strathavon, Scotland. Children: Eliza Alison,[7] b. at Kilwakening in 1876; at home. Jeanie Alison,[7] b. at Kilwakening in 1880; at home.

54. Andrew Alison,[6] b. at Kilwakening in 1831; d. in 1832.

55. William Alison[6] [46] (James,[5] John,[4] James,[3] Michael,[2] James[1]). He was born at Windyedge, in 1815, and in 1842 he married Eliza, daughter of William Thomson, of Boness. At the age of 21 he went to New South Wales, where he became one of the largest and most successful stockholders in Australia. He resided sometimes in Sydney, Australia, and sometimes in Dunavon, Avondale, Scotland. He was proprietor of several farms in Avondale, and in the parish of Ocheltree in Ayrshire. He was proprietor of Bonnytown estate, which included the farms of Bonnytown, Drumboy, Auchengee, Ravenscroft, and Waberton. He was a justice of the peace for Lanarkshire. His largest estate in Australia was Canonbar, and consists of 1,100,000 acres. It is grazed by 400,000 sheep. Three of Mr. Alison's sons are members of the legislative assembly of New South Wales. Mr. Alison is now deceased.

CHILDREN.

56. Ellen Alison,[7] b. in New South Wales, Australia, in 1843; m. in 1870 at Dunavon, Strathavon, Scotland, to George Russell, of Sydney, Australia; res. Dunside, Strathavon, county of Lanark, Scotland. The father of George Russell, late of Sydney, left Kirkcaldy, Fife, about 1814, and emigrated with his family first to Tasmania and then to Sydney, Australia. In Sydney he commenced a foundry and engineering business. Three of his sons succeeded him, and have come out of the firm with fortunes. Children: Eliza Alison Russell,[8] b. in 1872. Sydney Alison Russell,[8] b. in 1873. William Alison Russell,[8] b. in 1875. Leonard Alison Russell,[8] b. 1876; deceased.
57. Jennie Alison,[7] b. in New South Wales in 1845; res. at Dunside, Strathavon, Scotland.
58. Christina Alison,[7] b. in New South Wales in 1849; res. at Dunavon, Strathavon, Scotland, and owns the old family home.
59. Eliza Alison,[7] b. in New South Wales in 1852; m. Walter Vivian, member of the legislative assembly at Sydney, Australia; P. O. Parliament House, Sydney, Australia. Children: Alison Vivian,[8] b. in 1877. Isabel Josephine Alison Vivian,[8] b. in 1879; Edith Christine Alison Vivian,[8] b. in 1881; Winnifred Annetto Vivian,[8] b. in 1881; Violet Alison Vivian,[8] b. in 1883. Muriel Alison Vivian,[8] b. in 1885.
60. James Alison,[7] b. in Springbank, Strathavon, county of Lanark, Scotland, in 1853. At the death of his father, he succeeded to the estate of Bonnytown, county of Ayr, Scotland. That estate he sold for £20,000, and proceeded to Australia, where he became a stockholder in Queensland and New South Wales. He was educated in Bury St. Edmunds, England. He has held the office of justice of the peace, and is a member of the legislative assembly of New South Wales. His P. O. address is Union Club, Sydney, Australia.
61. William Alison,[7] b. in Springbank, Strathavon, county of Lanark, Scotland, and was educated in Bury St. Edmunds, England. He m. Ellen, daughter of James Wilson. Mr. Alison inherited his father's great estate of 1,100,100 acres at Canonbar, Australia, and is the second largest land-owner in Australia. He is a justice of the peace, and a member of the legislative assembly of New South Wales, Australia.
62. Charles Alison,[7] b. in 1859; m. in 1890, Constance, daughter of Dr. Cox, of Sydney, Australia. He is a barrister, and a member of the legislative assembly of New South Wales, Australia; res. Sydney. P. O. address, Hawkesbury, New South Wales, Australia.
63. Adaline Alison,[7] b. in 1864; m. Arthur Rowan.

64. Matthew Alison [6] [47] (James,[5] John,[4] James,[3] Michael,[2] James [1]). He was born at Kilwakening, Scotland, in 1817. At the age of 21 he went to Australia, where he became a large and successful squatter. After amassing what he considered a sufficient fortune, he returned to his native parish and built a house, which is called Sydney Villa, in Strathavon. There he resides in peace, plenty, and retirement, producing happiness to others by his generosity and kindness. He is unmarried.

65. George Alison [6] [48] (James,[5] John,[4] James,[3] Michael,[2]

James[1]).   He was born at Kilwakening, Scotland, in 1819.
He was educated at the College of Glasgow, and is a member of the University Court.   He was ordained as minister
of the United Presbyterian church at Kilbarchan, in Renfrewshire, in 1842, and there he has had a very long and successful ministry.   At his jubilee in 1891, he was presented by
his congregation with a check for upwards of £400, together
with many other valuable gifts from distant members of this
church.   He married Agnes, daughter of William Jamieson,
of Glasgow, Scotland.

CHILDREN.

66. Isabel Alison,[1] b. at Kilbarchan in 1857; m. John Gardner; res.
      Bunaw, near Oban, Argyleshire, Scotland.
67. George J. Alison,[1] b. at Kilbarchan in 1864; m. 1892, his cousin,
      Jane McEwen Alison, daughter of Rev. Archibald Alison, of
      Prestwick, Scotland.   He is a merchant, 95 St. John's Park,
      Blackheath, London, England.

68.   Alexander Alison[6] [50] (James,[5] John,[4] James,[3]
Michael,[2] James[1]).   He was born at Kilwakening, Scotland,
in 1822; married Helen, daughter of William Hamilton, of
Brownside; he married, second, Isabella, daughter of William Murray, of Fleckfield, East Kilbride, county of Lanark,
Scotland.   Mr. Alison is proprietor of Blackmoss, a farm,
and a portion of the original farm of Cairnduff, where the
Alisons first settled centuries ago.

CHILDREN.

69. James Alison,[1] b. in 1848 at Hallfield, Scotland; m. Jean, daughter
      of William Wiseman, of Hookhead.
70. John Alison,[1] b. at Blackmoss, Avondale, county of Lanark, Scotland, in 1850.
71. Alexander Alison,[1] b. at Blackmoss in 1852; m. Helen, daughter of
      James Hamilton, of Drumcloy, Scotland.
72. Isabella Alison,[1] b. at Blackmoss, in 1871.
73. Jeanie Alison,[1] b. at Blackmoss in 1872.
74. Eliza Alison,[1] b. at Blackmoss in 1874.
75. Christina Alison,[1] b. at Blackmoss in 1876.

76.   Archibald Alison[6] [51] (James,[5] John,[4] James,[3] Michael,[2] James[1]).   Rev. Archibald Alison was born at Kilwakening, Scotland, in 1825; married, in 1861, Mary, daughter of
Capt. J. H. Robertson, of Leith, Scotland.   He was educated
in Glasgow college, and is a member of the University
Court.   After receiving calls from the congregations of Leslie, Largo, and Baillieston, he was ordained in 1849 as minister of the West United Presbyterian church in Leslie.   In

1882 he was installed over the United Presbyterian church
in Prestwick, county of Ayr, Scotland, where he remains in
1893.   He believes that the Britons are descended from the
ten tribes of Israel.   Every month for a considerable period
he furnished articles to periodicals and magazines in proof of
this position.   Several of these articles have been published
separately.   The chief of these publications are the following :
   " Who are the Britons, and What is their Destiny?"
   "Jacob's Stone of Bethel, the British Coronation Stone in
Westminster Abbey."
   "The British, the Stone Kingdom of Nebuchadnezzar's
Image."

CHILDREN.

77.   James Alison,[1] b. at Leslie, Scotland, in 1862; m. in 1890 Mary
        Jack, of Watsonville, Queensland, Australia.   He is connected
        with the Queensland National Bank, Mount Albion, Herberton,
        Queensland, Australia.
78.   Jane McEwen Alison,[1] b. at Leslie in 1864; m. in 1892 her cousin,
        George Alison, son of Rev. George Alison.   He is a merchant,
        95 St. John's Park, Blackheath, London, England.
79.   John R. Alison,[1] b. at Leslie in 1865.   He is a merchant; res. Zan-
        zibar.   He is of the firm of Bonstead, Ridley & Co.
80.   Maggie Alison,[1] b. at Leslie in 1867; at home; res. Prestwick, Scotland.
81.   Mary Jane Alison,[1] b. at Leslie in 1869; at home; res. Prestwick,
        Scotland.
82.   Matthew Alison,[1] b. at Leslie in 1873; res. Prestwick, Scotland.
83.   Thomas Clark Alison,[1] b. at Leslie in 1874; res. Prestwick, Scotland.
84.   Christine J. Alison,[1] b. at Leslie in 1874; d. in 1875.
85.   Williamina Alison,[1] b. at Leslie in 1881; at home.
86.   Archibald Leslie Alison,[1] b. at Prestwick, Scotland, in 1883; at home.

   87.   James Alison, of St. David's street, Edinburgh, is a solicitor and notary public in excellent standing.   His father was
a house and estate agent in Edinburgh: was b. in 1807, d.
1855.   He was son of James Alison, of Alexandria, Dumbartonshire, who was b. 1784, and who m. Henrietta Crichton.
The father of Mr. Alison was James Alison, of Renfrew, who
m. Agnes Colquhoun.   The father of James (No. 25) was
John Alison (No. 23), of Muirhead, Avondale.   The father
of John was Michael Alison (see No. 8), of Windyedge, Scotland, and Londonderry, Ireland.

CHAPTER IV.

William Allison, aged 25, left London July 27, 1635, and lived in Virginia.

Lawrence Allison was in Windsor, Conn., in 1648; was living in Deerfield, Mass., in 1704, at the age of 84 years; wife unknown; had child, Richard Allison.

James Allison was in Boston, Mass., in 1644. He had a wife, Christian. They had a son, James Allison, born Oct. 20, 1650, and John Allison, who died April 2, 1658.

James Allison, of Boston, Mass. (perhaps the same as the above, son of James), married, May 26, 1674, Elizabeth Vasey, of Braintree, Mass.

Richard Allison, or Ellison, was of Braintree, Mass. He had a wife, Thomasin. Record of their children as taken from the *New England Historical Register*, born *Brantrey*, Mass.:

Mary Ellison, daughter of Richard and Thomasin Allison, b. 15 : 6, 1646.
Hannah Ellison, daughter of Richard and Thomasin Allison, b. 24 : 5, 1648.
John Ellison, son of Richard and Thomasin Allison, b. 26 : 6, 1650.
Sarah Ellison, daughter of Richard and Thomasin Allison, b. 4 : 10, 1652.
Thomas Ellison, son of Richard and Thomasin Allison, b. 1 : 1, 1655.
Experience Ellison, daughter of Richard and Thomasin Allison, b. 2 : 6 mo, 1657.
Richard Ellison, son of Richard and Thomasin Allison, b. 7. 2m. 1660.

It will be noticed that in the ancient record the parents are called *Allison*, while the names of their children are spelled *Ellison*.

Thomas Allison in 1645 went to America in the ship *Adventure*, and located in Virginia,

J. Allison owned a warehouse in Charlestown, Mass. In 1657 his estate was sold by R. Arrington.

One Lawrence Allison (or Ellison) removed to Hampstead, N. Y., and died there in 1665. His sons, Richard, Thomas, and John, administered on his estate.

[1] In the parish records of Kingston-on-Thames, England, is an item of thirteen shillings, four pence, paid in 1603, to James Allison and four others, for carrying the armour at Coronation.—*N. E. Historical Register, 1882.*

Ralph Allison was of Scarborough, Me., in 1678, and was a great landholder.—*Savage's Genealogical Dictionary.*

Thomas Alison, on June 14, 1679, had tickets granted to him from Barbadoes, for Jamaica, in the ship *Johns Adventure,* Edward Winslow, commander.

Thomas Allison came from Windsor, Conn., and settled in Deerfield, Mass.; was constable in 1692; called shoemaker that year, and trader in 1711; sold his home lot there in 1711 to Rev. John Williams. Thomas Allison was an inhabitant of Colchester, Mass., in 1713,—perhaps the Thomas of Deerfield.

Joseph Allison was a resident of Southold, Long Island, N. Y., in 1721, and was in Goshen, N. Y., in 1726.

Thomas Allison, of Deerfield, Mass., lived at Wapping in 1710, and in his old age was cared for by the town.

John Allison, of Deerfield, Mass., 1698; married, Aug. 4, 1698, Alice, daughter of George Jeffries, who died Dec. 81, 1780, aged 61 years. No children in 1704. He was employed in 1712 to sweep the meeting-house.—*Sheldon's History of Deerfield, Mass.*

William Allison was of Windsor previous to 1700.

Samuel Allison came from the county of Londonderry, Ireland, to America in 1718, and to Londonderry, N. H., in 1719.

John Alliston, of Hartford, Conn., purchased land there of Samuel Graham in 1726.—*Hinman's Settlers of Connecticut, 2d ed., pp. 47, 48.*

Elizabeth Allison, Comfort Allison, and Ann Allison, spinsters, of Boston, Mass., nieces of Madame Susannah Thatcher, of Milton, Mass., late deceased, received certain sums left by her will, of Rev. Peter Thatcher, May 24, 1725. —*Suffolk County, Mass., Records, Boston, Mass.* On the same records Andrew Allison, or Ellison (spelled each way), deeded land May 22, 1788.

"Thomas Allison, of Southampton, in Great Britain, Gentleman, and Susannah, wife of the said Thomas Allison, heretofore Susannah Caswall," and other heirs of Henry Caswall, late of Boston, Mass., sold property there July 24, 1749. Thomas Allison was late of London.—*Suffolk County, Mass., Records.*

---

[1] From the church records of the parish of Templemore, Londonderry, Ireland, which are kept in the ancient cathedral in that city, I took this record: "William Allison had his son Thomas Allison baptized, Feb. 9, 1668."

ELLISON.

Under the name of Ellison appears the following, and it may have a material bearing upon the history of the Allison family:

From John C. Hotten's lists of emigrants to America, 1600–1700:

John Ellison, living at Anchor's Hope, James City, Virginia, came in the *Prosperous* in 1623. Ellen, his wife, came in the *Charitie.*

George Ellison, a child, died at Anchor's Hope, Virginia, in 1623.

William Ellison, servant, aged 44; at Elizabeth City, 1624; came in the *Swan.*

The first settlers of Virginia were largely of English descent.

From the Suffolk county, Mass., unpublished records: On Sept. 4, 1654, John Ellison*n* gave a receipt to Robert Willis. On March 25, 1698, Mary Ellison and others sold property.

Those who spell this name Ellison appear to have come entirely from England. The larger part of those who spell their name *A*llison are from Scotland or the Scotch settlements in Ireland.

The names Ellison and Allison in America have been confused sometimes through the carelessness or ignorance of early transcribers, or by the choice of persons who bore them in later days. Some of those who spelled theirs *E*llison have changed it to *A*llison. Never, to my knowledge, has a single Allison or his descendants changed the orthography of his name to *E*llison.

CHAPTER V.

ALLISONS OF NEW HAMPSHIRE.

The ancient residents had heroic souls. They "conquered wood and
savage, frost and flame, and made us what we are."

1. Samuel Allison,[1] of sturdy form and Presbyterian faith,
was the progenitor of the Allisons of New Hampshire, the
honored founder of their house. He was of Scotch blood, a
descendant, and probably a son of one of those men and
one of those women of heroic mould who fled from religious persecution in Covenanting times in Scotland, from the
military and barbarous executions of Claverhouse, from other
fierce and persecuting adherents of Catholicism and of the
English Established Church, to the Plantation of Ulster in
Ireland. These persecutions and the scattering of the Scottish Allisons are given in chapter 8, pp. 21–25. The speech of
Mr. Allison, like that of "all his tribe," was the rich brogue
of the Lowland Scotch dialect. His people took that with
them from Scotland to Ireland, and he brought it to the
new settlement in Londonderry, New Hampshire. He
brought his Scotch traits of character with him,—frugality,
industry, persistence, integrity, and elevation of sentiment
and purpose. He was in the splendid strength of his young
manhood when he settled in the Granite State. He was a
member of a peerless company of emigrants who, with their
descendants, helped to develop, mould, and fashion the laws
and institutions of this state. All honor to that noble band!
  Mr. Allison was born in 1690, probably in the parish of
Aghadowey, county of Londonderry, Ireland, and in 1718
he with others accompanied Rev. James McGregor (who
was pastor of that parish from 1701 to 1718) to America,
and landed in Boston in August of 1718. In the succeeding
April he with others went to Nutfield, now Londonderry,
N. H., where he was one of the first sixteen settlers, and one

of the original grantees of land, or those to whom the charter of the town was given June 22, 1722, so he is called Charter Samuel Allison, and many of the name in Vermont and Massachusetts, as well as nearly all in New Hampshire, are descended from him.

Fourteen of the settlers of Londonderry, of which he was one, received a grant of five hundred and ninety-four acres of land, bounding on Corbett's Pond, in the Range, in that portion of Londonderry which is now Windham, on May 22, 1728. This Amendment land, which fell to Mr. Allison, he sold to Alexander Park, the emigrant ancestor of the Park family of Windham, Oct. 8, 1734, and it is, in 1893, the homestead farm of George Franklin Armstrong.

In 1758 he and his only son signed a memorial asking the number of taverns to be restricted. His home farm was situated about one half mile south-east of the church on the hill in East Derry, N. H., and between the farms of two other emigrants, John Morison and Thomas Steele. It is, in 1893, included in the large and spacious farm of Col. George W. Lane. It was situated upon that elevated ridge and swell of land which can be seen from distant points. He married, in Ireland, Katherine Steele, presumably a sister of his neighbor, Thomas Steele, who had married Martha Morison, a sister of John and James Morison, his neighbors. Upon that high elevation, commanding a magnificent view of the country for miles around, for many years Mr. Allison and these allied families lived in the closest intimacy and neighborly communion. There he and his wife died. His will was made Aug. 15, 1760, he being then very sick, and proven Sept. 10, 1760. Fac-simile of his autograph as shown in his will:

The ancient cemetery on the hill in East Derry, near where the first church stood, is holy ground to descendants of the first settlers of Londonderry. Its memorial stones are very rich in historic and family lore. A few rods from the main entrance, on the north side of the principal walk and near thereto, Samuel Allison, and his wife, Katherine Steele, lie sleeping. Near them rest James and John Morison, Justice James McKean, David Steele, Rev. James McGregor, who were their friends, relatives, neighbors, and pastor, in two settlements in different hemispheres, in Aghadowey, Ireland, and Londonderry, New Hampshire. Over them is a dark slate stone tablet bearing this inscription :

"Here lies the bodys of Mr. Samuel Alison & Mrs. Katherine Alison his wife. He departed this life 6th Sept. AD. 1760, in ye 70th year of his age. She departed this life 13th Jany AD. 1760, in ye 77th year of her age."

*John Morison was the ancestor of many of the Morisons of Peterborough, N. H., while James Morison was the ancestor of the Morrisons of Windham, being the father of the author's great-grandfather, Lieut. Samuel Morison, in this line: James,[1] Lieut. Samuel,[2] Samuel,[3] Jeremiah,[4] Leonard Allison Morrison.[5]

CHILDREN.

2. Janet Allison[2] (6), b. probably in Aghadowey, Ireland, in 1712 or 1713; m. Samuel, son of John Morison, who d. in 1736; res. Londonderry, N. H., and d. Jan. 8, 1800, aged 87 years.
3. Rebecca Allison,[2] b. about 1717; m. Robert Gray. They apparently removed to Biddeford, county of York, Me. On Oct. 10, 1757, Robert and Rebecca Gray, of Biddeford, sold land in Londonderry, N. H., to James Paul, of Londonderry.[1]
4. Martha Allison[3] (15), b. Londonderry,[4] N. H., March 31, 1720; m. Lieut. Samuel Morison, of Windham, N. H., and d. there Dec. 3, 1761, aged 41 years, 8 months, 4 days.
5. Samuel Allison[5] (21), b. in Londonderry, N. H., in 1722; m. Jennette, daughter of Andrew and Betty (Christy) McFarland; res. Londonderry, N. H., and d. June 5, 1792.

John Gray, of Londonderry, N. H., was one of the original proprietors. His home lot was in the English Range, near the west end of Beaver pond, and between the lots of Joseph Kidder and Benjamin Kidder. Some of his descendants are supposed to be in Worcester county, Mass.

There is a tradition in the New Hampshire family that there were three brothers of the name of Allison who landed in 1718. According to this authority, Samuel Allison located in. Londonderry, N. H., while, later, his brothers went to Jamestown, Va. One of them went to Savannah, Ga., and there died childless. The other remained in Jamestown, Va., and is the ancestor of many of the Allison name in Virginia, Tennessee, Kentucky, and Ohio.

1. The memorial stones to Thomas Steele and his wife record that he d. Feb. 22, 1748, and that she d. Oct. 9, 1759, aged 73 years.
2. John Morison,[2] with his family, removed to Peterborough, N. H., in 1750 or 1751, and was one of its first settlers. He d. there June 14, 1776, aged 96 years. His wife, Margaret Wallace, d. April 18, 1769, aged 82 years.

Aghadowey is near Coleraine, and at the present time the Morrisons, the Steeles, and Allisons are living as neighbors.

WILL OF SAMUEL ALLISON.

In the name of God amen the fifteen Day of August one thousand seven hundred and sixty I Samuell Allison of Londonderry within his Maj[es] provance of New hampshir in Newingland Yoman being very sick and weak in boday—but perfite Mind and Memery thanks be given to

God therfore Calling to Mind to Mortality of my bodey and Knowing
that it is appointed for all men once to Die Do make and ordain this my
last will and Tastament that is to say princapally and first of all I Give
and Recommend my soul unto the hands of God that Give it and my
bodey I Recommend to the Earth to be burid in a Desent Cristen burill
at the Discraition of my Exac" Nothing Doubting but at the generall
Resurrection I shall Recive the same again by the mighty power of God
and as Touching such worldly estat wherewith it hath plesed God to
bliss me in this life with I Give Demise and dispose of the same in the
following Maner and form ——
  Imprimesis after my Debts and funerall charges is payd I Give and
bequeth unto my Grand child Susanna Allison one single Johanna
which is six and thorty shillings starling
  I tam I Give and bequeth unto my Daughter in Law Janet Allison my
Cow ——
  Itam I Give and bequeth unto my Daughter Jannet Morison for hir
own use one single Johana of Gold —— —— ——
  Itam I Give and bequeth unto my Daughter Marth Morrison for hir
own use one single Johana of Gold.
  Itam I Give and bequeth unto my.Daughter Rebecca Gray for hir own
use one single Johanna of Gold.
  Itam I Give and bequeth unto my son Samuell Alleson what farming
utenshels I am possesed of with my Great bible and Grate pote —— —— ——
  Itam I allow a tombston in Good order to be put over my wife and me
out of my Estat in Equell shares amoungst my four Children (viz) Samll
Allison Janet Moreson Martha Moreson and Rebecca Gray and my will
is for them to to Destrebute it Equilly amoungst their children and I
leekwise Constute make and ordealn my three sons (viz) Samll Alleson
Samll Moreson of Windham and Samll Moreson of Derry to be my sole
Exacutors of this my last will and Tastament and my will is for them to
give the Revt Will" Davidson Six Dollers out of my estat and I do here-
by uterly Disallow Revock and Disanull all and Every other Tastaments
wills legeces and bequeths and Exac" by me in any wise before nameed
willed or bequethed Reatefying and Confirming this and no other to be
my last will and Tastament in witness whereof I have hereunto sate my
hand and sale the Day and year above writen signed sealed Published
Pronounced and Declaired by me the sd Samll Alleson as my last will
and Tastament in the presence of us the Subscribers

Samuel Allison (L s)

David Steel
David Craige
Mo' Barnett

Proved by the oath of Moses
Barnett in Common form the
10ᵃ Day of Sept. 1760.

15. **Martha Allison**[2] [4] (Samuel[1]). She was born on
the home farm in Londonderry, N. H. (now Derry), March
31, 1720, and was the first female child of European extraction born in that town. She married Lieut. Samuel Morison[3] (son of James,[2] and grandson of John Morison[1]). He
was born (in Aghadowey, Ireland, probably) in 1704; came
to Londonderry, N. H., in 1719, and his early home was
under the hill, on the farm owned by W. O. Noyes in 1893,
and which was near the house of Martha Allison. They
lived in Windham, on the Morison homestead now occupied
by their great-grandson, where Mrs. Morison died in her
comparative youth, Dec. 3, 1761. She was a person of good

mind and many lovable qualities. Mr. Morison was a lieutenant in actual service at Fort Cumberland, Nova Scotia, in 1760; an elder in the church, the first moderator, and on the first board of selectmen of Windham in 1743. He died Feb. 11, 1776, aged 72 years. In the ancient burial-place, at the head of Windham Range, near where the first church stood, and overlooking the clear, bright, sparkling waters of Corbett's pond, he and his dearly-loved wife, Martha Allison, rest together. The *old* headstones were nearly covered with moss, and time had nearly obliterated the record upon them.

Albert A. Morrison, Esq., his great-grandson, who occupies the Morrison homestead in Windham, originated the plan of having a new monument erected to their memory, and was one of the efficient managers in carrying it into execution. So, on Dec. 19, 1892, the ancient headstones, which for more than a century had withstood the buffeting storms of winter and the blasting heat of summer, were taken out, and four stone posts, so as to be below the frost, were sunk into the ground four feet. Between them, and flat upon the ground, were placed the ancient stones, and covered with earth. On these firmly-planted posts was placed by their descendants a heavy, substantial monument of Concord granite. It was finished in the early part of 1893. On the base, in raised letters, is the name MORISON. Above is this inscription:

LIEUT. SAMUEL MORISON,

Born in 1704;
Died in Windham, Feb. 11, 1776.

An inhabitant of two hemispheres, he became one of the Pioneers and Founders of Windham. A citizen of two governments;—a lieutenant in the French and Indian War, he was faithful to his king; on the abolition of Royal authority, he became an adherent of Popular Government. An elder in the Presbyterian church, he was a loyal subject of the King of kings.

MARTHA ALLISON,

His beloved wife, is here buried by his side. She was born March 31, 1720, being the first female child of European extraction born in Londonderry, N. H. She died Dec. 3, 1761.

They rest together till the day of the great awakening.

(On the reverse side.)

"I am the resurrection and the life."

Erected 1893.

CHILDREN BORN IN WINDHAM, N. H.

16. John Morison,[3] b. May 18, 1743; m., June 22, 1781, Jennet, daughter of William, and sister of the elder Gov. Dinsmoor, of Windham. She was b. March 8, 1756; d. March 13, 1807, aged 51 years. He d. Oct. 24, 1824, aged 81 years. He was in the French war, and War of the Revolution; was town-clerk for thirteen years; had strong mental powers; was a great reader, and a good talker. Children b. in Windham, N. H.: 1,

I. Samuel Morrison,[4] b. Nov. 15, 1784; d. Feb. 1, 1831; farmer; res. Windham, on Morrison homestead; was selectman two years. He m. Betsey, daughter of James Dinsmoor, of Windham; b. Aug. 12, 1796; d. July 7, 1845. Children b. in Windham, N. H.:

I. Catherine Morrison,[5] b. Dec. 21, 1818; teacher. She m., Sept. 27, 1847, Charles L. Haseltine, of Windham, and d. July 4, 1849. He was b. Nov. 26, 1820; d. June 29, 1881. Children b. in Windham, N. H.: Catherine Haseltine,[6] b. July 3, 1848; d. Sept. 14, 1848. Charles Haseltine,[6] b. July 3, 1848; d. Sept. 14, 1848.

II. James Dinsmoor Morrison,[5] b. Nov. 22, 1820; d. Sept. 7, 1877; carpenter; res. Boston, Mass. He m., Dec. 27, 1848, Elizabeth M., daughter of Ebenezer Stevens, of Boston, Mass. Mrs. Morrison res. Boston, Mass. Children: James Thornton Morrison,[6] b. Jan. 10, 1850; d. Aug. 14, 1864. Minnehaha Elisabeth Morrison,[6] b. Feb. 4, 1856.

III. William Allison Morrison,[5] b. Sept. 3, 1822; d. Knight's Ferry, Cal., Nov. 19, 1887; miner and farmer; went to California in 1849. He m., June 10, 1854, S. Garnier, who d. Feb 8, 1870; he m., 2d, Jan. 14, 1871, Fanny Jeffers, who d. Jan. 16, 1882. Children: Charles A. Morrison,[6] b. Sept. 10, 1855; res. Camp Harney, Oregon; farmer. Augusta Morrison,[6] b. March 11, 1857; m. Edward Kenney; res. Modesto, Cal. Three children. William H. Morrison,[6] b. Sept. 19, 1859; res. Camp Harney, Oregon; farmer. Frank P. Morrison,[6] b. March 24, 1861; d. April 15, 1865. James A. Morrison,[6] b. Nov. 15, 1862; res. Knight's Ferry, Cal.; farmer; m. Child: Albert Allison Morrison,[7] b. April 21, 1889. George F. Morrison,[6] b. Dec. 11, 1864; res. Modesto, Cal. Edwin L. Morrison,[6] b. Nov. 10, 1866; res. Modesto, Cal. Fred G. Morrison,[6] b. Aug. 10, 1868; on home farm at Knight's Ferry, Cal. Thomas J. Morrison,[6] b. April 8, 1872; at home, Knight's Ferry, Cal. Anna Belle Morrison,[6] b. Dec. 11, 1874; res. Modesto, Cal.

IV. Hannah Aurelia Morrison,[5] b. Jan. 1, 1825; educated at Derry, N. H.; teacher in early life. She m., Oct. 3, 1850, Joseph Thornton Greeley, of Nashua, N. H., where they resided. He was b. Nov. 19, 1823; d. June 3, 1881. She res. in Nashua. Children b. in Nashua, N. H.: Joseph Greeley,[6] b. Nov. 21, 1852; d. Nov. 10, 1864. Frederick Thornton Greeley,[6] b. Dec. 10, 1859; d. April 5, 1870. Ellen Dana Greeley,[6] b. July 20, 1862; m. June 15, 1887, Edward Jones Cutter, physician; res. Leominster, Mass. Katherine Morrison Greeley,[6] b. July 7, 1864; m., Oct. 7, 1885, Henry Arthur Cutter, lawyer; res. Nashua, N. H. Child: Janet Cutter,[7] b. Jan. 20, 1889.

V. Albert Augustine Morrison,[5] b. Sept. 14, 1827. He occupies the Morrison homestead in Windham, on which lived Martha Allison and Lieut. Samuel Morison, member of the choir for forty years; member of the legislature in 1871 and 1872. He m., June 7, 1877, Clarissa, daughter of Robert Park and Sally (Gregg) Dinsmoor, of Windham. She was b. Jan. 25, 1849; d. Aug. 13, 1878. One child b. and d. Aug. 11, 1878.

VI. Martha Morrison,[5] b. Feb., 1830; d. July 11, 1830.

2. William Morrison,[4] b. Oct. 18, 1786; d. Jan. 23, 1812.

3. Hannah Morrison,[4] b. Nov. 8, 1788; d. March 21, 1825.

4. **Allison Morrison,**[4] b. Jan. 31, 1792; d. May 7, 1830.
5. **Naomi Morrison,**[4] b. Oct. 12, 1794. "Aunt Naomi" resided on the homestead until her death in Dec., 1886. Her life was quiet and full of good works.
6. **Tennant Morrison,**[4] b. June 24, 1797; d. April 27, 1833.
7. **Eliza Morrison,**[4] b. Nov. 24, 1799; a teacher in early life. She m., Oct. 4, 1827, Dea. Theodore Dinsmoor, of Windham, N. H., and there resided. He was b. April 22, 1798; d. Aug. 26, 1870; farmer. Children b. in Windham, N. H.:

I. **Samuel Morrison Dinsmoor,**[5] b. May 31, 1831; carpenter; res. Yonkers, N. Y. He m. Adelia H. Banta, of New York, N. Y. Child: Theodora Belle Dinsmoor,[6] b. April 11, 1872.

II. **Edwin Orville Dinsmoor,**[5] b. Sept. 23, 1834; farmer and musician; res. on homestead in Windham; was organist in church and member of choir for about forty years; has been auditor, supervisor, and representative, 1887–'89; single.

III. **Martha Amanda Dinsmoor,**[5] b. Oct. 16, 1839; m., July 5, 1877, Horace Anderson; res. Windham, N. H., where she d. July 19, 1880; she was much beloved, and at her departure was much mourned.

IV. **Aurelia Jennette Dinsmoor,**[5] b. May 10, 1844; res. on the homestead in Windham, N. H.; single.

17. **Catherine Morison,**[3] b. Sept. 20, 1745; d. May 5, 1815; m. Benjamin, son of William Thom, the emigrant; res. in Windham, N. H., on farm owned in 1890 by Joseph W. Dinsmoor in the Range. He was b. in Windham in 1747; d. June 2, 1811. Children b. in Windham, N. H.:

1. **Samuel Thom,**[4] b. Aug. 29, 1775; d. Denmark, Iowa, Nov. 22, 1865. Removed to Ohio in 1816, to Denmark, Iowa, in 1840; shipbuilder and farmer; m., 1801, Elizabeth, daughter of William, and sister of the elder Gov. Dinsmoor; she was b. Dec., 1778. She was strong and vigorous, and retained her faculties until her death, Jan. 17, 1868, aged 90 years. Children b. Salem, Mass.:

I. **Catherine Thom,**[5] d. young.
II. **Eliza Thom,**[5] b. June 2, 1802; m., Jan. 15, 1820, Dr. Joseph P. Stevenson, of Meigs county, Ohio; removed to Denmark, Iowa, where he died. She d. there Oct. 22, 1842. Children:
Samuel T. Stevenson,[6] b. Oct. 11, 1821; m., April 26, 1842, Therese Guthrie, b. Dec. 14, 1822; res. near Oneida, Kansas. Children b. Denmark, Iowa: Charles G. Stevenson,[7] b. March 16, 1844; res. Oneida, Kansas; m., July 21, 1868, Eliza J. Porter, b. Dec. 6, 1843. Children: Amelia A. Stevenson,[8] b. Oct. 10, 1870: Charles H. Stevenson,[8] b. Nov. 7, 1871; Hanasy J. Stevenson,[8] b. April 19, 1873; Therese S. Stevenson,[8] b. May 28, 1877. Eliza Thom Stevenson,[7] b. July 16, 1845; m., Dec. 31, 1865, Nathaniel M. Fox, of Denmark, Iowa; res. in Denmark until 1881, since then in Seneca and Oneida, Kansas. Children b. Denmark, Iowa: Charles W. Fox,[8] b. March 18, 1867; teller in bank; res. Oneida, Kansas. Luella F. Fox,[8] b. Sept. 17, 1868; m., Oct. 8, 1889, William Allison Fox; res. Hinsdale, Ill.; he was b. July 1, 1864. Samuel E. M. Stevenson,[7] b. April 28, 1848; m., 1872, Celia Allen, b. 1854; res. near Oneida, Kansas. Children b. Denmark, Iowa: Dora Stevenson,[8] b. Jan., 1873. Celia Stevenson,[8] b. Dec., 1874; d. Jan., 1875. Timothy Stevenson,[8] b. Dec., 1875. Nannie E. Stevenson,[7] b. Nov. 23, 1849; d. Jan. 26, 1877. Seldon Stevenson,[7] b. Aug. 5, 1862; d. Aug. 18, 1862. George E. Stevenson,[6] b. Dec. 8, 1822; res. near Oneida, Kansas, m., March 20, 1844, Julia A. Rice, b. Aug. 31, 1824. Children b. Denmark, Iowa: Joseph P. Stevenson,[7] b. June 26, 1845; m., Feb. 3, 1870, Sarah Fox, b. Jan. 7, 1844; George W. Stevenson[7], b. April 8, 1860.

John Dinsmoor Stevenson,* b. July 11, 1825; m., Sept. 24, 1846, Celia
A. Rice, b. Aug. 30, 1829; res. near Oneida, Kansas. Children b. Denmark, Iowa: Amanda E. Stevenson,⁷ b. Aug. 24,
1847; d. Oct. 14, 1863. Jonas R. Stevenson,⁷ b. Feb. 1, 1849;
m., June 17, 1880, Lizzie Priest. Child: Myrta P. Stevenson,⁸ b.
Oct. 4, 1882. Eliza J. Stevenson,⁷ b. Jan. 18, 1851; m., May 11,
1871, Charles B. Humphrey, b. July 1, 1847. Children: Selden
D. Humphrey,⁸ b. Feb. 25, 1872. Sarah L. Humphrey,⁸ b. Aug.
4, 1875. Lewis E. Humphrey,⁸ b. June 25, 1878. Augusta C.
Humphrey,⁸ b. Sept. 18, 1881; d. Dec. 30, 1882. Julia A. Stevenson,⁷ b. Nov. 4, 1852; m. Joseph Alter. Clara D. Stevenson,⁷ b.
Feb. 11, 1855; d. Nov. 26, 1857. John D. Stevenson,⁷ b. May 23,
1857; m., Dec. 18, 1878, Eliza B. De Lashmutt, b. Nov. 3, 1854.
Children: Cornelia D. Stevenson,⁸ b. Sept. 21, 1879. Walter P.
Stevenson,⁸ b. June 28, 1881. Alma G. Stevenson,⁸ b. April 30,
1885. Lewis E. Stevenson,⁷ b. July 1, 1859. Sherman E. Stev-
enson,⁷ b. Nov. 25, 1861; m., Sept. 11, 1886, Abbie H. Woolman,
b. Oct. 18, 1867. Children: Roy Stevenson,⁸ b. April 4, 1887.
Herman A. Stevenson,⁸ b. Oct. 29, 1889. Clara E. Stevenson,⁷ b.
Nov. 21, 1864; m., Aug. 23, 1885, Edwin J. Humphrey, b. Nov.
26, 1863. Children: George S. Humphrey,⁸ b. Aug. 11, 1886.
Everett E. Humphrey,⁸ b. Nov. 11, 1889. Ada B. Stevenson,⁷ b.
Oct. 27, 1866. Nellie I. Stevenson,⁷ b. Feb. 7, 1870. Sumner S.
Stevenson,⁷ b. June 19, 1876.
Joseph E. Stevenson,⁶ b. Feb. 11, 1828; m., May 5, 1849, Eva C. Bolin;
res. Fort Madison, Iowa. Children: George E. Stevenson,⁷ b.
Jan. 24, 1851; d. Jan. 20, 1860. John P. Stevenson,⁷ b. March
25, 1852; m., Oct. 15, 1878, Laura B. Bush; res. Fort Madison,
Iowa. Child: Omillie B. Stevenson,⁸ b. April 7, 1880. Eva W.
Stevenson,⁷ b. Nov. 24, 1854; m., Feb. 25, 1874, William L. Bruce.
Children: John E. Bruce,⁸ b. Jan. 28, 1877. Mabel J. Steven-
son,⁷ b. March 7, 1880. Glen N. Stevenson,⁷ b. March 24, 1886.
2. William Wear Thom,⁴ b. Dec. 29, 1777; d., Dec. 16, 1870, at Mt. Des-
ert, Me.; ship-builder and farmer; served five terms in Maine
legislature; m., Sept. 10, 1807, Eliza Somes, of Mt. Desert, Me.,
b. Jan. 31, 1771; d. May 27, 1862. Children:
I.   Catherine Morrison Thom,⁵ b. July 3, 1809; d. Aug. 8, 1833.
II. Ann Somes Thom,⁵ b. May 9, 1811; d. April 7, 1812.
III. Ann Somes Thom,⁵ b. July 8, 1813; m., Jan. 12, 1834, Elisha Was-
gatt, of Mt. Desert, Me.
IV. Julia Maria Thom,⁵ b. Feb. 28, 1816; m. Thomas Mayo, Oct. 4, 1839;
d. Dec. 22, 1855.
V.   Benjamin Thom,⁵ b. April 9, 1819; res. Mt. Desert, Me.; d. 1889;
m., April 28, 1850, Emeline Smith, of that place, b. Jan. 21,
1833; nine children.
VI. William Wear Thom,⁵ b. Dec. 9, 1824; d. Dec. 19, 1824.
VII. Charlotte S. L. Thom,⁵ b. Aug. 1, 1826; m., May, 1871, Daniel G.
Somes, b. Sept. 15, 1825; res. Compton, Los Angeles county,
Cal.; four children.
3. Isaac Thom,⁴ b. Jan. 31, 1780; d. Jan. 29, 1832, at South Boston, Mass.;
manufacturer; member of city council; m., April 16, 1809,
Sophia Senter, of Windham, N. H., b. Feb. 29, 1789; d. March
3, 1849. Children:
I.   Eliza Thom,⁵ b. March 3, 1810; m., Dec. 6, 1831, Franklin F. Blood, b.
June 28, 1852. She died July 16, 1839. Child: Clarinda Blood,
b. Sept. 29, 1832; m. D. E. Fifield, of Janesville City, Wis.
II. George Senter Thom,⁵ b. Dec. 14, 1811; res. Boston, Mass.; had
charge of the electric machinery in the fire-alarm department,
and is deceased; m., Nov. 25, 1841, Mary B. Blaney. Children:
Mary Frances Thom,⁶ b. Oct. 10, 1842; m., Aug. 29, 1859, William C. Babbitt, who d. 1890; res. Dighton, Mass. Four chil-

4

dren: Caroline E. Thom,* b. July 5, 1845; d. Jan. 31, 1859.
George H. Thom.*

III. Mary Pinkerton Thom,* b. Sept. 28, 1813; m., Dec. 3, 1834, William
Aiken, b. Deering, N. H., Jan. 4, 1805; d. Worcester, Mass.,
April 18, 1808; she died at Newton, Mass., June 28, 1859. Chil-
dren: James S. Aiken,* b. Dec. 4, 1835. Mary F. Aiken,* b.
Sept. 10, 1839. William H. Aiken,* b. May 16, 1849; graduated
at Harvard college; res. Somerville, Mass.

IV. Catherine Morrison Thom,* b. Aug. 30, 1820; m. Lucius Greenslit,
b. April 16, 1834; res. Hampton, Conn. Child: Edward Greenslit,* b. April 3, 1843. Winslow Lewis Thom,* b. June, 1823;
d. Dec. 21, 1824. Isaac Thom,* b. Aug. 6, 1825; d. Aug. 4, 1830.
Sophia Thom,* b. Sept. 20, 1827; d. Oct. 7, 1828. Artemus S.
Thom,* b. Feb. 5, 1830; d. Jan. 5, 1832.

4. Benjamin Thom,* b. June 14, 1782; m., and lived in Charlestown,
Mass. He lost his wife and two children. He soon afterward
went West and was never heard from.

5. Elizabeth Thom,* b. Feb. 20, 1785; d. in Windham, N. H., February,
1839; m., 1807, John Hughes, of Windham, b. August, 1781; d.
March 31, 1851. Children b. Windham, N. H.:

I. Olivia Grey Hughes,* b. June 20, 1808; m., May 1, 1834, David Jones,
of Lunenburg, Mass., and d. July 4, 1852. He d. July 31, 1839.
Children: Mary Elizabeth Jones,* m. Enoch Merrill, of New-
buryport, Mass. Four children: Charles Moulton Jones;* res.
Dover, N. H.; m., Sept. 11, 1867, Lydia Blaisdell. Frances Ann
Jones,* b. Sept. 15, 1857; d. aged 18 years.

II. William Campbell Hughes,* b. Jan. 12, 1810; m. Lettice Merri-
weather Smith, of Dunnsville, Va.; res. Windham, N. H. He
d. Sept. 23, 1875; she d. July 11, 1880.

III. Martha Ann Hughes,* b. Jan. 20, 1812; m. Nathaniel Pillsbury, of
Newburyport, Mass. She m., second, Caleb Pike, of Salisbury,
Mass., who d. February, 1882. Children: Emily Wood Pills-
bury,* Harry Hughes Pillsbury,* Mary Evelyn Pillsbury.*

IV. Benjamin Harvey Hughes,* b. Aug. 10, 1814; res. Windham, N. H.;
m., Nov. 29, 1838, Betsey Jane Cochran; was selectman in
1860-'61; d. about 1888. Children b. Windham, N. H.: Ella
Frances Hughes,* b. Jan. 27, 1845; m., June 19, 1867, John B.
Pike; res. East Salisbury, Mass.; several children. Kate
Elizabeth Hughes,* b. July 23, 1847; m. Granville E. Plum-
mer; res. Londonderry, N. H.; no children. Charles Harry
Hughes,* b. Jan. 30, 1853; d. March 14, 1864. Florence Ardelle
Hughes,* b. Feb. 20, 1857; d. Oct. 1, 1871.

V. John Milton Hughes,* b. Aug. 10, 1814; d. 1831.

VI. Hannah Patterson Hughes,* b. Aug. 11, 1816; m., April 26, 1848,
William S. Jones, of Lunenburg, Mass., b. Dec. 5, 1813. Children: Herbert Mortimer Jones,* b. Feb. 13, 1849. Nellie Gertrude Jones,* b. Aug. 3, 1851. Clara Adalaide Jones,* b. March
10, 1853. Martha Eldora Jones,* b. March 12, 1855. Lizzie
Frances Jones,* b. March 11, 1859.

VII. Jacob Nesmith Hughes,* b. April 20, 1818; d. Dec. 3, 1837.

VIII. Catherine Hughes,* b. April 20, 1818; d. in infancy.

IX. Elizabeth Thom Hughes,* b. Nov. 8, 1821; m., April 27, 1852, Samuel Hartwell, of Lunenburg, Mass., b. Concord, Mass., 1820.
Children: Hattie Ann Hartwell,* b. September, 1877; d. aged
24 years. Arthur Clarence Hartwell,* d. 1857. Kate Alice
Hartwell,* d. January, 1881. Charlotte Elizabeth Hartwell.*

X. Sarah Adelaide Hughes,* b. March 23, 1824; m., Oct. 8, 1846, James
Cochran; res. Windham, N. H. He was b. July 4, 1820; farmer;
has been clerk, post-master, and member of the constitutional
convention. Children: James A. Cochran,* b. June 27, 1847;
m., January, 1873, Ella Lowd, of Plymouth, Mass.; merchant;
res. East Boston, Mass.; several children. Mary Alice Coch-

ran,[6] b. Nov. 11, 1848; m., January, 1873, Leroy A. Barker; res. Windham, N. H. Several children. John B. Cochran,[6] b. Jan. 29, 1850; res. Boston, Mass.; merchant. William B. Cochran,[6] b. Sept. 5, 1852; res. East Boston, Mass. Sarah A. Cochran,[6] b. March 16, 1854; m. Joseph Currier; res. Salisbury, Mass. Clara A. Cochran,[6] b. July 26, 1856; d. Oct. 3, 1859. Emma M. Cochran,[6] b. March 8, 1858. Ellen R. Cochran,[6] b. Sept. 16, 1860. Charles H. Cochran,[6] b. Oct. 10, 1865.

XI.   Samuel Orlando Hughes,[5] b. Oct. 23, 1865; m. Eunice Heckles; res. California. Children: Henry Hughes,[6] Mattie Hughes.[6]

XII.   Isaac Winslow Hughes,[6] b. Dec. 25, 1829; m., Sept. 7, 1858, Mary Merrill, of Newburyport, Mass.; res. Merrimac, Mass. Children: John William Hughes,[6] b. Oct. 25, 1860; Hattie Little Hughes,[6] b. Aug. 28, 1862. Martha Ann Hughes,[6] b. Aug. 24, 1864. Charles Harvey Hughes,[6] b. Dec. 14, 1866. Henry Merrill Hughes,[6] b. Feb. 16, 1869.

XIII.   James Barnet Hughes,[5] b. Nov. 27, 1832; res. Kalamazoo, Mich.

6. Martha Thom,[4] b. Sept. 24, 1787; m. Robert Boyd Dinsmoor; res. Windham, N. H. They died soon after marriage.

18. Samuel Morison,[3] b. Sept. 28, 1748; d. Jan. 2, 1816; res. on the farm in Windham, N. H., owned in 1890 by his grandson, Leonard Allison Morrison. He was a soldier of the Revolution, an elder in the church; was moderator, town-clerk, selectman, and representative. He m., May 20, 1779, Sarah, daughter of Robert Park, of Windham, b. Sept. 4, 1757; d. Dec. 27, 1789; six children. He m., Aug. 31, 1792, second, Mrs. Margaret (Dinsmoor) Armor, daughter of William Dinsmoor, and sister of the elder Gov. Samuel Dinsmoor, and widow of John Armor, of Windham. She was b. Oct. 14, 1759; d. Sept. 18, 1837. Children b. Windham, N. H.:

1. Martha Morrison,[4] b. Feb. 14, 1780; m. Dea. Jesse Anderson, b. Windham, July 7, 1777; res. Windham, and d. Aug. 10, 1859. She d. Jan. 23, 1859, after an active and useful life. No children.

2. Jane Morrison,[4] b. Oct. 22, 1781; m. Joseph Thom, of Salem, N. H., where she d. Aug. 24, 1810.

3. Samuel Morrison,[4] b. March 21, 1783; d. April 27, 1827.

4. Robert Morrison,[4] b. May 22, 1785; d. Nov. 3, 1860; res. Windham, N. H.; farmer. He was an intelligent and strong-minded man. He m. Nancy McCleary, b. April 21, 1792; d. Oct. 14, 1876. Children b. Windham, N. H.:

I.   Robert Park Morrison,[5] b. Dec. 27, 1828; lived on the home farm till 1873; since then in Lawrence, Mass.; grain merchant. He was clerk and selectman. He m., Nov. 24, 1859, Harriet Ann Kelley, of Windham, b. May 21, 1835. Children b. Windham, N. H.: Hattie Frances Morrison,[6] b. July 2, 1862; res. Lawrence, Mass. Sherman Howard Morrison,[6] b. Dec. 4, 1864; d. Aug. 24, 1876.

II.   Rev. Samuel Morrison,[5] b. April 22, 1830; clergyman; res. Charlton, Mass.; graduated at Amherst college in 1859 and Bangor Theological Seminary in 1864. He is an author of music, "Carmina Centum," published in 1882. He m., Sept. 17, 1884, Mrs. Rachel Frances (Hughes) Collins, widow of William Thomas Collins. She was b. at North Truro, Mass., Sept. 17, 1834.

III.   Rufus Anderson Morrison,[5] b. March 10, 1834; res. Washington, D. C.; graduated at Amherst college in 1859, and at Princeton Theological Seminary in 1862. His health failed, and he entered business life; is now an examiner in the Patent Office at Washington, D. C.; single.

IV.   John Morrison,[5] b. Oct. 22, 1837; res. Washington, D. C.; prepared for college; then gave his attention to music for several years; member of 22d Regiment N. J. Vols., and is, in 1893, in the second auditor's office, Treasury Department, Washington, D. C. He m. Belvidere Dodge, at Mount Joy, Penn. Children: Helen Dodge Morrison,⁶ b. Mount Joy, Penn., Dec. 14, 1873. Bertha Morrison,⁶ b. Washington, D. C., Jan. 5, 1877.

5. James Morrison,⁴ b. Nov. 17, 1786; d. Aug. 1, 1871; res. Plymouth, N. H.; farmer, elder in the church, and selectman of the town. He m. Miriam, daughter of Nathan Bean, of Candia, N. H.; she d. Sept. 6, 1845. He m., second, in 1850, Mrs. Betsey Brown, of Orford, N. H. Children b. Plymouth, N. H.:

I. Hannah Morrison,⁵ b. March 26, 1810; m, Chester F. Ellis. She d. in Haverhill, Mass., Jan. 14, 1886. Children: Sarah L. Ellis.⁶ Otis C. Ellis;⁶ res. Michigan. Albert O. Ellis;⁶ res. Haverhill, Mass. John M. Ellis;⁶ res. Haverhill, Mass.

II. Sarah Morrison,⁵ b. Nov. 4, 1812; m., —— George, who d. Jan. 1, 1849. She m., second, Lewis L. Hill; res. Plymouth, N. H. Three children: Amanda J. Hill,⁶ Henry Hill,⁶ Amanda N. Hill.⁶

III. Miriam Jane Morrison,⁵ b. Nov. 29, 1814; d. in Haverhill, Mass., March 6, 1886.

IV. James Otis Morrison,⁵ b. July 18, 1818; d. Oct. 23, 1824.

V. Martha Anderson Morrison,⁵ b. December. 1819; m., Feb. 18, 1842, Charles L. Hobart, who d. July 4, 1862; res. Plymouth, N. H. Four children: Abbie Adams Hobart,⁶ Emma Jane Hobart,⁶ Willie C. Hobart,⁶ Julia Eliza Hobart.⁶

VI. John Jay Morrison,⁵ b. March 22, 1822; d. Nov. 6, 1840.

VII. Maria M. Morrison,⁵ b. Feb. 23, 1825; m., Nov. 28, 1853, Damon G. Dearborn, who d. Jan. 2, 1857; res. Plymouth, N. H. Child: Annie M. Dearborn.⁶

VIII. Cyrena Morrison,⁵ b. May 14, 1827; d. Nov. 3, 1840.

IX. Eliza Ann Morrison,⁵ b. April 14, 1830; res. Haverhill, Mass.

X. James Morrison,⁵ b. April 14, 1830; res. De Smet, South Dakota; was in 36th Regiment Ia. Vols. He m., Sept. 29, 1852, Amanda Shaw, b. Salisbury, N. H., May 28, 1833. Children: Edward A. Morrison,⁶ b. June 13, 1853. Clara A. Morrison,⁶ b. May 9, 1856. John A. Morrison,⁶ b. Aug. 18, 1858; d. in California August, 1890. George A. Morrison⁶ and Mary A. Morrison,⁶ b. Feb. 3, 1860. Everett A. Morrison,⁶ b. Oct. 5, 1863. James W. Morrison,⁶ b. Jan. 17, 1865. Estelle A. Morrison,⁶ b. July 22, 1866. Sidney A. Morrison,⁶ b. Feb. 22, 1868. Joseph G. Morrison,⁶ b. March 27, 1871.

6. Stephen Morrison,⁴ b. July 26, 1788; d. at Saugatuck, Mich., about 1864. He res. at Barre, Vt.; m., March 31, 1812, Euridice Earle, b. 1806; d. Oct. 27, 1867. Children:

I. Stephen Augustus Morrison,⁵ b. May 18, 1815; res. Saugatuck, Mich.; m., May 7, 1842, M. E. Parkman, who d. 1860. Children: Julia E. Morrison,⁶ b. July 2, 1845; m. John Francis, April 13, 1870. Jessie S. Morrison,⁶ b. Oct. 23, 1853; m., Dec. 6, 1875, T. W. Leland; res. Saugatuck, Mich. Martha Morrison,⁶ b. Oct. 28, 1848; d. Jan. 15, 1849. Stephen Morrison,⁶ b. Dec. 3, 1849; d. 1849. Hattie Morrison,⁶ b. Sept. 5, 1856; d. Dec. 10, 1856.

II. Samuel Morrison,⁵ b. Sept. 28, 1818; d. in Topeka, Kan., in 1881. He m., April 28, 1845, Lucia Harrington, who d. Nov. 15, 1854. He m., second, Mrs. Delia W. (Trowbridge) White, of Chicago, Ill., who d. Dec. 6, 1876. Children: Lowson H. Morrison,⁶ b. June 26, 1847; m. Daidee Cowan, of Topeka, Kan. Martha E. Morrison,⁶ b. Nov. 21, 1850. Lulu Morrison,⁶ b. November, 1857; d. Jan. 1, 1862. Annie L. Morrison,⁶ b. Jan. 10, 1862.

III. Cyrus Morrison,⁵ b. June 29, 1820; d. April 4, 1821.

IV. Miles Morrison,⁵ b. April 18, 1822; farmer; res. Barre, Vt. He m., Jan. 25, 1847, Sabrina E. Gale, who d. Sept. 19, 1862. He m., second, Feb. 25, 1864, Emma M. Taft. Children b. Barre, Vt.: M. Eugene Morrison,⁶ b. Nov. 22, 1847; m. Minerva Allen.

Jermiah Morrison

III.
IV.

John Gale Morrison,⁵ b. Nov. 7, 1854; res. Barre, Vt. Maud
Myra Morrison,⁶ b. Aug. 28, 1871.
V. Martha Morrison,⁵ b. March 2, 1824; d. Sept. 22, 1847; m. Jan. 7,
1847, Isaiah C. Little.
VI. Myra Morrison,⁵ b. March 2, 1824; m. Jan. 7, 1847, L. B. Walker;
res. Chicago, Ill. Children: Stephen L. Walker,⁶ b. Dec. 6,
1851. Ida M. Walker,⁶ b. Sept. 4, 1855; m. F. Dennis; res.
Chicago, Ill. Willis P. Walker,⁶ b. April 12, 1862. George L.
Walker,⁶ b. April 7, 1865.
7. Margaret Morrison,⁴ b. Aug. 11, 1793; d. April 14, 1864; res. Belfast,
Me. She m., Nov. 10, 1823, Capt. Andrew W. Park, b. Wind-
ham, N. H., June 11, 1785, and d. in Belfast, Sept. 4, 1864. She
was a person of superior mind and conversational powers, and
was held in high regard. Children b. Belfast, Me.:
I. Agnes Park,⁵ b. Dec. 22, 1824; d. Dec. 29, 1824.
II. Agnes Park,⁵ b. Jan. 8, 1826; d. Nov. 23, 1832.
III. Margaret Mary Park,⁵ b. Jan. 11, 1828; m. Sept. 19, 1852, Isaiah
Dinsmoor of Windham, N. H., who was b. Sept. 19, 1824; res.
Windham, where he d. Sept. 20, 1881. She has been a writer
for the *Youth's Companion* and other periodicals. Children b.
Windham, N. H.: Arthur Wallace Dinsmoor,⁶ b. Jan. 25, 1854;
m. May 13, 1876, Anne Donegan, of Reading, Mass.; cabinet-
maker; res. Boston, Mass; he d. Nov. 27, 1892. Children:
Florence Edith Dinsmoor,⁷ b. Aug. 26, 1877; Wallace Park Dinsmoor,⁷ b. Feb. 20, 1881; Jennie Louise Dinsmoor,⁷ b. Dec. 28,
1883; Lillie May Dinsmoor,⁷ b. July 22, 1886; d. October, 1886;
Arthur Dinsmoor,⁷ b. June, 1887. William Weare Dinsmoor,⁶ b. Sept. 14, 1859; res. Boston, Mass. He m., Sept. 14,
1883, Anne Maria Macdonald, daughter of John Macdonald, of
Jamaica Plain, Mass.; res. Boston, Mass. Children: Willie
Bell Dinsmoor,⁷ b. July 29, 1886; Clarence Macdonald Dinsmoor,⁷ d. March 3, 1891. Allen Park Dinsmoor,⁷ b. Jan. 5,
1890; d. Aug. 11, 1890. Charles Henry Dinsmoor,⁶ b. March
21, 1862; artist; res. Windham, N. H. Horace Park Dinsmoor,⁶
b. May 3, 1863; res. Windham, N. H. He m. Helen Louise
Wheeler, daughter of Charles and Adaline (Gregg) Wheeler of
Windham, N. H. She was b. Derry, N. H., April 22, 1864.
Children: Sybil Louise Dinsmoor,⁷ b. Jan. 1, 1889; d. February, 1890. Sylvia Dinsmoor,⁷ b. Dec. 18, 1890.
IV. Martha Jane Park,⁵ b. May 17, 1832; res. Windham, N. H.
V. Louise Park,⁵ b. Sept. 24, 1834; res. Windham, N. H.
VI. Horace Park,⁵ b. Feb. 20, 1837; m., Jan. 29, 1868, Margaret Elizabeth Morrison, daughter of Jeremiah Morrison of Windham,
N. H. He is a farmer, and res. on home farm in Belfast, Me.;
has been a member of the city council. She was b. in Windham, Dec. 25, 1838, educated at academy in Bradford, Mass.;
teacher. Children b. Belfast, Me.: Mabel Agnes Park,⁶ b.
July 18, 1875. Edward Horace Park,⁶ b. Aug. 9, 1877.
8. Jeremiah Morrison,⁴ b. April 20, 1795; d. Nov. 24, 1862. He m., Jan.
27, 1836, at Bradford, Mass., Eleanor Reed, daughter of Job
and Elizabeth Reed Kimball, of Peacham, Vt. She was b. Jan.
8, 1808; d. of consumption, at Windham, Aug. 5, 1866. Her
life of gentleness was crowded with denial of self, full of good
works. Mr. Morrison possessed excellent judgment and an
untarnished reputation; was active in the church, town, and
religious society; was a justice of the peace many years, selectman, representative, member of constitutional convention, and
filled other offices. He res. Windham, N. H., and d. there
Nov. 24, 1862. Children b. Windham, N. H.:
I. Christopher Merrill Morrison,⁵ b. Dec. 2, 1836; fitted for college, and
while life was full of brightness and hope, he d. of consumption Dec. 22, 1857, aged 21 years, 20 days.

II.   Margaret Elizabeth Morrison,[5] b. Dec. 25, 1838; m., Jan. 28, 1868, Horace Park; res. Belfast, Me. (See Park family, p 53.)

III. Edward Payson Morrison,[5] b. Jan. 28, 1840; fitted for college at sixteen years of age; was a teacher; his powers of mind were the best. While life had so much apparently awaiting him, consumption laid its wasting hand upon him, and he died at Peacham, Vt., Aug. 5, 1858, aged 18 years, 6 months, 8 days.

III a. Roderick Donald Morrison,[5] b. Aug. 21, 1841; d. Sept. 19, 1841.

IV.   Hon. Leonard Allison Morrison,[5] b. Feb. 21, 1843; educated at Tilton, N. H. Seminary; has served as moderator fifteen years, and selectman of his town, representative 1885–'87, state senator 1887–'89, chairman of committee on education in both branches; traveled in Europe in 1884 and in 1889. Is author of "History of the Morison or Morrison family," published in 1880; "History of Windham in New Hampshire," published in 1883; "Rambles in Europe, with historical facts relating to Scotch-American Families gathered in Scotland and the North of Ireland," published in 1887; "Among the Scotch-Irish and through Seven Countries," published in 1891; "Biography and Lineage of the Norris Family," published in 1892; the "History of the Kimball Family " in preparation, and this "History of the Allison Family," also "Supplement to the History of Windham in New Hampshire," and "History and Proceedings of the Celebration of the 150th Anniversary of the Incorporation of Windham, N. H., held June 9, 1892," published 1892; degree of A. M. from Dartmouth college in 1884. Res. Windham, N. H.

9. John Morrison,[4] b. June 19, 1796; d. Sept. 12, 1865; res. Danvers and Lawrence, Mass. He d. in the latter place, Sept. 12, 1865. He m., May 24, 1826, Mary Ann Nutting, of Danvers, Mass., who d. in Lawrence, Nov. —, 1880. Children:

I.   Mary Elizabeth Morrison,[5] b. July 18, 1827; res. Lawrence, Mass.; d. 1887.

II.   Dennison Wallis Morrison,[5] b. March 8, 1830; treasurer of Warren's Chemical Manufacturing Co., New York city. He m., Nov. 4, 1857, Mary Jane, daughter of Luke Whitney, of Ashland, Mass.: res. New Rochelle, N. Y.; no children.

III. Sarah Marcia Morrison,[5] b. March 24, 1834; teacher. She m., May 21, 1857, Dr. A. D. Blanchard, b. Medford, Mass., March 4, 1828; res. Melrose, Mass. Children b. Lawrence, Mass.: Lucy Stanwood Blanchard,[6] b. March 4, 1858; artist; m. L. J. Bridgman, an artist; res. Melrose, Mass. She d. Jan. 26, 1862. Children: Blanchard Bridgman,[7] Neal Bridgman.[7] Andrew Denman Blanchard,[6] b. June 17, 1860; cashier of bank; res. Melrose, Mass. He m. Lucy Nutting, of Lynn, Mass.; one child. Mary Anna Blanchard,[6] b. Aug. 21, 1864. Annie Rea Blanchard,[6] b. July 29, 1869.

IV.   Anna Wallis Morrison,[5] b. March 8, 1837; teacher in public schools of Lawrence, Mass.

V.   Susan Coffran Morrison,[5] b. Nov. 8, 1839; teacher in public schools of Lawrence, Mass.

VI.   John Henry Morrison,[5] b. June 6, 1844; d. July 14, 1845.

10. Christopher Morrison,[4] b. Feb. 10, 1798; res. Plymouth, Salem, and Windham, N. H.; represented Salem in the legislature; filled offices in Windham, where he died Jan. 17, 1859; single.

11. Sarah Morrison,[4] b. Oct. 7, 1800; m. Dr. Milton Ward, May 7, 1832. He was b. Plymouth, N. H., Sept. 1808; d. Detroit, Mich., March 2, 1874; was an Episcopal clergyman. She had one child: Sarah Jane Morrison Ward,[5] b. Windham, N. H., May 12, 1833; was a teacher in the public schools at Lawrence, Mass.; res. Lawrence, Mass.

19. Robert Morrison,[3] b. Feb. 6, 1758; d. April, 1808; m., Feb. 6, 1783,

Agnes, daughter of James Betton. She was b. June 26, 1760;
d. July 1, 1792. Five children. He m., second, April 19, 1794,
Eunice Dow, b. Oct. 20, 1770; d. Feb. 7, 1854. Children:
1. Elizabeth Morrison,⁴ b. Dec. 12, 1783; m. Abel Dow, and died in
Windham, N. H., Sept. 28, 1865. He d. Oct. 23, 1824. Children:

I. Alva Dow,⁵ b. Feb. 13, 1812; d. Nov, 7, 1877; m., Nov. 30, 1876, Sarah
Rumney, of Biddeford, Me.; res. Marseilles, Ill. Children:
Vermelia C. Dow,⁶ b. May 19, 1838; d. July 28, 1878; m. Nelson
Rhines, of Marseilles. Children: Ella Mary Rhines,⁷ Sadie
Bell Rhines,⁷ Alva Dow Rhines.⁷ Gilman Corning Dow,⁶ b.
Jan. 4, 1840; res. Lynn, Mass.; m., Dec. 16, 1865, Hannah Jane
Kelley. Children: Alva N. Dow,⁷ Willie C. Dow,⁷ Frank H.
Dow,⁷ Lillian A. Dow.⁷ Sarah E. Dow,⁶ b. Feb. 18, 1844; m.,
Nov. 7, 1868, W. J. Burnett, of Marseilles, Ill. Children: Aleda
B. Burnett,⁷ William T. Burnett,⁷ Lizzie M. Burnett.⁷ Charles
A. Dow,⁶ b. Sept. 21, 1846; d. April 30, 1856. Emma F. Dow,⁶ b.
July 6, 1855; d. July 19, 1855.

II. Robert M. Dow,⁵ b. Sept. 3, 1813; res. Bellevue, Sarpy Co., Neb.
He m., Oct. 3, 1841, Ann W. Bennett, of Salem, N. H., b. Aug.
19, 1813; d. June 10, 1850. He m., second, May 4, 1855, Emily
R. Lane, b. March 2, 1827. Children: Olive H. Dow,⁶ b. July
12, 1842; Robert H. Dow,⁶, b. May 19, 1844; d. April 11, 1865;
• Willard W. Dow,⁶ b. July 20, 1846. Infant son d. July 10, 1850.
Lizzie J. Dow,⁶ b. Aug. 31, 1856. Jessie F. Dow,⁶ b. Jan. 13,
1858; d. Oct. 30, 1865. Cora L. Dow,⁶ b. Aug. 13, 1860. Nellie
C. Dow,⁶ b. July 18, 1862. Infant daughter,⁶ b. Dec. 13, 1863.
Jessie L. Dow,⁶ b. Aug. 13, 1865.

III. Nancy Betton Dow,⁵ b. March 30, 1815; m., Dec. 31, 1835, Jonathan
Massey, of Salem, N. H.; res. Morris, Ill. She d. April 18,
1875. He d. June 16, 1866. Children: Stillman E. Massey,⁶ b.
Oct. 28, 1836; res. Morris, Ill; m., July 31, 1872, Miriam R. Bar-
stow. Adeline B. Massey,⁶ b. June 12, 1841; m., Oct. 18, 1861,
J. N. Raymond; res. Morris, Ill. Children: Edward S. Ray-
mond,⁷ Howard Raymond.⁷ Myra S. Massey,⁶ b. June, 1844; m.,
Jan. 30, 1873, Joseph H. Pettitt; res. Morris, Ill. Child: Mur-
rell Pettitt.⁷ Horace S. Massey,⁶ b. Aug. 16, 1851. Lizzie H.
Massey,⁶ b. Sept. 24, 1852.

IV. Lucinda Dow,⁵ b. Oct. 22, 1816; m., Dec. 27, 1838, Gilman Corning,
of Salem, N. H.; res. Haverhill, Mass., where she died in 1889.
He res. Salem, N. H., 1893. Child: Albian James Corning,⁶ b.
Nov. 7, 1841; an apothecary; res. Baltimore, Md.; m., Nov. 12,
1871, Margaret Shepard Woodside, of Baltimore. Children:
John Woodside Corning⁷ and Charles Francis Corning,⁷ b. Dec.
10, 1872. Abram James Corning,⁷ b. July 27, 1876.

V. Betsey Dow,⁵ b. June 26, 1818; d. Dec. 27, 1854; m. (second wife),
Aug. 29, 1849, Ebenezer T. Abbott, of Windham, N. H., b. May
27, 1804; d. March 2, 1853. Child: Jacob Abbott,⁶ b. June 17,
1850; d. Sept. 20, 1857.

VI. Philena Dow,⁵ b. Sept. 8, 1820; m., Dec. 26, 1839, Samuel Carter
Jordan, of Kennebunk, Me., b. Jan. 26, 1818; res. Morris, Ill.
She d. Sept. 7, 1880. Children: Elizabeth Hannah Jordan,⁶ b.
May 15, 1841; d. Jan. 11, 1844. Alvah Reynolds Jordan,⁶ b.
Dec. 13, 1842; m., June 18, 1869, Sarah D. Parmelie; lawyer;
res. Morris, Ill.

VII. Hannah Dow,⁵ b. Dec. 27, 1822; d. Sept. 1842.

VIII. Abel Dow,⁵ b. Dec. 12, 1824; m., Sept. 28, 1849, Rhoda Ann,
daughter of Samuel Plummer, of Salem, N. H.; res. Windham,
N. H.; the owner and manager of Granite State Grove and
boats on Canobie lake; was representative in 1877, and again
in 1879 and 1880. Children b. Windham, N. H.: Martha Morrison Dow,⁶ b. Dec. 15, 1850; d. Aug. 27, 1852. George Plum-

mer Dow,⁴ b. Nov. 23, 1852; res. Windham, N. H. Charles
Allison Dow,⁶ b. Dec. 24, 1854; m., Dec. 24, 1878, Ada Dow,
daughter of William Colby, of Salem, N. H.; res. Windham,
N. H. Children: Charles Abel Dow,⁷ b. March 15, 1880. Lura
Edna Dow,⁷ b. April 24, 1881. Willard Elbridge Dow,⁶ b. Oct.
6, 1856; m., Dec. 14, 1880, Alice Heath, daughter of Lorenzo
and Sarah Elizabeth (Heath) Fairbanks, of Boston, Mass., b.
July 11, 1861; is in electric light business; res. Braintree,
Mass. Children: Alice Rebecca Dow,⁷ b. Dec. 8, 1881. Alvah
Morrison Dow,⁷ Clarence Dow.⁷ Lizzie Lucinda Dow,⁶ b. July
27, 1859; m., Dec. 30, 1880, Albert Onslow Alexander, of Windham, N. H., where he was b. May 22, 1857; store-keeper, post-
master, and station-agent at Canobie Lake, N. H. She d. Feb.
17, 1893. Children: Hannah May Alexander,⁷ b. Dec. 14, 1892.
George —— Alexander.⁷ Marion Louise Dow,⁶ b. Aug. 13, 1876.
2. Martha Morrison,⁴ b. April 24, 1785; d. Oct. 3, 1802.
3. Silas Morrison,⁴ b. March 4, 1787; d. April 7, 1814.
4. Samuel Morrison,⁴ b. July 1, 1789; d. aged 10 months.
5. Robert Morrison,⁴ b. June 5, 1791; d. aged 4 months.
6. Asa Morrison,⁴ b. Feb. 10, 1795; d. June 3, 1871. He m., Feb. 18,
1820, Lydia Allen, b. Salem, N. H., Jan. 28, 1828. He m., second, Nancy Scully, in 1838; res. Hopkinton, N. H., and Pokagon, Mich. Children:
I. Martha Ann Morrison,⁵ b. Aug. 12, 1821; m., Nov. 7, 1838, B. F. Silver, b. Hopkinton, N. H., Nov. 8, 1808; res. Pokagon, Mich.
Child: Helen Adalaide Silver, b. Sept. 3, 1845; d. May 27, 1874;
m. A. J. Sammon; res. Pokagon, Mich.
II. Nancy Morrison,⁵ b. Aug. 22, 1823; m., 1842, James Sullivan, grand-
son of Gen. John Sullivan, of Revolutionary fame, b. Exeter,
N. H., Dec. 6, 1811; lawyer; d. at Dowagiac, Cass Co., Mich.
She d. May 6, 1848. Child: Clara Sullivan,⁶ b. April, 1843; d.
Sept. 22, 1862.
III. Lydia A. Morrison,⁵ b. Jan. 21, 1828; m., Nov. 13, 1847, Henry Lind-
sey Rudd. She is dead. Res., 1882, Peoria, Oregon. Children:
Ellen N. Rudd,⁷ b. June 17, 1855; d. Oct. 21, 1857. Lura Allen
Rudd,⁷ b. May 9, 1860. Harry Z. Rudd,⁷ b. Aug. 27, 1862.
7. Nancy Morrison,⁴ b. Aug. 17, 1796; m. Rev. Abraham Dow Merrill,
Feb. 14, 1817. She d. Jan. 29, 1860. She possessed brilliancy
of thought and expression, and with remarkable fidelity per-
formed the arduous duties of a Methodist clergyman's wife.
He was b. March 7, 1896, and was one of the noted men of his
denomination. He d. April 29, 1878. Children:
I. Martha Mehitable Merrill,⁶ b. Salem, N. H., 1817; m., 1839, Samuel
Richardson Allen, who d. in Somerville, Mass., Jan. 22, 1852.
She d. there May 13, 1850. Children: Susan Amelie Allen,⁶ b.
1840; d. Feb. 8, 1860. Benjamin Franklin Allen,⁶ b. 1842; d.
March 8, 1860. Edward Everett Allen,⁶ b. Aug. 5, 1845; m.,
June 6, 1872, Fannie, daughter of Isaac Robbins, of Watertown,
Mass. Is connected with Downer Kerosene Oil Works, Water-
town, Mass.; res. Boston, Mass.
II. John Milton Merrill,⁶ b. Salem, N. H., 1819; m. Mary Bassett Par-
tridge Hills, of Holliston, Mass., b. Dec. 15, 1810. He was a
clergyman, 15 years in the ministry; his health failing, he
entered business life, and d. March 17, 1881. Children: Martha
R. Merrill,⁶ b. April 20, 1843. Mary S. Merrill,⁶ b. Dec. 25,
1844; m., April 26, 1871, Frederick Ernest Boden, of Corry
Plain. Children: John Merrill Boden,⁷ b. Nov. 25, 1872; Frederick Ernest Boden, Jr.,⁷ b. Aug. 4, 1874. Abraham D. Merrill,⁶ b. July 15, 1847; d. Aug. 12, 1847. Abram D. Merrill,⁶ 2d,
d. in infancy. John J. Merrill,⁶ b. Nov. 30, 1848; m., Nov. 20,
1875, Alice Ratcliffe, of Belmont, N. Y. He d. April 25, 1876,
Child: John Joshua Merrill,⁷ b. Sept. 1, 1876. Rufus B. Mer-

rill,⁴ b. March 16, 1852. Alva Morrison Merrill,⁵ b. May 15, 1854. Nathaniel C. Merrill,⁵ b. June 17, 1855. Wilhelmina Arabella Merrill,⁵ b. Jan. 23, 1861; m., July 18, 1881, Nathan Bushnell, of Bradford, Penn. Child: Rosalia Bushnell,⁷ b. Jan. 13, 1883.

III.   Jacob S. Merrill,⁵ b. Oct. 17, 1821; m. Harriet D. Barnes, of Boston, Mass., Sept. 1, 1842, who d. in Cambridge, Mass., Nov. 15, 1873, and was b. in Newton, Mass., Sept. 23, 1814; res. Wakefield, Mass. Children: George A. B. Merrill,⁶ b. Boston, Mass., Jan. 6, 1844; m. Eliza Isabel Peabody, of Salem, Mass., b. June 17, 1862; res. Wakefield, Mass. Child: Morrison Merrill,⁷ b. Dec. 8, 1881. Harriet E. Merrill,⁶ b. Cambridge, Mass., Dec. 31, 1847. Martha E. Merrill,⁶ b. Cambridge, Mass., Feb. 23, 1849. Caroline F. Merrill,⁶ b. April 20, 1851; d. Jan. 29, 1860.

IV.   Diantha F. Merrill,⁵ b. Oct. 2, 1824; d. March 2, 1827, in Barre, Vt.

V.   William B. Merrill,⁵ b. Barre, Vt., Aug. 15, 1826; m., June 9, 1853, Mary B. Dyer, of Boston, Mass., b. Oct. 8, 1830. He is a director and partner in the Downer Kerosene Oil Co., of Boston, Mass.; res. 147 West Concord St., of that city. Child: Adelaide Snow Merrill,⁶ b. June 22, 1854; m., June 26, 1876, Thomas E. Tuttle; res. Boston, Mass. Children: William Merrill Tuttle,⁷ b. April 15, 1879. Lizzie Holmes Tuttle,⁷ b. Nov. 12, 1888.

VI.   Joshua Merrill,⁵ b. Duxbury, Mass., in 1828; m. Amelia S. Grigg, of Boston, Mass., June 13, 1849, b. Boston, Dec. 25, 1830. Is permanently connected with Downer Kerosene Oil Co.: res. East Chester Park, Boston, Mass. Children: Isabella Morrison Merrill,⁶ b. April 10, 1850; m., Feb. 10, 1868, George H. Richards, Jr., of Boston, merchant; res. Boston, Mass. Children: Herbert Wilder Richards,⁷ and George H. Richards,⁷ d. in infancy. Joshua Merrill Richards,⁷ b. Jan. 12, 1873. William Bradley Merrill,⁶ b. Dec. 10, 1852; d. Oct. 9, 1853. Amelia Grigg Merrill,⁶ b. March 17, 1854; m., June 2, 1875, Mark Hollingsworth; res. Boston, Mass. Nellie G. Merrill,⁶ b. Sept. 22, 1858; d. Sept. 19, 1863. Gertrude B. Merrill,⁶ b. Dec. 11, 1862. Joshua Merrill,⁶ b. June 21, 1871.

VII.   Abraham H. Merrill,⁵ b. in Lynn, Mass., March 8, 1831; m. Martha A. B. Forbes, of Cambridge, Mass., Dec. 25, 1851, b. July 4, 1834; farmer, literateur, artist; res. Salem, N. H. Children: Alice E. Merrill,⁶ b. Feb. 21, 1858. Annie M. Merrill,⁶ b. March 28, 1864; d. June 19, 1864.

VIII.   Rufus S. Merrill,⁵ b. Lowell, Mass., July 5, 1833; m. Mary A. Stoddard, of Boston, Oct. 7, 1851; connected with the Downer Kerosene Oil Co., and has made many noted inventions; res. Arlington Heights, Boston, Mass. Children: Charles S. Merrill,⁶ b. March 27, 1853; m., June 27, 1878, Emma J. Abbot, of Hyde Park. Child: Mary Augusta Merrill.⁷ Rufus F. Merrill,⁶ b. Dec. 31, 1855; m., Oct. 16, 1869, Cora E., daughter of Horatio H. Hubbard, of Hyde Park, Mass. Willis C. Merrill,⁶ b. May 27, 1861. Walter E. Merrill,⁶ b. July 23, 1866. Mary A. Merrill,⁶ b. April 29, 1869. Nancy Merrill,⁶ b. Dec. 30, 1872.

8.   Ira Morrison,⁴ b. July 18, 1798; d. March 10, 1870; res. Ripley, Me., Salem, N. H., and d. in Braintree, Mass. He m. Sophia Colby, of Hopkinton, N. H., b. March 3, 1801; res. Braintree. She d. Oct. 16, 1891. Children:

I.   Catherine Colby Morrison,⁵ b. Jan. 10, 1825; m. John Whittaker, April 3, 1850; res. Braintree, Mass. Children: Horace F. Whittaker,⁶ b. May 31, 1851; d. March 30, 1881. Luella E. Whittaker,⁶ b. Nov. 20, 1853; m., Jan. 16, 1876, Francis French, of Brockton, Mass. She d. Feb. 2, 1883.

II.   Benjamin Lyman Morrison,⁵ b. March 28, 1828; m., Nov. 22, 1855,

Lydia Penniman; woollen manufacturer; res. Braintree, Mass.; d. Oct. 1886. Children: Lyman Willard Morrison,[6] b. Nov. 2, 1858; m. Cora I. Bates, of Braintree, Mass., Nov. 20, 1883. Helen Maria Morrison,[6] b. Sept. 7, 1867; res. Braintree, Mass.

III. Nancie Todd Morrison,[5] b. Dec. 26, 1836; teacher and artist; res. Rowley, Mass.

IV. Ira Plummer Morrison,[5] b. April 22, 1842; m., May 16, 1871, Mary Smith, of Weymouth, Mass.; res. Braintree, Mass. Children: Franklin Morrison,[6] b. May 17, 1872; d. May 16, 1877. Grace Morrison,[6] b. Jan. 20, 1875.

9. Mary Morrison,[4] b. March 25, 1800; m. Dea. Jonathan Cochran; res. Windham, N. H., and after 1842, in Melrose, Mass., where she d. March 18, 1885. He was b. June 9, 1781, and d. in Melrose, Mass., Jan. 6, 1885. Children b. Windham, N. H.:

I. Silas Morris Cochran,[5] b. June 24, 1819; d. Dec. 16, 1866; lawyer; res. Baltimore, Md., and was an associate justice of the court of appeals. He m. Mary Needham, of Baltimore. She d., and he m., second, Dec. 28, 1859, Charlotte Rockwood, of Cambridge, Mass., who res. at Newton, Mass. Children: Arthur Cochran,[6] b. Aug. 27, 1864. Agnes Langdon Cochran,[6] b. July 4, 1866.

II. Linus Cochran,[5] b. Jan. 8, 1821; d. Aug. 25, 1843.

III. Nelson Cochran,[5] b. Feb. 3, 1824; m., Jan. 24, 1850, Emily Green, b. Malden, Mass., May 24, 1829. He d. in Melrose, Mass. Children: Maurice G. Cochran,[6] b. Feb. 8, 1856. Clarence Cochran,[6] b. Feb. 26, 1858. Mary E. Cochran,[6] b. March 18, 1868.

IV. Isaac Augustus Cochran,[5] b. Nov. 21, 1826; d. May 24, 1841.

V. Emily Jane Cochran,[5] b. Aug. 29, 1832; m. Asa Dow, a business man; res. Chicago, Ill. Children: Alice Cochran,[6] Harold Cochran.[6]

10. Benjamin Morrison,[4] b. July 22, 1802; d. March 31, 1815.

11. Leonard Morrison,[4] b. May 4, 1804; d. April 26, 1875; a woollen manufacturer, and a man of much excellence of character; res. Salem, N. H., Lawrence, Mass., and Byfield, Mass.; d. in latter place. He m., April 8, 1827, Elizabeth, daughter of Arthur Bennett, of South Middleboro, Mass. She d. in 1882, in Braintree, Mass. Children:

I. Maria Elizabeth Morrison,[5] b. Nov. 16, 1828; m., April 26, 1849, Amos Dow; res. Salem, N. H. She d. Dec. 22, 1859. He d. Sept. 22, 1855. Children: Alvin Edson Dow,[6] b. March 15, 1852; d. Sept. 11, 1852. Maria Lizzie Dow,[6] b. Nov. 10, 1853; m., Sept. 19, 1875, George W. Adams, of Newbury, Mass. Child: Raymond Morris Adams,[7] b. Oct. 30, 1876. Lura Amanda Dow,[6] b. March 15, 1856.

II. Leonard Almy Morrison,[5] b. Oct. 29, 1835; m., April 5, 1857, Amanda Regina Huse, of Manchester, N. H. He d. July 2, 1872. She married again. Children: Almy Edson Morrison,[6] b. June 11, 1858. William Huse Morrison,[6] b. May 5, 1861. Ina Blanche Morrison,[6] b. May 8, 1871.

12. Hon. Alva Morrison,[4] b. May 13, 1806; d. May 28, 1879. He was a woollen manufacturer; res. Braintree, Mass. He possessed great energy of character and business capacity; was a member of the Massachusetts house and senate. He m., July 11, 1830, Myra Southworth, of Stoughton, Mass., b. Nov. 3, 1810, and she d. (1890) in Braintree, Mass. He d. there. Children:

I. M. Lurette Morrison,[5] b. Dec. 4, 1833; m., April 15, 1853, Horace Abercrombie; res. Braintree, Mass. Children: Helen M. Abercrombie,[6] b. June 13, 1855. Elmer Ellsworth Abercrombie,[6] b. April 27, 1861; m., June 6, 1889, Annie L. Coleman, of Boston, Mass.

II. Alva S. Morrison,[5] b. Nov. 9, 1835; m., Nov. 9, 1857, Lizzie A. Curtis, of Weymouth, Mass., who d. Jan. 7, 1874. He m., second, Rebecca Holyoke, of Marlborough, Mass., June 13, 1875. He is the senior member of the firm of A. S. Morrison & Bros., manufacturers; was a member of the legislature in 1888; res. Braintree, Mass. Children: Frank Russell Morrison,[6] b. April 6, 1860; d. Aug. 10, 1860. Anna Gertrude Morrison,[6] b. Sept. 23, 1862; m., Oct. 29, 1884, Aubry Hilliard; res. Braintree, Mass. Children: Carrie G. Hilliard,[7] b. Sept. 7, 1885. Curtis M. Hilliard,[7] b. Aug. 5, 1887. Ruth Hilliard,[7] b. May 25, 1888; d. Dec. 19, 1889. Walter Ellis Morrison,[6] b. May 16, 1864; m. June 14, 1887, Edith A. Follansbee, of Brookline, Mass.; res. Braintree, Mass. Child: Ibrahim Morrison,[7] b. Feb. 9, 1889. Fred Gilbert Morrison,[6] b. April 20, 1866; m. Anna Isabella Johnson, of Boston, Mass., Feb. 2, 1888; res. Braintree, Mass. Children: Norma Grace Morrison,[7] b. Oct. 16, 1888. Blanche Morrison,[7] b. Feb. 24, 1890. Mira Isabel Morrison,[6] b. Nov. 14, 1867; m., June 25, 1890, Albert E. Kingsbury, of Holbrook, Mass. Grace Curtis Morrison,[6] b. Dec. 30, 1870; d. Sept. 27, 1872. Alice Southworth Morrison,[6] b. May 20, 1878.

III.   Mary C. Morrison,[6] b. March 10, 1838; d. Dec. 29, 1839.
IV.   E. Adelaide Morrison,[5] b. Dec. 29, 1889; m., Jan. 15, 1862, Lewis Bass, Jr., of Quincy, Mass; res. Quincy, Mass. Children: Lewis Morrison Bass,[6] b. May 4, 1863; d. Aug. 26, 1863. Lewis Bass,[6] b. May 27, 1871. Alva M. Bass,[6] b. July 12, 1874.
V.   Robert Elmer Morrison,[5] b. May 12, 1843; res. Braintree, Mass.; firm of A. S. Morrison & Bros. He m., Jan. 5, 1870, Sarah R. Gregg, of Quincy, Mass. Children b. Braintree, Mass.: Mabel S. Morrison,[6] b. Sept. 3, 1871. Lizzie Curtis Morrison,[6] b. Jan. 14, 1875. Joseph Gregg Morrison,[6] b. Feb. 24, 1886.
VI.   Augustus M. Morrison,[5] b. Dec. 7, 1846; d. Nov. 17, 1875.
VII.   Ibrahim Morrison,[5] b. Oct. 21, 1848; res. Braintree, Mass.; woollen manufacturer of the firm of A. S. Morrison & Bros. He m., Jan. 20, 1870, Mary L. Rodgers, of East Marshfield, Mass.
20.   Martha Morrison,[3] b. Nov. 17, 1761; d. in Newburyport, Mass., Aug. 23, 1836; m. Rev. Gilbert Tennent Williams. He d. in Framingham, Mass. Children:
1.   Simon Tennent Williams,[4] b. May 20, 1790; res. Boston, Mass.
2.   Martha Williams,[4] b. July 29, 1792; m. Alfred W. Pike. Four children: Martha L. Pike,[5] Alfred W. Pike,[5] Samuel J. Pike,[5] Joseph G. W. Pike.[5]
3.   Samuel Morrison Williams,[4] b. Nov. 24, 1797; res. Lowell, Mass; d. about 1890.
4.   John Adams Williams,[4] b. Oct. 17, 1799; d. Aug. 9, 1865, in Boston, Mass.
5.   Constant Floyd Williams,[4] b. Nov. 11, 1801; d. Albany, N. Y., in 1832.

6.   Janet Alison[2] [2] Samuel.[1]   She was b., probably, in the parish of Aghadowey, county of Londonderry, Ireland, in 1712, and came to America in 1718, and settled in the township of Londonderry, N. H., in 1719, with her father's family. She m. Samuel Morison,[2] son by a late marriage, of John Morison[1] and Janet Steele, the patriarchal ancestor of the Morisons of Peterborough, the Morrisons of Windham, and many of the Morrisons of Derry and Londonderry, N. H., and Londonderry, Nova Scotia. This Samuel Morison was a half uncle of Lieut. Samuel Morison of Windham, who m.

Martha Alison, the sister of the subject of this sketch. Samuel Morison[2] was b., probably, in the parish of Aghadowey, Ireland (from which came Rev. James McGregor, and a portion of his flock, who settled in Londonderry, N. H.), in 1719, and came with his father previous to 1723 (but not in 1719) and settled on the farm which had been deeded to their "honored father," John Morison,[1] by Charter James Morison,[2] ancestor of the Morrisons of Windham, and Charter John Morison,[2] ancestor of the Morisons of Peterborough, N. H., and of Londonderry, Nova Scotia. On this farm, Samuel Morison[2] and his wife, Janet Allison, spent their lives. It is an exceedingly pleasant farm and locality, in Derry (Dock), N. H., owned by Charles Day. They lived to a rare old age, she dying Jan. 8, 1800, at 87 yrs. He d. June 21, 1802, at 92 yrs.

[For fuller record of Janet Allison's descendants, see pp. 246-254, " History of the Morison or Morrison Family."]

CHILDREN BORN IN LONDONDERRY (NOW DERRY), N. H.

7. Joseph Morrison,[3] b. 1742; single; lived on the homestead in Londonderry, N. H., where he died April 16, 1814, at 72 yrs.
8. Samuel Morison,[3] moved to Walpole, N. H., and d. there Dec. 8, 1833.

CHILDREN.

1. Jane Morrison,[4] b. April 10, 1780; m. John Cooper in 1808, who was b. Dec. 23, 1775, and d. in Alstead, N. H., April 1, 1854. She d. there July 12, 1857. Children:
    I.   Charles Lewis Cooper,[5] b. March 5, 1809; d. June 8, 1868.
    II. Laura A. Cooper,[5] b. June 30, 1810; d. Aug. 22, 1847; m. in Langdon, N. H., Esdras Smith.
    III. George W. Cooper,[5] b. Oct. 21, 1818; m. Katherine Buchanan; res. St. James, N. B.; d. Dec. 18, 1878. Four children.
    IV. James S. Cooper,[5] b. Oct. 18, 1820; res. St. James, N. B.; m. Janet Cameron. Nine children.
    V.   Mary Ann Cooper,[5] b. Nov. 15, 1820; m. William F. Kennedy; res. St. James, N. B. Eight children.
    VI. Margaret E. Cooper,[5] b. Nov. 23, 1823; m. William Barbour; res. St. James, N. B. She d. April 12, 1857. Three children.
    VII. Robert C. Cooper,[5] b. Dec. 8, 1828; m. Sarah J. Allen; res. St. James, N. B. Ten children.
2. Samuel Morrison,[4] lived and d. in Walpole, N. H.; single.
3. Robert Morrison,[4] b. Londonderry, N. H., Jan. 27, 1786; d. Alstead, N. H., in 1847; m. Sally Prouty. She d. Somerville, Mass., Aug. 30, 1856. Children:
    I.   Solon D. Morrison,[5] b. June 30, 1816; res. Alstead, N. H.
    II. Samuel J. Morrison,[5] b. Oct. 27, 1817; d. Boston, Mass.
    III. Sarah Ann Morrison,[5] b. Dec. 28, 1818; m. John S. Winn; d. Boston, Aug. 2, 1870.
    IV. Joseph H. Morrison,[5] b. Jan. 14, 1820; res. San Francisco, Cal.

V. Fanny Morrison,⁵ b. Sept. 13, 1821; m. George Case; res. San Fran-
        cisco, Cal.
VI. Milton D. Morrison,⁵ b. Dec. 21, 1822; d. Aug. 20, 1824.
VII. Mary D. Morrison,⁵ b. Dec. 21, 1822; d. Jan. 19, 1823.
VIII. Margaret E. Morrison,⁵ b. Dec. 28, 1823; d. Dec. 24, 1824.
IX. Charles W. Morrison,⁵ b. Dec. 28, 1824; d. Jan. 19, 1870, in San
        Francisco, Cal.
X. Caroline N. Morrison,⁵ b. Dec. 23, 1824; m. L. K. Whitcomb; res.
        Boston, Mass.
XI. Margaret C. Morrison,⁵ b. May 16, 1827; d. Dec. 28, 1867, in San
        Francisco, Cal.
XII. Betsey J. Morrison,⁵ b. April 16, 1829; d. 1849.
4. Mary H. Morrison,⁴ b. March 7, 1789; m. James C. Christie of New
        Boston, N. H.; res. St. James, N. B. where she d., Aug. 29,
        1858.
5. Joseph Morrison,⁴ d. in Wisconsin.
6. John Morrison,⁴ d. in Walpole, N. H.
7. Betsey Morrison,⁴ b. 1795; m. Luther Fay, who d., and she m., second,
        Calvin Chapman. of Keene, N. H., and d. Oct. 18, 1878.
9. Thomas Morison,³ b. 1747; d. April 2, 1804, in Londonderry, N. H.;
        single.
10. Catherine Morison.³ She m. John Reed, of Londonderry, N. H.
        She d. April 14, 1820. Seven children.
11. William Morison,³ b. 1745; removed to Walpole, N. H., and d. in
        Reading, Vt., in 1833, at 88 yrs. He m. Margaret Thompson,
        of Alstead, N. H., who d. Dec. 27, 1864, in Reading, Vt. Chil-
        dren:
1. Priscilla Morrison,⁴ b. June 27, 1802; m. Hiram Rice; res. Reading,
        Vt.
2. Calvin Morrison,⁴ b. Jan. 29, 1803; d. Cavendish, Vt., April 25, 1854.
        Four children.
3. Prudy Morrison,⁴ b. Nov. 21, 1805; d. July 21, 1821.
4. Mary Morrison,⁴ b. Jan. 21, 1807; d. Rockingham, Vt., June, 1881.
5. Sherburne Morrison,⁴ b. 1809; res. Boston, Mass.
6. George W. Morrison,⁴ b. June 11, 1811; a prominent business man;
        res. Rockingham, Vt. He m. Betsey Emery, b. July 23, 1812;
        d. April 15, 1871. Three children: George W. Morrison,⁵ b.
        Sept. 7, 1846; res. Rockingham, Vt.; m. Hattie Wetherbee;
        Three children. Mary J. Morrison,⁵ b. Aug. 26, 1850; m.
        Norman G. Gould, who d. July 31, 1874. Child: Melissa B.
        Gould. Sherburne C. Morrison,⁵ b. Sept. 1, 1854; res. Mabel-
        ton, Ia.
7. William L. Morrison,⁴ b. 1813; m., April 11, 1843, Sarah Hatch; res.
        Cavendish, Vt.
8. Jane H. Morrison,⁴ b. 1816; m. John Monroe, of Boston, Mass., and
        d. Sept. 10, 1854.
12. John Morison,³ b. and d. in Walpole, N. H.; single.
13. Jane Morison,³ b. Oct. 20, 1755; single; d. Londonderry, Dec. 9,
        1843.
14. Mary Morrison,³ b. 1757; lived on the homestead in Londonderry,
        N. H., and d. Nov. 13, 1835, aged 78 yrs.

21. Capt. Samuel Allison² [5], Samuel¹. He was born
in Londonderry, N. H., in 1722; married Janet, daughter of
Andrew and Betty (Christy) McFarland.¹ She was born in

¹ Andrew and Betty (Christy) McFarland fled from the troubles in Scotland to Londonderry (county or city), Ireland, and emigrated later to
America, landing at Boston, Mass., probably between 1718 and 1722,
where they were married. She is said to have been very beautiful, and
those of her descendants who possess that charming quality, attribute it

Rowley, Mass., in 1724; d. Oct. 16, 1809, in Weathersfield, Vt. (at the home of her son, James Allison, where she lived the latter part of her life), at 85 years, and is buried there; there is no stone at Weathersfield to mark her grave. Captain Allison died in Londonderry, June 5, 1792. He succeeded his father upon the home farm near Derry, East Village, and was prominent and active in town affairs; was intelligent and intellectual, and one of the best extempore speakers reared in that town. In their town meeting he was sure to be pitted against Jonathan Morison, an equally fluent speaker and ready talker. After one of their wordy encounters, when Morison had been rather worsted in the intellectual combat, he turned to Allison with the pithy remark, spoken in his rich Scotch brogue, "Ye are a braw speaker, but ye dinna tell the truth." When a young man of twenty two years, on July 3, 1744, he was one of the "Londonderry troopers" in Capt. John Mitchell's company raised for defence against the French and Indians; he served again in August, 1745. He served on the board of selectmen 1752, '53, '54, '55, '56, '57, 58, and '75, and was a signer of the Association Test in 1776, and was appointed coroner for Rockingham county in the latter year. His name appears

as a legacy from her. They removed to Rowley, Mass., and it is supposed that at a later date they settled in Londonderry, N. H. Their son, Andrew McFarland, b. 1734, d. 1754, and is buried near the tablets of the Allisons, in the old cemetery on the hill, at East Derry. Major Moses McFarland, with his wife, left their home in Londonderry, N. H., before 1769, and lived in Haverhill, Mass., and it is thought kept a tavern there. Their children, Robert McFarland, Nancy McFarland, Katherine McFarland, were left in charge of the home in Londonderry. Eunice McFarland, daughter of Major Moses McFarland, married in 1787 at eighteen years of age, and lived in Cambridge, Vt. She was the grandmother of Mrs. James Little of Tottenville, Richmond county, N. Y., who, in February, 1893, had collected material relating to the McFarlands. The clan McFarland once occupied Loch Sloy, on the north-western shore of Loch Lomond, in Scotland, and were neighbors of the "Rob Roy" McGregors of its south-eastern shores.

The proprietors of Suncook, now Pembroke, N. H., chose, in 1748, Andrew McFarland one of a board of commissioners to settle certain claims of the town of Bow. It is probable that this Andrew is the same as the settler of Rowley and Londonderry.

Rev. Asa McFarland, D. D., of Concord, N. H., was son of James, of Worcester, Mass., who was a son of Andrew. About the time the Londonderry, N. H., settlers emigrated to America, Andrew was a member of the Scotch colony in Ulster, Ireland. (N. H. Hist. Col., vol. 1, p. 195.) It *looks* as though these three Andrews were one and the same person, but it is not proven.

upon several petitions. He was buried in the cemetery at East Derry, N. H., by the side of friends and kindred.

CHILDREN BORN IN LONDONDERRY (NOW DERRY), N. H.

22. Katherine Allison,[2] b. November, 1747; d. Feb. 1, 1848, aged 8 months.
23. Samuel Allison[2] (34), b. April 2, 1749; m. Molly Barr; res. Dunbarton, N. H., and d. there Aug. 27, 1800.
24. Janet Allison[3] (46), b. July 13, 1752; m. James Stinson; res. Dunbarton, N. H., and d. there Dec. 10, 1843, at 92 yrs.
25. Andrew Allison[3] (54), b. Feb. 26, 1754; m. Sarah, dau. of Dea. Eli Moore, who d. 1801. He m. second, 1802, Mrs. Betsey Evans, of Dublin, N. H., where he d. May 28, 1841.
26. Margaret Allison[3] (60), b. April 1, 1756; m. David Quinton, of Walpole, N. H.
27. Susannah Allison,[3] b. Aug. 5, 1758; d. Aug. 6, 1758.
28. Susannah Allison[3] (63), b. Oct. 13, 1759; m. Lieut. John Moore, of Londonderry, N. H. She d. in Londonderry, April 28, 1809.
29. Kathreen Allison[3] (71), b. April 1, 1762; m., 1785, Nathaniel Holmes, of Peterborough, N. H., where she d. April 9, 1831, aged 69 years.
30. John Allison[3] (81), b. Aug. 15, 1764; d. before Sept. 24, 1800; res. Londonderry, N. H.
31. James Allison[3] (86), b. Feb. 22, 1767; removed to Weathersfield, Vt., and d. there Feb. 23, 1805.
32. Sarah Allison[3] (90), b. Dec. 17, 1769 or 1770; m., July 5, 1788, Daniel Abbot, of Peterborough, N. H. She d. in New York, N. Y., Nov. 22, 1837.
33. Stephen Allison,[2] b. July 10, 1772; m. his cousin, Betsey McFarland. It was not a happy marriage and they separated, and he went to North Carolina, where he d. at the age of 80 yrs. Child: Fanny Allison.[4]

34. Samuel Allison[3] [28], (Captain Samuel,[2] Samuel[1]). He was born in Londonderry, N. H., April 27, 1749; m. Molly Barr, and removed to Dunbarton, N. H.; became one of its first settlers, residing upon a farm a mile from the center of the said town, and said farm was owned in 1892 by John Ireland. Going there when a young man, he became thoroughly identified with the interests of the place and community. On March 14, 1775, he and several others entered their protest on the town book against the proceedings of a town meeting, believed by them to be illegal. When the Revolutionary war was calling for earnest effort on the part of the patriotic people, he was chosen, in 1777, one of a town's committee to hire soldiers for the war. He was interested in the religious matters of the town, and on May 26, 1789, he paid £7 : 2s for pew number 22, in the gallery of the meetinghouse "to be built." He died, in the prime of life, Aug. 27,

1800, and is buried in the cemetery at Dunbarton. He was 51 years 4 months of age.

CHILDREN.

35. Samuel Allison,[4] d. young.
36. John Allison[4] (95), b. March 23, 1776; res. Peterborough, N. H., and d. there Aug. 13, 1764, aged 88 yrs., 4 mo.
37. William Davidson Allison[4] (108), b. December, 1777; m. Amey Adlington; res. Boston, Mass., and d. 1842.
38. Elizabeth Allison[4] (113), b. Aug. 3, 1780; d. Manchester, N. H., Aug. 29, 1850; res. Manchester, N. H. She m. Daniel Hall.
39. Andrew Allison[4] (123), b. Sept. 18, 1782; d. Feb. 12, 1822; res. Dunbarton, N. H.; m. Sarah Bronson.
40. Polly May Allison,[4] m. David Culver; res. Weathersfield, Vt. They had children: one was named Eliza Culver.[5]
41. James Allison[4] (130), b. May 24, 1784; d. Feb. 2, 1867; res. Dunbarton, N. H.
42. David Clinton Allison[4] (146), b. April 27, 1787; m. Mary Bronson, a sister to Andrew's wife; res. Concord, N. H., and d. there July 1, 1851.
43. Margaret Barr Allison[4] (158), b. 1789; m. Samuel Evans, and d. Sept. 25, 1823.
44. Jane Allison.[4] She was never married, but lived to an advanced age, and d. in Warner, N. H., and is there buried. Her home was with her brother, James Allison.
45. Walter Harris Allison[4] (162), b. Dec. 30, 1792; m. Sarah Allen; res. Brookfield and Boston, Mass. He d. June 13, 1854.

46. Janet Allison[3] [24], (Captain Samuel,[2] Samuel[1]). She was born in Londonderry, N. H., July 13, 1751. She married, about 1782, James Stinson, of Dunbarton, N. H., born March 21, 1745. He was of Scotch descent, and his language clearly indicated his descent "from the land of Wallace, Bruce, and the bonny Dundee." He was noted for his honesty, uprightness, and integrity. He was a farmer, and the farm which he cleared, and in which he delighted, witnessed his closing days. He died April 5, 1827. Mrs. Stinson located with her husband in Dunbarton about 1775, and survived him some sixteen years, and received a pension for his Revolutionary services, which were rendered under General Stark at the battle of Bunker Hill. She was a strongminded and sensible woman, had a remarkably retentive memory, and her conversational powers were good. She retained her mind to the last of life, and died in Dunbarton, N. H., Dec. 10, 1848.

CHILDREN BORN IN DUNBARTON, N. H.

47. William Stinson,[4] b. Oct. 6, 1783; d. when about 23 yrs. of age; single.
48. Mary Stinson,[4] b. Nov. 30, 1785; d. Dunbarton, N. H., 1865.

49. Samuel Stinson,[4] b. Sept. 17, 1787; d. when a young man; single.
50. John Stinson[4] (166), b. Nov. 13, 1789; res. Dunbarton, N. H.
51. Archibald Stinson[4](170), b. March 14, 1791; res. Hammond, St. Lawrence county.
52. James Stinson[4] (181), b. July 20, 1794; res. Harbour Creek, Penn.
53. Jeremiah Page Stinson[4] (189), b. July 20, 1798; d. Sept. 5, 1827.

54. Andrew Allison[3] [25] (Captain Samuel,[2] Samuel[1]). He was born in what is now East Derry, N. H. (then Londonderry), on Feb. 26, 1754. He married, Feb. 5, 1784, Sarah, daughter of Dea. Eli and Sarah (Chenery) Morse, of Dublin, N. H. She was born in 1769, and died July 2, 1799. In 1783, he located in that town on lots Nos. 16 and 17, in the Sixth range, which had been purchased by his father, Samuel Allison. The home first established was on lot 16. Mr. Allison's second wife was Mrs. Betsey (Carter) Evans, of Peterborough, N. H., whom he married in October, 1802. In early life, in his father's home in Londonderry, Mr. Allison listened with delight to the stories and anecdotes told by Dr. Matthew Thornton, who was a visitor there, and he recounted them to his Dublin friends in the years of his mature life. He was large in size, fleet of foot, hot tempered, quick to take offence. In the town of his adoption he became a prominent actor, and frequently filled public positions; was moderator of the annual meetings in 1802 and 1810; town clerk in 1794, '95, '96, and '97, and selectman in 1795, 1802, 1803, and 1808; representative in 1808 and 1818. His death occurred in Dublin, May 28, 1841.

CHILDREN BORN IN DUBLIN, N. H.

55. Sarah Allison,[4] b. March 13, 1787; d. May 5, 1878, aged 91 yrs., 2 mos., 8 days. In young womanhood she engaged to marry a young man, a neighbor. Her household goods were ready; but consumption seized her lover. She tenderly cared for him during his sickness; she was faithful to her early love, and during a long life she waited in the joyous hope of meeting him in a land where there is no more death, and where partings are unknown.
56. Ebenezer Allison[4] (192), b. March 18, 1789; m. Phebe Phelps, in 1816; res. Brownville, N. Y.; son, Harlow Allison,[5] res. Lanark, Jefferson county, N. Y.
57. Eli Allison[4] (204), b. Dec. 25, 1791; res. Dublin, N. H.; d. March 25, 1860.
58. Samuel Allison,[4] b. March 20, 1795; m., Jan. 28, 1857, Mrs. Maria Piper, widow of Artemus Piper, dau. of Benjamin and Phebe

(Norcross) Mason, of Dublin, N. H. She was b. March 6, 1804.
He was selectman of Dublin in 1842,'43, '44; removed to Marlborough, N. H., and d. there July 31, 1880; no children.
59. Abigail Allison,⁴ b. April 20, 1804; m., Nov. 25, 1823, Cyrus Mason,
son of Benjamin Mason, of Dublin, and was his second wife.
He was b. Oct. 18, 1795; she d. Jan. 4, 1888. Children:
1. Betsey Evans Mason,⁵ b. Aug. 22, 1824; m., Feb. 8, 1849, Silas Pierce
Frost, of Dublin, N. H.; son of Benjamin, and b. Feb. 9, 1820;
res. Dublin, N. H. She d. April 3, 1887. Children: Walter
Clarence Frost,⁶ b. March 11, 1851; res. Colorado Springs, Col.;
m., July 3, 1878, Mary Ella, dau. of John Caldwell Hildreth.
She was b. New Ipswich, N. H., Oct. 7, 1853. He graduated at
Dartmouth college in 1876, taught at Woodstock, Vermont,
and at Newton, Mass.; organized Globe Investment Co.; went
to Colorado Springs, Col., in 1888, to regain his health, where
he now resides. His wife was a teacher in Newton, Mass.
Children born in Newton, Mass.: Hildreth Frost,⁷ b. Jan. 2,
1880; Hester Frost,⁷ b. June 9, 1884. Alfred Clinton Frost,⁶ b.
March 28, 1852; res. Dublin, N. H. He m. Henretta Frances,
dau. of Alonzo Patterson, of Henniker. Children: Edith C.
Frost,⁷ b. Dublin, N. H., July 20, 1884; Henry Walter Frost,⁷ b.
Dublin, N. H., May 16, 1886. Charles Mason Frost,⁶ b. Sept.
24, 1858; d. May 28, 1879. He was a young man of fine qualities of mind and heart. He had just commenced his career as
a teacher when he d. of pneumonia.
2. David Mason,⁵ b. Jan. 23, 1826; single; farmer. He served three
years in a New Hampshire regiment in the late war, and was a
highly respected soldier and man; is now in Concord, N. H.
3. Charles Mason,⁵ b. Nov. 5, 1836; d. Dec. 25, 1856.
4. Allison Zeman Mason,⁵ b. Aug. 13, 1839; res. Boston, Mass., business office, 19 Milk St. He m., Nov. 28, 1867, Emeline Sophia
Learned, b. Dec. 31, 1842; d. Jan. 16, 1883. She was dau. of
Calvin Learned, of Dublin, N. H. He m. second, June 17,
1885, Mary Frances, dau. of James Brown, of Boston, Mass.;
b. June 17, 1851. Children: Lucelia Learned Mason,⁶ b. July
9, 1870; Irene Elizabeth Whitney, b. and adopted March 14,
1886. She was the only child of Mrs. Allison's youngest sister.
Her parents d. at the time of her birth.
5. Henry Clay Mason,⁵ b. Feb. 22, 1842; d. Sept. 9, 1843.
6. John Henry Mason,⁵ b. Aug. 25, 1846; m., April 9, 1867, Abbie Smith,
of Marlborough, N. H.; res. Dublin, N. H. Children: Fred
Leslie Mason,⁶ b. March 29, 1868. Fannie Evalina Mason,⁶ b.
Dec. 20, 1869; d. Oct. 24, 1880.

60. Margaret Allison³ [26] (Captain Samuel,² Samuel¹).
She was born in Londonderry (now Derry), N. H., near the
church in the East Village, and on the land now included in
the farm of George W. Lane. Her date of birth was April 1,
1756. She married David Quinton, of Walpole, N. H., where
they a long time resided, but she died in Ohio.

CHILDREN.

61. Betsey Quinton,⁴ d. unmarried.
62. Samuel Quinton⁴ (211),

63. Susanna Allison[3] [28] (Capt. Samuel,[2] Samuel[1]).
She was born Oct. 13, 1759, and married, as his second wife,
Lieut. John Holmes, eldest son of Nathaniel and Elizabeth
(Moore)[1] Holmes, of Londonderry, N. H. He succeeded to
the home farm in Derry Lower Village. He was born in
1747, and died Nov. 2, 1794. She died April 28, 1809. His
first wife was his own cousin, Martha, daughter of Col. Robert Moore. (See p. 77.) She died Sept. 5, 1778, leaving a son
who died young, and a daughter, Molly Holmes, who married —— ——, living somewhere in Hillsborough Co., N. H.

CHILDREN BORN IN LONDONDERRY, N. H.

64. Martha Holmes,[4] b. in 1781; d. Dec. 25, 1834, aged 53 years; m.,
      about 1798, Col. William Moore[5] (Col. Daniel Moore,[3] of Bed-
      ford, N. H.), who was first cousin of her father on the Moore
      side. He d. March 25, 1839, and was b. in Bedford, Sept. 12,
      1778. He and his first wife were married at Bedford Centre,
      N. H. He was a brick manufacturer in Bedford; was a farmer
      and a colonel in the militia; selectman in 1833 and 1835, rep-
      resentative in 1832 and 1833. He m., second, Susan, daughter
      of Thomas Wallace, of Goffstown, in May, 1835. She d. at
      Henniker, Feb. 14, 1880, and is buried beside her first husband
      at Goffstown, N. H. Their children were.—
1. Daniel Moore,[5] b. Bedford, N. H., Feb. 23, 1801; m., April 1, 1828,
      Mary Shirley McQuesten, of Litchfield. She was his cousin.
      He d. Aug. 13, 1850. She d. Feb. 29, 1840, and he m., second,
      April 1, 1841, Sarah Stevens, of New Boston, N. H., who d.
      Jan. 13, 1855, aged 39 years. They are buried at Bedford Cen-
      tre, N. H. He was selectman of Bedford, 1832, 1837, 1838, and
      1839, clerk 1835, and clerk of Merrimack, N. H., in 1850, at
      time of his death. Children b. Bedford. N. H., except Ervin J.
      Moore:
I. William Clinton Moore,[6] b. Jan. 3, 1829; m., March 25, 1854, Martha
      Jane, daughter of William Moore. She was his cousin. He
      d. Aug. 16, 1854, aged 25 years, 7 months, 13 days.
II. James Clifton Moore,[6] b. April 8, 1830; m., Nov. 16, 1852, Mary A.
      Hodgman, of Bedford, N. H. He removed to Scranton, Penn.,
      in 1860, and manufactured brick. He enlisted, Feb. 13, 1864,
      in the 5th N. Y. Heavy Artillery; was taken prisoner, Oct. 19,
      1864, at the battle of Cedar Rapids, Va., and d. in Libby Prison,
      Richmond, Va., Dec. 25, 1864. His wife returned to Bedford,
      N. H.; m., second, William H. Gage, who d. July, 1879. Chil-
      dren: Mary Emeline Moore,[7] b. Bedford, N. H., Oct. 9, 1853:
      m., Oct. 24, 1872, George A. Powers, of Milford, N. H.; res.
      Milford, N. H. Child: Frederick E. Powers.[8] George Leroy
      Moore,[7] b. Jan. 16, 1858; d. at Pittston, Penn., Nov. 7, 1863.
      Sadie Jane Moore,[7] b. Scranton, Penn., June 30, 1861.
III. Martha Jane Moore,[6] b. June, 1832; d. Jan. 5, 1834.
IV. Daniel Leroy Moore,[6] b. Nov. 27, 1834; m., Sarah F. Chadwick, of
      Nashua, N. H. They lived in Nashua, and Wheeling, W. Va.
      Res. Cleveland, Ohio. She d. at Cleveland, March 2, 1872.

[1] She was the daughter of John[1] and Janet Moore, who came in 1723–
'24 from county Antrim, Ireland, to Londonderry, N. H.

He was a band-master in the late war. Children b. Cleveland, Ohio: Helen Leon Moore. Walter Leroy Moore,[7] b. 1866. Mildred Moore,[7] b. 1868. Alton Clifton Moore,[7] b. 1871.

V. George Burnham Moore,[6] b. in Bedford, N. H., Nov. 29, 1837; was a soldier in the Union Army; enlisted and served three enlistments; taken prisoner, confined in Libby Prison, never recovered from the starvation process inflicted by the rebels. He d. at the Soldiers' Home at Togus, Me., March 7, 1886, aged 48.

VI. Joseph Harrison Moore,[6] b. Feb. 4, 1840; m., July 15, 1875, Georgianna Ansell, of Manchester, N. H.; no children. He served through the war, and is now an engineer on the Boston & Maine Railroad.

VII. Ervin Jay Moore,[6] b. Nov. 24, 1844, in Merrimack, N. H.; m., March 28, 1872, Lydia Quimby, of Concord, N. H. Children: Frank Ervin Moore,[7] b. March 14, 1873, at Concord, N. H. Walter H. Moore,[7] b. Concord, N. H., Dec. 16, 1875; d. Oct. 22, 1878. Sarah Florence Moore,[7] b. Charlestown, Mass., March 27, 1879; d. Dec. 2, 1880. Mr. Moore served through the war; was taken prisoner, and escaped; returned to Weare, N. H., after his term had expired; then was in Concord, N. H., an engineer on Concord and B. & M. railroads. Three of these four brothers were wounded in the war (all save Daniel L. Moore). They were great-grandsons of Col. Daniel Moore, of Bedford, N. H., who was a captain at Bunker Hill under Gen. Stark and colonel of a New Hampshire regiment through the Revolutionary War, and was at Saratoga under Gen. Gates and in Rhode Island under Gen. Sullivan.

2. Nancy Cox Moore,[5] b. Feb. 19, 1803; m. her cousin, Thomas W. Moore, of Litchfield, N. H. She d. Feb. 8, 1869. He was b. April 12, 1792. He d. in Nashua on Feb. 10, 1878. He was representative from Bedford in 1853, selectman in 1844. Children:

I. William Moore,[6] b. Bedford, N. H., Oct. 19, 1824; d. Aug. 20, 1882; m., Nov. 27, Caroline A. Gage, of Bedford; no children. He was a captain in the militia and lieutenant in an independent company in Bedford during the war.

II. Martha Jane Moore,[6] b. Feb. 21, 1830; d. Sept. 11, 1832.

III. Annis Jane Moore,[6] b. April 15, 1834: d. March, 1836.

IV. Thomas Wallace Moore,[6] b. Bedford, N. H., Oct. 19, 1837; m., Feb. 19, 1861, Lura Smith, of New Boston, N. H. They were divorced in 1870, and she m., second, May 15, 1871, Nathaniel H. Weston, He m., second, May 6, 1880, Ella C. Edwards, of Dorchester, N. H.; res. Bedford, N. H. Child: Clara Ann Moore,[7] b. Bedford, N. H., Dec. 27, 1866; went to Michigan with her mother, and m., Dec. 25, 1885, Fred B. Dusett, of New Haven, Mich. They res. at Armada, Mich., in 1891. Children: Margie Moore Dusett,[8] b. New Haven, Mich., June 6, 1886. Harry Smith Dusett,[8] b. Armada, Mich., Aug. 6, 1890.

V. Margaret Ann Moore,[6] b. Oct. 10, 1839, in Bedford, N. H.; m., June 27, 1861, Luther Kittridge, of Merrimack, N. H., and lived in Nashua, N. H., till 1885; since then, at Reed's Ferry, Merrimack; no children.

VI. Olive Wallace Moore,[6] b. Nov. 2, 1841; d. Aug. 28, 1843.

3. Joseph Colby Moore,[5] b. April 7, 1805; d. Nov. 21, 1887. He m., 1832, Martha McQuesten, his cousin, of Litchfield, N. H. She d. in Goffstown, N. H., April 30, 1887, aged 75 years. Children:

I. Mary Shirley Moore,[6] b. Bedford, N. H., Dec. 16, 1833; m., April 10, 1851, Ziba A. Hoyt, of Goffstown, N. H.; res. Goffstown, N. H. Children: Martha A. Hoyt,[7] b. Merrimack, N. H., Aug. 13, 1853; m., April 10, 1871, Edward Gove, of Weare, N. H. Children b. at Weare, N. H.: Charles A. Gove,[8] b.

March 9, 1877; Gussie E. Gove,[8] b. June 28, 1880. Ella J. Hoyt,[7] b. Weare, N. H., Aug. 24, 1857; m., Aug. 29, 1877, Charles S. Parker, of Goffstown, N. H., and d. Feb. 3, 1878, at Goffstown, aged 21 years; no children. Frank Hoyt,[7] b. at Weare, N. H., Jan. 9, 1862; is a physician; res. Manchester, N. H., and in 1891 in New York city. Belle M. Hoyt,[7] b. Sept. 4, 1867, in Weare, N. H.; m., June 4, 1890, George F. Bartlett, of Weare, N. H.; res. Goffstown West Village, N. H. Adelie L. Hoyt,[7] b. at Weare, N. H., April 1, 1872; d. Jan. 10, 1888.

II.   Susan Jane Moore,[6] b. Aug, 22, 1836; d. 1838.

III. Martha Ann Moore,[6] b. Aug. 22, 1836; m., June 29, 1861, Nathan F. Hunkins, of Plaistow, N. H. Child: Mary Ella Hunkins,[7] b. April 29, 1865. He d. at Haverhill, Mass., Feb. 21, 1886, aged 21 years. Mrs. Hunkins and daughter reside on Jackson St., Haverhill, Mass. Mary Ella Hunkins,[7] m., June 4, 1890, Fred Rumery Moore, of Haverhill.

IV.   Abel Fletcher Moore,[6] b. June 12, 1837; m., Aug. 4, 1861, Eliza A. Simons, of Weare, N. H.; moved to Concord, N. H. He was roadmaster of the Concord Railroad from 1866 to 1877; resigned, and is now at Minneapolis, Minn. Children b. at Concord: Marietta Moore,[7] b. Aug. 25, 1864; m., Dec. 26, 1883, Frederic B. Luscomb, of Portland, Me. Children: Sadie Baker Luscomb,[8] b. Oct. 21, 1884. Horace Simons Luscomb,[8] b. Aug. 28, 1888. The family reside at Goffstown, N. H. Lena May Moore,[7] b. Aug. 2, 1868; d. March 30, 1871. Helen Frank Moore,[7] b. Oct. 30, 1872.

V.   David Rollins Moore,[6] b. Feb. 4, 1843; m., Oct. 16, 1880, Margaret Heskett, of Boston, Mass. They res. Amherst,· N. H. Children: Joseph Harrison Moore,[7] b. Goffstown. N. H., Oct. 29, 1882; d. April 19, 1883. Martha Ann Moore,[7] b. Aug. 31, 1884, Infant son,[7] b. and d. Feb. 16, 1886. Jenny Frances Moore,[7] b. Sept. 16, 1887. Carrie Belle Moore,[7] b. New Boston, N. H., Feb. 4, 1891. Mr. Moore was a member of Co. E, 4th Regt. N. H. Vols.; was in many battles; severely wounded; reenlisted; was in the service 4 years, 7 months, and 14 days; is a pensioner; res. New Boston, N. H.

4.   Susannah Moore,[5] b. Feb. 3, 1806; d. April 23, 1807.

5.   John Holmes Moore,[5] b. June 15, 1807; d. Jan. 23, 1812.

6.   Timothy Fuller Moore,[5] b. Bedford, N. H., June 16, 1809; m., Clarissa E. Emery, of Newbury, N. H., Jan. 9, 1838. She d. Oct. 14, 1885. He d. Jan. 28, 1889; res. Bedford, N. H. Children b. Bedford, N. H.:

I.   William Wilson Moore,[6] b. Bedford, N. H., June 17, 1839; m., Jan. 1, 1874, Sophia H. Babcock, of Groton, Mass., b. in Wilmot, N. H., May 1, 1851. They res. in Scranton, Penn. He is superintendent of B. Sweetser's brickyard. He is the compiler and author of this genealogical record of the Moore family. Child: Marian Moore,[7] b. Concord, N. H., April 10, 1875; d. Bedford, N. H., Dec. 1, 1888, aged 13 years, 7 months, 21 days.

II.   Sarah Jane Moore,[6] b. May 22, 1841; m., Feb. 17, 1873, Charles H. Wheeler; res. 20 Dunster St., Cambridge, Mass. Children: Charles Perley Wheeler,[7] b. July 17, 1874. Carrie N. Wheeler,[7] b. March 18, 1876.

III. Charlotte Ann Moore,[6] b. Oct. 13, 1842; m., Aug. 12, 1873, Edward E. Priest, of Cambridge, Mass.; res. 96 Winthrop St., Cambridge, Mass. Child: Clarissa A. M. Priest,[7] b. Cambridge, Mass., Nov. 23, 1874; m., Nov. 23, 1892, Everett Percy Ireland, of Corinna, Me.; res. Cambridge, Mass.

IV.   Phillips Quincy Moore,[6] b. Sept. 1, 1844; d. July 4, 1846.

V.   Amos Harvey Moore,[6] b. April 16, 1846; d. June 15, 1848.

7.   Elizabeth Moore,[5] b. Dec. 29, 1810; m., Sept. 27, 1831, Lancey Weston, of Antrim, N. H. He d. at Mt. Clemens, Mich., Dec. 9, 1877,

aged 77 years. She res. Mt. Clemens, now at Richmond, Mich. Children b. Antrim, N. H.:

I.   Nathaniel Holmes Weston,⁶ b. Antrim, N. H., July 21, 1833; m., Dec. 29, 1854, Hannah Holt, of Weare, N. H. Child: Willie Holmes Weston,⁷ b. Goffstown, N. H., April 16, 1860; m., Feb. 29, 1888, Eva A. Fuller, of Chesterfield, Mich., and res. Richmond, Mich. They res. Jan., 1891, at Osceola, Mich. Child: Jessie May Weston,⁸ b. July 19, 1889; d. July 28, 1890. Mr. N. H. Weston removed to Detroit, where Mrs. Weston d. June 30, 1862. He m., second, 1871, Mrs. Lura (Smith) Moore, the divorced wife of Thomas W. Moore, Jr. She d. March 19, 1889. Child by second marriage, Harvey Weston,⁷ b. Detroit, Mich., Aug. 19, 1872.

II. Leonard C. Weston,⁶ b. Dec. 13, 1834; d. Oct. 14, 1839.

III. Harrison C. Weston,⁶ b. Dec. 7, 1839; m., May 4, 1872, Mattie A. Ketchum. He res. at La Crosse, Wis. Children: Fred Weston,⁷ Frank Weston,⁷ b. in Michigan, Feb. 10, 1874.

IV. Clark W. Weston,⁶ b. Dec. 8, 1842; d. Dec. 4, 1861. He was a soldier in Co. I, 9th Regt. Mich. Vols., and d. of typhoid fever at West Point, Ky.

V.   George W. Weston,⁶ b. Aug. 4, 1846; m., Dec. 29, 1875, Jenny Bowman, of Chesterfield, Mich. Children: Charles C. Weston,⁷ b. March 2, 1881; d. Oct. 18, 1881. Winifred J. Weston,⁷ July 2, 1882. Clinton C. Weston,⁷ b. Feb. 23, 1887. Mr. Weston res. Richmond, Mich.; a sash and blind manufacturer.

8.   Nathaniel Holmes Moore,⁵ b. Bedford, N. H., Dec. 24, 1812; m., May 9, 1837, Jane Smith, at Bedford, N. H., and in 1846 removed to Cambridge, Mass., where she d. Jan. 6, 1847. He m., second, July 28, 1852, Susan E. Spencer, of Cambridge, Mass. He d. Nov. 25, 1880, at Manchester, N. H., to which he removed in 1876, and is buried in Cambridge. Children b. Cambridge, Mass.:

I.   Henry Holmes Moore,⁶ b. Feb. 23, 1856; m., Jemima Stewart, of Boston, Mass. Children: Elizabeth Marion Moore,⁷ b. Manchester, N. H., July 1, 1885. Walter Alexander Moore,⁷ b. March 9, 1887. Lillian Stewart Moore,⁷ b. Dec. 11, 1888; d. April 18, 1889. They res. in Manchester, N. H.

II. Lizzie Spencer Moore,⁶ b. June 29, 1853; d. Dec. 1, 1863.

III. Adelaide Frothingham Moore,⁶ b. Sept. 9, 1860; d. March 28, 1862.

IV. Ida Weston Moore,⁶ b. March 6, 1863; m., June 15, 1887, Alpheus Gray, of Dover, N. H.; res. Manchester, N. H.

V.   Ada White Moore,⁶ b. March 6, 1863; m., June 10, 1888, William F. Brent, of Manchester, N. H. Children: Ford Spencer Brent,⁷ b. Dec. 21, 1888. Percy Gray Brent,⁷ b. March 12, 1890. Arthur Thompson Brent,⁷ b. Dec. 8, 1891.

9.   William Moore,⁵ b. May 20, 1815; d. Oct. 20, 1880. He m. in 1836, Mary A. Kendall, of Merrimack, N. H.; res. Bedford, N. H.; was selectman in 1849, and a brick manufacturer. She d. Jan. 15, 1892, aged 77 years, 7 months, 22 days. Children b. Bedford:

I.   Martha Jane Moore,⁶ b. July 1, 1836; m. her cousin, William C., son of Daniel, who d. Aug. 16, 1854. She m., second, 1860, Aaron Q. Gage of Bedford, N. H. Children b. Bedford, N. H.: Carrie E. Gage,⁷ b. Feb. 26, 1861; m., Oct 14, 1885, Andrew McDougall; res. Manchester, N. H. Child: Roy Gage McDougall,⁸ b. Feb. 3, 1891. Annie Gertrude Gage,⁷ b. March 14, 1868. Mary Jane Gage,⁷ b. July 28, 1870. Mr. Gage is superintendent of the Horse Railway Co.; res. Manchester, N. H.

II. Elizabeth Marion Moore,⁶ b. March 14, 1839; d. Dec. 20, 1841.

III. Sarah Elizabeth Moore,⁶ b. Dec. 9, 1849; m., Dec. 24, 1873, George F. Barnard, of Bedford, N. H.; res. Bedford, N. H. He has been selectman and representative. Children: Henry George Barnard,⁷ b. Sept. 18, 1878. Alice Leone Barnard,⁷ b. Oct. 7, 1883.

IV. Estella M. Moore,* b. Dec. 15, 1854; m., Dec. 24, 1875, John W.
        Hoitt, of Goffstown, N. H.; res. Goffstown, N. H. Child:
        Ralph Henry Hoitt,* b. June 26, 1888.
10. Martha Jane Moore,* b. 1817; d. March 30, 1821.
11. Margaret Morrison Moore,* b. May 20, 1820; m., Dec. 29, 1842,
        Ephraim White, of Londonderry, N. H. He was a brick maker
        in Plaistow, N. H., where he d. April 12, 1854, aged 51 years.
        Mrs. White m., second, May 2, 1865, Gamaliel Gleason, of
        Andover, Mass., and res. in Andover, Mass. He d. March 24,
        1879. She d. Dec. 21, 1890, aged 70 years, 7 months, 1 day.
        Children:
I. Moores Ephraim White,* b. Bedford, N. H., Oct. 26, 1845; was a sol-
        dier in 1st N. H. Battery; res. Andover, Mass.
II. George G. White,* b. Plaistow, N. H., March, 1849; d. Jan. 5, 1851.
III. Mary Ella White,* b. Plaistow, N. H., Feb. 6, 1854; d. Cambridge,
        Mass., July 5, 1862.
12. Robert Cox Moore,* b. May 20, 1823; m. Nov. 20, 1845, Jane Sweet-
        ser, of Hooksett, N. H. She d. Sept. 9, 1887, aged 62 years.
        He lived in Plaistow and Manchester, N. H., till 1851; res.
        Scranton, Penn. He d. Aug. 25, 1890. Children:
I. Georgianna Moore,* b. Plaistow, N. H., July 28, 1850; m., July 4,
        1871, Levi S. Hackett, of Scranton, Penn., and res. there. Chil-
        dren: Burton Corbin Hackett,* b. Plymouth, Penn., June 25,
        1872. Frank Day Hackett,* b. at Scranton, Penn., Feb. 26, 1874.
II. Joseph Addison Moore,* b. at Scranton, Penn., Dec. 29, 1852; m.,
        July 5, 1876, Josephine A. Snow, of Hartford, Penn.; res.
        Scranton, Penn., and removed to Binghamton, N. Y., April
        1, 1891. Children b. Scranton, Penn.: Jessie M. Moore,* b.
        Feb. 27, 1877. Harry B. Moore,* b. March 15, 1880. Hattie
        Irene Moore, b. Sept. 25, 1892.
III. Edward A. Moore,* b. Jan. 10, 1855; d. March 20, 1855.
IV. Harry G. Moore,* b. Jan. 20, 1869; d. June 15, 1869.
V. Jennie Ruth Moore,* b. Feb. 21, 1870; m., May, 1888, Louis S. Ship-
        man, of Scranton, Penn., and res. there. He is superintendent
        of a button manufactory.
13. David McGregor Moore,* b. July 26, 1825; m., Aug. 9, 1851, Char-
        lotte E. Questen, of Amesbury, Mass.; res. Lawrence, Mass.
        Children:
I. Edward S. Moore,* b. Bedford, N. H., Dec. 2, 1853; he m. Laura Anna
        Clark, of Lawrence, Mass., Sept 16, 1874; res. Lawrence, Mass.;
        no children.
II. Frank E. Moore,* b. Bedford, Aug. 18, 1855; d. Sept. 27, 1856.
III. Marian Elizabeth Moore,* b. Bedford, Aug. 13, 1857; m., 1880,
        George H. Chandler, of Manchester, N. H.; res. Manchester,
        N. H. Child: Jenny Maud Chandler,* b. Nov. 24, 1884.
IV. Ellen Gertrude Moore,* b. Bedford, N. H., Sept. 14, 1859; m., Nov.
        4, 1886, Oscar Brown, of Lawrence, Mass. Children: Earnest
        Brown,* b. July 21, 1887, at Lawrence, Mass. Elmer Ray
        Brown,* b. Aug. 28, 1889, at Lawrence, Mass.
V. Elma A. Moore,* b. Manchester, N. H., Sept. 5, 1863; d. July 4, 1865.
VI. Martha Ann Moore,* b. Manchester, N. H., Nov. 10, 1865.
VII. Bertha Isabella Moore,* b. Manchester, N. H., Aug. 26, 1873.
14. Albert Wallace Moore,* res. Washington, D. C.; the son by the sec-
        ond wife of his father, Mrs. Susan (Bowman) Wallace, widow
        of Thomas Wallace. She d. in Henniker in 1885.
65. Janet Holmes,* daughter of Susanna Allison and Lieut. John
        Holmes, was b. 1782 or 1783; m. her cousin, Robert Holmes, son
        of Jonathan and Mary (Moore) Holmes of Londonderry, N. H.
        They went to Louisville, Ky., where they lived and died. She
        became insane in her last years. Children (two daughters died
        young):
1. Robert Holmes, Jr.* He was adopted by his great uncle, Robert

Holmes, of Elmgrove, near Georgetown, Scott Co., Ky., and at his death received a sum of money and a considerable estate. He m. Matilda Jenkins, of Kentucky, and died at Natchez, Miss., leaving an only child: Edwin Augustus Holmes,[6] now a prosperous trader at Mt. Sterling, Ky. He was b. in 1845; m. Eliza Tarleton Bowman, of that state. Children: Edwin A. Holmes,[7] Mabel Holmes,[7] Mary J. Holmes,[7] George B. Holmes,[7] Eliza T. Holmes,[7] Anna G. Holmes.[7]

66. Elizabeth Holmes,[4] daughter of Susannah (Allison) and Lieut. John Holmes, was b. May 11, 1788; m., May 16, 1811, Thomas Shepard, of Bedford, and res. in Bedford. She d. Oct. 18, 1853, aged 65 years. He d. Feb. 23, 1857, aged 77 years, and they are buried at Bedford Center. Children b. Bedford, N. H.:

1. John Holmes Shepard,[5] b. March 11, 1812; d. May 13, 1859; m., Dec. 21, 1841, Lucy Piersons, of Tewksbury, Mass. She d. April 9, 1845. He m., second, her sister, Sarah A. Piersons, who d. July 20, 1870. Children b. Bedford, N. H.:

I. John P. Shepard,[6] b. Nov. 21, 1844; d. Jan. 23, 1861.
II. William P. Shepard,[6] b. June 21, 1847, m., Nov. 21, 1871, Sophronia J. Farley, of Bedford, and res. there. Children: Jennie Louise Shepard,[7] b. Nov. 25, 1872. Florence May Shepard,[7] b. March 11, 1889.
III. Lucy A. Shepard,[6] b. May 21, 1849; d. Sept. 21, 1853.
IV. Lizzie A. Shepard,[6] b. May 5, 1851; m., Jan. 30, 1868, Charles P. Farley, of Bedford, N. H. She d. Aug. 9, 1887, aged 36 years, 8 months, 4 days. Children: John Hurlbert Farley,[7] b. Nov. 20, 1868; d. July 10, 1870. Annie Mabel Farley,[7] b. Oct. 12, 1871. Gracie Natalie Farley,[7] b. April 30, 1873.
V. Henrietta Shepard,[6] b. ——; d. June 20, 1853.
VI. Arthur M. Shepard,[6] b. ——; d. Dec. 13, 1885.

2. Charles Franklin Shepard,[5] b. Oct. 17, 1813; m., Feb. 20, 1838, Louisa A. Perry, of Amherst, N. H. Children:

I. Charlotte A. P. Shepard,[6] b. Dec. 27, 1838; d. March 21, 1849.
II. Nancy J. Shepard,[6] b. June 11, 1842; d. Sept. 30, 1842.
III. George F. Shepard,[6] b. April 20, 1845; m., Dec. 1, 1869, Delphina Jane Edwards Smith, of North Wayne, Me. She d. April 18, 1889, aged 43 years, 9 months, 20 days. He was selectman of Bedford, N. H., 1889–'90. Children b. Bedford, N. H.: Edith L. Shepard,[1] b. June 21, 1874. Hattie C. Shepard,[7] b. Nov. 14, 1875. Charles F. Shepard,[7] b. Feb. 24, 1878. Nellie F. Shepard,[7] b. Aug. 7, 1880.

3. George Shepard,[5] b. Jan. 20, 1816; d. Sept. 21, 1845; single.
4. James S. Shepard,[5] b. Sept. 24, 1818; d. Sept. 28, 1866; m., July 14, 1842, at Nashua, Gratia A. Moore, of Hancock, N. H. He d at Huntsville, Ala. Children:

I. Gratia Eloda Shepard,[6] b. Nashua, N. H., Jan. 11, 1845; d. Aug 2, 1845.
II. Ann Jane Shepard,[6] b. Nashua, N. H., Dec. 21, 1846; d. Dec. 31, 1846.
III. James Albert Shepard,[6] b. Nashua, N. H., Nov. 22, 1848; m., Jan. 1, 1872, Annie Gove, of Winchester, Mass.; res. Charlestown, Mass. Children: Annie Lois Shepard,[7] b. Oct. 8, 1874. Guy Albert Shepard,[7] b. Jan. 19, 1876. Ralph Myrick Shepard,[1] b. Feb. 1, 1878.
IV. William Monroe Shepard,[6] b. Nashua, June 25, 1851; m., Nov. 4, 1885, at Winchester, Mass., Abbie De Forrest, of Sand Lake, Rensselaer Co., N. Y.; res. Boston, Mass.; no children.
V. Eugene Everett Shepard,[6] b. Manchester, N. H., June 2, 1854; m., Dec. 4, 1877, at Winchester, Mass., Carrie Holton; res. 21 Boston ave., Medford, Mass. Child: Everett Holton Shepard,[1] b. Nov. 1, 1881.
VI. Frederick Carroll Shepard,[6] b. Lawrence, Mass., Aug. 18, 1856; m., Nov. 27, 1878, Clara Antoinette Pratt, b. Chelsea, Mass.; res.

Chelsea, Mass. Children: Frederick Stanley Shepard,[7] b. Feb. 27, 1880. Marion Shepard,[7] b. Dec. 23, 1881. Charles Gordon Shepard,[7] b. Aug. 28, 1886. Helen Antoinette Shepard,[7] b. Jan. 2, 1889.

VII.   Judson Shepard,[6] b. Lawrence, Mass., May 25, 1859; d. Dec. 12, 1875.

VIII. Harry Elmer Shepard,[6] b. Lawrence, Mass., Jan. 15, 1862; m., Sept. 14, 1881, Nellie Gertrude Teele, of Arlington, Mass. ; res. Arlington, Mass. Children: Elmer Shepard,[7] b. June 5, 1883; d. June 14, 1883. Marion Leslie Shepard,[7] b. Oct. 16, 1886.

IX.   Lillie Winnie Bell Shepard,[6] b. Feb. 3, 1865; d. Sept. 8, 1865.

5. Mary Jane Shepard,[5] b. Nov. 9, 1820; d. Oct. 22, 1864; m., Oct. 27, 1842, Hugh R. French. She d. Oct. 22, 1864. He was m. three times after her death, and d. Dec. 9, 1888. They had one son.

I.   George M. French,[6] b. Jan. 6, 1846, in Bedford, N. H.; m., Oct. 16, 1867, Mary F. Gillis, of Hudson, N. H. Children: Ervin R. French,[7] b. Sept. 16, 1869. Lizzie E. French,[7] b. Sept. 25, 1870. Leon F. French,[7] b. July 27, 1883. Mr. French d. Aug. 2, 1886, aged 40 years, 6 months, 27 days.

6. Nancy P. B. Shepard,[5] b. Aug. 15, 1822; d. June 19, 1880. She m., November, 1850 (see below), Alfred McAfee, her first cousin.

7. Thomas S. Shepard,[5] b. Aug. 5, 1826; m., Aug. 6, 1845, M. A. Moore, of Hancock, N. H. She d. Oct. 4, 1850, aged 25 years. He m. second, Mary H. Eames, of Lowell, Mass.; res. Winchester, Mass. Child: James Shepard,[6] b. 1850; d. 1850.

8. William M. Shepard,[5] b. Oct. 15, 1828; d. some years since. He was m. but had no children. His widow lives in Manchester, N. H.

9. Nancy P. B. (Shepard) McAfee. Her husband was Alfred McAfee, of Bedford, N. H. She d. June 9, 1880, at 57 years, 10 months, 4 days. He d. April 8, 1887, aged 71 years. Children b. Bedford, N. H.

I.   Emma Jane McAfee,[6] b. Dec. 11, 1851; d.   . She m., Jan. 1, 1874, George Chapman, and went to Point de Butte, New Brunswick. She is deceased. Children: Ellen Amelia Chapman,[7] b. Sept. 14, 1876. Charles Alfred Chapman,[7] b. Sept. 26, 1877. George William Chapman,[7] b. May 16, 1880.

II.   Charles A. McAfee,[6] b. April 7, 1855; m., Nov. 27, 1879, Susie E. Drucker, of Amherst, N. H.; res. Londonderry, N. H. Children: Alfred H. McAfee,[7] b. Nashua, N. H., June 4, 1882. Lizzie M. McAfee,[7] b. Londonderry, N. H., April 18, 1884. Carl A. McAfee,[7] b. Londonderry, N. H., May 14, 1887.

III.   John A. McAfee,[6] b. May 4, 1861; single ; res. Bedford, N. H.

IV.   Thomas E. McAfee,[6] b. March 2, 1863; m., April 23, 1885, Mary A. Pate, of St. John, N. B.; res. Nashua, N. H. Children: William Shepard McAfee,[7] b. Nashua, N. H., Aug. 28, 1887; d. Aug. 20, 1888. Hazel May McAfee,[7] b. Nashua, N. H., Sept. 2, 1888.

67. Susannah Holmes[4] [dau. Susannah (Allison), and Lieut. John Holmes], was b. in Londonderry, N. H., March 11, 1790; m., 1808, Thomas Atwood, who was b. in Bedford, N. H., July 22, 1786. After marriage they resided in Worcester, Mass., until 1819, then moved to Bedford, N. H., and in 1840 removed to Nunda, N. Y., and in 1860 he removed to Canaasaraga, N. Y., and d. there Jan. 19, 1865, aged 79 years, 6 months. After his death, Mrs. Atwood moved to Hornellsville, N. Y., and d. there April 25, 1866. Children:

1. Albert Atwood,[5] b. Worcester, Mass., June 23, 1810; m., August, 1833, Ann J. D. Colley, of Bedford, N. H. He d. Aug. 31, 1835. She res. Beloit, Wis. Children:

I.   —— Atwood,[6] a dau., b. 1833; d. in Beloit, Wis., in 1841, aged 8 years.

II.   —— Atwood,[6] b. 1835; d. 1838, aged 3 years.

2. Alvira Atwood,[5] b. at Worcester, Mass., May 22, 1812; m., 1836,

Humphrey Peabody. She d. at Canasaraga, N. Y. Children:

I. Charles A. Peabody.[6]
II. Harriet Peabody,[6] d. August, 1866.
III. Atwood Peabody.[6]
3. Susan H. Atwood,[5] b. at Worcester, Mass., Aug. 18, 1815; m., June 21, 1838, Lewis F. Rider. They removed to Nunda, N. Y., and afterwards to Hornellsville, N. Y. He d. Dec. 1,1885. She d. Aug. 21, 1889, aged 74 years, 3 days. Children:

I. Mary L. Rider,[6] b. at Rochester, N. Y., April 27, 1840; m., May 17, 1887, S. P. Wilcox, of Canasaraga, N. Y., and resides there; no children.
II. John A. Rider,[6] b. Nunda, N. Y., Jan 10, 1843; m., Nov. 2, 1869, Georgiana Davenport, and res. Wellsville, N. Y. He is a photographer, book-seller, and dealer in fancy goods and engravings. Children b. Wellsville, N. Y.: Leroy D. Rider,[7] b. Feb. 13, 1876. Albert L. Rider,[7] b. Jan. 10, 1878. Bessie A. Rider,[7] b. Dec. 8, 1879.
III. Francis A. Rider,[6] b. Nunda, N. Y., Aug. 13, 1849.
4. Harriet Atwood,[5] b. Worcester, Mass., Aug. 22, 1817; moved to Nunda, N. Y., with her parents, and m., Aug. 10, 1840, Dr. Barnabas Wright, who d. at Rochester, N. Y., May 10, 1861. She m. second, Feb. 13, 1866, Augustus Comstock, who d. 1886. She res. Dansville, N. Y. Child:

I. Everett Wright,[6] b. July 20, 1842; m., Sept. 24, 1867, Mary Squires, of Akron, Ohio. He d. at Buffalo, N. Y., Dec. 12, 1887, aged 45 years; no children.
5. Sarah D. Atwood,[5] b. Bedford, N. H., June 14, 1820; m., 1838, John D. Armstrong, and res. in Bedford, N. H. She d. August, 1849. He m., second, Jane M. Wells, of Bedford. He d. Nov. 14, 1868, aged 54 years, 1 month, 6 days. Children b. Bedford, N. H.:

I. William H. Armstrong,[6] b. Nov. 29, 1840; m. Elizabeth, dau. of Samuel Armstrong, Windham, N. H., who is deceased; res. Windham, N. H. Children b. Windham, N. H: Urvin S. Armstrong,[7] b. March 24, 1862. Eugene W. Armstrong,[7] b. Dec. 23, 1865. Ednah M. Armstrong,[7] b. Aug. 30, 1872. Almay A. Armstrong,[7] b. April 19, 1876.
II. John A. Armstrong,[6] b. Oct. 28, 1842. He was a member of Co. K, Third N. H. Vols., enlisted Aug. 23, 1861, and killed at Drury's Bluff, Va., May 13, 1864. By Mr. Armstrong's second marriage there were five children, George D., Edward F., Sarah J., Clara Almay, and Elmer E. Armstrong.
6. Martha J. M. Atwood,[5] b. July 7, 1822, moved with her parents to Nunda, N. Y.; m., at Grand Rapids, Mich., Charles Baker. She d. at Grand Rapids, Dec. 18, 1862. He d. Feb. 7, 1881. Children b. Nunda. N. Y.

I. Susan J. Baker,[6] b. July 21, 1849: m., Nov. 19, 1868, Henry C. Green; res. Wakawsa, Shawnee Co., Kansas; farmer. Children: Edward O. Green,[7] b. July 17, 1870. Fannie L. Green,[7] b. July 3, 1872; d. Oct. 6, 1883. Florence L. Green,[7] b. Dec. 22, 1878. Grace B. Green,[7] b. Aug. 29, 1884. Ina Green,[7] b. May 26, 1887.
II. Laura E. Baker,[6] b. May 6, 1853; m., Feb. 28, 1878, Charles H. Sandford; res. Dansville, N. Y. Children: Ray B. Sandford,[7] b. Dansville, N. Y., Jan. 29, 1879. Katie M. Sanford,[7] b. Dansville, N. Y., Jan. 28, 1881; d. March 16, 1882. Archie B. Sandford,[7] b. Dec. 23, 1885.
III. Charles A. Baker,[6] b. May 22, 1854; m., Nov. 22, 1881, Marietta Percival, of Topeka, Kansas, b. in Indiana, Jan. 9, 1861. He is a carpenter and builder; res. No. 425 North 2d St., Arkansas

city, Kansas. Children: Zella Baker,[7] b. July 18, 1883. Zona Baker,[7] b. Feb. 27, 1885. Newell Baker,[7] b. Sept. 27, 1888.

7. Thomas Atwood,[5] b. Bedford, N. H., Nov. 25, 1824; m., Oct. 14, 1846, Clarissa M. Clough, of Nunda, N. Y., b. Jan. 1, 1827, who, on April 1, 1891, was living in Avoca, N. Y. Mr. Atwood, while engaged in Ypsilanti, Mich., in erecting some shafting in a new building, lost his balance on the scaffolding, and fell, pulling the shafting with him, one end of which struck him upon the temple, pinning him to the floor below, and killing him instantly. Children:

I. DeLisle Atwood,[6] b. at Nashua, N. H., Sept. 5, 1848; m., Sept. 26, 1883, Mary A. McCord, of Big Flats, N. Y., b. March 27, 1861; res. Avoca, N. Y. Children b. Avoca, N. Y.: Albert Lewis Atwood,[7] b. Dec. 27, 1884. Carrie May Atwood,[7] b. Sept. 15, 1886. Minnie Maud Atwood,[7] b. May 3, 1888.

II. Fred. M. Atwood,[6] b. at Nunda, N. Y., May 26, 1852; m., March 13, 1870, Frances Taft, of Addison, N. Y., b. July 18, 1854; res. Avoca, N. Y. Children: Fred A. Atwood,[7] b. at Wyalushing, N. Y., Jan. 3, 1871. Edward T. Atwood,[7] b. at Addison, N. Y., Nov. 19, 1873.

III. Charles T. Atwood,[6] b. at Pike, N. Y., Nov. 9, 1861; m., Sept. 24, 1890, Leda E. Shults, b. at Wheeler, N. Y., Dec. 21, 1867. They reside at Avoca, N. Y.

8. Catherine McAfee Atwood,[5] b. Bedford, N. H., Feb. 2, 1827. She went with her parents to Nunda, N. Y., in 1840; m., Sept. 7, 1850, Jacob Smith, who d. Oct. 15, 1863, at Galesburg, Ill. She m. second, Dec. 13, 1865, Seymour M. Arnold, and res. at Galesburg, Ill. Child b. Galesburg, Ill.:

I. Jane B. Arnold,[6] b. July 21, 1870.

9. Charles G. Atwood,[5] b. Bedford, N. H., April 7, 1829; m. Marcelia E. Bradley; no children. He learned the printer's trade in Amherst, N. H. Left there in 1848, and was in Boston on the *Boston Daily Bee* for one year, then joined his parents in Nunda, N. Y., and for two years was editor and proprietor of the *Nunda Telegraph*; later was in Syracuse, N. Y., in charge of the *Daily Star*; went to Baltimore, Md., in 1853, and was employed on different papers till 1855, when he went to Chicago, Ill., and in 1856 to Mt. Morris, Ill., and started the *North Western Republican*, which he sold after the defeat of General Fremont for the presidency; was then in Galesburg, Ia.; run a newspaper, and was in the grocery and coal business, employing one hundred and fifty men. There, for a year, he bought and shipped horses to the principal cities in the country. Later he went to Quincy, Ill., built a horse railroad, managed it for one year, then sold it and went to Red Oak, Ia., in 1875, where he engaged in farming till July, 1890, when he sold his property, purchased an extensive orange ranch (paying $21,000) in Riverside, Cal., where he resided in 1891, and where he expects to end his days.

10. Ann Elizabeth Atwood,[5] b. July 7, 1831, at Bedford, N. H.; went with her parents to Nunda, N. Y.; m. William Wirt and res. at Hornellsville, N. Y.. She d. Sept. 6, 1884. He d. April 14, 1886. Children:

I. Katie Wirt,[6] b. Canasaraga, N. Y., Oct. 20, 1859; m., April 27, 1889, Charles W. Richardson, and res. at Dansville, N. Y. Child, b. Dansville, N. Y.: Mary Jenette Richardson,[7] b. Feb. 23, 1891.

II. Charles Wirt,[6] b. Sept. 26, 1861, at Canaseraga, N. Y. He is m., and res. at No. 10 Washington St., Hornellsville, N. Y.

III. Susan Wirt,[6] b. at Canaseraga, N. Y., Sept. 2, 1864; m., April 28, 1887, Fred H. Cowen; res. No. 88 Cypress St., Rochester, N. Y.; no children.

IV. Anna Bell Wirt,⁶ b. April 15, 1870; d. June 24, 1885.
11. Hannah F. Atwood,⁵ b. Bedford, N. H., Aug. 24, 1833; m., May 7,
        1859, A. H. Lemon, and res. in Dansville, N. Y. Children b.
        Dansville, N. Y.:
L. William H. Lemon,⁶ b. Sept. 8, 1860.
II. Minnie Allison Lemon,⁶ b. July 22, 1864; m., Dec. 1, 1886, Miller M.
        Fowler; res. Dansville, N. Y. Child: Harold G. Fowler,⁷ b.
        April, 1889.
III. Charles T. Lemon,⁶ b. Jan. 29, 1868.
68. Catherine Holmes⁴ [daughter of Susannah (Allison) and Lieut. John
        Holmes], b. in Londonderry, N. H., in 1792; m. Samuel Mc-
        Afee, of Bedford, N. H. He d. Nov. 5, 1855, aged 72 years, 7
        months. She d. Feb. 18, 1871, aged 78 years. Children:
1. Alfred McAfee,⁵ b. 1815; d. April 8, 1887. He m. his cousin, Nancy
        P. B. Shepard.⁵ (See her record.)
2. William McAfee,⁵ b. Dec. 20, 1816; m., March 16, 1865, Orline M.
        Flint, of Bedford, N. H.; res. in Merrimack, removed to Bed-
        ford, where they are now living. Child b. Merrimack, N. H.:
L. Ella Darrah McAfee,⁶ b. Dec. 11, 1866; m., Dec. 23, 1884, George L.
        Walsh, of Bedford, N. H.; res. Bedford, N. H. Child b. Bed-
        ford, N. H.: Wayland Flint Walsh,⁷ b. Nov. 25, 1888.
3. Adam McAfee,⁵ b. Bedford, N. H., Sept. 29, 1818; m., 1847, Elizabeth
        R. Brooks, of Putney, Vt., and lived in Newburyport, Mass.,
        and Boston, Mass. She d. at East Boston, Feb. 10, 1858. He
        m., second, Sept. 10, 1865, Helen F. Gilmore, of Bedford, N. H.,
        and in 1869 or 1870 removed to Bedford, N. H. He d. Sept. 23,
        1881. She d. Dec. 22, 1880, aged 57 years, 3 months, 23 days.
        Children by first wife, b. Newburyport, Mass.:
L. Franklin B. McAfee,⁶ b. July 2, 1848; m., Jan. 1, 1880, Maria Fisher,
        of Merrimack, N. H., and in Jan., 1891, resided in Grafton,
        Mass. Children: Emma Jane McAfee,⁷ b. Bedford, N. H.,
        Feb. 18, 1881. Adam Franklin McAfee,⁷ b. Oct. 12, 1882. Mary
        Elizabeth McAfee,⁷ b. Merrimack, N. H., March 20, 1886.
II. Elizabeth M. McAfee,⁶ b. July 2, 1853.
III. Ida Jane McAfee,⁶ b. East Boston, Mass., July 6, 1866; d. Dec. 2,
        1867.
IV. Nellie F. McAfee,⁶ b. East Boston, Mass., Sept. 28, 1868; d. Nov. 2,
        1868.
V. Annie L. McAfee,⁶ b. Bedford, N. H., June 16, 1870.
4. John Holmes McAfee,⁵ b. Bedford, N. H., Sept. 27, 1820; m., about
        1852, Sophia R. Kittredge, of Merrimack, N. H., resided and
        died in Bedford, N. H., June 19, 1878, aged 57 years, 8 months,
        22 days. She d. June 17, 1878, aged 47 years, 9 months, 14 days.
5. Jane McAfee,⁵ b. Bedford, N. H., July 2, 1823; m., Nov. 11, 1852,
        Eri Kittredge, of Merrimack, N. H.; res. Merrimack, N. H.,
        where he d. of pneumonia, Feb. 19, 1891. Child:
L. William F. McAfee,⁶ b. Sept. 8, 1855; d. of pneumonia in Merrimack,
        Feb. 16, 1891.
6. Catherine McAfee,⁵ b. in Bedford, May 22, 1825; m., Nov. 14, 1850,
        Joseph Kittredge, of Merrimack, N. H., and res. in Merri-
        mack, N. H. He d. Nov., 1891, aged 67 years, 10 months. Chil-
        dren:
L. Joseph W. A. Kittredge,⁶ b. in Merrimack, N. H., Sept. 3, 1859; m.
        June, 1879, Ella L. S. Fuller, of Merrimack. He d. Oct. 29,
        1881, aged 22 years, 1 month, 23 days. Children: Harry Kit-
        tredge,⁷ b. 1880. Ella Isabel Kittredge,⁷ b. Sept., 1881.
II. Katie Louise Kittredge,⁶ b. May 11, 1855; m., March 10, 1880, James
        F. C. Hodgman, of Bedford, N. H.; res. Merrimack, N. H.,
        where he was selectman in 1887, '88, '89. Child: Frederick
        J. Hodgman,⁷ b. Dec. 12, 1881.
7. Samuel Holmes McAfee,⁵ b. Jan. 7, 1828; d. July 7, 1847.
8. Ira J. Holmes McAfee,⁵ b. Aug. 2, 1829; d. Jan. 2, 1835.

9. Achsah Holmes McAfee,[5] b. Dec. 12, 1832, in Bedford, N. H.; m.,
      July 2, 1864, Charles A. Snell, of Boston, Mass., where they
      resided for a time, then lived in Bedford, N. H., and now live
      in Manchester, N. H., 25 Arlington St. Children b. Boston,
      Mass.:
I.   Sarah Elizabeth Snell,[6] b. May 5, 1865; m., May 5, 1885, at Manches-
      ter, N. H., David Conners, b. in Ossipee, N. H., Oct. 3, 1859.
      They res. in Nashua, N. H. Child b. Manchester, N. H.: Mabel
      Etta Conners,[7] b. Aug. 10, 1886.
II. Katie E. Snell,[6] b. May 24, 1867; m., April 9, 1888, Clinton A. Moore,
      of Manchester, N. H., and res. Manchester, N. H.
III. Charles A. Snell,[6] b. June 29, 1871; d. Oct. 19, 1891.
69. Samuel Holmes,[4] b. ——; d. when a child, in 1786, in Londonderry,
      N. H.
70. John Holmes,[4] b. 1786. By the will of his father, he received the
      home farm in Londonderry, N. H. He was a student in Dart-
      mouth college, class of 1814, and d. while a junior, June 1, 1818.

COL. ROBERT MOORE.

From Notes by Judge Nathaniel Holmes, Cambridge, Mass.

He was appointed lieutenant-colonel of Col. Samuel Hobart's second regiment of "Minute Men," being one of the
"four regiments of Minute Men" that were formed out of
the previous sixteen regiments of militia, on the 1st of September, 1775, and was taken out of "that of Colonel Bartlett," that "lately of Col. Matthew Thornton," that "lately
of Colonel Lutwyche," and that "lately of Colonel Kidder," whereof Samuel Philbrick was first major and Timothy Farrar second major (N. H. Prov. Papers, vol. 7, p.
608). He is called Col. Robert Moore upon his grave-
stone at Derry, and died in 1778. He was the great-grandfather of the Hon. O. C. Moore, of Nashua, N. H., an ex-
member of congress, and a brother of Elizabeth Moore, who
married Nathaniel Holmes, 2d, of Londonderry, N. H. In
1777, on the death of his father, he removed to the farm
of his •parents, John and Janet Moore, who, in 1723 or
1724, came from county of Antrim, Ireland, and in 1727
or 1728 settled on the farm where they lived and died, the
place more recently known as the "Jenness place," on the
Chester road, a little northwest of Beaver pond, in the English Range, and now owned by Mr. C. W. True. (See History of Bedford, N. H., for partial account of this family.)
    Mary Holmes, of Londonderry, married Joseph Morison[2]
(son of John[1]), and they were the parents of Abraham Morison. She was, probably, the daughter of Abraham Holmes,
of the West Parish, and thus perpetuated the Christian name
of her father in that of her son.
    Mary Holmes, daughter of Nathaniel and Elizabeth

(Moore) Holmes, of Londonderry (their second child), married Abraham Morison, and was born about 1746.

They quitclaimed, in a deed, all interest in the estate of her "honored father, Nathaniel Holmes, deceased," to his eldest son, Lieut. John Holmes, who bought out all the heirs, and succeeded to the home farm. Date May 13, 1771, acknowledged and recorded in 1776 (Book 107, p. 398 of County Records). They had a son, *Nathaniel*, named for her father.

71. **Kathreen Allison**[3] [29] (Capt. Samuel,[2] Samuel[1]). She was born at Londonderry, N. H., April 1, 1762, and married, in 1785, Nathaniel Holmes,[3] of Peterborough, N. H., son of Nathaniel and Elizabeth (Moore) Holmes,[2] of Londonderry, grandson of Nathaniel and Jane (Hunter) Holmes,[1] of Coleraine, Ireland. This Nathaniel Holmes,[1] after the death of his wife in Ireland, emigrated in 1740 to the Scotch settlement in Londonderry, N. H., where so many of his Scotch neighbors and kindred had gone before, being accompanied by his four sons, Nathaniel,[2] John,[2] William,[2] and Andrew Holmes.[2] Traditions say that he left his eldest son, Nathaniel Holmes,[2] in Londonderry, while he and his other three sons (who were then minors) went to Carlisle, Penn., and settled, and where he probably died. The three sons lived and had families at Carlisle, Penn.

Dea. Nathaniel Holmes was born at Londonderry, N. H., Sept. 5, 1759, and died at Peterborough, N. H., Sept. 10, 1832.

CHILDREN.

72. Jane Holmes,[4] b. Feb. 24, 1786; d. March 2, 1786.
73. Nathaniel Holmes,[4] b. May 4, 1787; m., Jan. 11, 1809, Sally, daughter of Maj. Jotham Hoar, b. June 24, 1787; d. June 14, 1887, within ten days of a century in age. He d. Jan. 23, 1840; res. at East Jaffrey, Meredith Bridge, and Tilton, N. H.; machinist and manufacturer. Children:
1. Katherine Allison Holmes,[5] b. Oct. 1, 1809; m., Nov. 5, 1835, Col. Zenas Clement, of Claremont, N. H. She res. Stamford, Ct. Children:
I. Sarah Clement,[6] b. May 8, 1840; m. Frank Kimball, Esq., attorney, who d. 1872. Child: Mary H. Kimball,[7] res. with her mother and grandmother in Stamford, Ct.
II. Nathaniel Holmes Clement,[6] of Brooklyn, N. Y., b. March 23, 1841; m., Oct. 24, 1871, Amelia C. Piper. Children: Erminia Augusta Clement,[7] b. Oct. 14, 1872. Arthur Wilford Clement,[7] b. March 17, 1878. Clara Louise Clement,[7] b. Jan. 26, 1880; d July 6, 1882. George Nathaniel Clement,[7] b. Sept. 17, 1883.
2. Artemus Lawrence Holmes,[5] b. East Jaffrey, N. H., July 9, 1814. Graduated at Dartmouth college, 1835; attorney-at-law and

merchant at Galena, Ill., St. Louis, Mo., New York city; m. Eliza Bloomer, of Galena, Ill., who d. leaving a daughter. He m., second, Mary M. Bloomer, of Galena. Children:

I. Eliza Augusta Holmes,[6] b. April 1, 1846; m. George H. Adams, attorney-at-law in New York city.

II. Artemus H. Holmes,[6] b. Galena, Ill., May 16, 1849. Graduated at Harvard college, 1870; attorney-at-law in New York city. He m. Elizabeth Allen, of Boston, Mass., who d. 1876. He m., second, May 20, 1880, Lillian, daughter of Henry Stokes, of New York city. Children: Artemus Holmes,[7] b. Oct. 16, 1881; Lillian Stokes Holmes,[7] b. May 6, 1884; Hilda Holmes,[7] b. March 11, 1890. Mr. Holmes d. in New York city, Nov. 29, 1891, leaving a large estate.

III. Robert Bloomer Holmes,[6] b. June 8, 1854. Broker in New York city; member New York exchange. He m., Nov. 1, 1877, Kate Rosaline, daughter of Seth W. Hale, of New York city. Children: Kate Hale Holmes,[7] b. Oct. 18, 1878; d. Feb. 4, 1881; Andres Holmes,[7] b. Feb. 2, 1882; Robert B. Holmes, Jr.,[7] b. March 3, 1884; Natalie Holmes,[7] b. June 2, 1885.

3. Abigail Evans Holmes,[6] b. Oct. 22, 1816; m. Edward A. Damon, merchant at St. Louis, Mo. She d. Aug. 30, 1857. He d. March 11, 1874. Children:

I. Edward Orne Damon,[6] b. Feb. 23, 1852; m. Florence R. Simpson, of Newburyport, Mass. Children: Edward Orne Holmes,[7] b. Sept. 24, 1876; Lucille Simpson Holmes,[7] b. March 7, 1879.

II. Henrietta Frances Damon,[6] b. March 24, 1854; m., June 13, 1877, Walker Gill Wylie, M. D., of New York city. Children: Juliet Agnes Wylie,[7] b. March 26, 1878; Luella Damon Wylie,[7] b. Aug. 3, 1879; Louis Gill Wylie,[7] b. March 27, 1882; Edward Alexander Wylie,[7] b. Feb. 27, 1887.

4. Edith Augusta Holmes,[6] b. Oct. 9, 1821; m. Hon. Samuel Swasey, of Haverhill, N. H., speaker of the New Hampshire house of representatives. Removed to Illinois; d. June 20, 1887. She d. Oct. 17, 1887, at Belvidere, Ill. Children:

I. Franklin Holmes Swasey,[6] b. Haverhill, N. H., Jan. 31, 1845; drowned in a mill pond June 30, 1853.

II. Charles James Swasey,[6] b. Haverhill, N. H., Sept. 3, 1847.

III. Katherine Swasey,[6] b. Dec. 29, 1849; d. March 5, 1852.

IV. Samuel Swasey,[6] b. Haverhill, N. H., March 8, 1852; d. at Fort Worth, Tex., Aug. 31, 1877.

V. Edith Augusta Swasey,[6] b. Portsmouth, N. H., Dec. 21, 1854; m. Alson Keeler, of Belvidere, Ill., Sept. 23, 1880. Child: Lawrence Swasey Keeler,[7] b. Dec. 23, 1882.

VI. Edward Holmes Swasey,[6] b. Chicago, Ill., Jan. 17, 1860.

5. Nathaniel Moore Holmes,[5] b. Feb. 20, 1823; d. May 2, 1828.

6. Daniel Avery Holmes,[5] b. at Meredith, N. H., Jan. 17, 1826; merchant at Galena, Ill.; m. Elizabeth A. Mackey, who d. March 1, 1874. Children:

I. Avery Nathaniel Holmes,[6] b. May 24, 1850; m. Eunice Brown, June, 1887; res. Union City, Wis.

II. Willie Mackey Holmes,[6] b. July 15, 1852; m., July 19, 1883, Miss J. H. Perley, of Galena, Ill. Child: Sherman Holmes,[7] b. April 12, 1887.

III. Albertine Merrick Holmes,[6] b. Nov. 8, 1855; m. E. C. Ripley, April 28, 1881, and d. May 15, 1884. Children: Albert Enos Ripley,[7] b. Feb. 5, 1882; Walter Ford Ripley.[7] Nathaniel Holmes Ripley,[7] b. Aug. 8, 1863.

IV. Abbie Damon Holmes,[6] b. Sept. 30, 1857; m. R. Martin, Oct. 8, 1884. Children: Abbie Mabel Martin,[7] b. June 8, 1886; Hazel Martin,[7] b. Oct. 20, 1887.

V. Isabel Holmes,[6] b. May 20, 1860.

VI.   Lizzie Lecompte Holmes,⁶ b. Jan. 27, 1864; m. Oct. 8, 1885, Q. Bixby.
VII. Henry Hooper Holmes,⁶ b. Nov. 11, 1878.
7.   Henry Greenleaf Holmes,⁵ b. Jan. 11, 1834. Merchant in St. Louis,
        Mo., and now of New York city; m. Georgie Kuhn. No chil-
        dren.
74. Samuel Holmes,⁴ b. Dec. 19, 1789; res. Peterborough, N. H., and
        then in Springfield, Vt., later in Peterborough, where he died.
        A manufacturer, machinist, and farmer. He m. Mary, daugh-
        ter of Rev. David Annan, March 31, 1813. She d. at Spring-
        field, Vt., Feb. 9, 1828, aged 38 years, 5 months. He m., sec-
        ond, Mrs. Fannie Moore Priest, widow of Dr. J. B. Priest. She
        d. Jan. 6, 1876, aged 85 years. He d. July 8, 1868. Children:
1.   Hon. Nathaniel Holmes,⁵ b. Peterborough, N. H., July 2, 1814. Hon.
        Nathaniel Holmes graduated at Harvard university in 1837.
        Received the degree of M. A. in 1859; was admitted to the bar
        in Boston, Mass., in 1839, and immediately commenced the
        practice of law in St. Louis, Mo. Was circuit attorney for the
        county of St. Louis in 1846. From 1853 to 1855 was counsellor
        of the board of public schools of St. Louis, and from 1862 to
        1865 was counsellor of the North Missouri Railroad company.
        In June, 1865, he was appointed one of the judges of the su-
        preme court of Missouri by Gov. Thomas C. Fletcher. He
        resigned in 1868 and accepted the Royall professorship of law
        in Harvard university, which he resigned in 1872 and resumed
        his profession in St. Louis. He published in 1866 "The Author-
        ship of Shakespeare," which has passed through several edi-
        tions. He was never married. Res. 7 Holyoke Place, Cam-
        bridge, Mass.
2.   David Annan Holmes,⁵ b. Peterborough, N. H., April 1, 1816; farmer;
        res. Bronson, Mich., where he d. Jan. 7, 1868; m. Nancy Tag-
        gart. Children:
I.   Mary Elizabeth Holmes,⁶ b. Sept. 6, 1842; m. M. B. Moore; divorced
        in 1871. She m., second, Capt. Frank M. Bissell, of Coldwater,
        Mich., June 10, 1872. Children: Edith L. Bissell,⁷ b. June 27,
        1873; Mabel Frankie Bissell,⁷ b. June 13, 1876; Gertrude Bis-
        sell,⁷ b. April 26, 1879. Mr. Bissell was wounded in the late
        war, and is a pensioner; res. Greencastle, Ind.
II.   Samuel Holmes,⁶ b. Nov. 31, 1844; res. with his mother in Bronson,
        Mich.
III. Frederick J. Holmes,⁶ b. Nov. 1, 1846; d. May 18, 1847.
3.   Elizabeth Holmes,⁵ b. Peterborough, N. H., Oct. 29, 1820; d. at Nashua,
        N. H., Aug. 31, 1861; m., 1846, John Leach, of Nashua, who d.
        Dec. 30, 1879, aged 71 years. Children:
I.   John Holmes Leach,⁶ b. Oct. 22, 1847. Graduated at Dartmouth col-
        lege in 1870; M. D. of Bellevue Medical college, N. Y., in 1874;
        city physician at Keene, N. H., and examining surgeon on the
        board of pensions; d. at Brooklyn, N. Y., Feb. 25, 1885. He
        m., Oct. 25, 1876, Emily M. Crossfield, daughter of Captain
        Crossfield, of Keene, N. H., who was killed at Gettysburg. She
        is a music teacher; was b. Dec. 31, 1854; res. Watertown, Mass.
        Children: Nathaniel Holmes Leach,⁷ b. Oct. 28, 1882; John
        Clark Leach,⁷ b. Aug. 11, 1884.
II.   Anne Frances Leach,⁶ b. at Nashua; N. H., May 2, 1851; res. San
        Francisco, Cal.
4.   Samuel Allison Holmes,⁵ b. at Springfield, Vt., Feb. 23, 1823; was
        fitted for college at Phillips Exeter academy (class of '38);
        entered the Sophomore class of Dartmouth college in 1841;
        left in his Junior year; studied law, and was admitted to the
        bar at St. Louis, Mo., in 1844. He was first lieutenant and
        adjutant of Lieutenant-Colonel Euston's St. Louis battalion in
        the Mexican war (1845–'47), and colonel of the 10th and 40th

Regiments of Missouri Volunteers in the late war, and commanded the 2d Brigade, 7th Div. of the 17th Corps in General Grant's campaign against Vicksburg; was engaged in the battles at Corinth under General Rosecrans, and at Jubra, Jackson, and Champion Hills, and with the 40th Missouri Regiment was in the battles at Franklin and Nashville, under General Thomas, and was afterwards sent to Mobile, and, after the capture of that city, was stationed at Montgomery, Ala., at the close of the war. At Champion Hills he received an injury on the left knee from the kick of a horse, which gave rise, some years afterwards, to a tumorous growth of bone in the joint, which was removed by a surgical operation in May, 1889, but had not healed up before the 16th of February, 1890, when the leg had to be amputated above the knee, and he recovered his health; he received a pension. After the war he was appointed judge of the land commissioner's court of the city of St. Louis, Mo., having jurisdiction of the condemnation of land for public streets, and held the place till 1872. He spent much time in reading and study, and indulged in writing. He d. of apoplexy in St. Louis, Jan. 5, 1892, and was buried with his relatives in Peterborough, N. H.

5. Sarah Smith Holmes,⁶ b. at Springfield, Vt., Sept. 4, 1825; m. Horatio Kimball, of Nashua and Keene, N. H., Sept. 16, 1847. Child:

I. Samuel Holmes Kimball,⁶ b. at Nashua, N. H., May 28, 1848; enlisted at sixteen in the N. H. Cavalry, and served a campaign in Virginia; res. Keene, N. H.

2. Edward Perry Kimball,⁷ b. at Keene, Oct. 21, 1855; printer; res. Keene, N. H.

6. Frances Sophia Holmes,⁵ b. Oct. 20, 1829; d. February, 1831. She was an only child by second wife, Fanny (Moore), widow of Dr. Jabez B. Priest, of Peterborough.

75. Jane Holmes,⁴ b. July 14, 1792; d. July 9, 1882; m., Dec. 25, 1815, Bernard Whittemore, merchant. He d. at Nashua, Aug. 8, 1846, aged 58 years, 11 months. Children:

1. Bernard Bemus Whittemore,⁵ b. in Boston, May 15, 1817; fitted for college at Phillips Exeter academy (class of '32), and graduated; Harvard College in 1839; studied law in the Harvard Law School in 1840–'41, and was admitted to the Bar in Hillsborough County, N. H.; practised at Palmer, Amherst, and Nashua, and in 1846 became, with his brother, F. P. Whittemore, proprietor and editor of the Nashua *Gazette*, until 1890. He was a member of the state senate in 1852–'53, alderman of the city of Nashua in 1860, and city treasurer in 1861. He d. in 1893.

2. Katherine Holmes Whittemore,⁵ b. July 12, 1819; m., Oct. 8, 1840, General Israel Hunt, of Nashua; he d. Jan. 11, 1889. Children:

I. Israel Thorndike Hunt,⁶ b. Oct. 12, 1841; M. D. of Harvard Medical College in 1870, and medical examiner for insurance companies in Boston; m. Evangeline Foisee, of Nashua, in 1883. Child: Katherine Evangeline Hunt,⁷ b. Aug. 13, 1886; res. Chelsea, Mass.

II. Frank Whittemore Hunt,⁶ b. April 26, 1849; res. Nashua.

3. Eloise C. Whittemore,⁵ b. Aug. 28, 1822; m., June 8, 1843, David F. McGilvray; merchant, of Boston. He d. Aug. 30, 1871. Children:

I. Alice E. McGilvray,⁶ b. Jan. 26, 1845; d. Feb. 22, 1869.

II. Jacob Bernard McGilvray,⁶ b. Aug. 13, 1850.

III. Katherine Holmes McGilvray,⁶ b. May 19, 1855; d. Nov. 7, 1879.

IV. David F. McGilvray,⁶ b. Oct. 5, 1858. Two sons and one dau. d. in infancy.

4. Francis Parkman Whittemore,⁵ b. March 29, 1825; printer; m., Jan. 27, 1851, Angeline H. Parks, of Palmer. Children:

I. Helen A. Whittemore,⁶ b. Nov. 5, 1851.
II. Alice F. Whittemore,⁶ b. 1853; d. young.
III. Frederick Parks Whittemore,⁶ b. Oct. 25, 1855.
5. Mary Jane Whittemore,⁵ b. July 29, 1827; principal of a ladies' school
        at Rome, N. Y., and lately resident at San Miguel, Cal.
6. Nathaniel Holmes Whittemore,⁵ b. Jan. 11, 1830; res. Marshfield
        (Brant Rock), Mass.
7. Ann Frances Whittemore,⁵ b. Aug 16, 1834; m., Feb. 22, 1864, Bloom-
        field J. Beach, Esq., of Rome, N. Y., where she d. Oct. 18,
        1867. Child:
I. John B. Beach,⁶ b. May 5, 1866; now res. at Indian River, Fla.
76. Andrew Holmes,⁴ b. Nov. 24, 1794; m. Jane Taggart, Feb. 12, 1818;
        she d.   ; he m. second, Abigail Phillips, of Derry. In
        early life he lost an arm in a cotton picker, and became a ped-
        dler of fancy articles, and d. at Turner's Falls in 1877. Chil-
        dren by first wife:
1. Caroline Holmes,⁵ b. Oct. 28, 1818; m. Joel Bruce. He d.; two chil-
        dren d. young.
2. Stephen Holmes,⁵ b. Dec. 2, 1820; m. Calista Dustan. Child: Charles
        Dustan,⁶ d. young, in Wilton. She d. Greenfield, June 18,
        1877. He d. in Peterborough, N. H., Nov., 1886 or 1887. He
        served as a soldier in the late war, and received a pension.
3. Margaret Holmes,⁵ b. March 6, 1823; m. Geo. Dickey, both d.
4. Jane Holmes,⁵ b. Dec. 14, 1825; m. Urick A. Hall, of Derry; he d.;
        one child.
5. Mary A. Holmes,⁵ b. Aug. 11, 1828; d. April 16, 1846.
6. Nathaniel Holmes,⁵ b. July 30, 1830; m. Angelia S. Mower, of Jaffrey,
        N. H., b. in 1829, and res. at Turner's Falls, Mass. Children:
I. Elizabeth Josephine Holmes,⁶ b. in 1854; m. George Starbush. Chil-
        dren: Amelia Angeline Starbush,⁷ b. in 1878. Joseph Nathan-
        iel Starbush,⁷ b. in 1880. George William Starbush,⁷ b. in
        1882.
II. Julian Augustus Holmes,⁶ b. in 1858; a commercial traveller.
III. Cora Roxana Holmes,⁶ b. in 1860; school teacher.
77. Elizabeth Holmes,⁴ b. March 23, 1797; m., Oct. 28, 1828, Daniel
        Adams (his second wife), of Jaffrey, b. May 22, 1798; moved
        to Springfield, Vt. She d. Nov. 10, 1836. He d. Dec. 15, 1851.
        Children:
1. Elizabeth Adams,⁵ b. June 6, 1831; m., in 1853, Maj. G. Peabody, b.
        in Littleton, N. H., in 1825; d. in 1868. He was a commis-
        sary for volunteers from Kansas in the late war. She m.
        second, Hon. Lawrence D. Bailey, of Lawrence, Kan. He was
        formerly a judge of the supreme court of Kansas. Children:
I. Richard Adams Peabody,⁶ b. 1854; d. 1855.
II. Frederick A. Peabody,⁶ b. 1856; d. 1866.
III. Alice Hubbard Peabody,⁶ b. June 22, 1857; m., June 25, 1884, Wil-
        liam Henry Sears, of Chillicothe, O., b. March 7, 1858.
IV. Carrie H. Peabody,⁶ b. 1862; d. 1863.
V. Elizabeth H. Peabody,⁶ b. 1864; d. 1865.
2. Helen Marr Adams,⁵ d. young.
78. Enos Holmes,⁴ b. at Peterborough, N. H., Dec. 14, 1799; m. Louisa,
        dau. of Daniel Adams, of Jaffrey, b. Dec. 14, 1806; moved to
        Springfield, Vt., and with his brothers Samuel and John, and
        brother-in-law, Daniel Adams, engaged in the manufacture of
        cotton for some years. After living in the state of New York,
        he removed to Buchanan, Mich., in 1846, where he bought a
        tract of land and made a farm. He d. there May 23, 1869. He
        was a man of clear intelligence, fond of reading, and a noted
        free thinker. She d. there Jan. 25, 1876. Children:
1. Katherine Holmes,⁵ b. at Springfield, Vt., October, 1826; m. John C.
        Marble, of Buchanan, Mich., and d. Oct. 2, 1872; no children.

2. Daniel Holmes,⁵ b. Springfield, Vt., May 28, 1829; m., Oct. 14, 1852,
      Sarah J. Baker, b. in Chautauqua county, N. Y., July 24, 1832.
      Children:
  I. Frank Holmes,⁶ b. July 27, 1853; d. Dec. 1, 1853.
 II. George Holmes,⁶ b. June 16, 1856.
III. Nathaniel Holmes,⁶ b. Aug. 17, 1857; d. March 7, 1863.
 IV. John Holmes,⁶ b. Dec. 24, 1858; d. Jan 1, 1875.
  V. Mary Louise Holmes,⁶ b. July 24, 1860; d. March 10, 1872.
 VI. Patrick Henry Holmes,⁶ b. Nov. 2, 1861.
VII. Katherine Allison Holmes,⁶ b. Jan. 4, 1864; d. Feb. 20, 1864.
VIII. Jane Holmes,⁶ b. March 16, 1865.
 IX. Twin girls,⁶ b. Feb. 22, 1866; d. 1866.
  X. Louisa Holmes,⁶ b. Feb. 14, 1867.
 XI. Enos Holmes,⁶ b. Aug. 1, 1869.
XII. Katherine Holmes,⁶ b. Sept. 22, 1870.
XIII. Harriet Holmes,⁶ b. May 9, 1871; d. Sept. 15, 1872.
3. Louisa Adams Holmes.⁵ b. May 4, 1831; m. Orson Marble, of Michi-
      gan, Dec. 25, 1851. He d.   Children:
  I. Willard B. Marble,⁶ b. Sept. 25, 1852; m., May 8, 1879, Sadie L. Grose.
        Children: Katie Grose,⁷ b. Feb. 20, 1880. Lemon Grose,⁷ b.
        Oct. 10, 1881. Elsie Grose,⁷ b. Oct. 20, 1883.
 II. Enos Marble,⁶ b. July 29, 1854; m. Verne Anderson, June 2, 1881.
        Child: Orson Leonard Anderson,⁷ b. May 3, 1883.
III. Sarah Katherine Marble,⁶ b. Sept. 26, 1856; m. Nathaniel Swan,
        June 27, 1880. Child: Carrie Mabel Swan,⁷ b. September,
        1882.
 IV. Mary Eloise Marble,⁶ b. April 23, 1859; m. Charles Matthews, Dec.
        12, 1878. Children: Alonzo Matthews,⁷ b. Sept. 8, 1879.
        Bertha Matthews,⁷ b. Nov. 5, 1881. Maud S. Matthews,⁷ b.
        May 11, 1884.
  V. Clarissa Myers Marble,⁶ b. Aug. 6, 1861; m. John B. Letchford,
        Nov. 18, 1880, of Frankville, Iowa.
 VI. Harriet Augusta Marble,⁶ b. June 4, 1863.
VII. Fanny Louisa Marble,⁶ b. March 7, 1865.
VIII. David Orson Marble,⁶ b. Aug. 12, 1867.
 IX. ⎰John Clarence Marble,⁶ b. May 8, 1870.
  X. ⎱Jessie Florence Marble,⁶ b. May 8, 1870.
        She m. second, John C. Marble, Oct. 12, 1873.
4. Mary A. Holmes,⁵ b. Jan. 16, 1834; d. July 19, 1834.
5. Charles A. Holmes,⁵ b. Sept. 11, 1835; d. March 15, 1836.
6. John A. Holmes,⁵ b. June 4, 1838; d. Feb. 25, 1845.
7. Enos Holmes,⁵ b. Aug. 11, 1841; m. Martha Barrows. Child:
  I. Alma Holmes,⁶ b. Feb. 2, 1881; res. Buchanan, Mich.
8. Harriet A. Holmes,⁵ b. Feb. 14, 1844; d. Aug. 23, 1844.
9. John G. Holmes,⁵ b. Oct. 4, 1852; m. Juliette Scidmore, Dec. 27,
      1876. Children:
  I. Grace Scidmore,⁶ b. Aug. 14, 1878.
 II. Clara Scidmore,⁶ b. June 11, 1881.
        He is editor and proprietor of the *Buchanan Record*, news-
        paper, Buchanan, Mich.
79. John Holmes,⁴ of Springfield, Vt., b. at Peterborough, N. H., May 8,
      1802; m., June 30, 1825, Hepsibeth Cutter, dau. of John Cutter,
      of Jaffrey, N. H., b. Dec. 2, 1803, who d. at Springfield, Vt.,
      Sept. 5, 1854; m., second, Emeline W., dau. of Nathaniel
      Cutter, of Jaffrey, Sept. 17, 1855, b. Sept. 7, 1828, and d. Spring-
      field, Feb. 8, 1857; m., third, Sybil Eliza Gates, dau. of Samuel
      Gates, of Peterborough, June 15, 1858; b. at Peterborough,
      April 14, 1819, and d. Springfield, April 3, 1863. He d. at
      Springfield, Sept. 24, 1874. Children:
  I. John Cutter Holmes,⁵ b. April 22, 1827; m. Marcia A., dau. of
        George Kimball, of Springfield, June 4, 1850, b. June 14, 1827;
        d. June 4, 1858. He m., second, Rebecca, dau. of Noah Saf-

ford, of Springfield, Vt., March 9, 1859. She was b. March 28, 1888. Children by first marriage:

I. Otto K. Holmes,⁶ b. June 2, 1854; d. Oct. 27, 1863.
II. Frank H. Holmes,⁶ b. Feb. 27, 1858.
        Children by second marriage:
III. Abbie Holmes,⁶ b. April 29, 1851.
IV. Henry Bigelow Holmes,⁶ b. March 12, 1868.
2. Emeline Duncan Holmes,⁵ b. March 7, 1830; d. Sept. 20, 1851.
3. Abigail Holmes,⁵ b. Aug. 21, 1836; d. April 20, 1854.
4. Nathaniel Cutter Holmes,⁵ b. Jan. 26, 1857; m., in 1881, Mary B. Smart, of Springfield. He was educated in the agricultural department of Dartmouth College, B. S. in 1879; studied law with Judge Nathaniel Holmes, and in 1883 was admitted to the bar in St. Louis, Mo., and Massachusetts in 1884, and began the practice of law at Gardiner, Mass., and d. of consumption at the home of his uncle, Lucius A. Cutter, at Jaffrey, N. H., June 24, 1887. He was a young man of much promise. Child:

I. Laura Rebecca Holmes,⁶ b. Gardner, Mass., 1886.
5. George Gates Holmes,⁵ b. July 15, 1857; d. Sept. 15, 1860.
80. Jonathan Holmes,⁴ b. Peterborough, N. H., June 8, 1807; m. Jane, dau. of Dea. Nathaniel Moore, of Peterborough, Feb. 4, 1830. She was b. Feb. 8, 1810; d. Aug. 19, 1831. He m., second, in 1831, Mary (Taggart) Robbe, widow of Cicero Robbe, of Peterborough, and dau. of John Taggart, of Dublin. He owned and lived till 1836 on the homestead in Peterborough, when he sold it, and removed to Bronson, Mich., where he established a large farm and acquired a large property. He was a bank director at Coldwater. He d. at Bronson, Dec. 11, 1884. Children:

1. Mary Jane Holmes,⁵ b. at Peterborough, N. H., in 1832; m. Freeman Lurdaw (?), of Bronson. She m., second, William Dougherty, of Winona, Minn. Children by first marriage:
I. Ellen A. Lurdaw⁶ (?), b. 1857; m. Mr. Cornell in 1878.
II. Emma Lurdaw⁶ (?), b. 1861; m. Mr. Hensley in 1878.
        Children by second marriage:
III. William Dougherty,⁶ b. 1869.
IV. Jenny Dougherty,⁶ b. 1873.
2. John Taggart Holmes,⁵ b. in 1836; m. Helen M. McMellon. He m., second, Sarah Van Aestine, in 1878. Children:
I. Nathaniel L. Holmes,⁶ b. 1872.
II. Mary Louise Holmes,⁶ b. 1874.
III. Jonathan Allison Holmes,⁶ b. 1881.
IV. Grace Holmes,⁶ b. 1884; res. Coldwater, Mich.
3. Cicero Jonathan Holmes,⁵ b. Nov. 13, 1844; m. Mary A. Strehlin in 1883; res. Bronson, Mich. Children:
I. Mary Jane Holmes,⁶ b. Aug. 7, 1884.
II. Cicero Jonathan Holmes,⁶ b. April 11, 1887.
III. Warren C. Holmes,⁶ b. October, 1888; d. Sept. 28, 1889.
4. Florence Holmes,⁵ b. 1853; m. Ezra E. Beardsley, in 1874; res. Bronson, Mich. Children:
I. Walton H. Beardsley,⁶ b. 1875.
II. Jessie Beardsley,⁶ b. 1877.

81. John Allison³ [30] (Capt. Samuel,² Samuel¹). He was born in Londonderry, N. H., in what is now Derry, near Derry east meeting-house. His father's homestead is included in the farm of George W. Lane, and he succeeded his father upon the home farm, and was a farmer and tavern-keeper. He died in the prime of early manhood or middle

life, before Sept. 24, 1800, and probably in 1799. He married Betsey Abbott, of Kingston, N. H., who died Nov. 8, 1799, aged 83 years. He and his family are buried in the cemetery at East Derry, near the burial-place of his father and grandfather and Rev. James McGregor, in the centre of the old yard. The administration of his estate was granted to Alexander McGregor, Sept. 24, 1800, and John Pinkerton was appointed guardian of his children.

CHILDREN BORN IN LONDONDERRY, N. H.

82. Betsey Abbott Allison[4] (214), b. April 3, 1788; m. Josiah Abbott, Jr., of Worcester, Mass., Dec. 30, 1808; d. April 30, 1830, in Lunenburg, Vt.
83. Sukey Prentice Allison,[4] b. Dec. 17, 1789. She became a governess in Boston, Mass. She was winning in looks, attractive in manners, and much beloved. She d. unmarried, April 12, 1844.
84. Naomi Pinkerton Allison,[4] b. March 28, 1796; d. June 15, 1799.
85. John Samuel Allison,[4] b. Sept. 3, 1788: d. March 30, 1799.

86. James Allison[3] [31] (Capt. Samuel,[2] Samuel[1]). He was born in Londonderry, N. H. (in the portion which is now Derry), Feb. 22, 1767. He married Anna Moore. He occupied a part of the homestead in Derry, and later removed to Weathersfield, Vt., and owned a farm near the southern foot of Ascutney mountain, where he died Feb. 23, 1805, aged 38 years, 1 day. Mrs. Allison was born April 23, 1765, in Londonderry, N. H., and died in Weathersfield, Vt., Oct. 26, 1834, aged 69 years, 6 months, 3 days.

CHILDREN BORN IN WEATHERSFIELD, VT.

87. Janet Allison,[4] b. Feb. 3, 1789; d. June 20, 1825, aged 36 years, 4 months, 17 days.
88. John Allison[4] (26), b. Feb. 26, 1790; m. Jerusha Swett, and, second, Anna Porter; res. Weathersfield, Vt., and d. there July 29, 1863.
89. Samuel Allison[4] (225), b. Aug. 12, 1791; res. Painesville, Ohio.

90. Sarah Allison[3] [32] (Capt. Samuel,[2] Samuel[1]). She was born in Londonderry, N. H., Dec. 17, 1766, and married July 5, 1795 or 1798, Daniel Abbot, of Peterborough, N. H., a trader, who was born in Lyndeborough, N. H., July 31, 1769. He was a carpenter in early life. Removed to Newburyport, Mass., and spent about five years; returned to Peterborough, which he left in 1834. He died in Westford, Mass., Jan. 27, 1854, aged 84 years, 5 months. Mrs. Abbot died in New York, N. Y., Nov. 22, 1737. She was a great reader, with a strong, active, and logical mind, and she and her husband attended the Unitarian church.

91. Jane Abbot,⁴ b. Peterborough, N. H., Sept. 30, 1800; d. in Brooklyn,
     N. Y., Sept., 1880. She m. John Scott, of Peterborough, N. H.,
     Aug. 24, 1842, as his second wife. (He was b. Feb. 18, 1797,
     son of William and grandson of William Scott, of Peterbor-
     ough.) They removed to Detroit, Mich. He d. Sept. 1, 1846;
     She had no children.
92. Sally Allison Abbot,⁴ b. Newburyport, Mass., Nov. 3, 1806; d. in
     Rutherford, N. J., Oct. 13, 1887. She m., May 6, 1830, Jeffer-
     son Fletcher, a grocer in New York, N. Y. He d. at Westford,
     Mass., July 17, 1852. Children:
1.   Sarah Jane Fletcher,⁵ b. June 11, 1831; d. at Peterborough, N. H.,
     March 2, 1834.
2.   Mary Louise Fletcher,⁵ b. at New York, N. Y., Oct. 15, 1835; m.,
     Aug., 1866, Robert B. Hallock, who d. in Brooklyn, N. Y.,
     March, 1878. Child:
I.   Julian Abbot Hallock,⁶ b. Feb. 3, 1868, and is employed on the *N. Y.
     Tribune* in the city of New York.
3.   Sarah Allison Fletcher,⁵ b. July 26, 1841; single; res. Rutherford,
     N. J.; business, typewriter; office, 8 Union square, New York,
     N. Y. She was a teacher for eleven years in Peterborough,
     N. H., Illinois, and Leominster, Mass.
4.   Edmund Abbot Fletcher,⁵ b. Oct. 15, 1849; single; res. Rutherford,
     N. J., and is connected with the *N. Y. Tribune*, being at the
     head of the proof-reading department. In early life he was
     for several years in the office of the Peterborough, N. H.,
     Transcript.
93. Daniel Abbot, Jr.,⁴ b. April 11, 1806; m., Feb. 15, 1838, Dorothy
     Evans Cutter, b. Sept. 20, 1809, and who d. in New York city
     Nov. 19, 1842. He was in the grocery business in New York,
     and removed there about 1833. He died in New York city Nov.
     2, 1854. Children:
1.   Clara Jane Abbot,⁵ b. June 2, 1840; d. Sept. 2, 1840.
2.   Laura Jane Abbot,⁵ b. Nov. 7, 1842; m., June 5, 1862, Albert Stevens,
     of Peterborough, N. H.; res. Leominster, Mass. Child:
I.   Ida Mabel Stevens,⁶ b. Aug. 17, 1866.
94. John Abbot,⁴ b. Peterborough, N. H., June 24, 1810; m., Jan. 2,
     1834, in Michigan, town of Monroe, Pamelia Beach. He was a
     farmer, and d. there Nov. 30, 1834, aged 24 years, 5 months.

95. John Allison⁴ [36] (Samuel,³ Capt. Samuel,² Samuel¹).
He was born in Dunbarton, N. H., March 23, 1776, and died
in Peterborough, N. H., Aug. 13, 1864, aged 88 years, 4
months. He married Rachel Ladd, of Dunbarton, in 1805,
who was born June 9, 1780, and died Sept. 3, 1824, aged
44 years. He married, second, Abigail Perry, of Rindge,
N. H., who was born May 15, 1791, and died at Sioux City,
Iowa, Feb. 13, 1873, aged 81 years, 8 months.

Mr. Allison located in Peterborough, Sept. 25, 1801, where
he spent the remainder of his life. He was a wood work-
man and turner, and for a long time was in the employ of
the proprietors of the factories in that town. As a man, he
was honest, upright, and respected.

96. Ira Allison,[5] b. June 11, 1806; graduated at Dartmouth college; was an expert writing-master; m. Catherine Gillis, who was b. Nov. 12, 1812. He res. in state of New York, and d. at Saratoga Springs. Mrs. Allison res. 1890, at North Argyle, N. Y.

97. Fanny Ladd Allison,[5] b. March 4, 1811; d. Feb. 24, 1847, aged 35 years, 11 months.

98. Mary B. Allison,[5] b. Jan. 31, 1813; m. Rev. Zebulon Jones, April 18, 1843. He is deceased. Children:

1. Maria Frances Jones,[6] m. —— Hurlburt; res. New Haven, Vt.
2. Ella Carrie Jones.[6]
3. Willie Allison Jones.[6]
4. Frank Irving Jones.[6]

99. Caroline P. Allison,[5] b. Sept. 9, 1817; m. Moses Wilkins, in Peterborough, N. H., Sept. 5, 1866; d. July 29, 1867, in Peterborough, aged 49 years, 10 months. Mr. Wilkins is deceased, and they left no children.

100. Abigail Maria Allison,[5] b. Sept. 22, 1827; d. Dec. 23, 1835, aged 8 years, 3 months.

101. Elizabeth Sarah Allison,[5] b. July 5, 1829; d. Dec. 21, 1864, aged 35 years, 5 months.

102. John Perry Allison,[5] b. July 28, 1831; m., May 20, 1858, Lizzie Ann Thing, of Exeter, N. H. He prepared for college at Phillips academy in Exeter, and graduated in 1854, at Cambridge, Mass. After his admission to the bar, he commenced the practice of his profession at Sioux City, Iowa, which became his home in April, 1857. Mrs. Allison was b. in Exeter, N. H., May 8, 1833; res. Sioux City, Ia. Children:

1. Fannie Allison,[6] b. July 31, 1859; m., Sept. 16, 1885, Edward Myron Ferris. He is a real estate operator. They res. at Bozeman, Montana.
2. Mary Olive Allison,[6] b. July 2, 1861; d. Sept. 21, 1862, aged 1 year, 2 months.
3. Hattie Allison,[6] b. May 6, 1863; res. at home.
4. Mabel Allison,[6] b. Aug. 11, 1867; m., May 20, 1886, Arthur J. More, of the firm of Harwich, Hess & More, wholesale druggists; res. Sioux City, Iowa.

103. William Davidson Allison[4] [37] (Samuel,[3] Capt. Samuel,[2] Samuel[1]). He was born Dec. 29, 1777, in Dunbarton, N. H. He married Amey Adlington, April 19, 1804, who was born June 18, 1787, and was a daughter of Elisha and Amey Adlington, of Boston, Mass. He was a furniture manufacturer, and lived in Castine, Me., while his brother was there. He removed to Boston, Mass., living in Temple St., where he died. He and his wife were attendants of the Baptist church, of which she was a member. His death occurred in 1842. His complexion was light with brown hair.

104. Amey Allison,[5] b. March 25, 1805; d. July 26, 1806.
105. William Francis Allison,[5] b. Sept. 9, 1806; d. Jan. 26, 1831. He was a seaman.
106. Amey Allison,[5] b. March 17, 1809: m. —— Fletcher; res. Boston, Mass. She d. April 12, 1860.

107. David Allison⁵ (236), b. June 13, 1812; d. June 20, 1850; m. Mary
     Kelley; res. Boston, Mass.
108. Walter Harris Allison⁵ (242), b. Oct. 31, 1814; d. Sept. 9, 1856.
109. M. Q. Allison,⁵ b. Jan. 26, 1817; d. Jan. 23, 1817.
110. Frederick P. Allison,⁵ b. Jan. 20, 1817; d. Jan. 22, 1817.
111. Sally S. Allison,⁵ b. Jan. 15, 1818; d. Jan. 17, 1818.
112. Mary Allison,⁵ b. July 1, 1823; m., Nov. 3, 1850, William Warren,
     son of Willard and Catherine (Cheney) Warren, of Dedham,
     Mass. He was b. in Roxbury, Mass., April 30, 1824. They
     lived after marriage in Rochester, N. H. He carried on an ex-
     tensive business as a leather manufacturer; removed to Brook-
     line, Mass., in 1855, and lived there twenty-four years, and
     while there suffered many financial losses. He is now em-
     ployed in New York, N. Y. Mrs. Warren, who is in feeble
     health, resides at 11 Hanson St., Boston, Mass. Child:
  1. Ella Frances Warren,⁶ b. Rochester, N. H., Sept. 12, 1852. She grad-
     uated from the Massachusetts Homeopathic Hospital Training
     School for Nurses in Boston, Dec. 31, 1887, and is now a pro-
     fessional nurse; res. 11 Hanson St., Boston, Mass.

113.   Elizabeth Allison⁴ [38] (Samuel,³ Capt. Samuel,²
Samuel¹).   She was born in Dunbarton, N. H., Aug. 3, 1780.
She was a communicant of the Presbyterian church. Her
complexion was light, with sandy hair. She died in Manchester, N. H., where her married life was spent, Aug. 29,
1850. She married Daniel Hall (son of Daniel, or John,
Hall and Jane Barr), of Manchester, N. H., where he was
born April 5, 1780. He was a farmer, lived in his native
town, and died there Aug. 8, 1853.

CHILDREN BORN IN MANCHESTER, N. H.

114. Jane B. Hall,⁵ b. Oct. 13, 1806; m. Jesse Poore⁶ (Samuel,⁵ Joseph,⁴
     Samuel,³ Henry,² John¹), of Goffstown, N. H. He was b. Oct.
     16, 1796; farmer; d. May 7, 1836, in Goffstown, in the part now
     included in Manchester, N. H. After his decease, she m., sec-
     ond, Enoch Ela, by whom she had a daughter. She d. July 12,
     1888, aged 81 years, 8 months, 30 days. Children:
  1. Charles Hall,⁶ b. Oct. 9, 1833; d., single, Dec. 19, 1858.
  2. Harris Jesse Hall,⁶ b. Feb. 23, 1836; m., June 17, 1869, Lizzie Rogers,
     daughter of Joshua Phippens and Mary Ellery (Rogers) Trask,
     of Hampden, Me. His married life has been spent in Manches-
     ter. Was a grocer until 1875, then an undertaker; res. corner
     Maple and Hanover Sts.; d. about 1885. Widow res. in Man-
     chester. Child: Mary Rogers Hall,⁷ b. May 11, 1872; d. April
     14, 1877.
  3. Mary Jane Hall.⁶
115. Maria A. Hall,⁵ b. Jan. 6, 1808; single; res. Manchester, N. H.
116. Daniel Hall,⁵ b. Nov. 12, 1810; dealer in real estate; res. Manches-
     ter, N. H.; d. Dec. 28, 1871.
117. Harris Allison Hall,⁵ b. Feb. 14, 1812; res. 170 Bellevue St., Boston,
     Mass. He went to Boston in March, 1832, where he has ever
     since resided. For more than forty years he did business in
     Faneuil Hall market; retired from business about 1880; is a
     Republican in politics; an attendant of the Orthodox Congre-
     gational church. He m., Jan. 9, 1844, Louise Wells, b. Sedg-
     wick, Me., April 29, 1812; d. Feb. 13, 1885. Children b. Bos-
     ton, Mass.:
  1. Mary Louise Hall,⁶ b. Oct. 20, 1844; d. June 23, 1849.

II.   William Harris Hall,⁶ b. Sept. 4, 1846; single; res. 170 Bellevue St.,
        Boston, Mass.
III. Charles Wells Hall,⁶ b. Feb. 22, 1851; m., March 21, 1877, Lottie How-
        land Smith, daughter of Barney and Betsey (Snow) Smith, of
        New Bedford, Mass., where she was b. Dec. 30, 1854; removed
        to Boston with her parents when three years of age. She and
        her husband were educated in the public schools of that city,
        and both are members of the Orthodox church. He is a com-
        mercial traveller; res. 170 Bellevue St., Boston, Mass. Chil-
        dren, b. in that city: Clara Sumner Hall,⁷ b. Dec. 20, 1879; Gor-
        don Hall,⁷ b. July 17, 1883.
IV.   Louise Clara Hall,⁶ b. July 10, 1854; d. May 17, 1857.
118. Margaret E. Hall,⁵ b. April 17, 1814; m. Varnum Greeley, who died
        many years since. He was a grocer in Manchester, N. H. She
        d. there, June 24, 1877. Children:
I.   Celesta Greeley,⁶ m. Dr. Carvelle; res. Manchester, N. H.
II.   Alexander (?) Greeley,⁶ res. Manchester, N. H.
119. Robert Hall,⁵ b. Sept. 15, 1816; single; res. Manchester, N. H. He
        was held in the highest regard by his acquaintances; d. March
        29, 1883.
120. Julia Ann Hall,⁵ b. Oct. 19, 1820; m. Dr. Guilford, of Thornton, N. H.;
        she d. Aug. 29, 1860. Child:
I.   Robert Guilford,⁶ farmer; res. Hooksett, N. H.; single.
121. Charles A. Hall,⁵ b. April 21, 1822; m. Susan Webster, of Manches-
        ter, N. H., who is deceased; farmer; resided at Manchester,
        N. H.; d. June 28, 1870. Children:
I.   Frederick Hall,⁶ res. in Manchester, then removed to Denver, Col.;
        m., but his wife is deceased.
II.   Charles Hall,⁶ d. when a youth.
III. William Hall,⁶ d. when a youth.
122. McGregor Hall,⁵ b. March 25, 1825; farmer; res. on the home farm
        in Manchester, N. H.; m. Lizzie, daughter of Israel Webster
        and sister of Charles A. Hall's wife. They were of Manches-
        ter. Child:
I.   Kate Hall,⁶ d. young.

123. Andrew Allison⁴ [39] (Samuel,³ Capt. Samuel,²
Samuel¹). He was born in Dunbarton, N. H., Sept. 18, 1782.
Married Sarah Carter Bronson. He died in Northport, Me.,
Feb. 12, 1822. She was born in Boston, Mass., June 15, 1789;
died in Concord, N. H., May 1, 1865. He left his native town
when a young man. He was a merchant in Castine, Me., as
early as 1810, and there the most of his active life was spent,
but he removed to Northport, Me., in the latter part of his
life. He and his wife were Congregationalists in their
church preferences and affiliations. After Mr. Allison's
death, his widow and family went to Dunbarton, N. H., and
lived eight years, and then settled in Concord, N. H.

CHILDREN.

124. Sarah Catherine Allison,⁵ b. Castine, Me., Nov. 22, 1810; m., April
        9, 1839, Rev. Henry S. Gerrish French, of Boscawen, N. H., and
        went to Bankok, Siam, as missionaries. They entered the mis-
        sionary work in 1839, and Mr. French d. in Siam in 1842, leav-
        ing a son. She returned to the United states, and d. in Greeley,

Col., April 9, 1882. She was a member of the North Congregational church in Concord, N. H., as well as her mother, sister,
and son. Child:

I. Henry Allison French,[6] b. Bankok, Siam, May 10, 1841. Came to the
United States with his mother when three years of age. Lived
in Concord, N. H. He was a printer, and worked in the *States-
man* and *Patriot* offices until 1873, when his health failed; went
to Greeley, Col., in the fall of 1873, purchased the Colorado
Sun, published it for ten years, and d. in Greeley, Col., April
26, 1889. He m., in 1883, Ellen M. Taylor, of Rutherford, N. J.
She still lives in Greeley, Col. Children b. Greeley, Col.:
Sarah Taylor French,[7] b. Aug. 24, 1884; Allison Taylor French,[7]
b. Oct. 9, 1885.

125. Mary Anne Allison,[5] b. Sept. 15, 1812; single. She was a very successful school teacher in Concord, N. H., and Montreal, Canada.
She was a literary person, wrote and published several works,
was active in all benevolent societies, and her life abounded in
good works. She was a most excellent, estimable, and beautiful woman, a devoted Christian, and considered by her friends
as one of the saints of the earth. She d. July 16, 1873.

126. Andrew Allison,[5] b. Dec. 28, 1814; was a painter; single; d. in
Concord, N. H., April 12, 1845.

127. Frederick Allison,[5] b. Castine, Me., May 11, 1817; farmer, bookbinder, and gardener; res. 93 N. State St., Concord. N. H.; m.,
Aug. 29, 1874, Mrs. Hannah Gove (Clark) Savory, b. July 18,
1826, in Weare, N. H.; d. Jan. 30, 1882. He m., second, July
28, 1883, Miss Jeannette Clark, daughter of Edward Gove and
Mehitable (Philbrick) Clark, of Henniker, N. H., where she
was b. Feb. 3, 1837, and was a sister of the first Mrs. Allison.
No children.

128. Harriet Allison,[5] b. Castine, Me., Sept. 18, 1819; d. Northport, Me.,
Sept. 19, 1821.

129. Harriet Adaline Allison,[5] b. Northport, Me., July 12, 1822; single.
She d. in young womanhood, in Concord, N. H., March 17,
1848.

130. James Allison[4] [41] (Samuel,[3] Capt. Samuel,[2] Samuel[1]). He was born in Dunbarton, N. H., May 24, 1784.
He married, Aug. 11, 1810, Mary, daughter of George and
Nancy (Fish) Holt, of Andover, Mass., Goffstown, and Dunbarton, N. H. She was born in Andover, July 7, 1791;
resided in Andover, Mass., before marriage, and in Dunbarton, N. H., afterward, where she died Nov. 28, 1835, aged 44
years, 4 months, 21 days. Mr. Allison married, second,
March 8, 1837, Mary, daughter of Jonathan and Molly (Mal-
let) Ireland, of Amesbury, Mass., and Dunbarton, N. H.
She was born in Salem, Mass., Aug. 4, 1798. Before marriage she resided in Salem, Mass., and Dunbarton, N. H.
She died October 29, 1870, in Concord, N. H., aged 72 years,
2 months, 25 days. Mr. Allison resided in Dunbarton until
1840; then in Warner, N. H., until 1846; then in Manchester, N. H., until 1853, and then in Goffstown, N. H., until
his death there, Feb. 2, 1867, aged 82 years, 9 months, 9
days.

Mr. Allison was an active, energetic, and influential per-

James Allison

sonage in his native town of Dunbarton, where the best years of his life were spent. He for many years kept a country store near the meeting-house; and, being a justice of the peace and post-master, he did a large part of the public business of the town. He also kept a hotel. He was town-clerk from 1819 to 1823, and from 1825 to 1832; selectman in 1822, 1823, 1825, 1826, 1830, and 1831, and represented Dunbarton in the legislature in 1827 and 1828. His home was a hospitable one. His memory was very retentive; his views were clear, and forcibly expressed; his mind was strong, as were his prejudices. He early espoused the temperance and anti-slavery causes, and upon the formation of the Republican party he forsook the Free Soil party and allied himself with its succeeding, and the successful, party of freedom, to which he ever after adhered. He was an attendant of the Congregational church.

CHILDREN BORN IN DUNBARTON, N. H., EXCEPT THE ELDEST AND
YOUNGEST.

131. Mary Ann Allison,⁵ b. Salem, Mass., Sept. 7, 1811; res. Dunbarton, N. H., where she d. May 23, 1828.
132. Caroline Brown Allison⁵ (249), b. Aug. 27, 1813; m., Nov. 12, 1840, Jonathan L. Allen; res. Hopkinton, N. H. She died there Aug. 24, 1863.
133. James Madison Allison,⁵ b. Nov. 9, 1814; was a merchant in Boston, Mass., where he d. single, Sept. 30, 1875, aged 60 years, 10 months, 21 days.
134. William Henry Allison⁵ (252), b. Sept. 18, 1816; m., Sept. 8, 1841, Mary Amelia Brown; res. Concord, N. H., and d. there May 15, 1887.
135. John Allison⁵ (257), b. June 26, 1818; m., May 10, 1845, Sarah Jane Richards; res. Boston, Mass., and d. there May 29, 1865.
136. Lavinia Holt Allison⁵ (260), b. Jan. 15, 1820; m., Jan. 7, 1841, John L. Weeks; res. Hopkinton, N. H. In 1890 she res. in Cambridge, Mass.
137. Margaret Jane Allison,⁵ b. Dec. 8, 1821. She was a teacher for many years in the public schools of Manchester, N. H., New Haven, Conn., and Boston, Mass. She was an excellent teacher, and a good elocutionist. She d. of typhoid fever, in Stoneham, Mass., Oct. 5, 1876.
138. Andrew Allison⁵ (262), b. March 12, 1824; m., Feb. 2, 1858, Martha Tozier; res. Winchester, Mass.
139. Elizabeth Hall Allison⁵ (269), b. March 24, 1825; m., Sept. 30, 1874, Rev. Cyrus Washington Wallace; res. Manchester, N. H.
140. Sarah Evans Allison,⁵ b. Nov. 13, 1827; d. in Warner, N. H., July 27, 1842, aged 14 years, 8 months, 14 days.
141. Mary Ann Damon Allison,⁵ b. Jan. 1, 1830; a teacher in the public schools of Manchester, N. H., for several years; res. Manchester, N. H.
142. Ignatius Allison,⁵ b. June 20, 1832; m., Sept. 15, 1880, Mrs. Eliza Ann McNaughten, who m. d. Sept. 7, 1890. He was a painter in the shops of the Union Pacific Railway Co. for several years; res. Manchester, N. H., in 1892; no children.

143. Franklin Allison,⁵ b. July 3, 1835. He was a merchant; res. Boston, Mass.; d. in New York, N. Y., Dec. 29, 1881, aged 46 years, 5 months, 26 days. He m. Elizabeth Favor, who is deceased; no children.
144. Susan Dickenson Allison,⁵ b. July 31, 1838; d. in Warner, N. H., March 1, 1842, aged 3 years, 7 months, 1 day.
145. George Augustus Allison⁵ (269 A), b. Sept. 14, 1843, in Warner, N. H.; m., Nov. 12, 1864, Julia Powers; res. Cambridge, Mass.

146. David Clinton Allison⁴ [43] (Samuel,³ Capt. Samuel,² Samuel¹). He was born in Dunbarton, N. H., April 27, 1787; married, Aug. 24, 1810, Mary Jackson Bronson, who was born in Boston, Mass., Feb. 8, 1891, and was a sister of Mrs. Andrew Allison. She died in Concord, N. H., June 10, 1842. Mr. Allison was a hatter; he learned his trade in Charlestown, Mass. For a time he lived in Castine, Me., but returned to his native state, and lived in Concord, where he died July 1, 1851, and is buried there. He was a person of great excellence of character. He married, second, about 1843, Mrs. Rider, who died July, 1892, in Dunbarton, N. H.

CHILDREN.

147. David Barr Allison,⁵ b. Salem, Mass., April 8, 1813. He was a printer, and carried on business at Sanbornton Square, Laconia, and Concord, N. H.; m. Pauline Moulton Lane, daughter of Joseph H. Lane, of Sanbornton, N. H., who was b. Feb. 28, 1822; d. 1850, aged 28 years. He m., second, Mrs. Elvira Tracy, in Claremont, N. H., 1851. He was a man of fine character. His death occurred at Bath, Me., July 16, 1866, aged 53 years, 3 months. Child:
I. Clara Elvira Allison,⁶ b. Concord, N. H., Aug. 15, 1854; m., Jan. 15, 1871, Benjamin Kimball Chase; farmer; res. Cornish, N. H. Child, b. Cornish, N. H., Everett Kimball Chase,⁷ b. June 29, 1889.
148. Mary Bronson Allison,⁵ b. Salem, Mass., Aug. 16, 1814. Much of her life was spent in Concord, N. H.; res. (1890) Norwood Park, Ill.; single.
149. Sarah Ann Allison,⁵ b. Peterborough, N. H., July 24, 1816; m., Feb. 15, 1843, William Thayer; res. Manchester, N. H. She d. in Peterborough, N. H., June 18, 1846, aged 29 years, 10 months, 24 days; no children.
150. Eliza Jane Allison,⁵ b. Peterborough, N. H., March 13, 1818; m., Dec. 31, 1840, Newell Abbott Foster, of Portland, Me., where she d. June 18, 1854. He was a publisher. Children:
I. Leroy Allison Foster,⁶ b. Portland, Me., March 15, 1843; d. at Denver, Col., March 29, 1882. He was a publisher. He m., Aug. 25, 1874, Emma S. Eastman, at Worcester, Mass. Children: Clifford Eastman Foster,⁷ b. Aug. 29, 1877. Cornelia Chase Foster,⁷ b. May 5, 1879.
II. Adelaide Eliza Foster,⁶ b. Portland, Me., Jan. 16, 1853; m. Austin Brainard, Oct. 23, 1886; res. Hartford, Conn., 15 Kenyon St. Child: Helen Allison Brainard,⁷ b. Dec. 5, 1889.
151. Henrietta White Allison,⁵ b. Concord, N. H., Jan. 24, 1820; m., Jan. 14, 1846, Rollin Fletcher, at Portland, Me., where they resided. He was a tailor, and d. at Morris, Ill., May 3, 1885. Mrs. Fletcher lives (1892) at Morris. Children:

I.   Eugene Bronson Fletcher,[6] b. Portland, Me., April 28, 1847; m., at Circleville, O., Nov. 29, 1869, Mary Rebecca Harris. Children: Lucy Harris Fletcher,[7] b. Jan. 5, 1871; d. Jan. 18, 1871. Inez Blanchard Fletcher,[7] b. Ashland, Ky., July 8, 1873. William Condit Fletcher,[7] b. Morris, Ill., Dec. 1, 1875.
II. Sarah Elizabeth Fletcher,[6] b. Portland, Me., Jan. 19, 1849: d. Aug. 18, 1851.
152. Henry Alexander Allison,[5] b. Concord, N. H., Sept. 30, 1822: d. there June, 1824.
153. George Allison[5] (270), b. Concord, N. H., July 30, 1824; m. Esther Noyes; res. Merrimacport, Mass.; d. Feb. 5, 1867.
154. Francis Augustus Allison,[5] b. Concord, N. H., Sept. 16, 1826; m., Dec. 31, 1855, at Circleville, O., J. G. McIntire. She d. April 6, 1856.
155. Henry Allison[5] (281), b. Concord, N. H., Nov. 7, 1828; m., Nov. 21, 1851, Mary L. Gallishun; m., second, Mary Garbet; res. Aurora, Ill.
156. Emeline Allison,[5] b. Concord, N. H., April 21, 1832; m., in Stratham, N. H., July 2, 1857, Charles Edwin Gilman. He is a blacksmith and farmer; was b. in Exeter, N. H., May 10, 1830. They lived in Merrimacport, Mass.; went to Wheeling, West Va., in the fall of 1860, to Illinois in 1861, and to Kansas in the spring of 1875. He d. Aug. 1, 1887. He was a son of Abijah and Harriet (Burley) Gilman, of Exeter, N. H.; res. Pittsburg, Kan. Child:
I.   Mary Ellen Gilman,[6] b. July 13, 1863, near Orange, Iroquois Co., Ill. She is a physician; res. Pittsburg, Kan., in January, 1891.
157. Ellen Maria Allison,[5] b. July 16, 1834; m., May 22, 1860, Dr. Asa F. Pettee, and d. March 16, 1863. He res. Boston, Mass.

158.   Margaret Barr Allison[4] [43] (Samuel,[3] Capt. Samuel,[2] Samuel[1]). She was born in Dunbarton, N. H., in 1789; died Sept. 25, 1828. She married Samuel Evans, of Peterborough, N. H., son of Asa and Dorothy (Bass) Evans, of that town. He was born May 2, 1786; died in Hopkinton, N. H., Jan. 27, 1868, aged 81 years, 8 months, 25 days. Mrs. Evans died in Concord, N. H., Sept. 23, 1828, leaving three children. Mr. Evans married, second, Sarah Chase, November, 1824, who was a devoted mother to the motherless children. She died Aug. 28, 1888; no children by second marriage.

CHILDREN.

159. Samuel Evans, Jr.,[5] b. October, 1811; d. Feb. 27, 1884, in Nashua, N. H., aged 72 years, 4 months.
160. Andrew Allison Evans,[5] b. Sept. 5, 1815; d. May 31, 1888, in Brookline, Mass., aged 72 years, 8 months, 26 days. He m. Agnes Kelt, of Boston, Mass., Sept. 15, 1845, who d. February, 1853. He m. second, November, 1862, Eliza Estabrook, who survives him; no children.
161. Susan Carlton Evans,[5] b. Sept. 10, 1817; m., April, 1851, John M. Kelt; res. Concord, N. H. He left for California in November, 1854, and she never heard from him after a year's time. In 1858 she was divorced, and resumed her maiden name.

162.   Walter Harris Allison[4] [45] (Samuel,[3] Capt. Samuel,[2] Samuel[1]). He was born in Dunbarton, N. H., Dec.

30, 1792; married, Sept. 26, 1817, Anna, daughter of John and Annie (Hamilton) Allen, of Brookfield, Mass., where she was born Jan. 18, 1793. She died in Boston, Mass., Aug. 28, 1868, aged 75 years, 7 months. She was living with her married daughter, Mrs. Lamb. Mr. Allison was a hatter; learned his trade in Charlestown, Mass.; went to Brookfield, Mass., in 1817, and there he made his home for thirty-two years; removed to Boston, Mass., where he was killed by the bursting of a boiler, dying in the Massachusetts General Hospital June 13, 1854. He and his wife were members of the Orthodox Congregational church.

CHILDREN BORN IN BROOKFIELD, MASS.

163. Walter Edwin Allison,[6] b. Nov. 27, 1818; d. March 4, 1819.
164. Sarah Stone Allison,[5] b. March 29, 1821; m., Oct. 1, 1843, Charles Churchill Lamb. He was b. in Phillipston, Mass., April 23, 1808, and is son of Jonas and Hannah (Sawyer) Lamb, of Phillipston, and grandson of Israel and Lucy (Wheeler) Lamb, of Templeton, Mass. Mr. Lamb was a book-keeper for more than fifty years, and retired Oct. 1, 1889; res. No. 125 Warren Ave., Boston, Mass. Children, b. Boston, Mass.:
I.   Sarah Anna Lamb,[6] b. Aug. 7, 1844; m., Nov. 19, 1872, Charles Frederick Wise, of Boston, Mass., b. October, 1844; clerk with Devoe & Co., paints and oils, New York city; res. No. 826 Union St., Brooklyn, N. Y. Child: Lester Drummond Wise,[7] b. Oct. 8, 1879.
II. Charles Allison Lamb,[6] b. Dec. 30, 1846; m., Sept. 17, 1874, Martha L., dau. of Joel Pike, of Boston, Mass. She was b. Dec. 25, 1848, in Philadelphia, Penn., but lived in Boston after her twelfth year. He is general manager of the National Tube Works, corner of Clinton St., Chicago, Ill.; res. No. 497 West Jackson St., Chicago, Ill. Children: Charles Holmes Lamb,[7] b. Cambridge, Mass., Sept. 7, 1876. Mabel Howard Lamb,[7] b. Boston, Mass., Sept. 26, 1877.
III. Edward Wheeler Lamb,[6] b. Nov. 28, 1849; d. March 14, 1850.
IV. Frank Hooker Lamb,[6] b. Sept. 2, 1851; res. No. 495 West Jackson St., Chicago, Ill. He is a book-keeper and cashier of the National Tube Works, corner of Clinton St., Chicago. He m., June 9, 1879, Clara Jane, dau. of William and Jane (Allen) Dane, of West Brookfield, Mass., where she was b. in 1853. Child, b. Chicago, Ill.: Roy Dane Lamb,[7] b. July, 1882; d. July, 1882.
V.   Nellie Florence Lamb,[6] b. Nov. 13, 1859; res. No. 125 Warren Ave., Boston, Mass.
165. Walter Harris Allison,[5] b. May 15, 1832; single; was a soldier from Chicago, in an Illinois regiment, and served during the war; was disabled in the service, and never recovered; is in the Soldier's Home, Chelsea, Mass. Before his enlistment he was in "Long John Wentworth's" printing office for nine years.

166. John Stinson[4] [50] (Janet Allison,[3] Capt. Samuel,[2] Samuel[1]). He was born in Dunbarton, N. H., Nov. 13, 1789; died Aug. 13, 1875. He married, Feb. 18, 1819, Betsey, daughter of David and Mary (Stark) Stinson, of New Bos-

ton, N. H., and his third cousin. He resided on the home
farm in Dunbarton; was appointed a colonel in the militia
in 1820, and often filled offices of trust in his native town.
He was town clerk in 1824, 1833–'44; selectman in 1846 and
1847; was appointed justice of the peace in 1830. He was
an intelligent and public spirited man.

CHILDREN BORN IN DUNBARTON, N. H.

167. Mary Jane Stinson,⁵ b. Feb. 11, 1820; m., 1845, David Story, and d.
      in Dunbarton, N. H., 1851. He is a farmer, and res. Dunbar-
      ton, N. H. Children:
I.   Mary Louise Story,⁶ d. young.
II.   Warren Story,⁶ b. July, 1854; res. San Bernardino, county of San
      Bernardino, Cal.; one child.
168. Nancy Chase Stinson,⁵ b. April 3, 1826; m., 1857, David Story, who
      had previously married her sister, and d. 1865, leaving one son.
I.   Lafayette Story,⁶ b. July, 1865; res. Nashua, N. H., near Hollis line.
      He m. Frances Helena Ryder; no children; farmer.
David Story m., third, his cousin, Sarah Ann Stinson. Children:
II.   David Story,⁶ b. 1871.
III. Charles Frederick Story,⁶ b. 1877.
169. John Chase Stinson,⁵ b. Sept. 4, 1834; m., May 2, 1867, Alice Beaty
      Coghill, at Gloucester City, N. J.; in 1855 removed to Chico-
      pee, Mass., and lived two years; removed to Gloucester City,
      N. J., April 15, 1857, and has been in coal, lumber, and hard-
      ware business ever since that time; a Democrat in politics; an
      Episcopalian; was five years a freeholder, for fourteen years
      a member of the board of education, and has been superin-
      tendent of city schools since 1885. Children:
I.   Abbie E. Stinson,⁶ b. Nov. 7, 1869.
II.   Charles Albert Stinson,⁶ b. Dec., 1871; d. July 4, 1872.
III. Mary Stinson,⁶ b. June, 1873; d. August, 1873.
IV.   Ellen Augusta Stinson,⁶ b. April 22, 1875.
V.   Henry Chase Stinson,⁶ b. Aug., 1877; d. Sept., 1877.

170. Archibald Stinson⁴ [51] (Janet Allison,³ Capt.
Samuel,² Samuel¹). He was born in Dunbarton, N. H.,
March 14, 1791. While in his young manhood, in 1817,
he went to Hammond, St. Lawrence county, N. Y., where
he was a school teacher. He married, in 1819, Sally Barker, daughter of Jeduthan (of Connecticut) and Lucy A.
(Pond) Barker, of Vergennes, Vt., born at Ogdensburg,
N. Y., Feb. 28, 1802. He owned a small farm where he
lived till about 1840, when he sold it and removed to Rossie,
St. Lawrence county, N. Y., where he lived for twenty years,
when he removed to the beautiful village of Gouverneur, St.
Lawrence county, N. Y. He attained a competence, was an
attendant of the Episcopal church, and a Democrat in his
politics. He died of small-pox, Jan. 24, 1872. He was a
soldier of the 1812–'15 war. Mrs. Stinson was a member of
the Episcopal church, and after the death of her husband
lived with her daughters. She was a strong-minded, ener-

getic woman, and died with her daughter, Mrs. Stone, in
Theresa, Jefferson county, N. Y., Nov. 3, 1882, and was
buried with her husband at Gouverneur, N. Y.

CHILDREN BORN IN HAMMOND, ST. LAWRENCE COUNTY, N. Y., EXCEPT
LAST.

·171. Janet Eliza Stinson,⁵ (285) b. March 2, 1820; m. Feb. 29, 1846, Loren
Stone; res. Theresa, Jefferson county, N. Y.
172. Mary Stinson,⁵ b. June 3, 1822; m. Feb. 25, John Wright; res. Can-
ton, N. Y.; d. Aug. 29, 1873. Children:
I. Luther L. Wright,⁶ b. 1855; m. Nellie Corning, April 21, 1881. Chil-
dren: Annie Corning Wright,⁷ b. April 24, 1882; Luther
McVichie Wright,⁷ b. Feb. 4, 1890.
II. Lucy L. Wright,⁶ d. Dec. 6, 1863.
III. Kate Emogene Wright,⁶ b. March 2, 1859; d. June 8, 1887; m. Joseph
Polacheck, June 17, 1885. Child: Kate Wright Polacheck,⁷ b.
June 8, 1886.
IV. John Wright, Jr.,⁶ d. Dec. 14, 1863.
V. Morris Wright,⁶ b. 1866; m. Susie L. Chappelle, Oct. 25, 1888.
VI. Harry Wright,⁶ b. 1868.
173. Lucy Stinson,⁵ d. in infancy.
174. Eleanor Hoag Stinson⁵ (293) b. June 25, 1825; m. Dec. 21, 1853,
Thomas Miller; res. Jersey City, N. J.
175. Lucy Pond Stinson,⁵ b. June 13, 1827; m. Feb. 11, 1852, Thomas
Ormiston; res. Kelseyville, Cal. He d. April 5, 1889. Children:
I. Sarah Blanche Ormiston,⁶ m. Dec. 3, 1873, John Griffitts; res. Kelsey-
ville, Cal. Children: Lucy Rebecca Griffitts,⁷ b. Nov. 13, 1874;
Jessie Esther Griffitts,⁷ b. March 30, 1877; Edward Stinson
Griffitts,⁷ b. April 19, 1879; Maud Melendy Griffitts,⁷ b. Oct.
4, 1883; Loren Keithly Griffitts,⁷ b. July 20, 1888.
II. Ann Eliza Ormiston,⁶ b. Jan. 31, 1862; m. D. H. Kirk, of Yuba
county, Cal., Dec. 26, 1882. Children: Hazel Thomas Kirk,⁷ b.
Oct. 11, 1883; Harvey Daniel Kirk,⁷ b. Oct. 11, 1883; Willie
Archibald Kirk,⁷ b. May 16, 1886; George Augustus Kirk,⁷ b.
Feb. 2, 1889; Blanche T. Kirk,⁷ b. Jan. 19, 1891.
III. Jettie Stinson Ormiston,⁶ b. Oct. 11, 1867; student at a medical col-
lege, San Francisco, Cal.
IV. Archie McGregor Ormiston,⁶ b. May 28, 1870; is pursuing a collegi-
ate course at Oakland, Cal.
176. Esther Blake Stinson,⁵ b. Oct. 1, 1830; m. Dec. 28, 1864, William N.
Buck; res. Waukegan, Wis. Children:
I. Dora Buck.⁶
II. Hershel W. Buck.⁶
III. Estella Amanda Buck.⁶
177. Sylvanus Barker Stinson,⁵ b. April 8, 1833; m. Dec. 2, 1862, Mary
Ann Rogers; res. Gouverneur, N. Y. They are members of the
Presbyterian church. He is a Democrat in politics. Children:
I. Frank Archibald Stinson,⁶ b. Jan. 1, 1865; is a merchant tailor; res.
Gouverneur, N. Y.
II. Henry S. Stinson,⁶ b. March 22, 1867; d. Jan. 26, 1889.
III. Clarence L. Stinson,⁶ b. July 16, 1869; shipping clerk in marble
works; res. Gouverneur, N. Y.
IV. Lena B. Stinson,⁶ b. April 7, 1872.
V. Roger B. Stinson,⁶ b. April 13, 1875.
VI. Glenn E. Stinson,⁶ b. July 19, 1878.
VII. Lynn M. Stinson,⁶ b. Jan. 12, 1882.
178. Sarah Elizabeth Stinson,⁵ b. Feb. 19, 1836; teacher; single; res.
Lakeport, Cal.

179. Louise Antoinette Stinson,[6] b. March 22, 1839; m. Feb. 13, 1859,
        George Clark; res. Springfield, Ohio. She d. July 6, 1878.
        He is deceased, having d. Sept. 16, 1879. Child:
I. Madge M. Clark,[6] b. May 10, 1861; m. April 6, 1882, Rev. Fred P.
        Sutherland, of White Plains, N. Y. They are missionaries;
        res. Saygang, Burmah, India. Children: Clark Stinson Suth-
        erland[7]; Elinore Miller Sutherland.[7]
180. Emogene Maligna Stinson,[5] b. Rossie, N. Y., Oct. 18, 1846; m. Oct.
        8, 1866, Clarence E. Dickinson. He is a druggist, a Republican,
        and city clerk; res. New London, Wis. Children:
I.   Clarke Jones Dickinson,[6] b. Oct. 7, 1867; d. Aug. 23, 1879.
II.   Archie Stinson Dickinson,[6] b. Nov. 24, 1868; d. Sept. 9, 1869.
III. Louise Dickinson,[6] b. April 19, 1870; d. Oct. 8, 1870.
IV.   Arnold Hayden Dickinson,[6] b. Oct. 8, 1871; d. Sept. 2, 1879.
V.   Roy Vene Dickinson,[6] b. Dec. 21, 1873.
VI.   Alice May Dickinson,[6] b. May 20, 1877.
VII. Baby Dickinson,[6] b. June 19, 1879; d. Sept. 2, 1879.
VIII. Harry John Dickinson,[6] b. July 31, 1881.
IX.   Claire Rogers Dickinson,[6] b. Dec. 16, 1882.
X.   Emogene Susie Dickinson,[6] b. Nov. 19, 1885.

181. James Stinson[4] [52] (Janet Allison,[3] Capt. Samuel,[2]
Samuel[1]). He was born in Dunbarton, N. H., Nov. 6, 1794;
married Jan. 25, 1818, Melissa, daughter of Abner Curtis,
born in the state of New York, Oct. 29, 1800, resided North
East, Penn., and died Jan. 7, 1832, at Harbour Creek, Penn.
He married, second, March 31, 1835, Mary, daughter of
Thomas and Dorcas Bell (Taylor) Greenwood, and granddaughter of Joseph Greenwood, born in England, and residing in Philadelphia. She was born in Paxton, Dauphin
county, Penn., Feb. 6, 1797, and died in Harbour Creek,
Penn., Nov. 3, 1878. He was a carpenter, and resided in
North East, Penn., from 1816 to 1819, and from the latter
date to his death, April 29, 1845, in Harbour Creek, Penn.

CHILDREN BORN IN HARBOUR CREEK, PENN., EXCEPT THE ELDEST.

182. William Stark Stinson,[5] b. North East, Penn., Feb. 27, 1819; Demo-
        crat; attends the Presbyterian church, and with his sisters res.
        on the old homestead in Harbour Creek, Penn. ; was in business
        for some years as a farmer and blacksmith, but is now retired;
        single.
183. Erastus Sheldon Stinson,[5] b. Harbour Creek, Penn., Feb. 3, 1822; m.
        Dec. 19, 1854, Ann Walker Carpenter; res. Dartford, Wis.,
        where d. Dec. 21, 1860. Children:
I.   Frank Stinson,[6] b. Nov. 14, 1855.
II.   Clara Stinson,[6] b. June 3, 1858; m. Bert Morris, Dec. 17, 1879. Chil-
        dren: Julia Ward Morris,[7] b. June 28, 1881; Harold Leigh
        Morris,[7] b. Aug. 29, 1883; Earl Morris,[7] b. April 16, 1889.
184. Mary Jane Stinson,[5] b. Oct. 18, 1824; res. Harbour Creek, Penn.,
        where she died June 29, 1846.
185. Jeremiah Page Stinson,[5] b. Oct. 9, 1827; m. Dec. 2, 1857, Irene
        Whitney, b. Nov. 17, 1831. He is a carpenter, and res. West-
        field, Wis. Children:
I.   Charilla Stinson,[6] b. Sept. 6, 1858; d. Oct. 12, 1864.

7

II.   Mary E. Stinson,⁶ b. April 18, 1865; m. April 8, 1889, George W. Roberts.
III.   Clara Stinson,⁶ b. Aug. 16, 1869.
186.   Charilla Twitchell Stinson,⁵ b. Feb. 17, 1831; res. on the homestead at Harbour Creek, Penn.
187.   Sarah Elizabeth Stinson,⁵ b. Feb. 24, 1836. She is post-mistress, and res. on the homestead at Harbour Creek, Penn.
188.   Joseph Greenwood Stinson,⁵ b. May 24, 1839; m. June 9, 1868, Catherine Tupper. He is a mechanic, and res. Harbour Creek, Penn. Children:
I.   Mary G. Stinson,⁶ b. Oct. 25, 1869.
II.   Albert E. Stinson,⁶ b. June 23, 1871.
III.   Margaret Stinson,⁶ b. March 5, 1875; d. Jan. 9, 1885.
IV.   James Stinson,⁶ b. June 19, 1878.
V.   Fred A. Stinson,⁶ b. July 13, 1879.
VI.   Ethel C. Stinson,⁶ b. Aug. 20, 1885.

189.   Jeremiah Page Stinson⁴ [53] (Janet Allison,³ Capt. Samuel,² Samuel¹). He was born in Dunbarton, N. H., July 20, 1798, and died Sept. 5, 1827. He was a carpenter and house builder. He married Nancy Clark, who was born in Londonderry, N. H., Oct. 29, 1796. They resided in Huevel, seven miles from and in Ogdensburg, N. Y., in 1823, with Archibald his brother, and in Pictou, and Smith's Falls, Ontario, Canada. She died in the latter place, Dec. 19, 1884, in her 89th year.

CHILDREN BORN IN OGDENSBURG, N. Y.

190.   Helen Mar Stinson,⁵ m. Abraham Edwin Dixon, a civil engineer; no children.
191.   Janette Clark Stinson,⁵ m., in 1858, James Trussel Frost, a foundry man or manufacturer. She d. Feb., 1865; res. Smith's Falls, Ontario, Canada. Children:
I.   Helen Elvira Frost,⁶ b. Feb. 18, 1859; m. George Frederick McKinnon, Jan. 30, 1889. Child: Charles Harvard McKinnon,⁷ b. Feb. 14, 1890.
II.   Caroline Lydia Frost,⁶ b. Jan. 15, 1861.
III.   James Edwin Frost,⁶ b. July 15, 1863; res. Smith's Falls, Ontario.

192.   Ebenezer Allison⁴ [56] (Andrew,³ Capt. Samuel,² Samuel¹). He was born in Dunbarton, N. H., March 18, 1789; married, in 1816, Phebe Phelps; carpenter and farmer. He resided at Brownsville, N. Y. Mrs. Allison was born March 16, 1797, and died Feb. 14, 1880. He died April 23, 1871.

CHILDREN BORN IN LIMERICK, N. Y.

193.   Sally Allison,⁵ b. July 1, 1817; m. Lloyd Sanford; res. Limerick, Jefferson Co., N. Y. She d. in Brownville, N. Y.
194.   Samuel Allison,⁵ b. Nov. 22, 1818; drowned at Limerick, N. Y., Sept. 6, 1826.

195. Polly Allison,[3] (316), b. Jan. 11, 1820, at Brownville, N. Y.; m. Henry Gibbs, who d. Oct. 30, 1890. She d. Sept. 3, 1890; res. Pelatuma, Saline Co., Col.
196. Esther Allison[3] (324), b. March 8, 1822; res. 501 Reed St., Milwaukee, Wis.
197. Julia Allison[3] (328), b. April 19, 1824; m. Edward Williston. She d. at Chicago, Ill.
198. Lavinia Jemima Allison[3] (330), b. June 25, 1826; m. Jacob Ellis Harmon; res. Watertown, N. Y.
199. Harlow Allison[3] (335), b. Oct. 21, 1828; res. Limerick, N. Y.
200. Jane Allison,[3] b. Oct. 3, 1830; m., March 17, 1856, Adam Hagan. He is a carpenter and farmer; res. Perch River, N. Y.; no children.
201. Simeon Allison,[3] b. Aug. 20, 1832; m., at Clayton, N. Y., Jan. 24, 1861, Helen Gloyd; farmer; res. Limerick, N. Y.; no children.
202. Hannah Allison,[3] b. May 21, 1836; m., Feb. 2, 1860, at Watertown, N. Y., Edward Spicer, a farmer. She d. at Perch River, N. Y., April 26, 1870. Child:
I. Jessie Spicer,[4] b. Oct. 17, 1865; d. Sept. 11, 1879.
203. William Henry Allison[3] (335), b. July 10, 1844; res. Limerick, N. Y.

204. **Eli Allison[4] [57] (Andrew,[3] Capt. Samuel,[2] Samuel[1]).** He was born in Dublin, N. H., Dec. 25, 1791; married, Dec. 30, 1817, Persis, daughter of John W. and Hannah (Wight) Learnard, of Dublin, N. H., who was born Dec. 3, 1797. They resided in their native town.

CHILDREN BORN IN DUBLIN, N. H.

205. Andrew Allison,[3] b. May 16, 1821; d. Jan. 17, 1850.
206. John Wilson Allison[3] (343), b. March 15, 1823; res. Boston, 121 Blue Hill ave., Roxbury district.
207. Samuel Allison,[5] b. June 1, 1825; d. Dec. 10, 1834.
208. Webster Allison,[3] b. July 12, 1827; d. Dec. 21, 1834.
209. James Allison[3] (351), b. March 13, 1830; m., March 19, 1854, Sarah Jane, daughter of William and Julia (Johnson) Darracott, of Dublin, N. H.
210. Sarah Jane Allison,[3] b. Jan. 21, 1835; d. July 16, 1841.
211. Persis J. Allison,[3] b. Nov. 15, 1837; d. July 16, 1841.

212. **Samuel Quinton[4] [62] (Margaret Allison,[3] Capt. Samuel,[2] Samuel[1]).** The name of his wife was not given.

CHILD.

213. Royal Bellows Quinton[5] (361); res. Denmark, Iowa.

214. **Betsey Abbott Allison[4] [82] (John,[3] Capt. Samuel,[2] Samuel[1]).** She was born in Londonderry (now Derry), N. H., April 3, 1788; married Josiah Abbott, Jr., of Worcester, Mass., Dec. 30, 1808, and died April 13, 1830, in Lunenburg, Essex Co., Vt. Mr. Abbott was born in New Boston, N. H., July 1, 1784, and died in Newark, Caledonia

Co., Vt., May 5, 1871. He was a son of Josiah Abbott, of Amherst, N. H., born in 1757 and died in 1830, and whose wife was Margaret Carr. She was his distant relative.

CHILD.

214a. A son b. Oct. 2, 1809; d. before being named.
215. John Allison Abbott,[5] b. March 5, 1811, in Roxbury, Mass. He is a painter and surveyor. He lived in Whitefield, N. H., from 1845 to 1850; since 1850 in Newark, Caledonia Co., Vt. He m., Dec. 3, 1845, Betsey Woodice Ordway, daughter of Nathaniel (b. Sept., 1791) and Olive (Willey) Ordway. His father d. in Newark, Vt., Aug. 16, 1853. His grandparents were John and Hannah Ordway, of Hopkinton, N. H. Mr. Abbott is a Democrat in politics. Child:
I.   Betsey Allison Abbott,[6] b. Newark, Vt., July 11, 1856; m. Alvin Pariss Drown, son of William and Sarah Jane (Allard) Drown, Feb. 26, 1876, a farmer. They res. in Newark, Vt. He was b. in Sutton, Vt., July 22, 1857. Children: Ella Jane Drown,[7] b. Sept. 7, 1877. Caroline Winch Drown,[7] b. May 4, 1882.

216. John Allison[4] [88] (James,[3] Capt. Samuel,[2] Samuel[1]). He was born in Weathersfield, Vt., Feb. 26, 1790, and died July 29, 1863, of heart disease, aged 73 years, 5 months, 3 days. He lived and died upon the home farm of his father in Weathersfield, Vt., which was in 1890 owned by his son, De Forrest Allison. Mr. Allison married, Jan. 1, 1824, Jerusha Swett, of Hanover, N. H., who died July 23, 1829, aged 34 years. She was born in Hanover in 1795. He married, second, in Feb., 1832, Mrs. Anna Porter, of Bradford, Vt., who was born Dec. 16, 1800, and died Feb. 20, 1845, aged 45 years, 2 months, 4 days.

CHILDREN BORN IN WEATHERSFIELD, VT.

217. Bolivar Allison,[5] b. Sept. 19, 1825; d. of croup, Aug. 12, 1830, aged 4 years, 10 months.
218. James Stockman Allison[5] (363), b. April 10, 1827; d. Newton, Mass., May 1, 1881, aged 54 years.
219. Jerusha Allison,[5] b. July 23, 1829; m., Dec. 22, 1863, Cyrus Piper, Jr., of Keene, N. H., b. Nov. 23, 1819. He d. Jan. 10, 1888; res. Northampton, Mass. Children:
I.   Mabel Elizabeth Piper,[6] b. Feb. 12, 1865; d. Oct. 17, 1875.
II. Louis Allison Piper,[6] b. Oct. 14, 1866; res. Keene, N. H.
220. Letitia Allison,[5] b. Jan. 10, 1833; d. Jan. 19, 1833.
221. John Quinton Allison,[5] b. Sept. 23, 1834; m., April 3, 1860, Mrs. Lutheria Bixby, of Denmark, Iowa; res. Dakota. Children:
I.   Carrie Allison,[6] m. Mr. Maxwell; res. Ballard, Washington.
II. Carroll De Forrest Allison.[6]
222. Almira Allison,[5] b. Nov. 23, 1836; m., Nov. 4, 1855, Albert Weston, a farmer, of Windsor, Vt. He was b. at Springfield, Vt., Aug. 19, 1830; res. Windsor. Child:
I.   John Albert Weston,[6] b. Dec. 31, 1856; d. Aug. 30, 1870, aged 13 years, 8 months.

223. De Forrest Allison,[5] b. Dec. 2, 1838; res. Kiowa, Barber Co., Kan., in 1890. He lived 32 years in Weathersfield, Vt., 7 years in Newton, Mass., 3 years in Topeka, Kan., and has lived in Kiowa, Kan., since 1882.
224. Cynthia Ann Allison,[5] b. Oct. 16, 1840; m., Feb. 3, 1873, David Fish, of St. Paul, Minn., who d. Aug. 21, 1874, aged 56 years, 6 months, 9 days. She m., second, July 22, 1880, John H. Bryant; res. St. Paul, Minn., and in 1890, Los Angeles, Cal. Children:
I.[*] Almira Weston Fish,[6] b. Nov. 13, 1873; res. Los Angeles, Cal.
II. Anna Allison Fish,[6] b. March 29, 1875; d. April 13, 1876, aged 1 year, 14 days.

225. **Samuel Allison[4] [89] (James,[3] Capt. Samuel,[2] Samuel[1]).** He was born in Weathersfield, Vt., Aug. 12, 1791. He resided in his native town until 1834, when he removed to Painesville, Ohio, where he died May 14, 1850, aged 58 years, 9 months, 2 days. He married, June 1, 1820, Mary Hulett, who died Nov. 20, 1854, in Painesville, Ohio. She was the mother of ten children. He was a Whig in politics.

CHILDREN.

226. Hannah Williams Allison,[5] b. Oct. 27, 1822; d. Aug. 1, 1848, in Perry, Lake Co., Ohio; single.
227. Clinton James Allison[5] (368), b. April 24, 1824; res. Olney, Ill.
228. Henry Allison[5] (374), b. Feb. 9, 1826; res. Hardinsburg, Ind.
229. Ann Moore Allison[5] (380), b. Nov. 14, 1827; m., Dec. 4, 1851, Carlos Mason, of Perry, Ohio; res. Painesville, Ohio.
230. Rodney Esbel Allison[5] (383), b. July 16, 1829; res. Perry, Lake Co., Ohio.
231. Orman Dutton Allison[5] (387), b. Feb. 3, 1831; res. Eight Mile, Oregon.
232. Walter Scott Allison[5] (394), b. July 9, 1832; d. Nashville, Tenn., July 27, 1864, aged 32 years, 17 days.
233. Oscar Hulett Allison,[5] b. April 15, 1834; d. Dec. 18, 1854, in Perry, Lake Co., Ohio.
234. Roland Hill Allison[5] (397), b. July 5, 1836; res. Clinton, Mo.; was a major in 63d Regt. Ill. Vols.
235. Lucian Osborne Allison,[5] b. Conneaut, Ashtabula Co., Ohio, Oct. 30, 1840; res. Eight Mile, Oregon; single; was living in Indiana when the war broke out, where he enlisted in 82d Indiana Vols., and served to its close. He was wounded in the service; is a Republican, and for 15 years a member of the Christian church.

236. **David Allison[5] [107] (William Davidson,[4] Samuel,[3] Capt. Samuel,[2] Samuel[1]).** He was born in Boston, Mass., June 13, 1812; married in 1837, Mary Ann Kelley, who died in Boston, June 21, 1849. She was born in 1813. He was a stage driver from Hingham to Boston. He lived in the West End, and died June 20, 1850, aged 38 years, 7 days.

237. Mary Ann Allison,⁵ b. July 19, 1839; res. Brockton, Mass. She m.
     Charles Bacon. He was a soldier, and is deceased; no chil-
     dren.
238. Laurinda Allison,⁵ b. July 28, 1843; m. Calvin Hilton, who was b.
     in Bowdoinham, Me., Jan. 9, 1834. He is a ship carpenter;
     res. Brooklyn, N. Y. Children:
  I. Annie Laura Hilton,⁷ b. Brooklyn, N. Y., Oct. 10, 1863; m., Feb. 26,
     1889, in Brooklyn, James Blair Bateman, who was b. in Balti-
     more, Md., Feb. 26, 1864; res. Brooklyn, N. Y.
 II. George William Hilton,⁷ b. Brooklyn, N. Y., May 10, 1865; d. July
     31, 1865.
III. Lovina Abbie Hilton,⁷ b. Bowdoin, Me., Jan. 9, 1867; res. Brook-
     lyn, N. Y.
 IV. Lizzie Debanfa Hilton,⁷ b. New York, N. Y., Dec. 6, 1869; d. July
     31, 1870.
  V. Albert Calvin Hilton,⁷ b. New York, N. Y., June 13, 1877; d. Nov.
     25, 1879.
 VI. Mabel Eleanora Hilton,⁷ b. Weld, Franklin Co., Me., June 29, 1882.
VII. Alice Merrill Hilton,⁷ b. Brooklyn, N. Y., Jan. 23, 1885; d. Jan. 23,
     1885.
239. Alice Bartlett Allison,⁵ b. July 5, 1845; m., June 25, 1868, William
     Henry Weld, b. Boston, Mass. She d. in Boston, June 2, 1888.
     They res. Boston, Mass. Child:
  I. William Weld,⁷ b. May 22, 1880.
240. Cornelia R. Allison,⁵ b. July 5, 1845; m., in Boston, Mass., July 8,
     1879, Winslow B. Morton, b. in that city, and who d. Jan. 7,
     1882. She d. in Boston, Mass., July 8, 1887.
241. Caroline E. Allison,⁵ b. June 1, 1848; d. Aug. 9, 1849.

242. Walter Harris Allison⁶ [108] (William Davidson,⁴
Samuel,³ Capt. Samuel,² Samuel¹). He was born in Boston,
Mass., Oct. 31, 1814; married, Feb. 7, 1836, Mary Whit-
marsh, who was born in Weymouth, Mass., Oct. 4, 1813.
He was a merchant tailor, and lived in Boston, Braintree,
Lexington, Wayland, and Weymouth, Mass., living for fif-
teen years in the latter place, where he died Sept. 9, 1856,
aged 41 years, 11 months, 22 days.

CHILDREN.

243. Caroline Allison,⁶ b. Braintree, Mass., Aug. 21, 1836; m., May, 1858,
     Luther Josiah Copeland; res. Weymouth, Mass., where she d.
     June 28, 1860. He d. May 19, 1859. Child, b. Weymouth, Mass.:
  I. Anna Harris Copeland,⁷ b. June 19, 1859; m., Dec. 16, 1885, Rev. John
     Loring Crane, of Braintree, Mass., b. Oct. 18, 1856. He is a
     Baptist clergyman, and preaches at Sheldonville, Wrentham,
     Mass. He graduated at Brown University in 1880, and from
     Newton Theological Seminary in 1883. Child: Florence Bin-
     ney Crane,⁸ b. Sheldonville, Mass., June 8, 1890.
244. Amey Allison,⁶ b. Weymouth, Mass., July 2, 1838; m., Nov. 22,
     1855, Samuel Frances Newcomb, who was b. in Braintree Neck
     (now Quincy), Mass., Feb. 3, 1831. He is the eighth genera-
     tion in descent from John Alden, and grandson of Samuel
     Newcomb, of Braintree Neck, a soldier of the Revolution, and

fought at Lexington and Bunker Hill. Mr. Newcomb has been in the grocery business for thirty-five years; res. Quincy, Mass. Children b. Quincy Neck, Quincy, Mass.:
I.   Amey Frances Newcomb,[7] b. Aug. 16, 1857; res. Quincy, Mass.
II.   Arthur Wilbur Newcomb,[7] b. Aug. 31, 1862; res. Quincy, Mass.
III.   Herbert Harris Newcomb,[7] b. May 3, 1856; res. Quincy, Mass.
245.   Mary Eliza Allison,[6] b. Dec. 26, 1839, in Boston, Mass.; m., Feb. 19, 1873, Elezar Bourk, of Weymouth, Mass. He was b. March 30, 1833, at St. Gregoire, Quebec, Canada. He does an express and livery business; res. Weymouth, Mass. Children, b. Weymouth, Mass.:
I.   Lila Mary Bourk,[7] b. July 13, 1874; d. July 25, 1875.
II.   Frank Eleazar Bourk,[7] b. Oct. 11, 1876; d. March 6, 1877.
III.   Hattie Evelyn Bourk,[7] b. Sept. 21, 1881.
246.   Harriet Kent Allison,[6] b. Wayland, Mass., Oct. 26, 1844; m., April 15, 1863, Simeon Waldo Gutterson, of Weymouth, Mass., b. Milford, N. H., Aug. 26, 1832. He is a deacon in the Baptist church and Sunday-school superintendent at Weymouth Landing, Weymouth, Mass., where he resides. Children b. in Weymouth, Mass.:
I.   John Harris Gutterson,[7] b. Oct. 14, 1864; organist in South Baptist church, Boston, Mass.
II.   Angie Mary Gutterson,[7] b. May 26, 1873.
III.   Charles Francis Gutterson,[7] b. May 14, 1876.
247.   William Allison,[6] b. Nov. 13, 1846; d. Nov. 14, 1846.
248.   Walter Balfour Allison,[6] b. Oct. 6, 1847; d. Quincy, Mass., Aug. 17, 1887.

249.   Caroline Brown Allison[5] [132] (James,[4] Samuel,[3] Capt. Samuel,[2] Samuel[1]).   She was born in Dunbarton, N. H., Aug. 27, 1813; married, Nov. 12, 1840, Jonathan Leach Allen; residence, Hopkinton, N. H. He was a son of David Allen, and grandson of Jonathan and Sarah (Dodge) Allen, of Manchester. She died in Hopkinton, Aug. 20, 1863, aged fifty years lacking seven days. Mr. Allen married, second, Mrs. D. J. Danielson. The date of his death was June 1, 1868, in Goffstown, N. H., where he had lived for four years.

CHILDREN BORN IN HOPKINTON, N. H.

250.   James Franklin Allen,[6] b. Aug. 13, 1841; res. Rockville, Ind. He graduated at Dartmouth college in 1862, at Columbian Law School, Washington, D. C., June 11, 1866; appointed to a clerkship in Treasury Department, Washington, D. C., Dec. 23, 1868; resigned Jan. 1, 1876; practised law until March, 1881, then was appointed to a clerkship in War Department, and resigned Feb. 14, 1882, to accept a clerkship in the Indian Office, Interior Department, which he held Oct., 1890. He is a member of St. Paul's Lutheran church, and prominent in Masonic circles. He m., Oct. 25, 1866, Julia Augusta Dow; res. Rockville, Montgomery Co., Md. Miss Dow was b. Dec. 21, 1837, in Thompson, Conn., and d. Nov. 10, 1886. She was a daughter of Jesse E. and Eliza (Stetson) Dow. He m., second, Aug. 28, 1888, Lilabel, daughter of Isaac and Mary (Greer) Maus. She was b. in Montgomery Co., Md., Oct. 20, 1853; no children.

251. **Henry Allison Allen,**[6] b. Hopkinton, N. H., May 8, 1849. He is a hotel manager, and now clerk in the Gault House in Chicago, where he has resided twenty years. He is a Republican, and an attendant of the Congregational church; single.

252. **William Henry Allison**[5] [134] (James,[4] Samuel,[3] Capt. Samuel,[2] Samuel[1]). He was born, Sept. 17, 1816, in Dunbarton, N. H.; married, Sept. 8, 1841, Mary Amelia, daughter of Dea. Philip and Lavinia (Currier) Brown, of Hopkinton, N. H., and granddaughter of Abram Brown. She was born in Hopkinton, N. H., April 19, 1820, and resides in 1892, in Concord, N. H. Mr. Allison was educated at the town schools in his native town and at the academy at Lyndon, Vt., and was a teacher in early life in Dunbarton and Hopkinton, N. H., Lyndon, Vt., and, in 1838, in South Carolina. In 1841 he engaged in the drug business, in which he continued until 1865, when ill health compelled him to relinquish it. He was tax collector from 1868 to 1875, when he engaged in the insurance business for three years. He was a member of the South Congregational church for more than fifty years, and was a deacon for several years; was superintendent of its Sunday-school from 1859 to 1863; residence, Concord, N. H., where he died May 15, 1887.

CHILDREN BORN IN CONCORD, N. H.

253. Mary Lavinia Allison,[6] b. Dec. 16, 1843; d. Aug. 8, 1844.
254. Philip Henry Allison,[6] b. Nov. 3, 1846; m., Oct. 7, 1880, Sarah Jennie Sloan. He is a book-keeper; res. Anniston, Ala. Children:
I. Mary Abbie Allison,[7] b. Nov. 29, 1881; d. Nov. 17, 1886.
II. Philip Arthur Allison,[7] b. Oct. 10, 1883.
255. Everett Brown Allison,[6] b. Oct. 23, 1852; d. Dec. 7, 1857.
256. James Edward Allison,[6] b. May 16, 1854; m., Dec. 1, 1876, Emma W. Curtis, daughter of George Henry and Harriet Kimball (Lougee) Curtis. Her parents were born in East Concord, N. H. House painter; res. Concord, N. H. Children:
I. Everett Curtis Allison,[7] b, July 16, 1877; d. May 13, 1884.
II. Henry Wallace Allison,[7] b. Oct. 23, 1878.
III. Edward Philip Allison,[7] b. June 30, 1881.
IV. William Bleckley Allison,[7] b. Aug. 20, 1882.

257. **John Allison**[5] [135] (James,[4] Samuel,[3] Capt. Samuel,[2] Samuel[1]). He was born in Dunbarton, N. H., June 26, 1818; married, May 10, 1845, Sarah Jane, daughter of Eliphalet and Sarah (McQueston) Richards, of Goffstown, N. H., where she was born July 13, 1820. She died in Boston, Mass., April 22, 1852. Mr. Allison resided in Boston, Mass. He was connected with the firm of Claflin, Saville & Co. His business faculties were of a high order, and he

acquired wealth. He was a Republican, and was a member
of the common council for several terms. He took a deep
interest in religious matters, and was a member of the Park
street church. He died in Boston, May 29, 1865.

CHILDREN.

258. Anna Josephine Allison,⁶ b. at Amoskeag, N. H., Oct. 27, 1848; m.
      Mr. Stirling, who is now deceased. She res. Plainfield, N. J.
259. Emma Jane Allison,⁶ b. Boston, Mass., Dec. 15, 1852; m., March 19,
      1872, Samuel W. Nettleton, b. Fulton, N. Y., March 18, 1841;
      merchant; res. Toledo, Ohio. Children b. Toledo, Ohio:
I.   Edward Allison Nettleton,⁷ b. Nov. 23, 1875.
II.   Roy Healey Nettleton,⁷ b. Feb. 10, 1877; d. June 22, 1880.
III. Florence Bowen Nettleton,⁷ b. Aug. 31, 1886.

260.   Lavinia Holt Allison⁵ [136] (James,⁴ Samuel,³ Capt.
Samuel,² Samuel¹). She was born in Dunbarton, N. H.,
Jan. 15, 1820; married, Jan. 7, 1841, John Langdon Weeks,
son of Maj. William Weeks, who was born March 26, 1819.
They resided in Hopkinton, N. H. He died Sept. 9, 1843.
She resides in Cambridge, Mass.

CHILD.

261. Sarah Lavinia Weeks,⁶ b. Aug. 14, 1843; m. William Franklin Stark,
      of Goffstown, N. H., b. Aug. 31, 1843; res. Cambridge, Mass.
      Children:
I.   Alice Holman Stark,⁷ b. March 1, 1869; d. Jan. 20, 1881.
II.   Elizabeth Allison Stark,⁷ b. Feb. 12, 1871.
III. William Everett Stark,⁷ b. Feb. 12, 1873.
IV.   Wallace Weeks Stark,⁷ b. April 27, 1877.
V.   Mary Lavinia Stark,⁷ b. April 20, 1879; d. May 14, 1884.
VI.   Margaret Allison Stark,⁷ b. Oct. 12, 1880.

262. Andrew Allison⁵ [138] (James,⁴ Samuel,³ Capt.
Samuel,² Samuel¹). He was born in Dunbarton, N. H.,
March 12, 1824; married, April 24, 1848, Melinda W.,
daughter of Hazen and Susan (Austin) Batchelder, of North-
field, N. H. She was born May 16, 1825, and died Jan. 3,
1857, in Boston, Mass. He married, second, Feb. 2, 1858,
Martha, daughter of Stephen and Joanna Tozier, of Water-
ville, Me., who is now living. She was born May 11, 1831.
Mr. Allison left Dunbarton with his parents in 1840, and
lived in Warner, N. H., three years. On March 9, 1843, he
commenced his individual lifework; went to what is now
Manchester, N. H., and for five years was a clerk in a store;
then carried on a dry goods and grocery business, which he
sold out, and then moved to Boston, Mass., in 1853, where

he has been since that date. He was of the firm of Claflin, Allison & Co., wholesale grocers; sold in 1886, and has been in the employ of Winslow, Rand & Watson, teas and coffees, 197 and 199 State St. They reside in Winchester, Mass.

CHILDREN.

263. Frank Allison,⁶ b. Lowell, Mass., May 10, 1853; d. Aug. 20, 1854.
264. Walter Irving Allison,⁶ b. Cambridge, Mass., June 20, 1860; clerk in the New York Dispatch Co., Summer St., Boston, Mass.; res. Winchester, Mass.; single; Republican.
265. Carrie Allison⁶ b. Boston, Mass., April 16, 1862; d. Aug. 20, 1864.
266. Stephen Tozier Allison,⁶ b. Boston, Mass., April 19, 1868; single; Congregationalist, and Republican; res. Winchester, Mass.
267. Fred Bird Allison,⁶ b. Cambridge, Mass., May 12, 1869; d. July 26, 1888. He was a young man of rare qualities of mind and heart.
268. Herbert Allison,⁶ b. Cambridge, Mass., Jan., 1872; d. July, 1872.

269a. Elizabeth Hall Allison⁵ [139] (James,⁴ Samuel,³ Capt. Samuel,² Samuel¹). She was born in Dunbarton, N. H., March 24, 1825. She was the first graduate of the high school in the city of Manchester, N. H., and received the first diploma. This was in December, 1848. She always was an energetic teacher, and followed her profession with marked success for a long period. She taught in Concord, N. H., for three years; in the Pinkerton academy at Derry, N. H., for three years; in the Ohio Female college, College Hill, Hamilton Co., Ohio, for thirteen years, the last three years of which she was the principal. In the Bennet Seminary for young ladies in Minneapolis, Minn., she was an instructor for three years, leaving there in 1874. On Sept. 30, 1874, she married Rev. Cyrus Washington Wallace, D. D., of Manchester, N. H., who was of the same Scotch race as herself, and whose Scotch ancestors had found a temporary home and abiding-place in Ireland before the settlement in Londonderry. He was a descendant of John Wallace, and his wife, Annis Barnett, who came in 1719 or 1720 from the county of Antrim, Ireland, and they were said to be the first couple married in Londonderry, N. H., May 18, 1721. He died in Manchester, N. H., Oct. 21, 1889. He was pastor of the First Congregational church for thirty-four years and preached his first and last sermon in that church edifice, just forty years apart, the first being in 1840, the last in 1880.

269. George Augustus Allison⁵ [145] (James,⁴ Samuel,³ Capt. Samuel,² Samuel¹). He was born in Warner, N. H., Sept. 14, 1848; married, Nov. 12, 1864, Julia L. Powers, daughter of Alanson Powers, of Berlin Heights, Erie County, O. She was born at Freedom, Portage County, O., June 17,

Geo. A Allison.

1842. Mr. Powers was a native of Woodstock, Vt. He married Sarepta Martin, a native of Rochester, Vt. Mr. Allison was educated in the public schools of Manchester, N. H., and at the academy at Pembroke, N. H. When about to enter college, he decided to engage in mercantile pursuits, and spent several years as a clerk in Concord, N. H.; in Jan., 1865, became a salesman in a wholesale establishment in Boston, Mass., and in January, 1869, became a partner. Since then he has been identified with Boston's business interests. For many years he was a member of the Boston board of trade, Boston commercial exchange, and a member of the Boston chamber of commerce since its organization; was a director of the last for five years, and its elegant building was built during that period. Cambridge, Mass., became his home in 1865, and there he has since lived. In the social, religious, and political circles of that city he has been active. He is a member of the North Avenue Baptist church, aided in establishing the Young Men's Christian association, and has been a member of the Cambridge and Colonial clubs since their formation. He was a member of the common council of his adopted city in 1881-'82, of the board of aldermen in 1885-'86, was twice elected for a term of three years each on the school board but after four years service by the pressure of other duties he resigned his position. His business office is in the Chamber of Commerce building, Boston, Mass. Residence, Cambridge, Mass.

CHILDREN.

1. Caroline Josephine Allison,⁶ b. Cambridge, Mass., Oct. 2, 1865; teacher; res. Cambridge, Mass.
2. Susan Allison,⁶ b. Cambridge, Mass., April 9, 1868; teacher in the public schools of Cambridge.
3. William Henry Allison,⁶ b. Somerville, Mass., Aug. 17, 1870. He entered Harvard University in 1889, in the class of 1893, where he expects to graduate.

270. George Allison⁵ [153] (David,⁴ Samuel,³ Capt. Samuel,² Samuel¹). He was born July 30, 1824, in Concord, N. H., where his life was mainly spent until his eighteenth year, when he went to Boscawen, N. H., to learn the trade of carriagemaker. He completed his apprenticeship in Merrimacport, Mass., then went to West Amesbury, where he lived the remainder of his life. He married, in Boscawen, N. H., Nov. 27, 1846, Esther Jane, daughter of Jeremiah and Martha (Jackman) Noyes of that town, where she was born Jan. 6, 1828, and who now lives a widow in Merrimacport,

108   HENRY ALLISON, OF AURORA, ILL.

Mass. Mr. Allison was a Republican in politics. He had light hair, sandy complexion and blue eyes. He and his wife were members of the Baptist church. He died of consumption in Merrimacport, Feb. 5, 1867, aged 42 years, 6 months, 6 days.

CHILDREN BORN IN MERRIMACPORT, MASS.

271. Clifton Orion Allison,[6] b. Jan. 31, 1848; machinist in Blood's Locomotive Works, Manchester, N. H.; has resided in Manchester twenty-seven years, going there in 1866. He m., Nov. 26, 1872, Alice A., daughter of Henry and Sally (Baker) Shultz, of Ellenborough, Clinton Co., N. Y., where she was b. Aug. 8, 1853; no children.

272. Roger Gilman Allison,[6] b. Feb. 10, 1850; m. Annie Hicks, of Granville, Nova Scotia; painter; res. Lowell, Mass.; no children.

273. Irving Russell Allison,[6] b. Oct. 19, 1853; single; painter; res. with his mother in Merrimacport, Mass.

274. Emma Frances Allison,[6] b. Jan. 17, 1855; d. June 17, 1855.

275. Willard Sumner Allison,[6] b. April 27, 1856; single; carriage trimmer; res. with his mother in Merrimacport, Mass.

276. Lawrence Edward Allison,[6] b. Sept. 7, 1857; m. Hannah Edminster, who lives a widow in Merrimacport, Mass. He d. May 22, 1886, aged 28 years, 8 months, 15 days. Child:
I.   Alice Allison.[7]

277. Mary Esther Allison,[6] b. Oct. 30, 1851; m., Sept. 30, 1879, Roswell Eaton, a silver-plater; res. Merrimacport, Mass. Children:
I.   Sarah Elizabeth Eaton;[7] d. when young.
II. Nellie Eaton,[7] b. June 5, 1881.
III. George Eaton,[7] b. March 18, 1883.
IV. Robert Irving Eaton,[7] b. May 11, 1884; d. young.
V.   Lizzie Eaton,[6] b. March 11, 1886.

278. Frederick Allison,[6] b. June 5, 1861: d. Aug. 31, 1861.

279. Clarence Thayer Allison,[6] b. Nov. 2, 1862; m. Bell, daughter of J. W. and Albert Preble; res. 19 Bromfield St., Newburyport, Mass. She was b. in Newton, N. H., Jan. 24, 1865. Child:
I.   Clara Izora Allison,[7] b. Aug. 5, 1884, in Merrimacport, Mass.

280. Sarah Ellen Allison,[6] b. Sept. 10, 1864; m. George F. Mason; res. Merrimacport, Mass. Children:
I.   Fred Davis Allison Mason,[7] lives with his grandmother.
II. Frank Allison Mason.[7]

281. Henry Allison[5] [155] (David Clinton,[4] Samuel,[3] Capt. Samuel,[2] Samuel[1]). He was born in Concord, N. H., Nov. 7, 1828, married, Nov. 20, 1851, Mary Little Gallishan, daughter of George K. W. and Elizabeth (Atkinson) Gallishan of Andover, Mass., where she was born Oct. 30, 1832. She died 1865. He married 2nd, Sept. 12, 1867, Mary Garbett, daughter of John Garbett, and born in England, May 2, 1846. Mr. Allison is a carriage maker. He lived in Concord, N. H., thirteen years, in Boston, Mass., two years, in Ohio eight years, in Chicago, Ill., eight years, and in Aurora, Ill., for several years. Residence, 114 South Lake St., Aurora, Ill. He enlisted Aug. 11, 1862, in the 114th Regt. Ohio Vols., mustered as third sergeant, promoted to

first lieutenant March, 1864, and afterward commanded the
company, till he was mustered out of the service in Aug.,
1865. He is a member of the New England Congregational
church in Aurora, Ill.

CHILDREN.

282. Mary Lizzie Allison,⁶ b. Sept. 1, 1852; m., in 1879, Frank R. Harris,
      who is a clerk, and they res. Norwood Park, Ill.
283. Edward Clarence Allison,⁶ b. April 30, 1856; d. July 8, 1856.
284. Fannie Allison,⁶ b. Jan. 29, 1858; d. July 27, 1859.

285. Janet Eliza Stinson ⁵ [171] (Archibald Stinson,⁴
Janet Allison³, Capt. Samuel,² Samuel¹). She was born in
Hammond, St. Lawrence County, N. Y., March 2, 1820;
married, Sept. 29, 1846, Loren Stone. He is a retired
farmer and they reside in the village of Theresa, Jefferson
County, N. Y.

CHILDREN BORN IN THERESA, JEFFERSON CO., N. Y.

286. James Archibald Stone,⁶ b. Sept. 16, 1847; d. Feb. 1, 1869.
287. John Wellington Stone,⁶ b. June 29, 1849; res. Silver City, New
      Mexico; broker; single.
288. Norris Stone,⁶ b. April 26, 1852; res. Theresa, N. Y., some three
      miles from the village, on his father's homestead. He m. Rox-
      ina Butler. Children:
  I.   Howard Stone,⁷ b. April 13, 1878.
  II. Blanche Stone,⁷ b. April 13, 1878.
289. Morris Stone,⁶ b. April 26, 1852; res. Forrest River, North Dakota;
      blacksmith; single.
290. Sarah Jane Stone,⁶ b. June 14, 1854; m. George Wilson Augsbury;
      merchant; res. Plessis, N. Y. Children:
  I.   Earl Stone Augsbury,⁷ b. Sept. 10, 1878.
  II. Reid Wilson Augsbury,⁷ b. July 12, 1883.
291. Nellie Louise Stone,⁶ b. Oct. 24, 1859; m. Dr. David Coe. He is a
      dentist; res. Theresa, N. Y. Children:
  I.   Annie Jenet Coe,⁷ b. Sept. 24, 1881.
  II. Pauline Belle Coe,⁷ b. Sept. 10, 1883; d. Aug. 24, 1884.
  III. Harper Allison Coe,⁷ b. Aug. 14, 1887.
292. Ada Emogene Stone,⁶ b. March 22, 1865; single; res. Theresa, N. Y.

293. Eleanor Hoag Stinson ⁵ [174] (Archibald Stinson⁴,
Janet Allison³, Capt. Samuel,² Samuel¹). She was born in
Hammond, St. Lawrence County, N. Y., June 25, 1825;
married, Dec. 21, 1853, Thomas Miller, born May 5, 1822, in
Baltimore, Md. Is an engineer. Residence, 59 Atlantic
St., Jersey City, N. J. She died April 14, 1891, at 65 years.

CHILDREN.

294. Archibald Stinson Miller,⁶ b. Oct. 30, 1854; d. Aug. 15, 1855.
295. Sylvanus Edward Miller,⁶ b. June 4, 1856; m., Aug. 27, 1879, Isa-
      bella H. Riley. He graduated at Packard's college, New York,
      N. Y.; is an electrician. Children:

I. Sylvia Edna Miller,[7] b. Jan. 8, 1881; d. Feb. 23, 1890.
II. Frank Eleanor Mabel Miller,[6] b Jan. 8, 1883.
III. Hazel Stinson Miller,[7] b. May 20, 1888.
296. Archie Woodworth Miller,[6] b. Aug. 3, 1863; m., Dec. 16, 1885, Eve-
        lyn C. Grattan.   He graduated at Hasbrouck Institute, in Jer-
        sey City, N. J.; is an electrician; res. Cordova, S. A.
297. Willie Grant Miller,[7] b. Jan. 11, 1865; d. Dec. 18, 1875.

298.   Sally Allison[5] [193] (Ebenezer,[4] Andrew,[3] Capt.
Samuel,[2] Samuel[1]).   She was born in Limerick, N. Y., July
1, 1817; married Loyal Sanford.   He was a farmer.   Residence Limerick, N. Y., and died there March 13, 1890.   She
died there Dec. 17, 1887.

CHILDREN.

299. Lucinda Sanford,[6] b. July 31, 1835.
300. Louisa Sanford,[6] b. Aug. 17, 1836.
301. Arvilla Sanford,[6] b. May 24, 1838.
302. Phebe Sanford,[6] b. Oct. 17, 1839.
303. Henry Sanford,[6] b. 1840.
304. Ebenezer Sanford,[6] b. Jan. 15, 1842.
305. Sarah Sanford,[6] b. July 25, 1844.
306. Mary Sanford,[6] b. 1846.
307. Andrew Sanford,[6] b. Jan. 2, 1848: m., Nov. 4, 1872, Libbie Mabey,
        of Ontario, Canada, b. there Aug. 12, 1857; d. Watertown,
        N. Y., Aug. 16, 1883. Children:
I. Irvin Sanford,[7] b. Syracuse, N. Y., Dec. 18, 1873; d. there Feb. 15,
        1874.
II. Maud Sanford,[7] b. Brownville, N. Y., Nov. 20, 1874; d. there Oct. 10,
        1875.
III. Jennie Sanford,[7] b. Brownville, N. Y., Aug. 12, 1876.
IV. Grace Sanford,[7] b. April 1, 1879.
V. Ida Sanford,[7] b. June 1, 1882.
        He m., second, Sept. 3, 1884, Maggie Clemens. She was b.
        March 7, 1858; no children. He is a farmer.
308. Carey Sanford,[6] b. June 17, 1850.
309. George Sanford,[6] b. March 20, 1852.
310. Adellaralette Sanford,[6] b. Oct. 7, 1853.
311. Simeon Sanford,[6] b. Dec. 6, 1854.
312. Helen Sanford,[6] b. July 17, 1856.
313. Lydia Sanford,[6] b. Feb. 16, 1858.
314. Robertus Sanford,[6] b. June 7, 1859.
315. Loyal Sanford,[6] b. July 17, 1860.

316.   Polly Allison[5] [195] (Ebenezer,[4] Andrew,[3] Capt.
Samuel,[2] Samuel[1]).   She was born in Brownsville, N. Y.,
June 11, 1820; married, Dec. 2, 1840, Henry Gibbs.   They
lived in New York, Wisconsin, and Trinity County, Cal., for
fifteen years; they located on a farm in Petaluma, Sonoma
County, Cal., where she died of dropsy, Sept. 3, 1890.   He
died there, at the age of 75 years, Oct. 30, 1890.

CHILDREN.

317. Amelia Ann Gibbs,[6] b. Jefferson Co., N. Y., April 5, 1842; m., Feb.
        12, 1860, Joseph Wooden, who d. in Portland, Oregon, Dec. 25,
        1888. She res. Portland, Oregon.

318. Orcelia Jane Gibbs,[6] b. Jefferson, Wis., Nov. 19, 1845; m., Sept. 22, 1867, Joseph C. Purvine; res. Petaluma, Sonoma Co., Cal.
319. Edward Gibbs,[6] b. Jefferson, Wis., March 13, 1847; m., April 11, 1883, Writta A. Sevedge. Is a teacher; res. Petulama, Cal.
320. Mary Catherine Gibbs,[6] b. Jefferson, Wis., Sept. 17, 1849; m., Dec. 28, 1878. George P. Manley; teacher; res. Petaluma, Cal.
321. Elbert Clark Gibbs,[6] b. Somona Co., Cal., April 9, 1860; m., Oct. 22, 1884, Ella D. Light. Farmer; res. Petulama, Cal.
322. Frederick Henry Gibbs,[6] b. Somona Co., Cal., May 18, 1861; m., Aug. 17, 1887, Silva N. Doss. Farmer; res. Petulama, Cal.
323. Carrie Elizabeth Gibbs,[6] b. Somona Co., Cal., July 16, 1863; m., Jan. 18, 1889, John B. Meloche. He is a book-keeper; res. Maderia, Fresno Co., Cal.

324. Esther Allison[5] [196] (Ebenezer,[4] Andrew,[3] Capt. Samuel,[2] Samuel[1]). She was born in Limerick, N. Y., March 8, 1822; married, 1841, Zeva M. Way. He was a paper manufacturer, who died March 25, 1860, at Watertown, N. Y. Three children. She married, second, Jan. 7, 1864, at Pulaski, Capt. Lewis W. Litts. He was a boat owner and captain on the lakes, and died at Milwaukee, Wis.

CHILDREN.

325. Emma Gertrude Way,[6] b. at Watertown, N. Y., Aug. 4, 1842; m. at Milwaukee, Wis., Sept. 13, 1880, Orson A. Thayer, a railway conductor; he died in Milwaukee, March 22, 1878. She m., second, at Columbus, Wis., Adolphus W. Ingalabe, Nov. 24, 1880, farmer.   Child by first marriage:
I. Gertrude Esther Thayer,[7] b. at Milwaukee, Wis., Oct. 21, 1871.
326. Kittie Esther Way,[6] b. Pulaski, Dec. 8, 1847; m. at Watertown, N. Y., June 27, 1871, John H. Roberts, merchant.   Child:
I. Lou-Lou Way Roberts,[7] b. Grand Rapids, Mich., June 28, 1872; d. Aug. 20, 1872.
327. George Z. Way,[6] b. Pulaski, July 5, 1854; d. there Sept. 2, 1855.

328. Julia Allison[5] [197] (Ebenezer,[4] Andrew,[3] Capt. Samuel,[2] Samuel[1]). She was born at Limerick, N. Y., April 19, 1824; m. Edward Williston, at Limerick, N. Y. He was a farmer. She died at Chicago, Ill., many years ago, and her daughter was brought up by her grandparents, the Allisons.

CHILD.

329. Isabel Williston,[6] b. Jan. 25, 1848; m. at Watertown, N. Y., Sept. 25, 1871, Linus Monson, farmer.   Children:
I. Julia Monson,[7] b. Oct. 10, 1872.
II. Jessie Monson,[7] b. March 8, 1874.
III. Eddie Monson,[7] b. Nov. 9, 1875.
IV. Bruce Monson,[7] b. June 14, 1878.
V. Lillian Monson,[7] b. Jan. 14, 1880.
VI. Jan Monson,[7] b. Nov. 2, 1882.
VII. George Monson,[7] b. March 14, 1890.

330. Lavinia Jemima Allison[5] [198] (Ebenezer,[4] Andrew,[3]

Capt. Samuel,[2] Samuel[1]). She was born in Limerick, N. Y.,
June 25, 1826; married, Feb. 21, 1850, Jacob Ellis Harmon,
son of James Harmon. He was born at Pulaski, N. Y., Jan.
6, 1826, where he resided about twenty-five years, and in
Watertown, N. Y., the rest of his life, and where he died
Aug. 20, 1881; machinist. Mrs. Harmon died at Utica, N.
Y., Dec. 16, 1888. They resided at Watertown, N. Y.

CHILDREN.

331. De Witt Clinton Harmon,[6] b. Pulaski, N. Y., Jan. 21, 1852; m.
      April 29, 1880, Margaret E. Richardson; was proprietor of ma-
      chine shop. Res. Watertown, N. Y., where he d. Dec. 10,
      1888. No children.
332. Herbert Edgar Harmon,[6] b. Adams, N. Y., Feb. 10, 1854; m., Oct.
      24, 1883, Helen J. Haven, clerk, res. Watertown, N. Y. No
      children.
333. Charles A. Harmon,[6] b. Watertown, N. Y., July 27, 1856; m. Nov.
      23, 1881, Clara E. Kenyon; locomotive engineer; res. Benson
      Mills, N. Y. Children:
I.   Ella J. Harmon,[7] b. Watertown, N. Y., Nov. 12, 1882.
II. Don K. Harmon,[7] b. Watertown, N. Y. Dec. 25, 1884.
334. George Allison Harmon,[6] b. Watertown, N. Y., March 1, 1866; in
      railroad employ ; res. Milwaukee, Wis.

335. Harlow Allison[5] [199] (Ebenezer,[4] Andrew,[3] Capt.
Samuel,[2] Samuel[1]). He was born in Limerick, N. Y., Oct.
21, 1828; residence, Limerick. He married Sarah Ann
Allen. He died at Limerick, Jan. 7, 1889.

CHILDREN BORN AT LIMERICK, N. Y.

336. Wayne Allison,[6] b. April 20, 1858; m., at Dexter, N. Y., Dec. 26,
      1883, Lillian E. Randall, who was b. Oct. 12, 1865. She d. Jan.
      15, 1889. He m. second, Anna Eva Darr, b. Germany, March 15,
      1870. They were m. at Brownsville, N. Y., Jan. 28, 1889.
      Children:
I.   Everet Allison,[7] b. Oct. 25, 1885.
II. Clara Elizabeth Allison,[7] b. June 30, 1887.
337. Elizabeth Allison,[6] b. Sept. 22, 1863; m., April 11, 1888, Luna Zim-
      merman, b. April 14, 1865. No children.

338. William Henry Allison[5] [203] (Ebenezer,[4] Andrew,[3]
Capt. Samuel,[2] Samuel[1]). He was born in Limerick, N. Y.,
July 10, 1844; married Mary Jackson June 30, 1864;
farmer; residence, Limerick, N. Y.

CHILDREN BORN AT LIMERICK, N. Y.

339. Frank Allison,[6] b. Aug. 16, 1866.
340. Etta L. Allison,[6] b. March 26, 1868; m., June 25, 1885, Wallace J.
      Patrick, farmer; child, b. Limerick, N. Y.:
I.   Ruth Esther Patrick,[7] b. Dec. 25, 1888.
341. William Allison,[6] b. Dec. 30, 1872.
342. Adelbert Allison,[6] b. May 22, 1875.

343. John Wilson Allison[5] [206] (Eli,[4] Andrew,[3] Capt. Samuel,[2] Samuel[1]). He was born in Dublin, N. H., March 15, 1823. On attaining his majority he left his native town, and in 1849 he joined the great flood of emigration to the gold fields of California. A few months' stay amid the hardships to which all were subjected, and the bad influence of the climate, brought on a severe sickness, compelling the abandonment of his plans and his return to New England. From that illness his system has never fully recovered. For three years he was connected with the postoffice in Boston, Mass. Since then he has been in active business life for others or for himself, and in 1893 was in the ships' stores and ships' chandlery business, of the firm of Allison & Mason, No. 1 and 2 Russia wharf, 270 Congress St., Boston, Mass. Is a Republican in politics.

CHILDREN BORN AT BOSTON, MASS.

344. Fred Lincoln Allison,[6] b. Dec. 31, 1854; d., of typhoid fever, Sept. 3, 1890. He res. Magnolia St., Roxbury Dist., Boston, Mass. He m. Emma Basset of Roxbury, who is still living. He was travelling salesman. Child b. Boston, Mass.:
I.　Chester Thorp Allison,[7] b. March 12, 1886.
345. Edwin Charles Allison,[6] b., 1856; d. at 6 mos.
346. Lillie Frances Allison,[6] b. June, 1858. Single. Lives at home.
347. Sadie Persis Allison,[6] b. Nov., 1861. Single. Res. at home, Boston, Mass.
348. Nellie Hope Allison,[6] b. May, 1865. Res. at home, Boston, Mass.
349. John Wilson Allison, Jr.,[6] b. Sept. 1, 1868. Res. Boston, Mass.
350. Charles Morrison Allison,[6] b. Sept., 1868; d. at 8 yrs. of age.

351. James Allison[5] [209] (Eli,[4] Andrew,[3] Capt. Samuel.[2] Samuel[1]). He was born in Dublin, N. H., March 18, 1830, where he has always lived. He married, March 9, 1854, Sarah Jane, daughter of William and Julia (Johnson) Darracott, who was born in Dublin, May 27, 1837; died there May 1, 1878. Her father was born in Shrewsbury, Vt., Feb. 17, 1804; died in Dublin, Aug. 28, 1884. Mr. Allison married, second, Dec. 3, 1878, Bessie Maria Darracott, a sister of his first wife. She was born in Dublin, April 29, 1839; and died in Dublin July 10, 1880. Mr. Allison was educated in the common schools and in early manhood taught school for several winters, and then settled on the homestead to care for his parents in their declining years. For nineteen years he has served as agent to invest and care for the trust funds of the town of Dublin, being elected in 1872. For twenty-eight years he has served as a trustee of the Appleton school fund, and has been a member of the school board for five years. A large amount of probate business is entrusted to him,

8

and many estates are settled, and he acts repeatedly as guardian for minors. Since 1874 he has held a commission as justice of the peace, was a selectman in 1870, '71, '72, '73, '75, '78, '80, '81, '82, '85, '86, and represented his town in the legislature in 1873, '74. In politics, he is a Republican; in religion, of the Unitarian faith, having been a deacon of the Unitarian church in Dublin more than twenty years, and agent for the care and investment of the trust funds of the First Congregational (Unitarian) society, of which he is a member. Residence, Dublin, N. H.

CHILDREN BORN AT DUBLIN, N. H.

352. William Andrew Allison,[6] b. May 4, 1855; d. Dublin, N. H., Oct. 5, 1862.
353. Annie Maria Allison,[6] b. March 7, 1859; teacher. Res. Dublin, N. H.
354. Flora Gertrude Allison,[6] b. April 2, 1860; teacher. She graduated, June, 1882, at State Normal school, Plymouth, N. H. Res. Revere, Mass.
355. John Learned Allison,[6] b. Aug. 2, 1861; m., Nov. 1, 1886, Myrtie Aurilla Pratt, dau. of Ira and——(Putney) Pratt. She was b. Feb. 3, 1867, in Marlborough, N. H. He is a carpenter in Colorado Springs, Colorado. Child:
I. Gertrude Mabel Allison,[7] b. Sept. 5, 1891.
356. Emma Jane Allison,[6] b. Jan. 24, 1864; teacher; res. Dublin, N. H. Educated at the State Normal school, Plymouth, N. H.
357. James Francis Allison,[6] b. March 29, 1865. He is a teacher; graduated at Cushing Academy, Ashburnham, Mass., June, 1886, and at Dartmouth college in 1891, and in 1892 is principal of Sherborn academy at Sherborn, Mass.
358. Henry Darracott Allison,[6] b. Feb. 2, 1869. He is a bookkeeper and postoffice clerk. Educated at Bryant & Stratton's business college, Boston, Mass. Res. Dublin, N. H. He m., Feb. 3, 1891, Florence Gowing Mason, dau. of Milton D. Mason; she was b. Dec. 16, 1871.
359. Edwin Sherman Allison,[6] b. Aug. 19, 1871; carpenter; res. Colorado Springs, Colorado.
360. Mabel Persis Allison,[6] b. March 26, 1874; at home.

361.   Royal Bellows Quinton[5] [213] {(Samuel,[4] Margaret Allison,[3] Capt. Samuel,[2] Samuel[1]). Residence, Denmark, Iowa; married,—— ——

CHILD.

362. Alfred Bixby Quinton[6] (398), b. Jan. 26, 1865; res. Topeka, Kan.

363.   James Stockman Allison[5] [213] (John,[4] James,[3] Capt. Samuel,[2] Samuel[1]). He was born in Weathersfield, Vt., April 10, 1827; married, Jan. 1, 1860, Sophronia Cole Butler, of Watertown, Mass., who died June 11, 1890, aged 62 years, 9 months, 15 days. She was born in Leominster, Mass., Aug. 27, 1827. Early in life he removed to Newton,

Mass., where the larger part of his time was spent. At one time he was in business in Faneuil Hall market, under the firm name of Porter & Allison. He was one of the leading business men of Newton, and was located in the provision business, on the spot now occupied by the Union Market National Bank, under the firm name of Allison & Bond. He was one of the directors of the Union Market National Bank for three years. He was a devoted member of the Congregational church, and by his courteous manners and upright Christian life won the confidence and love of many. He died at his home on California street, Newton, Mass., May 1, 1881, aged 54 years.

CHILDREN.

364. Edward Porter Allison,⁶ b. Dec. 17, 1860; d. Sept. 14, 1872, aged 11 years, 8 months, 28 days.
365. Albert Butler Allison,⁶ b. March 6, 1864; m., June 3, 1890, Mira Alma Graves, of Ludlow, Vt., b. Ascutneyville, Vt., Dec. 15, 1867. He was educated in the grammar and high schools of Newton, Mass., and received his musical education under teachers of note in Boston, Mass., and now devotes all his time to instruction in music. He is organist at the First Universalist church in Roxbury, Mass., and is a member of the Congregational church in Newtonville; res. 201 California ave., Newton, Mass.
366. Mary Allison,⁶ b. Jan. 9, 1865; d. Jan. 9, 1865.
367. James Stockman Allison, Jr.,⁶ b. Feb. 19, 1870; d. Aug. 19, 1872, aged 2 years, 6 months.

368. Clinton James Allison⁵ [227] (Samuel,⁴ James,³ Capt. Samuel,² Samuel¹). He was born in Weathersfield, Vt., April 24, 1824. When thirteen years of age, he went with his parents to Conneaut, Ohio, where he lived eight years; was in Indiana fourteen years; resides at Olney, Ill., and has resided there for thirty-one years. Manufacturer and farmer. He married, May 22, 1850, Hannah, daughter of Samuel and Chloe (Prather) Campbell. Her father was a native of Pennsylvania, born in 1775, removed with his father to Kentucky in 1784, and settled near Lexington, and removed to Jenning Co., Indiana, in 1816, and died there in 1856. She was born in Queensville, Ind., Nov. 29, 1830, and died in Jonesville, Ind., Dec. 25, 1855. He married, second, Nov. 25, 1858, Mrs. Sarah D. Webster, widow of Edward Webster, and daughter of Barnes Hubbard, of Massachusetts, who died in Conneaut, Ohio. She was born in Conneaut, June 29, 1824, and died in Olney, Ill., May 14, 1883. He married, third, May 1, 1887, Mary E. Whorf, who was born at Brownsville, Penn., April 14, 1847. She was the daughter

of James W. Whorf, who came from Yorkshire, Eng., when a child, settled at or near Brownsville, Penn., and married Mary Willis; resides at Olney, Ill. Mr. Allison is a Republican in politics, and a Baptist.

CHILDREN.

369. Walter Campbell Allison,⁶ b. Queensville, Bartholomew Co., Ind., April 15, 1852; d. Jonesville, Ind., March 20, 1856.
370. Eugene Hulett Allison,⁶ b. Jonesville, Ind., March 11, 1854. He is in the real estate and insurance business; res. New Decatur, Ala. He went to Olney, Ill., with his father, in 1858; removed to New Decatur in 1887. He m. Mrs. Mary Par.
371. Adelia Hannah Allison,⁶ b. Jonesville, Ind., Nov. 26, 1855; res. Olney, Ill.; m., Sept. 8, 1875, James E. Whorf, and has had five children, two deceased.
372. Clinton Lincoln Allison,⁶ b. Olney, Ill., May 11, 1860; res. Trout Lake, Wash.; is a printer, and editor of a newspaper.
373. Edward Roland Allison,⁶ b. Olney, Ill., June 11, 1864; res. Trout Lake, Wash.

374. Henry Allison⁵ [228] (Samuel,⁴ James,³ Capt. Samuel,² Samuel¹). He was born in Weathersfield, Vt., Feb. 9, 1826; married, Nov. 2, 1851, Sarah McConnell, who was born January 22, 1832, in Hardenburg, Ind. Mr. Allison resided in Weathersfield eleven years, in Conneaut, Ohio, eight years, and in Hardenburg, Ind., forty-five years; res. Hardenburg, Jennings Co., Ind.

CHILDREN BORN IN HARDENBURG, JENNINGS CO., IND.

375. Mary Allison,⁶ b. Aug. 28, 1853; m., Nov. 26, 1870, Harvey Graves, farmer; res. Hardenburg, Ind. Children:
I.   Rose Graves,⁷ b. Hardenburg, Jennings Co., Ind., April 10, 1872.
II. Carl Graves,⁷ b. Morocco, Newton Co., Ind., June 14, 1873.
III. Ward Graves,⁷ b. Morocco, Newton Co., Ind., Dec. 16, 1874.
IV. Boyd Graves,⁷ b. Hardenburg, Jennings Co., Ind., June 24, 1876.
376. Ora May Allison,⁶ b. Nov. 11, 1858; d. Sept. 27, 1861.
377. Della Allison,⁶ b. Sept. 5, 1862; m., April 23, 1889, Joel Wilson, farmer; res. Hardenburg, Ind. Child:
I.   Edith Wilson,⁷ b. Elizabethtown, Bartholomew Co., Ind., Dec. 2, 1890.
378. Edith Allison,⁶ b. Oct. 6, 1866; m., April 14, 1887, Hugh Berkshire, telegraph operator; res. Rising Sun, Ind.
379. Hoyt Allison,⁶ b. Feb. 28, 1870; farmer; res. Hardenburg, Ind.

380. Ann Moore Allison⁵ [229] (Samuel,⁴ James,³ Capt. Samuel,² Samuel¹). She was born in Weathersfield, Vt., Nov. 14, 1827, where she lived ten years, then in Conneaut, Ohio, nine years, in Perry, Ohio, five years, and for thirty-nine years has been a resident of Painesville, Ohio, which is still her home. She is a member of the M. E. church. She married, Dec. 4, 1851, Carlos, son of John and Dameras

Bolles) Mason, of Perry, Lake Co., Ohio, and grandson of Elijah Mason. He was born in Perry, Nov. 26, 1822, where he lived twenty-nine years, and since then in Painesville, Ohio. He is a farmer, and a Republican in politics. He resides some three miles from the village, in Painesville.

CHILDREN BORN IN PAINESVILLE, OHIO.

381.   Katie Mary Mason,⁶ b. Nov. 9, 1854; m., Jan. 17, 1884, Henry Neff;
          res. Painesville, Ohio.
382.   Jessie Allison Mason,⁶ b. Dec. 27, 1869; res. Painesville, Ohio.

383.   Rodney Esbel Allison⁵ [230] (Samuel,⁴ James,³ Capt. Samuel,² Samuel¹). He was born in Weathersfield, Vt., July 16, 1829; married, Dec. 1, 1853, Malvina Tyler, daughter of Ralph and Maria (Gordon) Tyler. Her father was born in Marcellus, N. Y., Sept. 23, 1810, and died Nov. 17, 1871. She was born in Mayfield, Ohio, June 16, 1833, and was residing in Perry, Lake Co., when married. Mr. Allison lived in Weathersfield eight years, in Conneaut, Ohio, ten years, and in Perry, Ohio, forty-three years. P. O., Painesville, Ohio. In early life he was a teacher; is now a farmer and a justice of the peace; does public business to some extent, and settles many estates; residence, Perry, Lake Co., Ohio.

CHILDREN BORN IN PERRY, LAKE CO., OHIO.

384.   Genevieve Maria Allison,⁶ b. Dec. 28, 1864; m., July 18, 1889, Harry
          Graves, b. March 24, 1866; merchant; res. Geneva, Ashtabula
          Co., Ohio.
385.   John Tyler Allison,⁶ b. May 8, 1870; d. May 17, 1872.
386.   Gertrude Mary Allison,⁶ b. Jan. 23, 1872.

387.   Orman Dutton Allison⁵ [231] (Samuel,⁴ James,³ Capt. Samuel,² Samuel¹). He was born, Feb. 3, 1831, in Weathersfield, Windsor Co., Vt.; married, April 15, 1857, Mary Elnora Hause, daughter of Harris E. and Lucinda (Maynard) Hause. Her father was born in New York, Jan. 15, 1816; died, Feb. 12, 1879, at Six Mile, Jenning Co., Ind. Mrs. Allison was born at the latter place, April 8, 1840. Mr. Allison lived in Perry, O., for seven years; twelve in Spencer, Jennings Co., Ind.; two in Noble, Richland Co., Ill.; eight in Frankfort, Kan.; four in Montrose, Henry Co., Missouri; one year in Live Oak, Sutter Co., Cal. Farmer. Residence, Eight Mile, Morrow Co., Oregon, which has been his home for eight years.

CHILDREN.

388. Carrie Bell Allison,[6] b. Perry, Lake Co., Ohio, June 4, 1858 ; m.,
      Oct. 6, 1874, Franklin P. Vaughan, farmer. Members of Chris-
      tian church. Res., Frankfort, Kansas, and res., 1890, Eight
      Mile, Morrow Co., Oregon. Children:
  I. Mertie M. Vaughan,[7] b. Sept. 15, 1875 ; d. May 4, 1880.
 II. Nellie G. Vaughan,[7] b. Sept. 9, 1877.
III. John Vaughan,[7] b. June 18, 1883.
 IV. Charles Vaughan,[7] b. Feb. 24, 1887.
389. William Orman Allison,[6] b. Madison, Lake Co., Ohio, Jan. 7, 1860 ;
      m., Dec. 1, 1880, Aurilla Snow. Farmer ; res. Montrose, Mo.
      They res., 1890, Eight Mile, Morrow Co., Oregon. Children:
  I. Walter Allison,[7] b. Nov. 10, 1881.
 II. Pearl Allison,[7] b. Nov. 12, 1883.
390. Emma Ann Allison,[6] b. Six Mile, Ind., Sept. 27, 1862 ; m., Jan. 10,
      1882, Alfred Doolittle. He is a carpenter. Children:
  I. Elmer Allison Doolittle,[7] b. April 22, 1883.
 II. Ermie Doolittle,[7] b. Oct. 9, 1885.
III. Lester Doolittle,[7] b. Jan. 10, 1887. Mr. Doolittle res. North Bend,
      King Co., Washington.
391. Gertrude Allison,[6] b. Six Mile, Ind., March 28, 1864 ; d. there May
      4, 1864.
392. Oscar Hause Allison,[6] b. Noble, Richland Co., Ill., Oct. 13, 1867 ;
      farmer ; res. Eight Mile, Morrow Co., Oregon.
393. Cora Lucinda Allison,[6] b. Frankfort, Kansas, June 25, 1873 ; res.
      Eight Mile, Morrow Co., Oregon.

394. **Walter Scott Allison**[5] [232] (Samuel,[4] James,[3] Capt.
Samuel,[2] Samuel[1]). He was born in Weathersfield, Vt.,
July 9, 1832 ; married, Oct. 9, 1857, Rebecca McConnell,
born at Hardenburg, Ind. He went to Ohio when eight years
of age, where he lived fifteen years, and in Vernon, Jennings
Co., Ind., nine years. Machinist. He was a soldier in the
Union army in Sixth Regiment Indiana volunteers, and died
at Nashville, Tenn., July 27, 1864.

CHILDREN BORN IN NORTH VERNON, JENNINGS CO., IND.

395. Frank Ellsworth Allison,[6] b. June 9, 1861 ; farmer ; res. Pittsburgh,
      Kan. ; m. Clara Ann Hoffman, b. Jersey Co., Ill., Nov. 8,
      1861. They were married at Gerard, Kansas, Aug. 16, 1882.
      Children:
  I. Bessie Blanche Allison,[7] b. Pittsburgh, Kan., Jan. 16, 1884.
 II. Ellsworth George Allison,[7] b. Leon, Butler Co., Kan., Aug. 21, 1885.
III. Walter M. Allison,[7] b. Leon, Kan., Oct. 10, 1886.
396. Flora Dell Allison,[6] b. June 2, 1863 ; m., Oct. 10, 1882, at Harden-
      burg, Ind., Morton Oathout, b. Hardenburg, Ind., Oct. 2,
      1861. Res. Ewing, Jackson Co., Ind. Children:
  I. Walter Oathout,[7] b. Queensville, Jennings Co., Ind., June 12, 1883.
 II. Ralph Logan Oathout,[7] b. Queensville, Ind., March 21, 1888.
III. Hazel May Oathout,[7] b. Ewing, Jackson Co., Ind., Oct. 5, 1890.

397. **Roland Hill Allison**[5] [234] (Samuel,[4] James,[3] Capt.
Samuel,[2] Samuel[1]). He was born in Weathersfield, Vt.,
July 5, 1836 ; married, Oct. 5, 1862, Theodocia W., daughter

of Rev. Martin E. and Clarissa (Tousley) Cook, and grand-daughter of Josiah Cook of Windham, Vt. Her family lived in Massachusetts, Bellville, N. Y., Dayton, O., and her father died in Streetsboro', O., Oct. 4, 1841. She was born at Dayton, O., Dec. 27, 1887. Mr. Allison left Ohio in 1854, and lived in Jennings Co., Ind., with his brother, Clinton J., until 1856; removed to St. Louis, Mo., living there until '59; then was in trade in Ottawa, Ill., until Aug., 1861, when he enlisted in Company B., Fifty-third regiment, Illinois volunteers; was promoted to first lieutenant, then to captain, and two years later was commissioned major of the same regiment, and resigned in 1865. He participated in the siege of Corinth, Miss., of Vicksburg and of Atlanta, and was in Sherman's March to the Sea, ending at Savannah, Ga., in Dec., 1864. He is a Republican in politics, is engaged in the sale of machinery and agricultural implements, and he and his family are Baptists in their religious faith; res. Clinton, Henry Co., Mo. No children.

398. Alfred Bixby Quinton [6] [362] (Royal Bellows Quinton,[5] Samuel Quinton,[4] Margaret Allison,[3] Capt. Samuel,[2] Samuel [1]). He was born in Denmark, Iowa, Jan. 26, 1865; married, Jan. 25, 1882, Georgie Helen, daughter of George A. and Helen M. (Crane) Hoffman, of Topeka. Her father was born in Lyons, N. Y., in 1830, a son of Charles Ogden Hoffman, who died in New York city, in 1885, and grandson of Ogden Hoffman. She was born in Rochester, N. Y., Sept. 9, 1867. Mr. Quinton graduated at Michigan University, at Ann Arbor, in 1876. He then located in Topeka, Kan., and has been in the active practice of his profession as an attorney. He has been county judge for four years; resides at Topeka, Kan.

CHILDREN BORN IN TOPEKA, KAN.

399. Helen Hoffman Quinton,[7] b. April 5, 1882.
400. Georgie Fay Quinton,[7] b. Oct. 24, 1885.
401. Eugenie Quinton,[7] b. Jan. 15, 1888.
402. Alfred Bixby Quinton, Jr.,[7] b. Aug. 17, 1890.

ALLISONS, OR ELLISONS, OF NEW HAMPSHIRE.

403. Mrs. Mary Allison (or probably Ellison), of Nottingham, N. H., died Jan. 17, 1859, in the 109th year of her age. She was born in Lee, N. H., May 20, 1750. She, at her death, had eight daughters living. The youngest was sixty years of age, three of them were over eighty years of age.

and the eldest was in her eighty-sixth year. (N. E. Hist. Reg., 1859, vol. 13.)

404. Richard Allison (or Ellison), of New Hampshire, was arrested on suspicion of conspiring against the state during the War of the Revolution. On June 9, 1777, a committee of the General Assembly was chosen to investigate, and they reported in favor of sending him to jail for safe keeping. (N. H. Town Papers, vol. 8, p. 580.)

405. Joseph Allison enlisted April 26, 1781, for three years, or for the war, in the army of the Revolution.

405a. Ebenezer Allison, (or Ellison), of Deerfield, N. H., refused to sign the Association List, in 1776.

CHAPTER VI.

ALLISONS OF PENNSYLVANIA.

The name Allison occurs quite frequently among the Scotch-Irish who settled in the south-western part of Chester county, Pennsylvania, from 1718 to 1740, at about the same dates as the emigrations from the same localities in the north of Ireland occurred to New Hampshire, Massachusetts, and to Maine. (See Futhey & Cope's Hist. of Chester Co., Penn.) The surnames, with the same Christian names of the early Scotch-blooded settlers in New Hampshire, were often duplicated at the same dates in the Scotch settlements in Pennsylvania, and among them are Allison, Park, Morrison, Cochran, Boyd, Dickey, McAllister, Stewart, Wilson, Mitchell, Steele, Campbell, and others. Nor is this strange when we remember "that as early as 1718 no less than five vessels of immigrants from the north of Ireland arrived on the coast of New England, but, forbidden to land at Boston by the intolerant Puritans, the immigrants moved up the Kennebec and there settled. The winter of 1718-'19 being one of unusual severity, the great majority of these settlers left the Kennebec and came overland into Pennsylvania, settling in Northampton county."—Letter of Wm. H. Egle, M. D., of Harrisburg, Penn., dated April 13, 1878. He is the author of the "Illustrated History of the Commonwealth of Pennsylvania," published in 1876.

ALLISONS OF ALLEN TOWNSHIP, PENN.

406. James Allison, Sr., in 1780, lived in the Scotch-Irish settlement of *Allen township*, Northampton county, Penn., and was there taxed. He lived on the property owned a few years ago by Daniel Saegar. This settlement included Weaversville and the adjacent localities. In relation to this settlement, Rev. J. C. Clyde, D. D., in his "History of the Allen Township Presbyterian Church, Northampton County, Penn.," says, that "as early as 1717 [it was 1718] no less

than five vessels of immigrants from the north of Ireland arrived on the coast of New England, but forbidden to land at Boston by the intolerant Puritans, the emigrants moved up the Kennebec and there settled. The winter of 1717-'18, being one of unusual severity, the great majority of these settlers left the Kennebec, and came overland into Pennsylvania, settling in Northampton county." (See p. 44, note to Samuel Allison, No. 1, of Londonderry, N. H.) It was at this very time that one portion of those emigrants went from the Kennebec, and founded the Scotch settlement of Londonderry, N. H.

In the Scotch settlement of Allen township were the following Allisons, all presumably the children of James Allison, Sr. Mr. Allison was a farmer.

CHILDREN.

407.   James Allison, Jr. He was a farmer; res. in Allen township, and was taxed in 1780.
408.   John Allison. He was a farmer; a resident of Allen township, and was taxed in 1780.
409.   Sarah Allison, m. Joseph Horner.
410.   Mary Allison, m. Joseph Hays.
411.   Jeannie Allison, m. William Scott.
412.   Margaret Allison.
413.   Ann Allison, m. James Wilson.

REV. FRANCIS ALISON AND HIS DESCENDANTS.

414.   Rev. Francis Alison, D. D., was perhaps the most influential person of this family name in Chester county at that early period. He was born in 1705, in the parish of Leck,[1] county of Donegal, Ireland; educated at the University at Glasgow, Scotland; emigrated to America in 1735; licensed as a Presbyterian minister in 1736 or 1737; installed over the church in New London, Chester county, May 25, 1736, and remained fifteen years; went to Philadelphia in 1752, took charge of the academy there, and became vice-provost of the college of Pennsylvania, afterwards University of Pennsylvania, on its establishment in 1755. He was professor of moral philosophy and assistant pastor of the First Presbyterian church in Philadelphia, Penn. In 1756 the degree of A. M. was given him by Yale college, and in 1758 the degree of D. D. was conferred upon him by the University of Glasgow, Scotland. It is asserted that he was the

[1] Leck is a parish on the direct road between Letter Kenney and Raphel, and some three miles from Letter Kenney. There is a church there, and Rev. A. W. Smyth was the incumbent in 1892.

first clergyman in this country to receive the degree of D. D. He married Hannah, daughter of James Armitage, of Newcastle, Delaware, and died Nov. 28, 1779, in his 74th year. The father of Mrs. Alison was a son of Benjamin and Mary Armitage, who came from Holmfirth Parish, Yorkshire, Eng., and resided near Bristol, Penn.

CHILDREN.

415. Francis Alison,[2] d. in infancy.
416. Ezekiel Alison,[2] d. in infancy.
417. Benjamin Alison,[2] d. unmarried about 1782.
418. Frances Alison, Jr.[2] (421), b. in 1751; res. Chatham, Chester Co., Penn., May 11, 1813. He m. Mary Mackey.
419. Mary Alison,[2] d. unmarried.
(See foot note.[1])

421. Francis Alison, Jr.,[2] [418] (Francis[1]). He was born in Chester county, Penn., in 1751; married Mary Mackey, who was born in Chester county, Penn., in 1757. She died in Chatham, Penn., in 1827.[2] Mr. Alison was graduated in arts from the University of Pennsylvania (then the college of Philadelphia) in 1770; studied medicine, and was a surgeon during the Revolution. He was a physician of eminence, and died in Chatham, Chester county, Penn., where he resided May 11, 1813.

CHILDREN BORN IN CHESTER COUNTY, PENN., PROBABLY IN CHATHAM.

422. Francis Alison,[3] d. 1794, aged 14 years.
423. Rachel Alison,[3] d. April 13, 1843, aged 62 years; single.
424. Sarah Alison[3] (432), m. Alexander Adams; res. Chester Co., Penn.; d. June, 1843, aged 60 years.
425. Horatio Tates Alison,[3] d. 1808, aged 25 years; single.
426. Agnes Alison,[3] d. 1800, aged 13 years.
427. Oliver Alison,[3] d. Oct. 14, 1855, aged 66 years; single.
428. Robert Alison[3] (435), b. 1789; m., May 27, 1839, Elizabeth Aitken. He d. May 4, 1854.
429. Maria Alison,[3] m. William Hesson; res. Chester Co., Penn., and d. in 1811, aged 21 years. They had a son, Horatio Hesson,[4] who married Margaret Downing. They had children who went west and married there, namely,—

[1] OTHER ALLISONS. 420. Anne Allison, of Donegal, Penn.; m. Thomas Anderson, Nov. 30, 1774. 420 a. Miss Allison, of Bemis's Valley, Penn.; m. Oct. 30, 1879, Frank Stewart, a. in Bellefonte, Penn. 420 b. Robert Alison was made a lieutenant in a Pennsylvania regiment, Feb. 8, 1747–'48. He was a nephew of Rev. Francis Alison, on the authority of Dr. Robert S. Allison, of Ardmore, Penn. 420 c. James Allison was a resident of Pennsylvania, June 6, 1758.

[2] She was the daughter of John and Rachel (Elder) Mackey, who lived near New London, of Chester county, Penn., and granddaughter of Robert Mackey, of the same place. Her grandfather was lieutenant of the Provincial forces of 1747–'48, and her father, John Mackey, was a member of the constitutional convention in 1776.

I.   William Hesson.[5]
II. Jeanette Hesson,[5]
III. Wright Hesson.[5]
IV. Madge Hesson.[5]
430. Louisa Alison,[3] d. ——, aged 70 years; single.
431. Julia Alison,[3] d. June 27, 1854, aged 49 years; single.

432. Sarah Alison[3] [424] (Francis,[2] Francis,[1]). She was born in Chester county, Penn., and married Alexander Adams.

CHILDREN.

433. Thomas Adams,[4] (439) b. Feb. 24, 1810, in Londonderry, Chester Co., Penn.; m., 1835, Ruth A. England.
434. Mary Adams,[4] b. Feb. 24, 1810; m. Samuel Ramsey. Children:
I.   Margaret Ramsey.[5]
II. Adams Ramsey.[5]
III. Francis Ramsey.[5]
IV. Horatio Ramsey.[5]
V.   Lucetta Ramsey.[5]

435. Robert Alison[3] [428] (Francis,[2] Francis[1]). Dr. Alison was born in Chester county in 1789. He graduated in medicine at the University of Pennsylvania in 1819, and practised his profession until his death, May 4, 1854. He resided in Chatham, and Jennerville, Chester county, Penn. He married, May 27, 1839, Elizabeth Aitken, daughter of John and Jane Aitken, of Chester county. Jane Aitken was the daughter of Capt. James and Sarah (Gettys) McDowell of Chester county, Penn. (See Futhey & Cope's history of Chester county, Penn.). She was born in 1807; died Aug. 21, 1851, in Wilmington, Delaware.

CHILDREN BORN IN JENNERVILLE, CHESTER CO., PENN.

436. Louisa Jane Alison,[4] b. 1841; d. Aug. 21, 1850.
437. Francis John Alison,[4] (446) b. May 16, 1843; lawyer; res. Philadelphia, Penn.
438. Robert Henry Alison,[4] (450) b. June 8, 1845; physician; res. Ardmore, Penn.

439. Thomas Adams[4] [433] (Sarah Alison,[3] Francis,[2] Francis[1]). He was born in Londonderry, Chester county, Penn., Feb. 24, 1810. He married, 1835, Ruth A. England.

CHILDREN.

440. Sarah Adams.[5]
441. Mary Adams,[5] m. Joseph Pratt. Children:
I.   Nathaniel Pratt.[6]
II. Adams Pratt.[6]
442. Robert Adams,[5] m. Elizabeth Strawbridge. Children:
I.   Anna Adams.[6]
II. Sarah Adams.[6]

III. Louisa Adams.[6]
IV. Robert Adams.[6]
V. Edwin Adams.[6]
443. Louisa Adams,[5] m. Andrew J. Young; res. 1330 Spring Garden St., Philadelphia, Penn. Children:
I. Edwin Stanton Young.[6]
II. James Thomas Young.[6]
444. Oliver Adams.[5]
445. Emmeline Adams.[5]

446. Francis John Alison[4] [437] (Robert,[3] Francis,[2] Francis[1]). He was born in Jennerville, Chester county, Penn., May 16, 1843; married, Sept. 6, 1877, Sophia Dallas Dixon, who was born in Philadelphia, Penn., Dec. 28, 1853. She was the daughter of Fitz Eugene and Catherine Chew (Dallas) Dixon. Her father was born in Amsterdam, Sept. 4, 1820; resided in Farley, Bucks county, Penn., and died in Philadelphia, Penn., Jan. 22, 1880. He was the son of Thomas Dixon, Jr., and his wife, Mary B. Dixon, who was born Jan. 26, 1781, in Westminster, London, Eng.; resided in Boston, Mass., where he died Sept. 15, 1849. He was the son of Thomas Dickson (or Dixon), born Nov. 6, 1739, in Perthshire, Scotland; resided in Amsterdam; married Elizabeth Mann, and died in Amsterdam, Oct. 25, 1824.

Mr. Alison graduated from the academic department of Harvard University, Cambridge, Mass., in 1865; was admitted to the bar of the city of Philadelphia, Penn., June 7, 1875, and practises his profession as a lawyer at 216 South 4th St., of that city; resides at 327 South 18th St., Philadelphia, Penn.

CHILDREN BORN IN PHILADELPHIA, PENN.

447. Catherine Dallas Alison,[5] b. June 11, 1878.
448. Mary Elizabeth Alison,[5] b. June 17, 1880.
449. Frances Armitage Alison,[5] b. March 27, 1889.

450. Robert Henry Alison[4] [438] (Robert,[3] Francis,[2] Francis[1]). He was born in Jennerville, Chester county, Penn., June 8, 1845. He graduated in arts at Yale College, New Haven, Conn., in 1867, and in medicine, from the University of Pennsylvania, in 1869. He is a physician. From May, 1871, to Oct., 1872, he was a resident physician of the Pennsylvania Hospital in Philadelphia. From Feb., 1883, to Nov., 1884, when he resigned, he was port physician of the port of Philadelphia. He removed to Ardmore, Montgomery county, Penn., Nov. 4, 1884; unmarried; resides at Ardmore, Penn.

OTHER ALLISONS OF PENNSYLVANIA.

Rev. James Allison, of Pittsburgh, Penn., in a personal letter, Dec. 17, 1890, says: "Part of the Allison family, to which I belong, went to Mecklenburg county, North Carolina, nearly one hundred and fifty years ago. Many of the descendants are still there (see sketch of Allisons of North Carolina, No. 579). Another part went to Virginia, and thence passed on into Indiana (see Allisons of Indiana, No. 463). One family of the part that went to North Carolina returned to Cecil county, Maryland, and afterwards removed to Washington county, Pennsylvania. One of its number (Hon. James Allison, No. 485), afterward going to Beaver county, Pennsylvania, served in the Eighteenth congress and was reëlected to the Nineteenth, but declined on account of ill-health. The late Hon. John Allison, register of the United States Treasury. was his son (see sketches of Hon. James Allison, and of his son, Hon. John Allison, No. 486). The father of Hon. William B. Allison, United States senator from Iowa, removed from the Cumberland valley, Pennsylvania, to Bellafonta, Pennsylvania, and then to the Western Reserve, Ohio, where William B. Allison was born (see sketch of Hon. William B. Allison, No. 489). One of my grandfather's brothers went from the Cumberland valley to Erie, Pennsylvania, where his descendants still live (James Allison and his descendants of Lake Pleasant, Erie county, Pennsylvania, may be of this family. See notice of them, No. 490). Another went to Butler; and my grandfather himself removed to the south side of the Monongahela river, near this city, in 1810, and afterward to a place ten miles north of this city, where he resided until his death."

460. James Allison [4] (James,[3] George,[2] —— Allison [1]).[1] Rev. James Allison was born in Pittsburgh, Penn., September 27, 1823; married, August 6, 1851, Mary Jane, daughter of Robert Anderson, who was born in Lancaster county, Penn., and who lived in Washington, Washington county, and in Sewickley, Alleghany county, Penn. Mrs. Allison was born and died in the latter place. He married, second, November 6, 1855, Caroline, daughter of Hon. John M. Snowden. She was born in Pittsburgh, Penn. Mr. Allison graduated at Jefferson College, Penn., in the class of 1845, taking the first honor. He studied theology in the

[1] He is the son of James and Elizabeth (Brickett) Allison, grandson of George and Susan (McRoberts) Allison, son of —— Allison, an emigrant from the north of Ireland.

Western Theological Seminary, Alleghany, Penn. In 1848 he took charge of the Presbyterian church at Sewickley, Penn., fourteen miles from Pittsburgh, where he continued to be pastor until 1864. During his pastorate the church had grown to be the strongest in the county outside of Pittsburgh. In 1864 he resigned, and became editor and proprietor, in connection with the late Robert Patterson, of The *Presbyterian Banner*, at Pittsburgh, of which from 1856 to 1861 he had been one of the editors and proprietors. This paper was started in Chillicothe, Ohio, July 5, 1814,—one of the very first religious newspapers of its kind,—and is very widely circulated. Mr. Allison is its editor in 1891. He was one of the original signers of the memorial on the subject of the reunion between the old and new school Presbyterian churches in 1864, and was the author in 1868 of the platform by which the union was effected in 1869. Much of the time during the War of the Rebellion he was in the field with the Pennsylvania troops, though not a soldier. From 1865 to 1890 he served on the General Assembly's Board for Freedmen, acting as treasurer, without salary, from 1870 to 1889.

CHILDREN BORN IN SEWICKLEY, PENN.

461. Lizzie Allison,[a] b. in 1852; m., in 1875, S. W. Reinhart; res. Brookline, Mass.
462. John M. S. Allison,[a] b. in 1857; m. Miss M. B. Laughlin; was an editor; res. Pittsburgh, Penn.; d. Dec. 27, 1877.

ALLISONS OF INDIANA—A BRANCH OF THE PENNSYLVANIA FAMILY.

The account of the Allisons as furnished by this family is that there were six brothers:

463. George Allison[1] settled in Iredell Co., N. C.
464. William Allison[1] settled in Charlotte, N. C.
465. John Allison[1] settled in North Carolina.
466. Thomas Allison[1] settled in North Carolina; was a teacher.
467. Robert Allison[1] settled in North Carolina; see sketch of North Carolina Allisons.
468. James Allison,[1] (469) m. Miss Young; res. Donegal, Penn.

469. James Allison[1](468). He settled in Donegal township, Penn., near where Harrisburg now stands. He was an elder in the Presbyterian church. He married Miss Young. He had three sons, and perhaps other children.

CHILDREN.

470. William Allison² (473). Settled near Staunton, Va.
471. John Allison.² He was a colonel in the Revolution, it is said.
472. James Allison.²

William Allison ²[470] (James¹). He left his father's home in township of Donegal, Penn., and settled near Staunton, Va. In the Revolutionary army he was a lieutenant, and was with General Washington in his retreat through New Jersey. After his settlement in Virginia he was for many years an elder in the Presbyterian church, for like most of the Allisons he was a pronounced adherent of that church.

CHILDREN.

474. James Allison³ (476). Deceased.
475. John Allison.³ Deceased.

476. James Allison ³ [474] (William,² James¹). He went West, and married, near Cincinnati, O., Sarah Cox, a lady of German descent, who died before Mr. Allison. He had several children. Among them were:

CHILDREN.

477. William Allison.⁴ Res. Toledo, Ohio.
478. Mary Ann Allison,⁴ m. James Shevoel; res. Lawrenceburg, Ind.
479. James Young Allison,⁴ (480) b. in Jefferson Co., Ind.; res. Madison, Ind.

480. James Young Allison ⁴ [479] (James,³ William,² James¹). Hon. James Y. Allison was born in Jefferson county, Ind., Aug. 20, 1823; married Antoinette McIntire. He was educated at Hanover college, Jefferson county, Ind.; studied law with Joseph G. Marshall, of Madison, Ind.; was admitted to the bar in Sept., 1847; served three terms as prosecuting attorney, one term as a state senator, and was elected judge of the fifth judicial circuit in Oct., 1873, for six years, and was reëlected for six years more in 1878. He resided in Madison, Ind., in that year.

CHILDREN.

481. Edward Allison.⁵
482. James Graham Allison.⁵
483. Antoinette M. Allison.⁵
484. Charles B. Allison.⁵

485. Hon. James Allison. He was born in Cecil county, Maryland, Oct. 14, 1772; lawyer. Acquired a high legal position in western Pennsylvania, was elected to 18th con-

HON. WM. B. ALLISON,
UNITED STATES SENATOR FROM IOWA.

gress from Pennsylvania, reëlected to 19th.   After practising his profession for fifty years he died in June, 1854.

486.   Hon. John Allison, son of the foregoing James Allison, was born in Pennsylvania Aug. 5, 1812.   Studied law but never practiced.   Was elected to the assembly of Pennsylvania in 1846-'47 and '49, and was a member of the 33d and 34th congresses, house of representatives, from Pennsylvania.   He was appointed registrar of the treasury of the United States in 1869; and died while in office, March 23, 1873.

487.   John Allison, his son, is living on a ranch in Montana.   (See letter of Rev. James Allison, preceding No. 460.)

488.   Hon. Robert Allison was born in Pennsylvania, and was a representative to congress from that state from 1831- • '33.   (From Charles Lanman's "Biographical Annals of the United States Government."   The sketch of W. B. Allison is from Harper's Weekly, March 17, 1888).

489.   Hon. William B. Allison,[3] United States senator from Iowa.   He was born in Perry, Wayne county, Ohio, March 2, 1829, and is the son of John Allison,[2] who was born in Bellefonte (or its neighborhood), Penn., in 1798, and who removed to Ohio about 1824, and resided on a farm in Perry. John Allison[2] was the son of Archibald Allison[1], who migrated from the county of Monaghan, Ireland, in 1783, and settled in Centre county, Penn.

Senator Allison spent his early years upon a farm and was educated at Allegheny college, Penn., and at Western Reserve college, Ohio.   He studied law, and practiced in Ohio till 1857, when he located in Dubuque, Ia., which has been his home since April, 1857.   He began his public career when the war broke out as a member of the staff of the governor, and his first task was to aid in the organization of the volunteer regiments that were destined to serve in the War of the Rebellion.   He was sent to congress while the war was going on, and has been representative and senator from that time to the present, except between 1871 and 1873, when he declined an election, so that he has participated in all the legislation that has been enacted during and since the great conflict.   He has done his full share in it all, and his impress is on the statutes which have framed and modified our fiscal and banking systems, our methods of taxation, as it was on the laws which gave to Mr. Lincoln the power to put down the rebellion, and which readjusted their relations to the Union of the once insurrectionary states.   His biography is

9

part of the history of the times in which he has lived.
Through them Mr. Allison has accurately represented the
sentiments and opinions of his section and of his party. He
has performed the duties imposed upon him with calmness
and caution. He was one of the congressmen depended upon
by the president and secretary of the treasury to devise ways
and means needed for the support of the government. After
the war he continued to be a radical Republican, always acting with his party, opposed to Johnson, and a believer in the
reconstruction measures which were intended to revolutionize
the political complexion of the conquered South, and to make
the freedman a citizen and a voter.

Senator Allison is one of the safe men of the Republican
party. He is without passion, prejudice, or very strong
friendships. He has not made the mistake, so common of
recent years, of allying himself to a faction. He is not weak,
nor a trimmer, nor a man of undecided views. It is not for
any one of these qualities that he fails to make enemies ; it is
because he is never carried away by the passions of the
moment, but is so moved and dominated by his judgment
that the public men who know him and have been associated
with him realize that his action is always the result of his
matured opinion.

There are very few men who have been so long in public
life as he who are so scrupulously devoted to their work.
Men like him are oftener found in the British parliament,
where tenure of place is more secure. Practically, Mr.
Allison's tenure has been as strong as theirs, and his familiar-
ity with the business of legislation is as accurate and thorough
as that of the under-secretaries of the British cabinet. This
is especially true of his acquaintance with fiscal matters. On
his first entrance into congressional life he came to the front
in the consideration of all questions affecting the treasury,
the banks, and taxation. He was a member of the ways and
means committee of the house of representatives very early,
if we take into consideration the very large majority which
his party had in congress at the time, and the number of able
men in both houses. The reputation that he then made for
himself for accurate information and sound judgment has not
been lost. He has not been tempted to endeavor to shine
in the discussion of other questions. He has been content
to be easily the first authority on all bills relating to expenditures. Some of his short speeches have indicated that he
might have been a leading debater on questions of constitutional law and on taxation and bank policy. So far as the

last two subjects are concerned, he has been prominent, and
there are very few public men of his party whose opinions on
all fiscal matters are more respected than Mr. Allison's ; but
of recent years he has been chairman of the appropriations
committee, and none but the most reckless undertake to
question his statements of fact concerning the expenditures
of the government.

As chairman of the appropriations committee he has been
of very important service to the cause of sound administration. He is a wise economist. This means judicious lib-
erality as opposed to an extravagant saving. The modern
deficiency bill, and the urgency bill, which has only recently
become one of the appropriation bills to be reckoned with at
every session of congress, would not exist, or would involve
inconsiderable amounts of money, if Mr. Allison's views about
the regular and stated bills always prevailed. The chairman
of the senate appropriations committee knows what each
branch of the public service needs for its proper maintenance,
and is willing to take the responsibility of advocating its
appropriation. The spirit in which he performs this vital
public function is directly, opposed to that which moves very
many members of congress, who do not appreciate their
responsibilities to refuse appropriations, and thus lower the
aggregate, when the refusal will not attract public attention
and arouse popular protest. Not many years ago the member of the house committee who had charge of the diplomatic
appropriation bill refused to allow the secretary of state any
money for postage or cable charges, and thus threatened to
cut off the state department from all correspondence with
our representatives in foreign countries. This incident illus-
trates the tendency and attitude of certain persons who seek
to figure before the country as savers of the people's money,
and who have wider reputations as economists than Mr.
Allison ; but Mr. Allison is neither sordid nor extravagant.
He does not advocate loose and unguarded expenditure, and
he is always desirous that every department and division of
the government shall have all that it needs. It is not exag-
gerating to say that when he is ready to sign a report of his
committee on an appropriation bill he knows as much of the
requirements of the objects for which the proposed expenditures are to be made as the executive officer who is at the
head of the department. And in all the years during which
he has acted in his present capacity there has not been a
whisper injuriously affecting his reputation.

Mr. Allison's influence on general legislation has been felt because he insists on having a reason for his votes. He is largely influenced by the feeling and opinions of his section of the country. This has made him an advocate of lower rates of tariff duties, and a consistent friend of the land-grant railroads. In 1870, after he had declined a reëlection to the house of representatives, and just before he was chosen to be Senator Harlan's successor, he took a very prominent part in the debate on Mr. Schenck's tariff bill. In the course of a speech on that measure, he said,—"The tariff of 1846, although confessedly and professedly a tariff for revenue, was, so far as regards all the great interests of the country, as perfect a tariff as any that we have ever had."

Perhaps the following extract from the same speech will best illustrate his tariff views of that time : " Our policy should be so to cheapen manufactured products that we can revive our export trade, now swept away because we cannot compete with other nations in the markets of the world. If we could restore what we have lost, and in addition greatly enlarge our exportations of manufactures, we would then have an enlarged home market for our agricultural products in a concentrated form, in exchange for other commodities which we do not and cannot produce."

He is really the author of the existing silver law, although he did not bring forward and advocate the measure as an original proposition. As the Bland bill passed the house of representatives it was a free coinage measure, and the senate finance committee was equally divided for and against it, Mr. Allison neither approving nor opposing it. Some silver legislation was inevitable, and Mr. Allison suggested the measure which was adopted. He is a bimetallist, but not of the Bland kind, and the law as it stands to-day (1888) ought to bear Mr. Allison's rather than Mr. Bland's name. The measure was probably the most conservative that could have been adopted at the time it became a law.

Mr. Allison's friendship for the land-grant roads, which came into existence during the beginning of his service in the house, was shown by his opposition to the Thurman act. There was no question as to the sincerity of his position, however. He voted and spoke against the bill because he believed that it would be injurious to the interests of the roads which had done very much for the building up of the material interests of his state.

For the rest he has always been a strong friend of the national bank system, and the treasury has leaned upon him as one of its wisest and most influential friends in congress.

It is one of his excellent traits that he never deals with the
public business in a partisan spirit.   As a legislator he is pre-
eminently a man of affairs.   He manages the subjects entrusted to him with the view of doing the best that is possible
for the government.   It is because he is determined to do
the best that is in his power that he confines himself so closely to one class of subjects.   He is not brilliant.   He does not
address the galleries nor the country, and while his speeches
are not works of art, they are very earnest, and very interesting and informing to those who desire to obtain a thorough
knowledge of the question under discussion.   Perhaps the
most popular speech that he ever made in congress was that
on the tariff, from which excerpts have been given.   His
argument on the silver question was full of learning.   The
part he has taken in the political debates which have been
made in the senate, especially those of the special session in
1879, when both houses of congress were controlled by the
Democrats, and when there was a bitter conflict between
them and President Hayes, has been that of a questioner and
suggester; and in that way he has had more influence upon
legislation than many a senator whose appearance upon the
floor has furnished entertainment for the idlers of the capitol.

While he has not filled any executive office, his Republican
colleagues regard him as a man of exceptional executive
capacity.   When Mr. Garfield was elected president, Mr.
Allison might have been secretary of the treasury.   There
was then a general consensus of opinion that, next to Mr.
Sherman, he was the best equipped of his party for that office.
The relations between the president and himself were very
close.   They had served together in the house, and they had
acted together on almost every question of public policy,
with the exception, perhaps, of that involved in the silver
bill.   Mr. Garfield was desirous that the Iowa senator should
be his finance minister, but the latter was unwilling to quit
the senate, and Mr. Windom was appointed.

In the interesting and exciting times that followed the in-
auguration of his friend, he never permitted himself to turn
from the duties with which he was charged to take part in
the factional strife.   He was consulted by both sides in the
confident belief, which was never disappointed, that he would
not betray the councils of either.   He is too thoroughly
devoted to the public business to permit party politics to in-
terfere with it, and too strongly devoted to his party to do
anything to divide it into factions.

He is as quiet in his social life as he is in the senate, and yet he is a man who loves society. For many years, while Mrs. Allison was alive, his comfortable house on Vermont avenue was one of the social centres of the capital. His hospitality was generous, but not profuse. He is a kindly, agreeable man, an excellent listener, and a general favorite. His fortune is ample, his tastes are refined, and those who know him best like him most. He has a repose and restfulness which make him a pleasant comrade, and many a nervous man finds it a great comfort to be with him, even if he does n't say a word.

He has a sturdy frame and a fine face. He comes from strong Scotch-Irish stock. His ancestors settled in Pennsylvania, where his father was born. When he began his professional and public life he had the vigor which has kept him young, for his sixty-four years sit lightly upon him. He has been a leading candidate for the Republican nomination for the Presidency. He married Annie Carter; married second, Mary Heally. Resides Dubuque, Iowa.

OTHER ALLISONS OF PENNSYLVANIA.

490. James Allison[1] (see letter of Rev. James Allison previous to No. 460), born in Pennsylvania; lived in Maryland.

490 a. William Allison,[2] his son, born Baltimore, Md.; resided at Lake Pleasant, Erie county, Penn.; married Nancy Gilchrist of Harrisburg, who died March 27, 1846. He died at Lake Pleasant, Nov. 25, 1825. His son,

490 b. William Allison,[3] b. in Erie county, Penn., Jan. 18, 1808; resided at Lake Pleasant, Erie county, Penn.; married Harriet H. Carson, who was born at Wattsburgh, Erie county, Penn., Oct. 2, 1805. Mr. Allison died at Lake Pleasant, Dec. 29, 1889.

CHILDREN BORN AT LAKE PLEASANT, PENN.

491. John Allison,[4] b. 1837; d. Lake Pleasant, April 4, 1843.
492. Catherine R. Allison,[4] b. 1839; d. Lake Pleasant, April 6, 1843.
493. Infant son,[4] b. 1840; d. 1840.
494. Mary Amelia Allison,[4] b. 1842; m. Martin Van Buren Gifford; res. Cassewago, Penn., and Erie, Penn.
495. Rachel R. Allison,[4] b. 1843; m. George W. Gifford; res. Madison, Ohio.
496. James Wallace Allison,[4] b. 1846; m., Sept. 15, 1874, Clarissa Adell Frith; res. Erie, Penn.

497. George Allison[1] located in Philadelphia, Penn., and was a blacksmith.

498. Matthew Allison,[1] his brother, is thought to have located in the state of New York.

George Allison,[1] above-named, had

CHILD:

500. George Allison,[2] never married.
501. Matthew Allison,[2] removed to Maryland; married, and had a large family.
502. Elijah Allison,[2] married in Pennsylvania, res. there several years; then removed to Kentucky, thence to Ohio, thence to Indiana, thence to Illinois, where he died, aged 97 years. The maiden name of his wife was Margaret Shepherd.

CHILD.

503. Solomon Allison,[3] m., at Cincinnati, Ohio, Elizabeth, dau. of Philip Sloat, a Revolutionary soldier. She was b. in N. Y. Children:
504. George Allison,[4] m., went to Iowa, and died there.
505. Amanda Allison,[4] m. Hon. E. R. Allen, an influential man in Pike Co., Ohio. No children.
506. Sarah E. Allison,[4] m. William Hammauer, a farmer, who d. without issue.
507. Mary Allison,[4] m. William Rotroff, farmer. Two children.
508. William L. Allison,[4] m., in Washington, D. C., Mary Sypherd; was recorder of deeds for Pike Co., Ohio. Res. Waverley, Pike Co., Ohio.

ALLISONS FROM THE COUNTY OF LONDONDERRY, IRELAND.

There landed in Philadelphia, Penn., about the first of July, 1750, three emigrants of Scotch blood and Presbyterian faith. They came from the County of Londonderry, Ireland. They were brothers, named Andrew Allison, Robert Allison, James Allison. From them have sprung many descendants, who are widely scattered, residing in Pennsylvania and many of the western states. They are mostly Presbyterians. As a family they have been healthy and long lived; the earlier generations were mostly farmers. Many professional men were in the later generations.

509. James Allison,[1] one of the three brothers, settled in Franklin county, Penn.

510. Andrew Allison [1] settled in Lancaster county, Penn.

511. Robert Allison [1] resided in Cumberland county, Penn., for some years; then removed to Indiana county where he passed the remainder of his days, and died in 1805. He married, in 1752, Rebecca Beard, who came in the same ship with him across "the deep blue sea." She was a granddaughter of one Charles Stewart (or Stuart), a soldier, who was wounded in the hand at the "Battle of the Boyne."

512. John B. Allison,[3] grandson of Robert, died in 1878,

aged eighty-two years. He lived on the farm on which he was born till he was seventy years of age, when he moved to Indiana, the county seat of Indiana county, Penn., where he died. His

512. Rebecca A. Allison,[4] res. Indiana, Indiana Co., Penn.

HON. JOSEPH ALLISON OF PHILADELPHIA, PENN. — HIS BRANCH OF THE ALLISONS.

513. Mr. Allison, of Scotch blood, lived in a double cabin some three miles from Londonderry, Ireland. He had relatives of the name of Knox and McIllvaine, who lived there in 1867. He had several children. Among them were three daughters, names not known to the compiler, who lived and died in Ireland.

514. His son, Joseph Allison,[2] lived at the old home near Londonderry, Ireland, and died there about 1870.

515. William Allison,[2] another son, emigrated to America when eighteen years of age; landed at Wilmington, Del., and immediately joined his relatives by name of Mac Beth, or MacBeg, near Harrisburg, Penn. He had no known Allison connections in this country. He became a successful hardware merchant in Harrisburg, where he spent the active years of his life. He finally joined his son, Judge Joseph Allison,[3] in Philadelphia, and lived the life of a retired business man, and died there. He married, in Harrisburg, Penn., Mary Andrews, who when a child was brought to this country from Armagh, Ireland, by her parents. She died in Harrisburg about 1848. She had a sister who married Mr. Irwin, of Scotch blood, and they lived in Winchester, Va., where she died, and her large family later went to Missouri. Her brother, in early life, settled in the city of New York. William Allison[2] had six sons and one daughter, all deceased except Judge Allison, of Philadelphia. Among them were:

516. Robert Henderson Allison,[3] a physician, who died about 1855, in Charleston, Coles county, Illinois.

517. James Irwin Allison[3] was for many years a magistrate in Philadelphia, Penn.

518. Arthur David Allison[3] was a merchant in Philadelphia, Penn.

519. Joseph Allison,[3] born August 31, 1819; named for his uncle. He studied law in Harrisburg, Penn.; admitted to the bar of Dauphin county in 1843; elected solicitor of

Residence and Grounds of T. J. ALLISON, Esq., Sheriff of Iredell County, Near Statesville.

Spring Garden in 1846, and held the office many years, till he was elected an associate law judge of the court of common pleas of the first judicial district of Pennsylvania. In 1865 he succeeded to the presidency of the court, and has to the present (1892) held that position—a period of forty years. Has been five times elected, the last two times without opposition, receiving at the last election 145,000 votes with none against him. He married in 1843, and has a family. Residence Philadelphia, Penn.[1]

520. Samuel Allison[1] was born in Northumberland county, Penn., about 1785, and it is said his father was a chaplain in the Revolutionary army. Mr. Allison was in the 1812–'15 war. He married Annie Caldwell, of Northumberland county, Penn., and about 1816 he took up military lands in Greene county, Ohio.

HIS SON.

521. James Allison,[2] born about 1817, was a prosperous merchant and banker; was prominent in constructing the first railroad in that locality, and built the first gasworks in Xenia, Ohio. He m. Anne, dau. of Captain Matthew Corey. He d. June, 1864. They had but one child.

522. Matthew Corey Allison,[3] b. in Xenia, Ohio, Dec. 18, 1840; manufacturer and banker, at Xenia, Ohio; educated at Wittemburg; and m. Frances, dau. of Rev. John Elkin, D. D. He d. May 2, 1888. Children:

523. James Ekin Allison,[4] b. Xenia, Ohio, May 10, 1865; graduated at Harvard University in 1887. Removed to Nashville, Tenn., in 1888, and resides there in 1893. He is a member of the Hermitage Club.

524. Frederica Lee Allison,[4] b. Xenia, Ohio, July 30, 1866; m. George Gill Whitaker, of St. Louis, Mo., in 1889.

525. Matthew Herbert Allison,[4] b. Xenia, Ohio, Oct. 30, 1867; m. in 1886, Mary Pettengill, of Ithaca, Mich.

ALLISONS OF RAMELTON, COUNTY OF DONEGAL, IRELAND, MIDDLETOWN, PENN., AND TRENTON, N. J.

These Allisons descended from a Scotch family who came over from Scotland at the time of the Plantation of Ulster; they left their native land during the religious persecution. There was one woman of the Allison family, called Isabella Allison, who with another, called Marion Harvey, was put to death. They were chained out in the sea till the tide came in, and when it was surging into their mouths, were

[1]This unsatisfactory record is as full as the information furnished me after repeated requests.   L. A. M.

asked, "Will you recant now, and kiss the pope?" They held up their hands, saying :

"For Zion's King, and Zion's cause,
And Scotland's covenanted laws."[1]

and died.[1]

526.   Robert Allison[1] came first to Ramelton from Scotland, and took a farm called Louchras (?), but lost the same through some chicanery.   Ramelton is fifteen miles west of the city of Londonderry, a town of considerable note, and was peopled by the Scotch and English.   The Lough Swilly river flows into the town.

CHILDREN.

527.   Samuel Allison[2] (528) lived and died in Ramelton, Co. Donegal, Ireland.   He m. Lydia Curran.

528.   Samuel Allison[2] [527] (Robert[1]).   He was born in Ramelton, county Donegal, Ireland; lived in that place, where he and his wife were members of the Presbyterian church. They were excellent people, and gave their children the best possible education.   He married Lydia Curran, a cousin of the brave John P. Curran.   Mr. and Mrs. Allison died in Ramelton, and are buried in the churchyard there.

CHILDREN, BORN RAMELTON, COUNTY DONEGAL, IRELAND.

529.   William Allison[3] (536), b. Sept. 18, 1777; res. Middletown, Penn.
530.   Robert Allison[3] (545), res. Ramelton, Ireland; m. Nancy, dau. of Richard McConnell.   She had a brother, Richard McConnell.
531.   John Allison[3] emigrated to America some years after his brother, William Allison.
532.   Samuel Allison,[3] res. New Mill, Ramelton, Ireland.   He m. Elizabeth Lockhart.   He had a son, William Allison, who was in the British army and went abroad, and of whom there is no knowledge.   Another son emigrated to America; and daughters Ellen Matilda Allison,[4] Eliza Ann Allison,[4] who m. Frank Anderson, res. Glasgow, Scotland, and had son, Frank Anderson,[5] res. Australia, and Isabella Allison.[4]
533.   Lydia Allison,[3] m. Robert Jackson, and emigrated to America. Settled in New York city, and had sons John Jackson,[4] Robert Jackson,[4] and Samuel Jackson.[4]
534.   Isabella Allison,[3] m. McNaught.   He d. in Ireland.   She emigrated to Philadelphia, Penn.   Children:
I.   Samuel McNaught;[4] res. Philadelphia, Penn.
II.   Mary Ann McNaught;[4] res. Philadelphia, Penn.
535.   Mary Ann Allison,[3] m. John Jackson.   She d. in Ireland.   He with his family emigrated to America, he dying upon the passage. The family settled in New York city.

[1]From letter of John Allison, Clooney Cottage, Ramelton, Ireland, Jan. 14, 1892.   An old gentleman of 86 years of age.

586.   William Allison[3] (529) (Samuel,[2] Robert[1]).   He was
born in Ramelton, county of Donegal, Ireland, where he
received a fine education.   He was a friend and correspondent
of the celebrated and unfortunate Emmet.   Mr. Allison came
to America about 1800—at about 23 years of age, as he was
born Sept. 18, 1777.   He settled in Middletown, Penn., and
he said that he was of the same stock as the Allisons who, at
an early date, settled in Pennsylvania, and traditions are in
the family of their descent from Scottish ancestors.   As he was
acquainted with the then secret art of blistering steel, he
went into partnership with Thomas Stubbs, in Middletown,
Dauphin county, Penn.   It was claimed that they manufactured the first steel in America.   He was a man of consequence
in his locality, and was a director in the Saratoga bank.   He
married, Sept. 26, 1801, Ruth, daughter of Thomas and Elizabeth Stubbs, a granddaughter of Thomas Stubbs, born March
9, 1784; died March 25, 1818.   He married, second, Juliana,
daughter of Charles and Mary Brandon, March 14, 1819.
He died Nov. 2, 1825, and is buried in a private burial lot on
the Fisher estate.   Mrs. Allison was born March 6, 1785;
died March 21, 1870, at Wheeling, W. Va.

CHILDREN.

537.   Elizabeth Allison,[4] b. Sept. 29, 1802; d. Oct. 7, 1805.
538.   Samuel Stubbs Allison,[4] b. July 29, 1804; d. Oct. 7, 1805.
539.   Sarah Ann Allison,[4] b. Aug. 7, 1808; died Sept. 9, 1810, at Middle-
         town, Penn.
540.   Thomas Stubbs Allison[4] (550), b. May 21, 1810; d. Feb., 1871.
541.   Lydia Curran Allison,[4] b. July 29, 1812.
542.   Phebe Caroline Allison,[4] b. Oct. 15, 1814.
543.   William Winfield Scott Allison,[4] b. Feb. 11, 1817; d. July 17, 1817,
         at Middletown, Penn.
544.   Charles William Brandon Allison[4] (558), b. Dec. 12, 1820; d. at
         Wheeling, W. Va., Dec. 5, 1876.

545.   Robert Allison [3] [530] (Samuel,[2] Robert [1]).   He was
born at or near Ramelton, county of Donegal, Ireland;
married Nancy ————, and died in 1870; she died in 1858.
They were Presbyterians and lived in Ramelton, Ireland.

CHILDREN.

546.   John Allison [4] (564), b. Dec. 25, 1806; res. Clooney cottage, Ramel-
         ton, county of Donegal, Ireland.
547.   Elizabeth Allison,[4] m. Richey Gallagher, and lived in Londonderry,
         Ireland; she is deceased; three sons and two daughters.
548.   Isabella Allison,[4] lives with her brother at Clooney cottage, Ram-
         elton, Ireland.
549.   Nancy Allison,[4] m. William Gallagher and is deceased; her husband
         subsequently came to America.

550. Thomas Stubbs Allison [4] [540] (William,[3] Samuel,[2] Robert [1]). He was born in Middletown, Dauphin county, Penn., May 21, 1810; married, Dec. 19, 1833, Margaret, daughter of Henry Sigismund Gatzmer, who was born, 1729, in Berlin, Germany, and who with his wife, Agnes Schutz lived in Bound Brook, N. J., where he died Dec. 24, 1844. He was the son of Frederick Ernest Gatzmer, of Berlin, Germany. Mrs. Allison was born in Bound Brook, N. J., July 16, 1811 ; resided in Trenton, N. J., with her family, where she died May 21, 1864. Mr. Allison lived in Somerville, N. J., from 1831 to 1851, and then in Trenton, N. J. He was an editor, then secretary of state for the state of New Jersey. He was made a paymaster in the United States army, and died in Atlanta, Ga., Feb. 1, 1871.

CHILDREN BORN IN SOMERVILLE, N. J., EXCEPT THE YOUNGEST.

551. Mary Elizabeth Allison,[5] m., Oct. 25, 1867, William G. Cook; res. Trenton, N. J.; an officer in two banks. He is dead. No children.
552. Augusta Allison,[5] res. 222 West State Street, Trenton, N. J.
553. Margaret Gatzmer Allison,[5] m., March 14, 1867, Ferdinand W. Robeling, a native of Saxonburg, Penn. He was a son of John A. Robeling, the architect of the Brooklyn bridge. Mr. Robeling is an engineer and largely engaged in the iron works of Trenton, N. J. Res. 222 West State street, Trenton, N. J. Children b. Trenton, N. J:
I. Margaret J. Robeling,[6] b. July 22, 1868.
II. Charles G. Robeling,[6] b. July 7, 1873.
III. Augusta Henrietta Robeling,[6] b. Sept. 20, 1875.
IV. Ferdinand William Robeling,[6] b. Sept. 30, 1879.
554. Ellen McGowan Allison,[5] m., Jan. 26, 1871, Dr. A. K. Smith. He was from Hartford, Conn., and b. there, Feb., 1826. He was an army surgeon, and retired, on account of age, Feb., 1889. His rank was that of a colonel. Res. Dobbs' Ferry, N. Y. Child:
I. Thomas Allison Smith,[6] b. July, 1872. He is a cadet at West Point Military academy.
555. William Allison,[5] d. May 27, 1845.
556. Florence Allison,[5] m., Aug. 26, 1869, Harry R. Anderson, son of William Marshall Anderson, of Circleville, Ohio. He is a nephew of Gen. Robert Anderson of Fort Sumter fame. Mr. Anderson is a first lieutenant in 4th Artillery, U. S. regular army. Children:
I. William Allison Anderson,[6] b. June, 1871; res. Trenton, N. J. He is in the iron works with his uncle, Mr. Robeling.
II. Davis Catlin Anderson,[6] b. Jan., 1873. Student.
III. Duncan McArthur Anderson,[6] b. Jan., 1874.
IV. Margaret Allison Anderson,[6] b. Oct., 1877.
557. Emily Allison,[5] m., Sept. 30, 1874, Frank A. Briggs, son of Hon. James F. Briggs of Manchester, N. H. Mr. Briggs was a graduate of West Point Military academy. He is treasurer of iron works of John A. Robeling's sons. Res. Trenton, N. J. Child:
I. Frankland Briggs,[6] b., Trenton, N. J., June 4, 1877.

558. Charles William Brandon Allison[4] [544] (William,[3] Samuel,[2] Robert[1]). He was son of Major William Allison and was born, Dec. 12, 1820, in Middletown, Dauphin county, Penn.; removed to Ohio in 1831. He was raised upon a farm; was placed at hard work there, and later was a mechanic. During this time he attended the district school, and studied at night, preparing himself for his lifework. In 1889 he commenced the study of law, and was admitted to the bar in Columbus, O., in Dec., 1841. He formed a partnership with Hon. Augustus Hall, late member of congress from Iowa and chief justice of Nebraska, and later with Otway Curry. In 1851 he removed to Bellefontaine, O., and formed a partnership with Congressman Benjamin Stanton. Was a Whig, and then a Republican, in politics. In May, 1862, he enlisted for three months in the army, and was made captain of Company E, Eighty-sixth regiment, Ohio volunteers, and a few days afterwards, was commissioned as colonel of the Eighty-fifth regiment Ohio volunteers, and his company was transferred to that regiment. In October, 1862, he was appointed colonel of the rendezvous for drafted men at Camp Dennison, where he remained in command until that service was closed, Jan. 1, 1863. He was a member of the Ohio house of representatives convened January, 1864, and was chairman of the committee on military affairs, and a member of the judiciary committee. He was elected a member of the Ohio state senate, and was chosen its president. In 1866 he with Mr. Stanton opened an office in Wheeling, West Va., and removed there with their families April 1, 1867, where they carried on a most extensive and lucrative practice. Mr. Stanton died June 2, 1872. Mr. Allison continued in practice till his death, Dec. 5, 1876. He was a self-made man. He preferred to follow the convictions of his judgment rather than to act from considerations of policy. He had a discriminating and investigating mind, and ranked high as a lawyer. He married, Nov. 5, 1844, Sophronia, daughter of Dr. Elisha S. and Elizabeth Lee, of Marysville, O., who died Aug. 26, 1848. She was born in Knox county, O., Oct. 24, 1825. He married, second, May 21, 1851, Mary, daughter of Hon. Benjamin Stanton, son of Elias and Martha (Wilson) Stanton, grandson of Benjamin and Mary Stanton, his law partner of Bellefontaine, O. Mrs. Allison was born at Mount Pleasant, O., Dec. 27, 1830, and now lives at No. 36 15th St. Wheeling, West Va.

CHILDREN.

559. Julia Sophronia Allison,⁵ b. Marysville, O., Aug. 15, 1845; m., Feb.
      24, 1865, Owen J. Hopkins, b. Bellefontaine, Logan Co., O.,
      June 14, 1844; was son of Daniel and Sarah (Carter) Hopkins.
      His grandfather is said to have been killed at Ft. Meigs, O.,
      1813, and his great grandfather was Stephen Hopkins of Rhode
      Island, b. March, 1707; d. 1785; a signer of the Declaration of
      Independence. Mr. Hopkins was four years in the army. Is
      now a bookkeeper. Res. 1330 Huron St., Toledo, O. Children
      b. Toledo, O.:
  I. Annie Allison Hopkins,⁶ b. 1866; res. Toledo, O.
 II. Oliver Perry Hopkins,⁶ b. 1868; res. Toledo, O.
III. Frederick Livingstone Hopkins,⁶ b. 1870; d. 1872 in Toledo, O.
 IV. Cordelia Oswald Hopkins,⁶ b. 1873; res. Toledo, O.
  V. Charles Benjamin Hopkins,⁶ b. 1882.
 VI. Julia S. Hopkins,⁶ b. 1887.
560. Otway Allison,⁵ b. Marysville, O., April 2, 1848; d. there Oct. 5,
      1848.
561. Kate Allison,⁵ b. Bellefontaine, O., May 29, 1852; res. No. 36 15th
      St., Wheeling, West Va.
562. Benjamin Stanton Allison,⁵ b. Bellefontaine, O., Dec. 18, 1854; res.
      No. 36 15th St., Wheeling, West Va., and is not married. He
      graduated at the University at Wooster, O., in June, 1876, at the
      law school at Albany, N. Y., in May, 1878, and the same month
      he was admitted to the bar in Wheeling, W. Va. He then
      formed a law partnership with William Erskine, and is now
      engaged in the active practice of the law. He is a Republican
      in politics and has been the candidate of his party for mayor of
      the city.
563. Ann B. Allison,⁵ b. Bellefontaine, O., Jan. 10, 1858; d. there Aug.
      16, 1863.

564. John Allison⁴ [546] (Robert,³ Samuel,² Robert¹).
He was born in Ramelton, county of Donegal, Ireland, Dec.
25, 1806; resided Clooney cottage, Ramelton, Ireland, on Jan.
14, 1892. He and his family are all Presbyterians. Mr.
Allison is a farmer, having sixty acres near Ramelton.

CHILDREN.

565. Robert Allison,⁵ b. Dec. 29, 1838; emigrated to Melbourne, Aus-
      tralia. Single.
566. Thomas William Allison,⁵ b. Jan. 18, 1840; emigrated to America,
      and died in Wisconsin. He married Jane McClure; no children.
567. John Allison,⁵ b. April 21, 1844; emigrated to America, and died.
      He was married, but left no children.
568. James Allison,⁵ (570) b. Feb. 23, 1846; residence Ramelton, Ireland.
569. Joseph Allison,⁵ b. May 4, 1848; has for twenty years been a mem-
      ber of that splendid body of men, the Royal Irish Constabulary,
      and has been promoted. He is loyal to his queen, and is re-
      spected by his acquaintances. He lives in the county of Wex-
      ford, Ireland, in town of Crohan.

570. James Allison⁵ [568] (John,⁴ Robert,³ Samuel,²
Robert¹). He was born in Ramelton, Ireland; resides at

Clooney cottage, Ramelton, Ireland.   He married Mary Jane
Malseed ; they have seven daughters.

CHILDREN.

571. John Allison,* b. Aug. 28, 1876; res. Ramelton, Ireland.
572. Bella Allison,* b. April, 28, 1878.
573. Jean Ann Allison,* b. Feb. 12, 1880.
574. Mary Elizabeth Allison,* b. April 28, 1882.
575. Margaret Allison,* b. April 28, 1884.
576. Agnes Allison,* b. June 28, 1886.
577. Martha Allison,* b. Nov. 3, 1888.
578. Josephine Allison,* b. Jan. 17, 1891.

CHAPTER VII.

Five brothers by name of Allison, born in Pennsylvania[1]
(one account says in Ireland), lived on the Yellowstone river
in that state, and between 1760 and 1770, and before the
War of the Revolution, they moved to North Carolina, while
their brother, James Allison, remained in Pennsylvania.
They were of that strong Scotch stock which went from Scotland to Ireland, and later to Pennsylvania, New Hampshire,
and the southern states, and who have been such magnificent
builders of states and commonwealths. They settled in Iredell
and Mecklenburgh counties, where the name to-day is very
common. The names of these emigrants to North Carolina
were:

579. William Allison[1] (586), who resides at Bethany
Church, N. C.

580. John Allison,[1] married, first, a sister of Colonel Richard Allison, of Iredell county, N. C. The relationship between
them is not known. There was no issue by this marriage.
He married a second time.

581. Polly Anderson,[2] his daughter, married her cousin,

582. James Allison,[2] son of Robert Allison.[1] Mr. Allison
lived at Poplar Tent, Mecklenburgh county, N. C.

583. George Allison,[1] settled in Mecklenburgh or Iredell
county, N. C.

584. Thomas Allison,[1] born 1743, was never married. He
was a school teacher of renown, and was widely known as
"Master Allison." He died in Nov., 1811, aged 68 years.
A sister of these five Allisons married a Mr. Todd, settled
in Mecklenburgh, N. C., and their descendants live in that
county today.

585. Robert Allison[1] (588), born in 1750; married Sarah
Graham; resided on Clark's Creek, Cabarrus county, N. C.;
died in 1804, aged 54 years.

---

[1]See notice in account of the Allisons of Pennsylvania, in letter of Rev.
James Allison, which precedes No. 460.

ALLISONS OF NORTH CAROLINA.

586. William Allison[1] [579], one of the five emigrants from Pennsylvania, and a brother of Robert Allison, as stated in a record by Robert Washington Allison, of Concord, N. C., April, 1887. He was born in Pennsylvania, and his people from Ireland, like all of the residents in Ulster, were weavers. He resided in Pennsylvania, removed to North Carolina with his brothers, and was one of the earliest settlers in Iredell county, and one of its first purchasers of land. He owned a plantation which has been in possession of his descendants for more than one hundred years. Residence at Bethany Church, N. C., where he died.

CHILD.

587. Thomas Allison[2] (597); res. Bethany Church, N. C.

588. Robert Allison[1] [585], one of the five brothers who went south from Pennsylvania, between 1760 and 1770, probably, was born in 1750, and settled near Charlotte, N. C., and married Sarah Graham.[1] Mrs. Allison was a sister of Joseph Graham, the father of Hon. William A. Graham, once governor of North Carolina, and candidate for vice-president of the United States on the ticket with General Winfield Scott, in 1852. Mrs. Allison was the aunt of Miss Graham, sister of Hon. William A. Graham, who married Rev. Hall Morrison, D. D., and one of their daughters married General D. H. Hill, and another married General Thomas J. Jackson, known as "Stonewall" Jackson. In 1790, Mr. Allison removed to Poplar Tent on Clark's creek, in what is now Cabarrus county, and was a ruling elder in the church there. He died in 1804, aged 54 years. Mrs. Allison was delicate in appearance, had great energy, and was a fine manager and a strong Presbyterian.

CHILDREN.

589. William Allison[2] (599), born Oct. 7, 1780; m. Peggy Young; res. Charlotte, N. C.
590. James Allison,[2] m. his cousin, Polly, dau. of Uncle John Allison.[3]
591. Mary Allison,[2] m. James Young, a brother of Mrs. Thomas and Mrs. William Allison. Their sons
I. John Young,[3] lived in Concord, N. C., in 1887.
II. Joseph Young,[3] lived in Concord, N. C., in 1887.[2]

[1] She was a daughter of Widow Graham, of Pennsylvania, who, with slender means and five small children, John Graham, George Graham, Joseph Graham, Sarah Graham, and Ann Graham, removed to Mecklenburgh, N. C., about 1765.

[2] The Youngs were of the same Scotch blood who came from Ireland to Pennsylvania, and later to North Carolina.

10

592. Thomas Allison² (605), born March 5, 1785; m. Sarah Young, a sister of his brother William's wife; res. Poplar Tent, Cabarrus Co., N. C.
593. Anne Allison,² m. Sandy McKinley, of Rocky River, N. C., and d. young. Child:
I. Fanny McKinley,³ who m. Rev. Cyrus K. Caldwell.
594. John Graham Allison,² m. Almira, dau. of John Johnston. They died without children.
595. Sarah Allison,² m. W. C. Johnston, son of John Johnston. Their son,
596. Robert Allison Johnston,³ m. a Miss Reeves.

597. **Thomas Allison² [587] (William¹).** He was a farmer and tanner. Residence at Bethany Church, N. C. Married Miss Kerr; married, second, Miss Matthews. He died at Bethany Church, N. C., in 1844.

CHILD.

598. William M. Allison³ (620), b. June 28, 1816; res. Bethany Church, N. C.

599. **William Allison² [589] (Robert¹).** He was born Oct. 7, 1780, and was a merchant in Charlotte, N. C. He married, Nov. 7, 1805, Peggy Young; born July 13, 1784. He died Feb. 25, 1816, and she married second Mr. Gillespie, and had two children. She died Oct. 30, 1850.

CHILDREN.

600. Sarah Maria Allison,³ b. 1806; d. 1834. She m. Mr. Erwin, and lived in Kentucky. They left three children.
601. Robert Washington Allison³ (622), born April 24, 1809.
602. Margaret Allison,³ born 1811; m. David Kistler. She d. in 1868, leaving three married daughters.
603. Jane Allison,³ b. 1813; m. Henry C. Owens. She d. 1867. Children:
I. William A. Owens,⁴ lawyer; res. Charlotte, N. C.
II. James Henry Owens⁴ was another son.
604. Anne Allison,³ b. July 4, 1815; m., in 1836, Charles Overman; d. in 1874, leaving three daughters and two sons. Children:
I. Margaret Eliza Overman,⁴ m. A. H. Tate; has had eight children. One only living.
II. Mary Cornelia Overman,⁴ m. Thomas R. Tate, who d. in 1872. Two children.
III. William W. Overman⁴ is a shoe merchant; res. Newark, N. J.
IV. Hamilton Overman⁴ is a merchant in Reidsville, N. C.

605. **Thomas Allison ² [592] (Robert ¹).** He was born March 5, 1785; was a farmer, and a person of moral and industrious habits, and accumulated a considerable property. He married, in May, 1810, Sarah Young, who died Sept. 16, 1847. They were members of the Poplar Tent Presbyterian church, in Cabarrus county, N. C., and lived within the limits of that congregation.

FOURTEEN CHILDREN.

606. Sarah Caroline Allison,⁵ b. April 27, 1811; m., Dec., 1833, William
       Young, who d., and she m., second, David G. Holbrooks. She
       d. Dec., 1861.
607. Mary Ann Allison,⁵ b. Jan. 17, 1813 ; m. Henry Farr in Jan., 1834,
       and d. in Oct., 1847.
608. Margarette Allison,⁵ b. Jan. 5, 1815; d. Oct., 1815.
609. Robert Allison,⁵ b. Sept. 19, 1816; d. Aug., 1824.
610. Thomas Franklin Allison,⁵ b. Nov. 29, 1818; d. Nov., 1845.
611. Elizabeth Jemima Allison,⁵ b. Jan. 15, 1821; d. Feb. 9, 1885.
612. James Allison,⁵ (632) b. April 29, 1823; res. Davidson College, N. C.
613. Martha Jane Allison,⁵ b. Dec. 27, 1825; m., Dec., 1859, John F.
       Sloan, and d. in June, 1885. Two children—one living—Mrs.
       Margarette Johnston.⁶
614. John Graham Allison,⁵ b. April 27, 1828; d. in Aug., 1854.
615. Ruth Minerva Allison,⁵ b. June 8, 1830; m., in May, 1862, W. F. Stilll,
       who is deceased. She still lives at Davidson College, N. C.
616. Agnes Henrietta Allison,⁵ b. Oct. 1, 1832; m., Jan., 1851, J. Fisher.
       She d. June 12, 1853.
617. Robert William Allison,⁵ b. Nov. 9, 1834; d. in California in May,
       1877.
618. Silas Young Allison,⁵ b. Jan. 23, 1837; m. Harriet Moore; d. Dec.,
       1862.
619. ——— Allison,⁵ b. Jan. 23, 1837; d. Feb. 15, 1837.

620. William M. Allison ³ [598] (Thomas,² William ¹).
He was born at Bethany Church, N. C., June 28, 1816. He
owned and lived upon the homestead of his father at
Bethany Church, or Turnersburg, N. C., and was a farmer,
who also carried on the tanning business. He married Elizabeth B. Johnston, and died at Turnersburg, N. C., June 20,
1870.

CHILD.

621. Thomas Johnston Allison,⁴ (636) b., Feb. 2, 1849, at Bethany Church,
       N. C.; res. Statesville, N. C.

622. Robert Washington Allison ³ [601] (William,²
Robert ¹). He was born in Charlotte, Mecklenburgh county,
N. C., April 24, 1809; married, May 31, 1842, Sarah Ann
Phifer of Cabarrus county, N. C.; resided at Concord, N. C.
In 1828, Mr. Allison left Charlotte, N. C., his native place,
and entered the store of his uncle, Joseph Young, in Concord,
N. C., where he ever afterwards lived. He was a farmer and
merchant, and filled public positions of trust and importance.
He was a delegate to the state constitutional convention, a
member of the state legislature, clerk and master of the court
of equity for a number of years, a justice of the peace, and
chairman of the board of county commissioners, which position he held in 1878. Like most of the Allisons he was a
Presbyterian—an elder in that church. His wife was a
daughter of a prominent citizen of Mecklenburgh county. In

a letter dated Dec. 9, 1878, he said: " I have never regretted
my name ; have always been thankful that my lot has been
cast in this country ; that my forefathers emigrated to America, and that they settled in this beautiful country between
the Yadkin and Catawba rivers, where we have good land,
fine water, a healthy and delightful climate, peaceable and
quiet citizens; where we can worship God according to the
dictates of our own consciences, with none to molest or make
us afraid."

CHILDREN.

623.   Esther Phifer Allison,[4] b. 1843; m., in 1866, Capt. Samuel E. White
         of South Carolina.
624.   Joseph Young Allison,[4] b. 1846. He was educated at Davidson col-
         lege, N. C., and at the University of Virginia, and became a
         lawyer ; practised three years, disliked the profession, studied
         for the ministry at Columbia, S. C., graduated in 1876, and
         became a clergyman; in 1887 was pastor of a church in Baton
         Rouge, La. He m. Carrie Davant, of South Carolina, in 1876.
         He was a delegate to the General Assembly of the church at
         Knoxville, Tenn., in 1878.
625.   John Phifer Allison,[4] b. 1848 ; m., 1880, Annie Craige, of Salisbury,
         N. C.; merchant. He succeeded his father in business in Con-
         cord, N. C.
626.   Mary Louise Allison,[4] b. 1850 ; d. 1879.
627.   E. Adaline Allison,[4] b. 1852; m., in 1875, Col. John M. White of
         South Carolina, who d. in 1877.
628.   William Henry Allison,[4] b. 1854 ; d. 1854.
629.   Caroline Jane Allison,[4] b. 1855 ; d. 1857.
630.   Ann Susan Allison,[4] b. 1857; d. 1859.
631.   Robert Washington Allison,[4] b. 1862 ; d. 1865.

632.   James Allison[3] [612] (Thomas,[2] Robert[1]). He was
born April 29, 1823, at Poplar Tent, Cabarrus county, N. C.;
married, Aug. 3, 1847, Mary Clarissa Johnston. He settled
on a farm in Cabarrus county, eleven miles northeast of Concord, N. C. Mrs. Allison and her husband were members of
the Bethpage church. She was fond of Sunday-school work,
and was a teacher of a large class of ladies in that church.
She was a strong-minded and pious woman. She died Jan.
17, 1860, and is buried in the cemetery at Poplar Tent
church. He surrendered with Lee at Appomattox, walked
to his home, and on April 26, 1865, married Mary L. N.
Kilpatrick. She died in June, 1887, and he married, third,
in Aug., 1890, Mary S. Scott, of Taylorsville, N. C. Since
the fall of 1868 he has been a merchant at Davidson College,
N. C., where he resides.

CHILDREN.

633.   Thomas Johnston Allison[4] (643), b. May 30, 1849; clergyman; res.
         at Way Cross, Ga.
634.   —— Allison,[4] b. July 9, 1854; d. July 9, 1854.
635.   Victor Alexander Allison,[4] b. July 14, 1856; d. Dec. 25, 1856.
635a. Minnie Louisa Allison,[4] b. Nov. 17, 1858; d. Oct. 12, 1863.

636. Thomas Johnston Allison[4] [621] (William M.,[3] Thomas,[2] William[1]). He was born at Bethany Church, N. C., some ten miles north of Statesville, Feb. 2, 1849; married, Nov. 23, 1870, Bettie Crawford Chunn, daughter of Matthew Lock and Caroline (Foard) Chunn, and granddaughter of William and Mary (Lock) Chunn, of near China Grove, Rowan county, N. C. Mrs. Allison was born Aug. 31, 1853, near Salisbury, N. C. Mr. Allison was born on the plantation where his great-grandfather settled more than a century ago, and which was owned by his grandfather and his father. The Allisons were the first to acquire land in the opening of the settlement, and the first deeds given in the county were given to Allisons. They were large real estate owners, often buying and rarely selling land. Mr. Allison received a portion of his education at Davidson college, N. C. He was a farmer and tanner, the same as his predecessors. He added the manufacture of harness and saddlery to his business, and dealt in saddlery and hardware till 1884. He has served as county commissioner; was elected sheriff of Iredell county, N. C., in 1884, and held the position till he was appointed by President Cleveland, in 1893, United States marshal for the Western District of North Carolina. Residence, Statesville, N. C.

CHILDREN BORN IN TURNERSBURG, N. C.

637. Carrie Allison,[5] b. Jan. 1, 1874.
638. William Lock Allison,[5] b. March 20, 1876.
639. Edgar Matthews Allison,[5] b. June 5, 1880.
640. Lizzie Allison,[5] b. March 23, 1885.
641. Raymond Allison,[5] b. Sept. 2, 1886.
642. Mary Allison,[5] b. Nov. 20, 1888.

643. Thomas Johnston Allison[4] [633] (James,[3] Thomas,[2] Robert[1]). He was born at the homestead in Cabarrus county, N. C., May 30, 1849, and lived there till his father's removal to Davidson College, N. C., in 1868. He entered Davidson college in 1867, and was graduated in 1871, with the degree of A. B., and received the degree of A. M. in 1874, and in the spring of 1868 united with the Davidson College Presbyterian church. In 1871 he entered the Union Theological seminary at Hampden Sidney, Va., and graduated in 1874; was licensed by the Concord, N. C., presbytery in 1874, and in August accepted a call to the Presbyterian church at Tarboro, N. C. He was ordained and installed on Nov. 8, 1875, preaching once a month at Kingston, and at Rocky Mount. On Sept. 12, 1876, he married Jeannette, daughter of Rev. John Tillett. Resigning his charge in 1877, he preached at Rockingham and Lumberton, N. C. In 1879 he was installed over the church

at Mebaneville, N. C., and continued there eight years. His work there, as at his former parishes, was greatly blessed. Resigning in 1887, his next pastorate was over the Third Creek and Fifth Creek churches, his home being at Elmwood, N. C. He labored there till April, 1891, when he resigned, and is now engaged in evangelistic work in the Savannah (Ga.) presbytery, and resides at Waycross, Ga.

CHILDREN.

644. Minnie Laura Allison.⁵ b. Aug. 3, 1877; d. Feb. 1, 1885.
645. Thomas Tillett Allison,⁵ b. April 26, 1879.
646. James Cumming Allison,⁵ b. April 6, 1881.
647. Charles Walter Allison,⁵ b. Feb. 4, 1883.
648. Wilbur Graham Allison,⁵ b. Oct. 30, 1888.
649. Julius Hartell Allison,⁵ b. Oct. 14, 1890.
650. Henry Johnston Allison,⁵ b. Aug. 11, 1892.

ALLISONS OF NORTH CAROLINA—BRANCH NUMBER TWO.

651. Thomas Allison¹ went south to North Carolina about 1750, from Pennsylvania. He was born April 14, 1722; died May 5, 1794, at Statesville, N. C. He married Magdaline Neil, who was born Aug. 31, 1725. He was of the Allisons of Scotland, his ancestors going to Ireland, and emigrating from Ireland to America.

CHILDREN.

652. Theophilus Allison,² b. Feb. 1, 1748; d. early.
653. Alexander Allison,² b. Nov. 27, 1749; d. May, 1781.
654. Magdaline Allison,² b. Dec. 28, 1751; m. —— Knox, and d. Nov. 27, 1802.
655. Theophilus Allison,² b. May 30, 1754; d. Nov., 1805.
656. Margaret Allison,² b. Aug. 29, 1756; d. Sept. 24, 1779.
657. Thomas Allison² (662), b. Jan. 18, 1759; d. Nov., 1799.
658. Richard Allison² (668), b. Sept. 20, 1761; d. June 14, 1823.
659. Mary Allison,² b. Sept., 1764; m. —— Kerr; d. Aug. 24, 1839.
660. John Allison,² b. Feb., 1767; d. June 26, 1804.
661. Ann Allison,² b. —— ——; m. —— Neill. She d. Feb. 11, 1809.

662. Thomas Allison² [657] (Thomas¹). Ne was born Jan. 18, 1759; married, March 11, 1790, Esther Neill. He died Nov., 1799. Farmer.

CHILDREN, BORN NEAR STATESVILLE, N. C.

663. Roxannah Allison,³ b. May 16, 1791.
664. Magdaline Allison,³ b. Sept. 12, 1792; m., Jan. 13, 1813, James Ramsey. She d. Oct. 13, 1821.
665. Thomas Alexander Allison³ (681), b. Dec. 19, 1794; d. June 8, 1879, at Statesville, N. C.
666. Esther Allison,³ b. Jan. 23, 1797.
667. Margaret Allison,³ b. April 12, 1799.

668. Richard Allison[2] [658] (Thomas[1]). He was born Feb. 20, 1761; died June 14, 1823. He married, July 24, 1785, Lettice Neill, born Feb. 9, 1766; died Oct. 13, 1824.

CHILDREN.

669. Thomas Allison,[3] b. Jan. 1, 1787; d. Sept. 13, 1830.
670. Roxannah Allison,[3] b. Aug. 23, 1788; m. —— Matthews. She d. Dec. 29, 1844.
671. Andrew Neill Allison,[3] b. July 23, 1790; d. Jan. 28, 1867.
672. Magdaline Simonton Allison,[3] b. Dec. 24, 1792; d. Dec. 29, 1858.
673. Margaret Allison,[3] b. Dec. 18, 1794; d. April 9, 1795.
674. Lettice Allison,[3] b. Jan. 19, 1790; m. —— ——; d. Oct. 18, 1877.
675. Margaret Allison,[3] b. Jan. 6, 1798.
676. Richard Allison,[3] b. March 25, 1800; d. Jan. 20, 1832.
677. Sarah Adaline Allison,[3] b. April 10, 1802; d. June 29, 1829.
678. John Allison,[3] b. Aug. 16, 1804.
679. Jenny Lucinda Allison,[3] b. Nov. 13, 1806.
680. Mary Allison,[3] b. May 25, 1809; m. —— Davis. Her child, Elnathan Hayne Davis,[4] b. Nov. 25, 1833. Mrs. Davis d. Jan. 14, 1838.

681. Thomas Alexander Allison[3] [665] (Thomas,[2] Thomas[1]). He was born Dec. 19, 1794; died Feb. 24, 1854. He married, Sept. 19, 1816, Lettice, daughter of Richard Allison, and his own cousin. She was born June 19, 1796; died June 8, 1879, at Statesville, N. C. Before the war he was one of the largest land owners and farmers in Iredell county. For a number of years he was a member of the state legislature, an elder in the Presbyterian church, and noted for his piety and strong character.

CHILDREN.

682. Evaline Allison,[4] b. July 26, 1817; m., Nov. 12, 1833, Miles M. Bailey. She d. July 17, 1852.
683. Esther Selina Allison,[4] b. May 25, 1819; m. Rev. Thaddeus C. Crawford. Sept. 1, 1847, and d. May 23, 1848. No children.
684. Richard Monroe Allison[4] (691), b. April 22, 1821; m., Oct. 27, 1842, Elizabeth C, Hampton; res. Statesville, N. C.
685. Letitia Allison,[4] m. Dr. Richard Carson.
686. Margaret Adaline Allison,[4] b. Oct. 29, 1826; m., Sept. 1, 1848, Augustus C. Houston, and d. Aug. 13, 1850. He d. Feb. 20, 1850. One son, John Augustus Houston,[5] b. June 11, 1848.
687. John Andrew Allison,[4] b. July 26, 1828; d. Sept. 13, 1830.
688. Andrew John Amos Allison[4] (699), b. Oct. 10, 1830; physician; res. Mississippi; m. Mary Locke; m., second, Laura Matthews.
689. Roxannah Allison,[4] b. Aug. 4, 1833; d. Aug. 11, 1833.
690. Joseph Cornelius Allison,[4] b. Sept. 28, 1834; d. Dec. 15, 1836.
690a. Thomas Alexander Allison, Jr. He was killed by a falling tree.

691. Richard Monroe Allison[4] [684] (Thomas Alexander,[3] Thomas,[2] Thomas[1]). He was born April 22, 1821, in Iredell county, N. C. Married, Oct. 27, 1852, Elizabeth Carmichael Hampton, born Jan. 14, 1835, at Cedar Hill, near Jonesville, Yadkin county, N. C., and daughter of Henry Gray and Charlotte Temple (Doby) Hampton, of Cedar Hill. Her

father was son of Thomas, and grandson of Henry Hampton. Mr. Allison was educated at the state university at Chapel Hill, N. C., studied law under Chief Justice Pearson, and was admitted to the bar in Jan., 1852. He was a practicing lawyer, county attorney for Iredell county, and died, after a brief illness, at Statesville, N. C., April 30, 1884. He was cast in a heroic mould, a man of most positive convictions, and was never false to friend or client, and no one was more unswerving in adherence to principle. He was buried with Masonic honors.

CHILDREN, BORN AT STATESVILLE, N. C.

692.   Thomas Hampton Allison,⁵ b. Sept. 4, 1854; m., Nov. 30, 1881, Nannie Gaines; tobacco manufacturer; res. Mooresville, N. C.
693.   Andrew John Allison,⁵ b. June 16, 1856; m. Colie Baggette; farmer; res. Era, Ark.
694.   Letitia Evaline Allison,⁵ b. Dec. 11, 1858; m., Sept. 12, 1882, David Francis Stevenson; res. Statesville, N. C.
695.   Richard Monroe Allison,⁵ b. July 8, 1861; d. Sept. 15, 1861.
696.   Wade Hampton Allison,⁵ b. July 3, 1865; merchant; res. Statesville, N. C.
697.   Mary Selina Allison,⁵ b. Dec. 7, 1867; m., Oct. 12, 1889, John B. Gill; res. Statesville, N. C.
698.   Richard Preston Allison,⁵ b. June 24, 1870; res. Statesville, N. C.

699.   Andrew John Amos Allison⁴ [688] (Thomas Alexander,³ Thomas,² Thomas¹). He was born Oct. 10, 1830. Married, Oct. 21, 1856, Mary E. Locke, of Alabama; she died Feb. 12, 1863. He married second, in Tuscaloosa, Ala., Laura Matthews, Dec. 14, 1865, who died about 1880. He entered Davidson college, N. C., in 1851, graduated in 1854; received the degree of M. D. from Jefferson Medical college, in Philadelphia; was a physician in Lowndes county, Miss., till 1861, when he returned to Philadelphia and took a special course in surgery. During the war he practiced at home, and in the hospitals in Virginia. In 1864 he opened a hospital for the sick and wounded soldiers at Statesville. Residence, Statesville, N. C.

CHILDREN, BORN IN NORTH CAROLINA.

700.   Margaret Torrence Allison,⁵ b. April 20, 1867; m. Walter H. Torrence, who died in May, 1891; physician; res. Statesville, N. C.
701.   John Matthew Allison,⁵ b. May 20, 1869.
702.   Robert Hugh Allison,⁵ b. March 11, 1871.
703.   Mary Allison,⁵ b. Sept. 4, 1873.
704.   Charles Allison,⁵ b. 1874.

Andrew John Allison   Richard Preston Allison   Thomas Hampton Allison

Mary Selina Allison   Evalina Allison Stevenson

Wade Hampton Allison   Elizabeth Carmichael Allison   Richard Monroe Allison

ALLISONS OF NORTH CAROLINA. BRANCH NUMBER THREE.

The emigrant ancestor of this family, of Scotch blood, Christian name not known, came from the north of Ireland and settled in Pennsylvania or Maryland. His son,

705. William Allison,[2] according to my information, was born in Maryland, lived in Wilkes county, N. C., where he raised a large family, which remained there till each member arrived to mature age, and soon after that period became scattered. He was a Revolutionary soldier.

CHILDREN BORN IN WILKES COUNTY, N. C.

706. Ephraim Allison,[2] (713) m. Elizabeth Coffee; d., 1845, in Cooper Co., Mo.
707. Hugh Allison[2] (721). He was b. Feb. 11, 1771; res. Cooper Co., Mo.
708. Benjamin Allison,[2] rem. to Miller Co., Mo.
709. Samuel Allison.[2]
710. Daniel Allison.[2]
711. William Allison.[2]
712. Thomas Allison,[2] rem. to Cooper Co., Mo.
712a. —— Allison,[2] his dau. m. Mr. Petty.
712b. —— Allison,[2] his dau. m. Mr. Perkins; had 18 children and their descendants are numerous in Central Illinois.

713. Ephraim Allison [3] [706] (William,[2] —— Allison [1]). He was born in Wilkes county, N. C.; married Elizabeth Coffee. Upon arriving at manhood he removed to a spot near Booneville, Cooper county, Mo., where he spent his life, and died about March, 1845. His first halting place in Missouri (to which he and his two brothers removed in 1815), was at New Franklin, Howard county.

CHILDREN.

714. Thomas Allison,[4] (727) b. Oct. 24, 1800; d. Feb., 1845, in Saline Co., Mo.
715. Lucy Allison,[4] b. —; m. Vincent Johnson. They are deceased.
Child:
I. Elizabeth Johnson,[5] m. Mr. Kirkpatrick; res. Butler, Mo.
716. Nancy Allison,[4] m. James Harvey; res. Sedalia, Mo.
717. Rebecca Allison,[4] m. Thomas Jones. They are deceased.
718. Elizabeth Allison,[4] m. John Chambers. They are deceased. Joseph Chambers,[6] Booneville, Mo., is a grandson. Frank Chambers,[7] county clerk, Booneville, Mo., is a great grandson. William H. Allison,[6] of Clinton, Henry Co., Mo., is a grandson.
719. Matilda Allison,[4] m. Thomas L. Johnson, and both are dead.
720. William Allison,[4] d., unmarried, of yellow fever at New Orleans, La.

721. Hugh Allison [3] [707] (William,[2] —— Allison [1]). He was born near Jacksboro', Wilkes county, North Carolina, Feb. 11, 1771 ; resided at Ft. Boonesborough, Madison county,

Ky., after 1797, and lived in Cooper county, Mo., after March, 1821, where he died April 25, 1846. He married, Nov. 5, 1788, Rebecca Sanders Hartt. Hugh Allison was a fair business man. Was elected coroner of Cooper county, Mo., August, 1824, and again in 1828, serving eight years in all. As a military man he served three years in Colonel Whitley's regiment of volunteers in 1812-'13-'14, and was in Harrison's army, was at the battle of Lundy's Lane. After his discharge he was commissioned a captain in the Kentucky militia. He always declared that he would gladly have fought three years longer rather than to have let Great Britain have one foot of ground in America. He was a fiery patriot and was ever ready to serve his country. He was a believer in a sound national currency that was worth one hundred cents on a dollar anywhere on earth. In 1840, by appointment, he met and spent a short time with Gen. W. H. Harrison, the Whig candidate for president, at Vincennes, Indiana. On July 4, 1840, he was present at the grand Whig rally at Rochefort, Mo., it being one of the largest political gatherings ever held in the state. There are said to have been 17 steamboats loaded with people who came to attend. Mr. Allison was a great friend and admirer of President Harrison, and was greatly overcome when the news reached him in 1841 of the death of his old commander. He was a farmer, and a dealer in fat cattle and hogs. Was a Baptist. Was an uncompromising Whig. He took an active part in the election of General Harrison to the presidency in 1840. He favored the extension of the charter of the U. S. bank; he also favored a protective tariff.

CHILDREN.

721a. Rebecca Allison,[4] b. about 1791; m. James Pearce, and after the close of the war of 1812-'15, they settled in Illinois, and some of this family lived in Alhambra, Madison county, Ill.

722. Jesse Allison,[4] b. Sept. 29, 1791; m. Mary Snodgrass, in 1809; served in the U. S. army in 1812-'13-'14. Went to Illinois in 1821, Co. Madison; rem. to Cooper Co., Mo., in 1840, and later to Arrow Rock, Saline Co., in fall of 1859, and d. there about March 1, 1860. James Allison, Yuba Dam, Yuba Co., Cal., and Dr. John L. Allison, Poplar Bluff, Butler Co., Mo., are of that branch of the family.

723. Lucinda Allison,[4] is deceased; she was b. Feb. 6, 1793.

724. Thomas Allison,[4] b. in North Carolina, Sept. 4, 1795. Res. Wilkes Co., N. C., Madison Co., Ky., and in St. Charles Co., Cooper Co., Pettis Co., and Lawrence Co., Mo. He enlisted in the militia against the rebels in 1863, being over 66 years of age, and was killed near Mount Vernon, in Lawrence Co., Mo., about May, 1863. He m. Roxanna Snyder in 1816. He m. second, Nancy Orr, in 1856. Children: Nathaniel T. Allllison,[5] Greene P. Allison,[5] Martin S. Allison,[5] Hugh Allison,[5] Elizabeth

Allison,⁵ Rebecca Allison⁵, Lucinda Allison⁵, John L. Allison⁵ (was a soldier in the state militia during the war), Thomas F. Allison,⁵ Frances Allison,⁵ Mary Allison,⁵ Louisa Allison,⁵ Henry C. Allison⁵, Roxanna Allison⁵, who m. Frank Payne, Hughesville, Mo. Mrs. Absalom McVey was of this family; res. Sedalia, Mo. —— Allison,⁵ his dau., m. James Lapsley; res. Diamond Grove, Newton Co., Mo. Monroe Allison,⁶ grandson of Thomas Allison,⁴ lives in Silverton, Colorado.

725. Nathaniel Thompson Allison,⁴ (735) b. Ft. Boonesborough, Madison Co., Ky., April 29, 1798; m. Ruth Goodrich, and d. March 18, 1877.

726. John L. Allison,⁴ b. in North Carolina, Aug. 22, 1801. He lived in Wilkes Co., N. C., Madison Co., Ky., St. Charles Co. and Cooper Co., Mo. Farmer. He d. about 1844. Children:
I. Shelton R. Allison,⁵ went to Richmond, Ft. Bend Co., Texas, about 1859.
II. Lucinda Allison⁵ removed to Richmond, Ft. Bend Co., Texas, about 1859.

727. Thomas Allison⁴ [714] (Ephraim,³ William,² —— Allison¹). He was born in North Carolina Oct. 24, 1800, and emigrated with his parents to Missouri when fifteen years of age. He married Lydia Jones; resided in Henry county, Mo., and died in Saline county, in Feb., 1865.

CHILDREN.

728. Josephine Allison,⁵ m. William Claycomb, and lives at Herndon, Saline Co., Mo.
729. Selinda Allison,⁵ m. William Adkisson, and died at Warrensburg, Mo., in 1885.
730. Alfred J. Allison,⁵ lives near Marshall, Saline Co., Mo.
731. Sarah Allison,⁵ m. Thomas Dysart, and lives in Granbury, Hood Co., Texas.
732. Ephraim Allison,⁵ b. Saline Co., Mo., Nov. 27, 1835; m. May 28, 1868, Ruth. dau. of Edward Cresop and Mary E. (Brown) McCarty of Virginia. She was b. in Saline Co., Mo., April 7, 1842. She was granddaughter of P. and Ruth (Cresop) McCarty, and great granddaughter of Edward and Ann (Miller) McCarty, of Virginia. Mr. Allison is a merchant, and res. Clinton, Mo. Children b. Clinton, Mo.:
I. Charles S. Allison,⁶ b. May 15, 1869.
II. Thomas E. Allison,⁶ b. May 8, 1871; d. Sept. 6, 1872.
III. Mary L. Allison,⁶ b. July 6, 1873.
IV. William B. Allison,⁶ b. July 18, 1875; d. Sept. 12, 1876.
V. Anna M. Allison,⁶ b. Feb. 7, 1877.
VI. Nellie B. Allison,⁶ b. Aug. 3, 1878.
733. Matilda Allison,⁵ m. Thomas Ferry; and d. about 1882, in Clinton, Mo.
734. William H. Allison,⁵ res. Clinton, Mo.

735. Nathaniel Thompson Allison⁴ [724] (Hugh,³ William,² —— Allison¹). He was born in Fort Boonesborough, Madison county, Ky., April 29, 1798. Married, May 19, 1822, Ruth Goodrich, who was born in St. Charles county, Mo., Feb. 6, 1806, and was daughter of Elijah (or Elisha) Goodrich, a liberally educated man, and a native of Hartford, Conn. Mr. Allison had a good education; was a farmer and stock

raiser, and at the commencement of the war was in good circumstances. He resided in Cooper county, Mo., and was a justice of the peace; assessor in Cooper county in 1858. He had a fine memory, and was a good conversationalist. He was a Whig, then a Republican in politics, and a Baptist in his religious faith. He lived a blameless life. He was a staunch Unionist during the war. He kept open house for his neighbors and strangers for fifty-five years. He was a great hunter, and could use his rifle almost to perfection. He was six feet two and one half inches in height and weighed 185 pounds. He died March 18, 1877, at his son's in Pilot Grove, Mo.

CHILDREN.

735a. Ann Eliza Allison,⁶ b. Dec. 27, 1823; d. April 30, 1844.
735b. Elizabeth Allison,⁶ b. Dec. 23, 1825; d. Dec. 21, 1838.
735c. Mary Ann Allison,⁶ born Jan. 7, 1828; m., July 8, 1847, Lewis Feck Evans, and d. Oct. 8, 1851. He was b. in Baltimore, Md., Dec. 25, 1823. He was a farmer in Saline Co., Mo., and d. March 13, 1876. Child:
1. Eliza Evans,⁷ b. Aug. 20, 1849; m. James Thornton; res. Arrow Rock, Saline Co., Mo.
735d. Hugh Allison,⁶ b. July 25, 1829; d. Sept. 12, 1829.
735e. Lucinda Allison,⁶ b. Sept. 7, 1830; d. Aug. 21, 1839.
735f. Margaret Allison,⁶ b. Sept. 23, 1833; m., Nov. 18, 1855, William G. Hindman; b. Oct. 8, 1828; farmer; res. Napton, Saline Co., Mo. Children:
I. Nathaniel Thomas Hindman,⁷ b. Jan. 24, 1857; d. April 14, 1863.
II. Ruth Goodrich Hindman,⁷ b. Feb. 21, 1868.
III. William Rea Hindman⁷, b. Oct. 22, 1872.
735g. Paulina Allison,⁶ b. Oct. 27, 1835; m. Jan. 19, 1858, James M. Morton; b. in Madison Co., Ky., April 26, 1835; res. Iconium, St. Clair Co., Mo.; farmer. Children:
I. William Henry Morton,⁷ b. May 28, 1859; d. Aug. 9, 1878.
II. James Quinn Morton,⁷ b. Sept. 18, 1861; m., June 22, 1885, Elizabeth Riddle.
III. Mattie Morton⁷, b. July 26, 1868; m., July 26, 1891, Harrison Grant Nida.
735h. Nancy Jane Allison,⁶ b. March 19, 1838; m., Sept. 17, 1857, Thomas J. Morton. He was born March 30, 1834; d. in Alton, Ill., Dec., 1864. She m., second, May 17, 1868, William F. Foreman. She d. Feb. 22, 1874. Thomas Jefferson Morton's children, b. Cooper Co., Mo.:
I. Marietta Margaret Morton,⁷ b. Oct. 4, 1859; m.,Nov., 1878, Robert Baise.
II. Matilda Maud Morton,⁷ b. Oct. 13, 1861; m., Oct. 27, 1878, Joseph Crawford.
III. Mary Madora Morton⁷, b. Dec. 24, 1862; m., Oct. 3, 1887, Joseph Tuttle; res. Booneville, Mo.
IV. Nannie Thomas Morton,⁷ b. Jan. 8, 1865; m., May 5, 1884, James Campbell. She d. Aug. 10, 1886.
735i. Matilda Caroline Allison,⁶ b. April 4, 1840; m., Nov. 10, 1870, Andrew J. Howard; res. Iconium, St. Clair Co., Mo. Children:
I. Florence Mary Howard,⁷ b. Aug. 23, 1871; m., March 13, 1890, Martin Harvey.
II. Alice May Howard,⁷ b. Jan. 25, 1874.
III. —— Howard⁷, b. Aug. 1, 1877; d. Aug. 1, 1877.
IV. John Allison Howard,⁷ b. Oct. 5, 1878.

Ruth R. Allison.   Hugh N. Allison.   Fletcher J. Allison.

735j.   William Henry Harrison Allison,⁶ b. Nov. 18, 1842, in Cooper
county, Mo.; m., April 13, 1873, Mae Amanda Williams,
daughter of Samuel K. Williams, of Fairfield county, Ohio,
and McDonald county, Mo., who died Feb., 1886. She was
born Aug. 2, 1852, in Lancaster, Fairfield county, Ohio. Mr.
Allison was educated in the common schools and two years in
an academy. Was a teacher, then a lawyer. He was assistant
United States marshal for taking the ninth census in the north
half of Cooper county, Mo. He was deputy assessor and deputy collector in the same county in 1868-'69. Justice of the
peace for four years, and in Nov., 1870, was elected superintendent of registration of voters for Cooper county on the Republican ticket, but did not qualify. He went to Neosho,
Newton county, Mo., in Aug., 1871, and practised law. Went
to Colorado in 1876, and engaged in business, as the state of
his health demanded active life. He removed to New Mexico
in 1879, which is now his home, and is in business. He served
in the home guard, in Col. Parker's regiment, in the fall of
1864, at Sedalia, Mo., and thinks that "treason should be
made odious." He voted for Lincoln in 1864. He is a Republican in politics, a Methodist in religion. Has served as superintendent of Sabbath school, and class leader. Residence,
Albuquerque, New Mexico. Children:

735k. Hugh Nathaniel Allison,⁷ b. Feb. 21, 1874. He is a steam
engineer.

736. Nannie Kate Allison,⁷ b. July 4, 1876; d. Oct. 12, 1876.

737. Fletcher James Allison,⁷ b. March 20, 1878. In school.

738. Ruth Goodrich Allison,⁷ b. June 7, 1880. In school.

739. Seldon Coke Allison,⁷ b. Jan. 20, 1882; d. June 29, 1884.

740. Nathaniel Thompson Allison,⁶ b. Cooper county, Mo., Jan. 24, 1846.
Printer and teacher. He served a year in the 28th Regiment
Illinois Volunteers in the late war. He enlisted March 13,
1865; was discharged March 13, 1866. He has the degrees of
A. B. and A. M. He is one of the publishers of the Columbus Star-Courier. Resides Columbus, Kansas. Is a Democrat in politics. He married, November, 1868, Nannie, daugh-
·ter of Guinn and Artamasia (Ellison) Morton. Her father was
a native of Kentucky. She was born in Cooper county, Mo.,
May 16, 1848; died in Bolivar, Mo., Nov. 20, 1879. He married,
second, Mrs. Nannette (Martin) Cook, daughter of James Martin, a native of Poughkeepsie, N. Y., a resident of St. Louis,
Mo., and his wife, Anna Mayfield (Waton) Martin. Mrs. Allison was born in Cole county, Mo., Oct. 2, 1845. Resided in
Clinton, Mo., and now in Columbus, Kan. Children:

CHILDREN.

741. Lou Ella Allison,⁷ b. April 13, 1870; d. May 25, 1872.

742. Olive Allison,⁷ b. Feb. 20. 1874.

743. Ruth Allison,⁷ b. May 8, 1876; d. June 12, 1878.

744. Hortense Allison,⁷ b. Bolivar, Mo., Nov. 10, 1879.

745. Harriet Ann Allison,⁶ b. Oct. 18, 1848; m., May 31, 1868, George
Rothwell Potter, b. July 30, 1846. Res. Blackwater, Cooper
Co., Mo. Children:

I.   William Allison Potter,⁷ b. March 3, 1869; m., Oct. 5, 1890, Mary Ann
Jones.

II.   Webster Greene Potter,⁷ b. Dec. 5, 1870; d. Oct. 14, 1871.

III. Edward Louis Potter,⁷ b. Sept. 10, 1874; d. April 27, 1875.

IV.   Eva Leona Potter,⁷ b. Dec. 28, 1876.

ALLISONS OF GLASGOW, SCOTLAND, NORTH CAROLINA AND VIRGINIA—FOURTH BRANCH.

746. David Allison[1] of Glasgow, Scotland, said to be a brother of the noted William Allison of that city, emigrated to Ashe county, North Carolina His wife was Nancy Black. He was a farmer and stock raiser; a member of the Masonic order. Their son,

747. Samuel Allison,[2] born in Glasgow, Scotland, married Rebecca Scott; lived and died in Ashe county, North Carolina; was a farmer and stock raiser. His death was a tragic one—an insane man stole into his room in the dead of night and cut his head off with a corn cutter. His son,

748. Robert Allison,[3] removed to Broad Ford, Smythe county, Va., where he lived in 1892. He married, in 1847, Anna Mary Reedy, daughter of Samuel and Susan Reedy, of Grayson county, Virginia. He purchased a farm of 300 acres, and raised a family of eight sons and a daughter. Mr. Allison has held many public offices, and was collector of internal revenue for the second district of Virginia, in 1892.

CHILD.

749. William Jefferson Allison,[4] b. Sept. 22, 1848; m., April 5, 1868, Jane Hill of Ashe Co., N. C.; removed to Ohio in 1871; became a student of medicine; graduated in 1876 from the school of physicians and surgeons in Cincinnati, and successfully practised his profession. Mrs. Allison died in 1881. Mr. Allison is a member of the "Church of Christ, or Disciples." He became a minister, traveled over fourteen states and one territory, preaching the gospel, and received many into the church. In 1887 he married, near Marion, Va., Susan Messer, and in Oct., 1890, settled in or near Heber, Cleburne, Co., Ark., and resided there in 1892—a practising physician and preacher. His express office is Searcy, White Co., Ark. Children:

750. Arley Spencer Allison.[5]
751. Christopher Columbus Allison.[5]
752. John Fielden Allison,[5] m. Jane Bastie near Charleston, W. Va.; and has six children; farmer; res. Charleston, Kanawha Co., W. Va.
753. David Jesse Allison,[5] teacher of music; m. Lizzie Brown, of Chillicothe, O.; he is in the mercantile business at Greenfield, Ohio.
754. James Noah Allison[5]; m. Susan, dau. of Maxie Goffe, Knawha Co., W. Va; farmer; res. Charleston, W. Va.
755. Zilpha Catherine Allison,[5] m. Rev. Millard Fillmore Marsh, son of William Marsh, attorney, Wythe Co., Va., a Methodist clergyman; res. Blaine, Marshall Co., Kan.
756. Samuel Frederick Allison,[5] spent several years as teacher of vocal and instrumental music; m. Miss Harmon, and is now a farmer in the fine blue-grass region of Baptist Valley, Tazewell Co., Va.; has held several public offices.
757. Thomas Madison Allison,[5] farmer; res. on the home farm at Broad Ford, Va.; single.

758. Addison Alexander Allison,[6] m. Joanna Wilkinson, of Charleston, W. Va. He is a machinist in railroad employ; res. Charleston, W. Va.
759. Robert Franklin Allison[6] is principal of a business college at Waverly, O., and Point Pleasant, W. Va.; res. Jackson Court House, W. Va.

ALLISONS OF NORTH CAROLINA—FIFTH BRANCH.

760. Andrew Allison[1] had a son,
761. Theophilus Allison[2] who was born in 1747; settled in Iredell county, N. C. There is a tradition that he was born in Scotland, that he first settled in Pennsylvania, lived for a time in Georgia, and then made North Carolina his home. He married Sarah Simonton, and died Oct. 5, 1815.

CHILDREN.

762. Thomas Jefferson Allison[3] (765), b. Oct. 25, 1801; d. Jan. 28, 1839; res. in North Carolina.
763. Robert Allison,[3] b. in Georgia; is deceased. His son,
I. 764. John A. Allison, res. Granite Hill, N. C.

765. Thomas Jefferson Allison[3] [762] (Theophilus,[2] Andrew[1]). He was born in North Carolina, Oct. 25, 1801; resided at Troutman's, Iredell county, N. C. He was prominent in his locality, was a member of the Associate Reformed Presbyterian church, and was an elder in one of the oldest churches in that section of North Carolina. He married Jane, daughter of William and Ann (Allison) Neill, of Lincoln county, N. C. Her grandfather was Andrew Neill, of Rowan county, N. C. Mrs. Allison was born Oct. 17, 1808; died June 9, 1860. He died Jan. 28, 1839.

CHILDREN.

766. Theophilus Washington Allison,[4] b. Nov. 6, 1827; res. Salisbury, N. C.
767. William Lafayette Allison,[4] b. June 8, 1826; m., July 25, 1861, Asenath Cavin, and is still living; res. Troutman's, N. C. Children:
I. John Washington Allison,[5] b. June 3, 1868; m. Laura Cornelia Sherrill, Dec. 22, 1889. She was b. March 12, 1865.
II. Thomas Young Allison,[5] b. Feb. 3, 1867.
III. William Elmore Allison,[5] b. Jan. 12, 1868; res. Leesburg, Fla.
IV. Jennie Cordelia Allison,[5] b. Aug. 1, 1869.
768. Andrew Neill Allison,[4] b. May 11, 1829; m., Aug. 21, 1861, Jane Elizabeth White; res. Iredell Co., N. C.
769. Richard Allison[4]; is deceased.
770. Thomas Jefferson Allison[4]; is deceased.
771. Julia Ann Allison,[4] b. May 31, 1833; d. of consumption, June 5, 1861. She and her sister were devoted Christians, and noted for their kindness and philanthropic principles.
772. Sarah Keziah Allison,[4] b. Oct. 4, 1838; d. Oct. 16, 1858.

778. Andrew Neill Allison [4] [768] (Thomas Jefferson,[3] Theophilus,[2] Andrew[1]). He was born May 11, 1829; married, Aug. 21, 1861, his cousin, Elizabeth White. His parents were wealthy, and his early life passed in ease and luxury. He attended the public school, but the educational facilities in the south were very limited, and received so little approbation that his education was quite limited. The war freed the slaves belonging to the family, so that when it closed he was compelled to work on the farm; but work did not go as hard with him as with many, and he became a successful and prominent farmer. He still lives on the Allison homestead. He is prominent in county politics; an elder in the Associate Reformed Presbyterian church; a man of good judgment and spotless character; residence, Troutman's, Iredell county, N. C.

CHILDREN.

774. Thomas Calvin Allison,[5] b. June 9, 1862; d. June 12, 1863.
775. Maggie Ann Allison,[5] b. April 23, 1864; d. Jan. 29, 1887.
776. Sarah Jane Allison,[5] b. Oct. 19, 1865; d. May 29, 1871.
777. Mary Etta Allison,[5] b. April 19, 1867; d. in infancy.
778. James White Allison,[5] b. Dec. 11, 1868; railroad employé.
779. William Theophilus Allison,[5] b. Sept. 25, 1870; student.
780. Julia Bell Allison,[5] b. Aug. 7, 1872; d. Nov. 4, 1874.
781. Elver Lorannah Allison,[5] b. April 14, 1874; student.
782. Frances Cremiler Allison,[5] b. Sept. 4, 1876; student.
783. Andrew Neill Allison,[5] b. Oct. 26, 1878; d. Oct. 15, 1879.

CHAPTER VIII.

ALLISONS OF VIRGINIA, KENTUCKY, TENNESSEE, AND LOUISIANA
—ALLISONS OF LIFFORD, COUNTY DONEGAL, IRELAND, AND TEN-
NESSEE, U. S.

784. Robert Allison.[1] He was born about 1730, and was
was living in Iredell county, N. C., in 1757. In the year
1781 he removed to the eastern part of Washington county,
Va., one and one half miles from Glade Spring. There he
reared three sons and two daughters. About 1811 he and
his two sons, Robert and James Allison, removed to Logan
county, Ky., leaving his son William and his two daughters
in Washington county, Va. He resided in Logan county,
Ky., the last of his life, and died there.

CHILDREN.

785. William Allison[2] (790), b. in Iredell Co., N. C., in 1757; d., 1818, in
Washington Co., Va.

786. Robert Allison,[2] res. in Logan Co., Ky.

787. Mary Allison,[2] m. William Beattie, of Washington Co., Va. They
reared a large family, and many of them located in the great
West.

788. Elizabeth Allison,[2] m. Ezra Hayter in Washington Co., Va. They
reared a large family, and their descendants are mostly in the
West.

789. James Allison,[2] res. in Logan Co., Ky.

790. William Allison[2] [785] (Robert[1]). He was born
in 1757, in Iredell county, N. C.; resided in Washington
county, Va., where he died in 1818, having emigrated to Virginia with his father in 1781. He married Susannah Hayter,
born in Washington county, Va., and died there in 1835.

CHILDREN.

791. William Beattie Allison[3] (799), b. March, 1800, in Washington Co.,
Va., where he d., 1849.

792. Elizabeth Allison,[3] m. William Hayter b. Washington Co., Va.;
they removed to Tennessee, and later to Missouri. They are
deceased.

793. Robert Allison,[3] d. in Washington county, Va., when comparatively
young; his family moved to Missouri, in 1839. His wife's
name was Lucy Scott, of Washington Co., Va.

794. Josiah Allison.[3] He never married; lived in Washington Co., Va.,
and d. when an old man.

795. Hiram Allison,[3] m. Ellen Thomas. They had one daughter who is
deceased.

11

796. James Allison,[3] m. Sarah Williams, removed to south-west Missouri,
        and reared a family.
797. Abram Hayter Allison,[3] m. Susie Meek, of Washington Co., Va.,
        reared a large family, and in 1844 removed to north-west Mis-
        souri. They are deceased.
798. Israel Allison,[3] d. unmarried.

799. William Beattie Allison[3] [791] (William,[2] Robert[1]).
He was born in Washington county, Va., March, 1800; re-
sided Washington county, Va., where he died May 7, 1849.
He married, March, 1827, Mary, daughter of Robert and
Martha (Harvey) Clarke, of Argyleshire, Scotland. Her
parents died in Washington county, Va. She was born in
Argyleshire, and died in Washington county, Va., Nov. 23,
1863. He was a farmer and dealer in live stock.

CHILDREN.

800. Robert Clark Allison[4] (805), b. Washington Co., Va., Feb. 23, 1828;
        res. Glade Spring, Washington Co., Va.
801. William White Allison[4] (812), b. Dec. 14, 1829, in Washington Co.,
        Va.; res. Washington Co., Va.
802. Martha Harvey Allison,[4] b. July 3, 1834; m., Dec., 1858, Benjamin
        D. Ligon; res. Glade Spring, Washington Co., Va. No children.
803. Samuel Duane Allison[4] (820), b. Jan. 6, 1839, in Washington Co.,
        Va.; res. Glade Spring, Va.
804. John Beattie Allison[4] (824), b. June 6, 1841; d. Jan. 21, 1879.

805. Robert Clark Allison [4] [800] (William Beattie,[3] William,[2] Robert[1]). He resides at Glade Spring, Washington
county, Virginia. He was born, Feb. 23, 1828, in Washington county, Virginia. He was educated, but did not graduate, at Emory and Henry college, and is a surveyor and
teacher. Has served as county supervisor. He married,
Aug. 29, 1867, Rebecca Jane Clark, daughter of Andrew
Jackson and Margaret (Rains) Clark, of Wythe county, Va.
She was born June 18, 1844.

CHILDREN BORN WASHINGTON COUNTY, VA.

806. Mollie Clark Allison,[5] b. July 23, 1868; m., March 27, 1889, George
        W. Gilliam.
807. Rose Stribling Allison,[5] b. Jan. 28, 1870.
808. Robert Hamilton Allison,[5] b. Aug. 8, 1871.
809. Jennie Kate Allison,[5] b. Feb. 21, 1873.
810. William Andrew Allison,[5] b. Nov. 16, 1875.
811. Freddie Allison,[5] b. July 4, 1882.

812. William White Allison [4] [801] (William-Beattie,[3]
William,[2] Robert[1]). He was born in Washington county,
Va., Dec. 14, 1829, and still lives there; farmer. He married, Feb., 1867, Mary Jane Ayres, daughter of John Preston
and Mary (Whitaker) Ayres, of Washington county, Va.

She was born in Saltville, Smythe county, Va., March 11, 1845. Residence, Glade Spring, Va.

CHILDREN BORN WASHINGTON COUNTY, VA.

813. William Beattie Allison,⁵ b. Nov. 30, 1867.
814. Mary Rachel Allison,⁵ b. Feb. 13, 1871. She graduated at Sullins's
      college, June, 1891, and is now a teacher of music in Wartburg
      Female seminary, at Graham, Va.
815. Martha Harvey Allison,⁵ b. Feb. 4, 1874; she is a student at Sullin's
      college.
816. Bettie Ayres Allison,⁵ b. Jan. 12, 1876.
817. Lavinia Allison,⁵ b. Oct. 23, 1877.
818. Susanna Virginia Allison,⁵ b. Dec. 31, 1880.
819. Janie Jacques Allison,⁵ b. Aug. 20, 1884.

820. Samuel Dunn Allison⁴ [803] (William-Beattie,³ William,² Robert¹). He was born in Washington county, Va., Jan. 6, 1839. Resides at Glade Spring, Washington county, Va. He is a farmer and trader. He married, Jan., 1861, Susan Cate Stevens, born Aug. 22, 1839, daughter of Thomas Hity and Jane (Wade) Stevens.

CHILDREN BORN AT GLADE SPRING, WASHINGTON COUNTY, VA.

821. Charles Edward Allison,⁵ b. Aug. 18, 1865.
822. Benjamin Curtis Allison,⁵ b. Feb. 23, 1868.
823. Martha Wilmouth Allison,⁵ b. July 19, 1871.

824. John Beattie Allison⁴ [804] (William-Beattie,³ William,² Robert¹). He was born, June 6, 1841, in Washington county, Va. He was a farmer and trader, and died Jan. 21, 1879. He married, 1865, Sarah Ellen Wright, daughter of James Edward and Sarah Mariah (Thompson) Wright. She was born Dec. 31, 1841. Resides at Glade Spring, Va.

CHILDREN.

825. Abraham Greenfield Allison,⁵ b. Feb. 26, 1867; m., Nov., 1887,
      Mattie Lee Taylor.
826. Lelia Blanche Allison,⁵ b. Oct. 20, 1869; m., March 25, 1885, Roland
      P. Johnson. He is a railroad conductor.
827. Nellie Grant Allison,⁵ b. Dec. 13, 1872.
828. James Clinton Allison,⁵ b. Jan. 15, 1874.
829. Gordon Hampton Allison,⁵ b. Oct. 26, 1876.

ALLISONS OF VIRGINIA.

830. James Allison,¹ born, 1770, in Wythe county, Va.; residence in the east end of that county. He married Jane Craig, born in 1779, who died in 1840. He died in 1845.
831. Halbert McClure Allison,² born Oct. 8, 1800, in Wythe county, Va.; residence in the east end of that county; married Mary Beattie Sayers, born April 5, 1805, in Virginia,

and died in Wytheville, Va., June 9, 1882. He died Aug.
31, 1866, in his native county. Their son,

832. John Craig Allison,[3] born in Wythe county, Va.,
Oct. 5, 1828; married Minerva, daughter of William and
Jane (Rayburn) Guthrie, of Dublin, Pulaski county, Va.
She was born there Sept. 28, 1831; died in Wytheville, Va.,
Jan. 13, 1885. [She was granddaughter of Richard and Eliza-
beth (McIntosh) Guthrie, of Maryland. He was born April
2, 1767; died in 1840, in Dublin, Va.; and was grandson of
James Guthrie, born in Ireland, lived in Maryland, who married Esther Giles, and died in Rockbridge county, Va.]   Mr.
Allison married, second, Matilda Ann Sanders, daughter of
Stephen and Mary Craig (Allison) Sanders, born in Wythe
county, Va., Jan. 26, 1840. Mr. Allison was a farmer before
the war; was severely wounded the day General Lee surrendered. He was elected county treasurer of Wythe county, Va.,
and served for fourteen years; residence, Wytheville, Wythe
county, Va. Mrs. Minerva (Guthrie) Allison died a tragic
death by a kerosene explosion. She was true to her Scotch
blood and was proud of her people. A noble Christian
woman, "she died a triumphant Christian death; her voice-
less lips are sealed in silence by the words, 'I am the resurrection and the life.'"

CHILDREN.

833. John Lee Allison,[4] b. Pulaski Co., town of Dublin, Virginia, Sept.
5, 1863. He was educated in the high school at Wytheville,
Va.; graduated at King college, Bristol, Tenn., at twenty years
of age, and from the Union Theological seminary at Hampden,
Sidney, Prince Edward Co., Va. Is a Presbyterian clergyman,
and is settled over a Presbyterian church at Radford City, Va.,
where he resides. He m., Feb. 28, 1888, Laura B. Stanley.
Children, b. at Wytheville, Va.:
834. Mattie Lee Allison,[5] b. Aug. 7, 1889.
835. Laura B. McClure Allison,[5] b. Oct. 10, 1890.

ALLISONS OF TENNESSEE AND LOUISIANA.

836. Thomas Allison.[1] According to my information, he
was from Philadelphia, Penn., and his forefathers were living
in Pennsylvania before the Revolution. Mr. Allison lived in
South Carolina, then in Smith county, Tenn. He had two
brothers; one was Samuel Allison, of Carthage, Tenn., who
at different times was a member of the legislature, sheriff,
and clerk of the court for Smith county.

CHILD.

837. Joseph B. Allison[2] (838), b. May 28, 1800; res. Smith county, Tenn.

838.   Joseph B. Allison[2] [837] (Thomas[1]).   He was born in South Carolina, May 28, 1800; married Sarah, daughter of Joseph Reasonover, and emigrated to Smith county, Tennessee, where he was reared.

CHILD.

839.   Daniel Brown Allison[8] (840), b. April 28, 1844; res. Morgan City, La.

840.   Daniel Brown Allison [8] [889] (Joseph B.,[2] Thomas[1]). He was born April 28, 1844, in Panola, Miss.   He left his native state, and located at Franklin, parish of St. Mary, La. He was elected sheriff, and served in 1872; was elected clerk of the court, and served in that capacity.   Later he removed to Morgan City, La., and was for three years assistant collector of United States customs.   He married, Jan. 14, 1870, at Pine Prairie, parish of St. Laudry, Mary Adelia Adams, born in the parish of St. Martin, La., Nov. 8, 1852.   Residence, Morgan City, La.

CHILDREN, BORN IN MORGAN CITY, LA.

841.   Melissa Emma Allison,[4] b. March 8, 1871.
842.   Adelia Alice Allison,[4] b. Jan. 26, 1880.
843.   Sarah Gertrude Allison,[4] b. Nov. 17, 1881.
844.   Edna Clarina Allison,[4] b. Oct. 24, 1883.
845.   Andrew Calvin Allison,[4] b. Sept. 25, 1885.
846.   Rupert Lester Allison,[4] b. Nov. 19, 1887.
847.   Opal Ruth Allison,[4] b. July 20, 1890.

ALLISONS OF THE PARISH OF LIFFORD, COUNTY OF DONEGAL, IRELAND, AND OF TENNESSEE, U. S.

848.   Andrew Allison,[1] of Scotch blood, lived at Churchminster, near Ballandreat, in the parish of Lifford, county of Donegal, Ireland.   This parish is a few miles southwest of the city of Londonderry, on the border of the county of Tyrone, and in the province of Ulster, so noted for its settlement by Scotch and English colonists more than two centuries ago.   Lord Lifford owns much landed property at this place, and is its chief inhabitant.   From the small railway station we can see on a high, ledgy adjacent hill a flagstaff, which is flagless when his lordship is absent, but from which a flag flutters in the breeze when his lordship is at home. In this locality lived Mr. Allison and his family.[1]

[1]Alexander Porter, of Churchminster, near Ballandreat, parish of Lifford, county of Donegal, Ireland, was of the Scotch Presbyterians, that strong, sturdy race, which leaves its imprint and influence on men and institutions wherever planted.   He had a daughter, Matilda Porter, who

849. Andrew Allison[2] (850), b. Dec. 26, 1775; d. at Carthage, Tenn., Sept. 29, 1818. He married Matilda Porter, of Lifford, Ireland.

850. Andrew Allison[2] [849] (Andrew[1]). He was born in the parish of Lifford, county of Donegal, Ireland, Dec. 26, 1775. He married, about 1798, Matilda, daughter of Alexander Porter, of Churchminster, near Ballandreat, parish of Lifford, Ireland; who was some six years his junior. It is to be presumed that Mr. Allison was not fully satisfied with his home locality, nor with the prospect of reaping great harvests from the rocky and sterile soil of Lifford, for in his young manhood, somewhere about 1802, he settled in Hartsville, Tenn. He died at Carthage, Tenn., Sept. 29, 1818. He was a merchant. He organized the first lodge of Masons in that section, and was master of the lodge at his death.

CHILDREN.

851. Alexander Allison,[3] b. in Lifford, Ireland, about 1800. Res. Nashville, Tenn., where he was a successful wholesale dry goods merchant, and was prominent in all its public enterprises. For three terms he was mayor of that city, and d. in 1862, leaving no issue. He m., in 1824, Cynthia Hart, daughter of James Hart. Alexander Allison, after the death of his wife, Cynthia Hart, m. Madeline Allcom. He had one son, by his first wife, who was killed at the battle of Monterey, Mexico, and one son by his last wife, who d. about 1845. Mrs. Allison d. about 1878.
852. Andrew Allison[3] (855), b. in Hartsville, Tenn., Sept. 24, 1805; d. in Nashville, Tenn., Dec. 24, 1860. He m. Rebecca Greer Allen in 1832.

---

married Andrew Allison, and in 1798 (see his record). His son, Rev. James Porter, a Presbyterian clergyman, distinguished for his learning, ability, and zeal, was a patriot in the troubles of 1798, and was condemned to an ignominious death, and executed before his church door by the unjust decision of a court-martial. His two sons were cared for by his uncle in Tennessee. One became an able jurist in Louisiana. The other sons of Mr. Porter, of Lifford, were Alexander Porter, Robert Porter, and William Porter, who came to the United States in August, 1798, with their sister, Mrs. Andrew Allison. Alexander first settled in Wilmington, Del., and finally in Nashville, Tenn., and was a successful merchant. He d. of Asiatic cholera, at Dresden, Tenn., in April, 1833. His wife was Susan Massingill, of East Tennessee. Their son, Dr. James Armstrong Porter, was born in Nashville, Tenn., in 1800; married Sally Ann Murphy. Resided at Nashville, where he died in 1853. He was a man of distinguished ability, and held a professorship in the university at Nashville. His son, Alexander James Porter, was born in Nashville, Tenn., June 6, 1822, residence, Nashville, where he died Feb. 11, 1888. He married Martha Watson. Their daughter, Mary Amanda Porter, b. Jan. 14, 1851, m. Joseph Webster Allison, her relative, June 12, 1872 (see his record), their marriage thus reuniting the branches of this family in the fourth and fifth generations. Their son, Alexander Porter Allison, born Memphis, Tenn., July 13, 1876, revives the name and blood of the common ancestor of his parents in Ireland, who died more than a hundred years before.

853. James Porter Allison,[3] b. about 1807. He graduated at West Point military academy, but resigned his commission after a short term of service in the army. He studied law and commenced its practice in Nashville, Tenn., then removed to Bowling Green, Ky., where he d., without issue, about 1834. He m. in 1830, Elizabeth Garnet of Clarksville, Tenn. He was a merchant and planter.
854. Robert Porter Allison[3] (862), b. at Hartsville, Tenn., July 25, 1809; res. Lebanon, Tenn. He m. Alithea Sanders.

855. Andrew Allison[3] [852] (Andrew,[2] Andrew[1]). He was born in Hartsville, Tenn., Sept. 24, 1805; married, May 24, 1832, Rebecca Greer Allen, daughter of Robert Allen of Carthage, Tenn. He was a dry goods merchant, and succeeded to his father's business. Later he removed to Carthage, Tenn., and engaged in the manufacture of cotton goods. He erected a large factory, which was destroyed by fire in 1850, rebuilt and again destroyed in 1852. He then removed to Nashville, and engaged in the wholesale dry goods business, being of the firm of Allison, Anderson & Co. He died in Nashville, Tenn., Dec. 24, 1860.

CHILDREN.

856. Dixon Allen Allison.[4]
857. Rebecca Allison,[4] m. Alexander J. Porter; res. Nashville, Tenn. He d. about 1884. She res. in Nashville, and three children.
858. Robert Allen Allison[4] (870), b. Carthage, Tenn., Nov. 28, 1836; m. Isabel Kilso; res. Jackson, Tenn.
859. Alexander Allison.[4]
860. Andrew Allison.[4]
861. Joseph Webster Allison[4] (873), b. Lebanon, Tenn., May 24, 1848; m. Mary Amanda Porter; res. Memphis, Tenn.

862. Robert Porter Allison[3] [854] (Andrew,[2] Andrew[1]). He was born in Hartsville, Tenn., July 25, 1809. He was a student of medicine, and graduated at Jefferson college, Philadelphia, Penn. After practising his profession in Sumner county, he removed to Lebanon, Tenn., and became a druggist. He married, in 1839, Alithea, daughter of James Sanders, of Sumner county, Tenn.; resided at Lebanon, Tenn., in 1892, and is retired from business.

CHILDREN.

863. Alexander Allison,[4] b. May 15, 1840; druggist; res. Knoxville, Tenn. He married and has three children.
864. Andrew Allison,[4] b. Feb. 6, 1842. In 1865 he graduated at the law school at Harvard College, Cambridge, Mass., and became an attorney of the firm of Smith, Baxter & Allison in Nashville, Tenn.; was judge of the chancery court in 1892. He m. Nettie, daughter of Dr. Granville P. and Leonora (Cheney) Smith, Dec. 13, 1867; res. Knoxville, Tenn. Children:
865. Granville S. Allison,[5] b. Sept. 13, 1868; lawyer; res. Nashville, Tenn.
866. Mary Allison,[5] b. Nov. 25, 1873.

867. James Porter Allison,⁴ b. 1852. He is a druggist; res. Huntsville,
       Alabama. He m. Mattie Higins (?) of Huntsville, Ala.
868. Madeline Allison,⁴ m. Mr. Humphreys. She res. with her father in
       Lebanon, Tenn. She has one son:
       Allison B. Humphreys,⁵ aged 16 years in 1892.
869. Sallie Allison,⁴ m. H. H. Buckman, a lawyer; res. Jacksonville,
       Fla. Three children.

870. Robert Allen Allison⁴ [858] (Andrew,³ Andrew,²
Andrew¹). He was born in Carthage, Smith county, Tenn.,
Nov. 28, 1836. His home was in Lebanon, Tenn., from 1838
-'56, in Nashville from 1856-'66; in Memphis from 1866-'76;
in St. Louis, Mo., from 1876-'81; and Jackson, Tenn., from
1881 to the present time. In 1857 he graduated at Cumberland university at Lebanon, Tenn., and the same year entered
his father's store as bookkeeper and cashier; in 1860 formed
a partnership in the wholesale hat business. After the war,
which had divested him of his property, he opened a cotton
commission house with his brother Alexander as partner, in
Nashville, and was successful; removed to Memphis, and
with three brothers engaged in the wholesale hardware business; and was for a time successful. In 1873 the firm lost
heavily, and he gave up the business later and engaged in
other business in St. Louis. He is now in business, and resides in Jackson, Tenn., where he is an elder in the First
Presbyterian church. He married, Feb. 14, 1861, Isabel
Kelso, born at Fayetteville, Lincoln county, Tenn., Feb. 1,
1840. She was daughter of Henry and Rebecca (Rutledge)
Kelso. Her father was born Sept., 1818; died June, 1866.
He was a son of Henry Kelso, who was born near Kelso, in
Scotland, who married Ruth Wells of Kentucky, and he died
in 1831, in Lincoln county, Tenn.

CHILDREN.

871. Isabel Kelso Allison,⁵ b. Nashville, Tenn., Dec. 29, 1862; m., 1889,
       Charles Hunter Raines, a banker. They res. in Memphis,
       Tenn.
872. Anne Dixon Allison,⁵ b. Nashville, Tenn., Aug. 2, 1867; d. in Jack-
       son, Tenn., Feb., 1882.
873. Rebekah Rutledge Allison,⁵ b. Memphis, Tenn., Dec. 28, 1871; res.
       Jackson, Tenn.

874. Joseph Webster Allison⁴ [861] (Andrew,³ Andrew,²
Andrew¹). He was born in Lebanon, Wilson county, Tenn.,
May 24, 1848. He lived in his native town seven years; in
Nashville, thirteen years; in Jackson, seven years; and for
fourteen years has been a resident of Memphis, Tenn. The
war interfered with his early opportunities for education.
He attended a boarding school, and upon the occupation of

Nashville by the United States troops he returned to his home, and soon secured a clerkship in a hardware store in Nashville, which he retained till the close of the war. He then returned to the university at Lexington, Va., graduated after a four years course, and then united himself for the next nine years at Memphis, Tenn., in the wholesale hardware business with his brothers, who were established there. He then engaged in the cotton-seed oil manufacture at Jackson, Tenn., and in 1886 sold his business to the American Cotton Oil Trust, and returned to Memphis to assume control of the company's oil business in that locality, a position he still holds. Residence, Memphis, Tenn. He married Mary Amanda, daughter of Alexander James Porter. She was born in Nashville, Tenn., Jan. 14, 1851, and is still living.

CHILDREN.

875. Rebekah Allison,[s] b. Nashville, Tenn., Dec. 27, 1873; res. Memphis, Tenn.
876. Alexander Porter Allison,[s] b. Memphis, Tenn., July 13, 1876. At home.
877. Andrew Allison,[s] b. Jackson, Tenn., April 23, 1879. At home.
878. Joseph Webster Allison,[s] Jr., b. Memphis, Tenn., March 26, 1890. At home.

CHAPTER IX.

879. Joseph Allison.[1] He was born about 1747, in Cumberland county, England. He resided in Moser, Cumberland county, England. He married Miss Jane Fisher, daughter of Joseph Fisher, about 1775. Her father was a country squire, and a noted fox hunter, who owned three estates. Joseph Allison's children are unknown to the compiler, except one son. It is said that Mr. Allison had three half brothers, namely,

880. Peter Allison.[1]
881. John (?) Allison.[1]
882. Henry Allison.[1]

Joseph Allison[1] had a child

883. John Allison[2] (884), b. at Brigham, Cumberland Co., Eng., 1777; d. at Goat, near Cockermouth, Cumberland Co., about 1845.

884. John Allison[2] [883] (Joseph [1]). He was born in Brigham, Cumberland county, England, in 1777; married Jane Shaw, July 19, 1808. They lived in Moser, and he died near Cockermouth, Cumberland county, England, about 1845. He held the position of clerk of the parish of Moser Chapel. Mrs. Allison was born in "Lowerby Water of Ayr, Scotland," in 1779, and died at Goat, near Cockermouth, England, about 1850. She had one sister, and three half brothers, namely: John Shaw, James Shaw, William Shaw, and Mary Shaw.

CHILDREN.

885. Joseph Allison,[3] b. Aug. 5, 1804; emigrated to America in 1835.
886. Grace Allison,[3] b. Oct. 17, 1805.
887. John Allison,[3] b. May 4, 1807; d. Feb. 25, 1830.
888. Peter Allison,[3] b. April 26, 1809. He is said to have emigrated to America, and to have settled in one of the Eastern states. History not known.

MRS. SARAH A. EICK.

889. Isaac Allison,² b. April 14, 1811.
890. William Allison,² b. Jan. 25, 1813; d. April 27, 1831.
891. Fisher Allison² (895), b. Aug. 13, 1815, at Keswick, Cumberland Co.,
        England; m. Jane Gelleland Van Buskisk.
892. Sarah Allison,² b. June 10, 1818.
893. Jacob Allison,² b. Dec. 6, 1823.
894. Henry Allison,² b. March 7, 1827; d. July 14, 1831.

895. Fisher Allison³ [891] (John,² Joseph¹). He was
born in Keswick, Cumberland county, England, Aug. 13,
1815 ; married, Oct. 25, 1837, Jane Gelleland, daughter of Isaac
Van Buskisk. She was born June 7, 1816, in Fairview,
Guernsey county, Ohio, and still lives, in Jan., 1892; her
father was born in Virginia: her people were originally from
Holland. He worked upon a farm near Moser, England,
until his 19th year, when he emigrated from Keswick to
Vaughan, a place near Toronto, Canada, in 1835. He removed
to Dixon, Ill., in 1840, and on September 6 of that year he
removed to Elkhorn Grove, Carroll county, Ill., where he
resided till his death, March 8, 1878. He was chairman of
the board of supervisors of Carroll county, Ill., for a number
of years. In the early days of Carroll county, churches
were few, and ministers regularly installed were scarce. Mr.
Allison often officiated as a local Methodist minister in a
gratuitous manner to appreciative congregations. He raised
a family of thirteen children. Four of his sons went into
the Union army; two were killed and another seriously
wounded in the service.

CHILDREN.

896. Joseph Fisher Allison⁴ (909), born in Toronto, Canada, Oct. 19, 1838;
        res. Mount Carroll, Carroll Co., Ill.
897. Henry Allison,⁴ b. Toronto, Can., Feb. 27, 1840. He was a soldier
        of the Union army, and was a member of Company K, 15th
        regiment, Illinois infantry. He enlisted May 24, 1861. After-
        ward he was in railroad employ. His wife died April 20, 1878,
        leaving a daughter five years of age. Mr. Allison is now a car-
        penter, and resides at Fort Worth, Texas. He is a member of
        the Masonic fraternity, and other orders.
898. John Huss Allison,⁴ b. at Milledgeville, Ill., Dec. 3, 1841. He was
        a soldier of the Union, in Company G, 39th regiment, Illinois
        infantry, and was killed at Suffolk, Va., Sept. 15, 1862.
899. William Allison,⁴ b. at Milledgeville, Ill., July 10, 1843. He was a
        member of Company H, 55th regiment, Illinois infantry. He
        was not married, and was killed in a railroad accident at Dixon,
        Ill., in March, 1865.
900. Sarah Ann Allison,⁴ b. in a little log cabin, on the prairie at Elkhorn
        Grove, Ill., March 26, 1845, and remembers vividly all the scenes
        and incidents of pioneer life in that then new and undeveloped
        country. She was educated at Milledgeville, Ill., and at the
        seminary at Rock River. Then she commenced a new life as a
        school teacher, which occupation she followed till her mar-

riage. Early in life she united with the Methodist Episcopal church, and has been a consistent and active member. She is positive in her convictions, and believes that there should be no sex in citizenship, and believes that the surest method for the suppression of the liquor traffic and kindred evils is to place the ballot in the hands of women. For more than twenty-seven years she has shared with her husband all the joys and sorrows of life. She m., Oct. 11, 1865, George T. Eick. Mr. Eick was b. Jan. 19, 1841, in Middlebush, Summerset Co., N. J. Went with his father to Illinois in 1856, and in 1859 settled in Jordan, Ill., where he was married. In 1874 he removed with his family to Adams Co., Ia.; and in 1881 sold his farm; and in Feb., 1882, settled in Diller, Gage Co., Nebraska, where he has since resided. He has won the high regard of all by his consistent Christian life. He is an elder in the Presbyterian church, and has at heart the best interests of church and community. He is an upright citizen, and worthy officer of the church. Children:

I. William Milton Eick,[5] b. Jordan, Ill., June 14, 1867; farmer; res. Diller, Nebraska.
II. George Francis Eick,[5] b. Jordan, Ill., Aug. 29, 1868; farmer; res. Diller, Nebraska.
III. Allison Alphonso Eick,[5] b. Jordan, Ill., April 1, 1873; at school.
IV. Sarah Elizabeth Eick,[5] b. Grant, Adams Co., Ia., Jan. 11, 1876; at school.
901. Mary Allison,[4] b. Milledgeville, Ill., in 1847; m., Dec. 7, 1870, Howard O. Barber, a merchant; res. Milledgeville, Ill. Children:
I. Cora Barber,[5] aged 18 years.
II. Frank F. Barber,[5] aged 13 years.
III. Harry Barber,[5] aged 10 years.
IV. Price Barber,[5] aged 6 years.
902. Charles Wesley Allison[4] (914), b. Milledgeville, Ill., in 1849; res. Milledgeville; farmer.
903. Jacob L. Allison,[4] b. Milledgeville, Ill.; res. Milledgeville, Ill. Unmarried. Since his father's death he has lived, the larger part of the time, with his mother.
904. Isaac Allison,[4] b. Dec. 7, 1852, at Milledgeville, Ill.; res. Milledgeville, Ill. He m., April 30, 1878, Sarah E. Vandusen. Child:
I. Ray Allison, aged 13 years.
905. Maria Elizabeth Allison,[4] b. March 27, 1853, at Milledgeville, Ill.; res. Milledgeville, Ill.; m., March 20, 1880, Joseph Newton Musser; b., Jan. 1, 1854, in Jefferson, Wis.; farmer; res. Rock Grove, Ill. Children:
I. Joseph Newton Musser,[5] b. Feb. 2, 1881.
II. Violet Musser,[5] b. Feb. 12, 1882.
III. Jane Allison Musser,[5] b. Sept. 4, 1883.
IV. Grace Leilah Musser,[5] b. Jan. 21, 1886; d. Sept. 21, 1886.
V. Fisher Allison Musser,[5] b. Feb. 11, 1890.
906. Susanna Allison,[4] b. Milledgeville, Ill.; d. there in 1862.
907. James Allison,[4] b. Milledgeville, Ill.; d. there in Dec., 1860.
908. Frances Allison,[4] b. Milledgeville, Ill.; d. there in Dec., 1860.

909. Joseph Fisher Allison[4] [896] (Fisher,[3] John,[2] Joseph[1]). He was born in Toronto, Canada, Oct. 19, 1838. Married, Sept. 28, 1866, Hariet Adaline, daughter of Darius and Martha Ann (Foster) Dodge, of Rockford, Winnebago county, Ill. Mr. Dodge was born in 1816, and was son of Elijah and Laurena (Thayer) Dodge. His father was born in Vermont in 1790. Mrs. Allison was born in Perkins, Ohio,

June 27, 1846. Mr. Allison worked till his majority upon
his father's farm. In 1859 he entered the Mount Morris
seminary of Ogle county, Ill., intending to prepare himself
for the legal profession. The war, breaking out in 1861, broke
up his life plan. He entered the military service as an enlisted man, eight days after the attack on Fort Sumter, en-
listing April 22, 1861, in Company H, Fifteenth regiment,
Illinois infantry. He was wounded in both hands at the
battle of Hatcher's River, Oct. 5, 1862, losing his left hand
and third and fourth fingers of the right, and again in the
right ankle at Champion Hills, Miss., Feb. 4, 1864. He
served six years, seven months, and seven days, and was hon-
orably discharged as a first lieutenant, Jan. 1, 1868. He was an
officer of the Freedmen's Bureau, North Carolina, after the
war. He has held the office of special examiner of the
United States pension office. He has been circuit clerk and
recorder, and county clerk of Carroll county, Ill., for thirteen
years, and was first assistant clerk of the House of Representatives of Illinois for the twenty-eighth and thirty-third General Assembly. He resided at Toronto, Canada, till April,
1840, then in Milledgeville, Carroll county, Ill., till 1868;
since 1868, in Mount Carroll, Carroll county, Ill. He receives
a pension of $30 per month, and is a Republican, having cast
his first vote for Abraham Lincoln.

CHILDREN BORN IN MOUNT CARROLL, CARROLL COUNTY, ILL.

910. Frances Cora Allison,⁵ b. June 15, 1870; res. Mount Carroll, Ill.
        Student.
911. Waite Fisher Allison,⁵ b. Aug. 10, 1872; res. Mount Carroll, Ill.
        Student.
912. Martha Allison,⁵ b. Feb. 27, 1882, at home.
913. Joseph Foster Allison,⁵ b. April 21, 1884, at home.

914. Charles Wesley Allison⁴ [902] (Fisher,³ John,²
Joseph¹). He was born in Milledgeville, Ill., March 26,
1850. Married, Oct. 19, 1875, Mary Emma Horning, born
Dec. 13, 1855, in Collegeville, Montgomery county, Penn.;
lived at Malvern, Whitesides county, Ill. She was daughter
of Samuel Eisenburg, and Elizabeth (Grater) Horning, and
grand-daughter of Henry and Hannah (Eisenburg) Horning
of Montgomery county, Penn. Mr. Allison has lived in
Mount Carroll, Ill., and Wymore, Nebraska. He is a teacher
and farmer; resides Milledgeville, Ill.

CHILDREN.

915. Charles Horner Allison,[5] b. April 2, 1877, in Milledgeville, Carroll
    county, Ill.
916. Frank Fisher Allison,[5] b. Milledgeville, Ill., Dec. 20, 1888.
917. Olive Emma Allison,[5] b. Milledgeville, Ill., April 20, 1881.
918. John Earle Allison,[5] b. Wymore, Gage Co., Neb., July 19, 1883.
919. Edna Derr Allison,[5] b. Milledgeville, Ill., Oct. 6, 1887.

ALLISONS OF HALIFAX, YORKSHIRE, ENGLAND.

·920. Joseph Allison,[1] born in Halifax, England, about
1778. Married Elizabeth Shaw. They lived and died in
Halifax, England, and their sons were all brought up in the
cotton and woollen manufacturing business.

CHILDREN.

921. William Allison.[2]
922. Joseph Allison.[2]
923. Elizabeth Allison.[2]
924. Martha Allison.[2]
925. John Shaw Allison,[2] b. Halifax, Eng., June 29, 1808; emigrated to
    America in 1827; m. Elizabeth Clark; res. in Philadelphia,
    Penn., and there died Nov. 22, 1888. Was engaged in the cotton
    and woollen manufacturing business. Mrs. Allison was b. in
    Wigton Co., Cumberland, England, Nov. 29, 1808, and was
    daughter of an officer in English army who was in garrison in
    St. Helena at the period of Napoleon's imprisonment. He sold
    his commission, and with his family came to America in 1818.
    Mrs. Allison was an Episcopalian, while her husband was a
    Presbyterian. The remarkable aggregate height of Mr. Alli-
    son and his five sons was 36 ft. 6 in.

CHILDREN.

926. Joseph Allison,[3] m. Louisa Hines. Children:
927. William Niles Allison,[4] d. in infancy.
928. Jesse Virginia Allison,[4] d. in infancy.
929. Thomas Nixon Allison.[4]
930. Albert Henry Allison.[4]
931. Frank Niblo Allison.[4]
932. Jane Allison[3] is deceased.
934. Jane Elizabeth Allison[3] is deceased.
935. John Smick Allison[3] is deceased.
936. William Henry Allison[3] was a Union soldier. He m. Catherine
    Riemshart; one child living.
937. Elizabeth Allison.[4]
938. John Allison,[4] deceased.
939. Jennie Allison,[4] deceased.
940. Ellen Allison[3] is deceased.
941. Albert Clark Allison[3] was a Union soldier. He m. Millie Ann Mc-
    Clennan. Children:
942. Willie May Allison.[4]
943. Walter Allison.[4]
944. Douglass Allison[3] was a Union soldier. He m. Catherine Hoffman.
    Children:

945. Blanche E. Allison.[4]
946. Eleanor H. Allison,[4] deceased.
947. Arthur Algernon Allison,[3] b. Philadelphia, Penn., Jan. 29, 1849;
m., Sept. 22, 1881, Ellen Toon Maslin, of London, England; b.
there June 9, 1853. She is dau. of Charles and Harriet (Salter)
Maslin, of Leicester, England, and later of Montreal, Canada.
He was son of John Maslin of Leicester, England. Mr. Allison
is a printer and clerk. Res. Washington, D. C. He has lived
in Philadelphia, Penn., and College Green, Md. Children b.
Washington, D. C.:
948. Albert Childs Allison,[4] b. July 9, 1881.
949. John Franklyn Allison,[4] b. Sept. 16, 1886.

ALLISONS OF ILLINOIS.

950. William Allison [1] (or John), an offshoot of the Pennsylvania family, lived in Kentucky, and married, in Grayson
county, a Miss Huntress, or Montrose (?); and after the
birth of his two sons, he went further south, joined the army,
and was in the battle of New Orleans, under General Jackson.
He was seldom heard from after that date. He had a brother,
Samuel Allison, who lived in Pennsylvania. Mrs. Allison
died about this time, and the children were brought up by
her relatives.

CHILDREN.

951. William Allison[2] (953), b. Grayson Co., Ky., in 1794; res. Coles Co.,
Ill., and d. there in 1854.
952. John Allison,[2] res. in Hardin Co., Ky., and raised a family. He
visited his brother's family about 1832, after which the families
seldom or never saw one another. He d. about 1872; P. O.,
Horse Valley, Ky. He was a person of much intelligence,
weighed some 200 pounds, was muscular, and a model of physical manhood, with a ruddy complexion. He was a lover of the
military profession in old militia days. He had two sons who
were Democratic and Secessionist in their sympathies.

953. William Allison [2] [951] (William [1]). He was born
in Grayson county, Ky., in 1794; married, Oct. 17, 1818, in
Hancock county, Ky., Eliza B. Lewis. He was an itinerant
Methodist preacher for six or eight years, and was three times
a delegate to the general conference at New York city; then
he studied medicine, became a physician, and practised his
profession till his death; commenced his practice in 1832.
When Illinois was comparatively a wilderness, he moved to
Etna, Coles county, in that state, in May, 1833. She died
in 1870. He died in 1854. He was muscular, weighed some
200 pounds, and physically was a model of manhood. At
his death he had nine children living.

CHILDREN.

954. William L. Allison,³ res. Neoga, Cumberland Co., Ill.; m. Emily
——.
955. John L. Allison,³ m. Deborah ——; res. at Mattoon, Coles Co., Ill.;
he was killed near Vicksburg, Miss., in 1864.
956. Joseph L. Allison³ (963), b. Oct. 7, 1823, in Hancock Co., Ky.; lawyer;
res. Marshall, Clark Co., Ill.
957. Francis A. Allison³ (970), b. in Ky., Feb. 11, 1825; lawyer and farmer;
res. Mattoon, Coles Co., Ill. He m. Zippora ——.
958. Susan E. Allison,³ m. John Miller; res. Nashville, Tenn.
959. Eliza B. Allison,³ m. Capt. James Hart; both deceased, leaving four
children.
960. Alfred E. Allison³ was killed in the battle of Perryville, Ky., in 1862;
res. Paradise, Coles Co., Ill. He m. Martha ——, and they had
one child. His widow was again married to William Green
Vault; res. Etna, Coles Co., Ill.
961. Charles W. Allison³ was a private in Company I, 123d regiment, Illinois Volunteers, and served three years; is a justice of the
peace; res. Etna, Coles Co., Ill.
962. Ann Mary Allison,³ m. Walter Hadley; res. Bell Air, Crawford Co.,
Ill.

963. Joseph L. Allison³ [956] (William,² William¹). He
was born in Hancock county, Ky., Oct. 7, 1823; married,
March 1, 1847, Harriet A. Easton, in Clark county, Ill. He
lived there in April, 1855; removed to Marshall, Clark county,
Ill.; residence, Marshall, Ill., in 1878.

CHILDREN.

964. Annie E. Allison.⁴
965. Joseph L. Allison,⁴ photographer.
966. Sarah M. Allison,⁴ school teacher.
967. Charles C. Allison,⁴ printer.
968. Edgar L. Allison.⁴
969. Laura Mary Allison.⁴

970. Francis A. Allison³ [957] (William,² William¹).
He was born in Kentucky, Feb. 10, 1825, and in the following
year was taken by his parents to Indiana, and in the spring
of 1834 went with his parents to Etna, Coles county. He
has lived in or in the vicinity of Mattoon, Coles county,
for many years. Lawyer and farmer. He is said to be a
second or more remote cousin to Judge James Young Allison,
of Madison, Ind. (See Allisons of Indiana). Mr. Allison
is a strong Republican, and made a warm canvass for Lincoln,
in 1860. He and his brothers were very active politicians,
good speakers, and able organizers; all Republicans. The
Allisons of this family are mostly Presbyterians, and Meth-
odists. They are muscular, have broad shoulders, fair com-
plexions, with light brown or black hair and blue eyes, and
are peaceable and law-abiding people.

CHILDREN.

971. John S. Allison,⁴ m. Sarah E. —— ; res. Mattoon, Ill.
972. Eliza B. Allison,⁴ m. Dr. J. W. Weis; res. Mattoon, Ill.
973. Alice A. Allison.⁴
974. A. F. Allison.⁴
975. J. W. Allison.⁴

ALLISONS OF NEW JERSEY.

976. Burgess Allison, born in Bordentown, N. J., Aug. 17, 1753; died in Washington, D. C., Feb. 20, 1827. Clergyman ; Baptist; studied in what is now Brown University, Providence, R. I., in 1777, and had charge of a small parish in Bordentown, N. J., where he established a classical boarding-school, which attained great repute. In 1796, he gave his attention to inventions, and several improvements in the steam engine, and its application to navigation are due to his efforts. "In 1801, he resumed his school, and soon afterward his pastorate, but ill health compelled him to relinquish both. In 1816, he was elected chaplain of the house of representatives, and later became chaplain of the navy yard at Washington, D. C., where he remained till his death. He was at one time one of the secretaries of the American Philosophical society, and was a constant contributor to periodical literature." (From Appleton's Encyclopedia of American Biography, Vol. I, p. 58.)

ALLISONS OF CONNECTICUT.

977. William Allison¹ was an emigrant from Ireland, and his native place was near Omagh, in the county of Tyrone, and was of the Scotch stock. He came to America soon after the close of the Revolution, locating in Hartford, Conn. ; later, he removed to Holland Patent in western New York, took up land, and lived upon it till his death, about 1830.

CHILDREN.

978. Margaret Allison,² m. —— Duprea, and went south.
979. Sallie Allison,² m. —— Winslow, of Holland Patent.
980. Jane Allison,² m. —— Tarwood, of Holland Patent.
981. Nancy Allison,² m. —— Mildrum, of Middletown, Conn.
982. Andrew Allison,² never married; lived and died at his father's home.
983. Samuel Allison² (984), res. Middletown, Conn.

984. Samuel Allison ² [983] (William¹). He served his time as soap- and candle-maker with a Mr. Nichols, of Hart-

ford, Conn., till 1807. Then he removed to Middletown, Conn., and established the soap and candle manufactory, which has ever since been successfully carried on by himself and his descendants. He managed the business till 1828, when he died, aged 42 years.

CHILDREN.

985. William P. Allison,[3] b. March 15, 1806; hardware manufacturer; res. Cromwell, Conn.; d. in 1874.
986. J. D. Allison,[4] his son, is a hardware manufacturer; b. in 1833; res. Cromwell, Conn. Another son, res. Georgetown, Col.; editor of Georgetown *Courier*.
987. Samuel S. Allison,[3] b. Sept., 1809; res. Middletown, Conn.; carried on the soap manufacturing business till 1856, and retired, giving place to his sons, Samuel and Abel Allison. He was living in 1879. Children:
988. Samuel Allison,[4] res. Middletown, Conn.
989. Abel C. Allison,[4] res. Middletown, Conn. Two other sons, res. Middletown, Conn. Three daughters, res. Middletown, Conn. Two sons in California; farmers.

ALLISONS OF MARYLAND.

989a. James Allison was a lieutenant in the third Maryland regiment, and signed a flattering memorial to General John Sullivan, Oct. 13, 1777.

ALLISONS OF LAWRENCE, MASS.—A BRANCH OF THE LONDONDERRY, N. H., FAMILY OF ALLISONS.

990. Samuel Allison [5] (Samuel,[4] James,[3] Capt. Samuel,[2] Samuel [1]). He was related to the Whittemores by his mother, Polly, a member of that family. He was born in Weathersfield, Vt., Oct. 7, 1812; married, Dec. 11, 1836, Mary Ann, daughter of Clark and Martha (Reed) Preston, of Weathersfield, Vt. (The Reeds were of Westford, Mass., and the Prestons of Mansfield, Conn.) Mrs. Allison was born, Dec. 2, 1815, at Weathersfield, and now lives at No. 60 Newbury street, Lawrence, Mass. In May, 1850, they removed to Lawrence, Mass., where Mr. Allison died Sept. 5, 1879. He was buried in Weathersfield, Vt. His age was 66 years, 10 months, 28 days.

CHILDREN.

991. Charles Allison,[6] b. Bridgewater, Vt., Feb. 24, 1838; enlisted in the 4th Massachusetts regiment, and died of disease at Baton Rouge, La., April 16, 1863, aged 25 years, 1 month, 23 days.

992. Martha Ann Allison,* b. Bridgewater, Vt., Feb. 27, 1840; m. Jason
Wright, of Waltham, Mass.; merchant; res. San Jose, Cal.
Child:
993. Jason Allison Wright.⁷
994. Ellen Maria Allison,* b. Cavendish, Vt., Jan. 16, 1847; d. March 27,
1847, aged 11 weeks, 5 days.
995. George Henry Allison,* b. Cavendish, Vt., May 29, 1849; m., July
5, 1871, Ellen C., dau. of Jotham Sewell and Maria Bugbee
(Stoddard) Preston, of Edmunds, Me., where she was b. Jan. 21,
1851. Mr. Allison is a "commercial tourist," and res. at No.
60 Newbury street, Lawrence, Mass. Child:
996. Mabel Preston Allison,⁷ b. Lawrence, Mass., June 24, 1875.

CHAPTER X.

THE ALLISONS OF MAGILLEGAN AND LIMAVADY, COUNTY OF LONDON-
DERRY, IRELAND, AND OF NOVA SCOTIA AND NEW BRUNSWICK.

997.   John Allison[1] was born in 1652, and lived at Drumnaha, Magillegan, near Newton–Limavady, in county of Londonderry; in and near also the waters of Lough Foyle, some
twenty miles distant from the city of Londonderry, and about
equidistant between that place and the parish of Aghadowey
in the same county.   From the latter evidently emigrated, in
1718, Samuel Allison, the progenitor of the New Hampshire
Allisons, together with the first settlers of Londonderry, N.H.
Limavady is a place of great antiquity, is well built, and
has a population of several thousand.   At Drumnaha, Magillegan, Mr. John Allison was a prominent citizen, and died in
1786.   He is buried in Magillegan, in the family burying-
ground.   This place is in county of Londonderry, about eight
miles from Limavady, and situated in the angle made by the
junction of Lough Foyle and the Atlantic ocean.   There several generations of this family of Allisons are buried, and there
their living connections, as well as being the connections of
the numerous Allisons of this branch in Nova Scotia, are living in 1893.   On Mr. Allison's tombstone is this inscription:
"Here lieth the body of John Allison, who departed this life
on the 19th of November, 1786, aged 84 years; here also lieth
the body of Jane Clarke, first wife of the above John Allison,
who departed this life 10th May, 1684, aged 24 years.   Also
lieth the body of Mary Fleming, second wife to the aforesaid
John, who departed this life 17th March, 1733, aged 78
years."

CHILD.

998. William Allison[2] (999), b. in Drumnaha, Ireland, in 1680; resided
there, and d. there June 20, 1766.

999.   William Allison[2] [998] (John[1]).   He was born in
Drumnaha, county of Londonderry, Ireland, where he lived
and died.   In the family cemetery there he is buried, and

above him is this inscription: "Also here lieth the body of William Allison, son to the above John, who departed this life on the 20th June, 1766, aged 86 years. Here also lieth the body of Rebecca Caldwell, wife of the above William, who departed this life 11th March, 1751, aged 66 years." William and Rebecca (Caldwell) Allison had several children, among them were,—

CHILDREN BORN AT DRUMNAHA, IRELAND.

1000. Joseph Allison² (1002), b. about 1720; emigrated to Horton, Kings Co., Nova Scotia, and d. in 1794.
1001. William Allison² (1009), b. in 1724; m. Mary Lawrence, lived in Drumnaha, and d. there Nov. 24, 1798.

1002. Joseph Allison³ [1000] (William,² John¹). He was born in Drumnaha, near Limavady, Ireland, about 1720, and when he reached manhood's estate, he rented a farm belonging to a London corporation, paying yearly rates, which were collected by an agent in Ireland. On one of these visits of the agent he was invited by Mr. Allison to dine with him. The best the house afforded was given to him as an honored guest. On that day silver spoons were used. Turning to Mr. Allison the agent said,—

"I see that you can afford to have silver on your table. If you can afford this, you can afford to pay more rent. Your next year's rent will be increased."

"I will pay no more rent," said Allison. "I will go to America first."

The agent increased the rent, which Mr. Allison would not pay. He sold all his property, and, with his family and six children, in 1769 left the home of his fathers and the graves of his kindred, and embarked from Londonderry for the New World, intending to land at Philadelphia. He had relatives in Pennsylvania with whom he had corresponded, who had urged him to come to them in that state and bring his family. Their names were Pollock, the children of Mrs. Allison by her first marriage; they settled in Pennsylvania about 1760. Their passage was rough, and the vessel was wrecked on Sable Island, and he and his family were taken to Halifax, Nova Scotia. It was then difficult and expensive to journey from one section of the country to another. A few years previous to the arrival of Mr. Allison in Halifax, the French people had been most cruelly expelled from their Acadian homes, and their lands thrown open to settlement. Through the persuasion of Admiral Cochrane, then admiral on that coast and station, and by the liberal offers made to them by the authorities, these sturdy people of Scotch blood were induced to go in and occupy. Of those who came with the Allisons, the McHeffys settled in Falmouth, N. S., the Magees in Aylesford, the McCormicks in Annapolis, and Mr. Allison purchased a farm in Horton, Kings county, Nova Scotia, on the border of the historic Grand Prè, where he lived till his death in 1794. He was a Presbyterian, though many of his descendants have departed from the ancient faith, and belong to other denominations. He married in Limavady, county of Londonderry, Ireland, Mrs. Alice Polk (or Pollock) Caldwell, who survived him for several years. She gave the historic silver spoons to her youngest child, a daughter who lived to be ninety years old. They are now in the possession of her great-grandson, Hon. Leonard Shannon, of Halifax, N. S.

CHILDREN BORN IN LIMAVADY, COUNTY OF LONDONDERRY, IRELAND.

1003. Rebecca Allison[4] (1020), b. in 1751, d. in 1842. She m. Col. Jonathan Crane; res. Horton, Kings Co., Nova Scotia.
1004. William Allison[4] (1026), b. in 1752; d. about 1815.
1005. John Allison[4] (1031), b. in 1753; d. March 1, 1821; res. Newport, Hants Co., N. S.
1006. Joseph Allison[4] (1044), m. Alice, dau. of Israel Harding, a Loyalist in the Revolution; res. Horton, N. S.
1007. James Allison[4] (1054), b. in 1765; d. in 1849; m. Margaret Hutchinson.
1008. Nancy Allison,[4] b. 1768; d. in 1858. She was less than a year old when brought to Nova Scotia. She m. Major Samuel Leonard, but left no children. Her husband was a native of New Jersey, espoused the Loyalist side during the Revolutionary War, and was a captain in the New Jersey volunteers. He was a major of the militia in Nova Scotia, in 1807–1808, which garrisoned the forts at Halifax when the regulars were withdrawn to the aid of Wellington in the peninsula.

1009. William Allison[3] [1001] (William,[2] John[1]). He was born in Drumnaha, county of Londonderry, Ireland, in 1724, lived in his native town, and died Nov. 24, 1798, at 74 years. He married Mary Lawrence, "who departed this life 8th July, 1796, aged 62 years." They are buried in Drumnaha, Ireland. The tombstone above them records these facts: "They lived united in the honourable state of matrimony 48 years, and brought up a numerous family in the principles of religion, morality, and truth. He was a man of the strictest integrity. She possessed all the amiable qualities that are the best ornaments of her sex."

CHILDREN BORN IN DRUMNAHA, IRELAND.

1010. Samuel Allison[4] (1063), lived in Drumnaha, Ireland; b. 1755; d. Dec. 3, 1818, "in the 64th year of his age."
1011. William Allison[4] obtained a large fortune, lived privately at No. 3 Edward St., Bath, England. He was a surgeon, and attained high rank in the East India company's service. Res. Bath, Eng., and d. there in 1850. His nephew, Samuel Allison of Magillegan, Ireland, wrote a letter Oct. 2, 1819, stating that his uncle William Allison had two children. Children:
1012. Mary Allison.[5]
1013. John Allison.[5]
1014. Rebecca Allison[4] m. a farmer, and lived in Ireland. Was living in 1819.
1015. Elizabeth Allison[4] was unmarried Oct. 2, 1819.
1016. Ann Allison[4] was m. and lived in Ireland in 1819.
1017. Eleanor Allison[4] was m. and lived in Ireland in 1819.
1018. Esther Allison[4] was deceased on Oct. 2, 1819.
1019. Mary Allison[4] was deceased on Oct. 2, 1819.

1020. Rebecca Allison[4] [1008] (Joseph,[3] William,[2] John[1]). She was born in Limavady, Ireland, in 1751, and was in the bright flush of young womanhood when she with her father's family emigrated to Nova Scotia in 1769. She married Col. Jonathan Crane, and resided in Horton, Kings county, N. S., where she died in 1842. She was the first of the Allison family in Nova Scotia to join the Wesleyan Methodist church. Colonel Crane for nearly forty years represented Kings in the provincial assembly. They had a large family.

CHILDREN.

1021. William Crane,[5] res. in Sackville, New Brunswick, where he d. in 1851. He possessed brilliant parts, accumulated a large fortune, and became one of the wealthiest men in the province. He entered politics, was a member of the legislature of that province, and was chosen to the speakership.
1022. James N. Crane,[5] farmer; he lived and died at Horton, N. S.
1023. Silas Crane,[5] merchant; res. Economy, N. S.
1024. —— Crane,[5] m. Mr. Dennison.
1025. —— Crane,[5] m. Mr. Taylor.

1026. William Allison[4] [1004] (Joseph,[3] William,[2] John[1]). He was born in Drumnaha, near Limavady, Ireland, in 1752, and died in Pleasant River, Digby county, N. S., in 1834. He married Humility Rathbun, of Horton, N. S., and had issue by this marriage. He married, secondly, Mrs. Eliphal Lee. His life was mostly spent in Horton, N. S.

CHILDREN BORN IN HORTON, N. S.

1027. Elizabeth Allison,[5] m. Rev. William Bennett, a missionary of the Wesleyan Methodist church, and moved from place to place.

They had a large family of children. He settled in Newport,
N. S., where he lived some twenty years. The last years of his
life were passed.in Halifax, N. S. Mrs. Bennett died soon after
they settled in Newport.   Children:
I.   William Allison Bennett,⁶ b. 1812; farmer; res. 1892, in Newport, N. S.
II.   Martha Bennett,⁶ m. Robert, second son of John Allison. She d.
1889.
III.   Joseph B. Bennett,⁶ merchant; res. Halifax, N. S., and d. years ago.
IV.   Jane Bennett,⁶ m. William Coffin; res. Barrington, N. S.
1028.   William Allison,⁵ d. young.
1029.   Amos Allison,⁵ d. young.
1030.   Nancy Allison⁵ (1074), m. James Noble Shannon; res. Halifax,
N. S.

1031.   John Allison⁴ [1005] (Joseph,³ William,² John¹).
He was born near Limavady, Ireland, in 1753, and came to
America with his father's family when he was sixteen years
of age, and settled on the shores of Acadia, bringing with
him the loyalty and religion of his ancestors.   From 1769 to
1804 he lived in Horton, N. S., where he successfully contended with all the privations and difficulties incident to a new
settlement, and while there, and later in life, by great perseverance, industry, frugality, and integrity, secured for himself and family a respectable competency.   In 1804, he removed to Newport, Hants county, N. S., which was his home
the remainder of his life.   He was a trader, and later on became one of the most successful farmers in Nova Scotia.
He was a man of solid virtues, of good sense, excellent judgment, and a pleasant conversationalist.   Being a magistrate,
he exerted his powers oftentimes successfully for the settlement of differences.   Brought up a Presbyterian, in his later
years he was an active member of the Methodist church.   He
was a.friend of God, and delighted in the duties of religion.
For many years he represented Newport in the provincial
parliament.   By his efforts the Hants Branch Bible society
was reorganized, and new life infused into the organization.
This was his last public work.   He told his family that the
fear of death was past, and died in peace March 1, 1821, and
went over the river to be reunited with many beloved friends,
and to join " that great multitude which no man can number."
Mr. Allison married in 1779, Nancy, daughter of John
Whidden, a leading magistrate in Cornwallis, Nova Scotia.¹

¹ John Whidden emigrated to Truro, N. S., with the New Hampshire
settlers in 1761. He married a Miss Longfellow of Gorham, Me., who
was closely related to the family of the poet Henry W. Longfellow. Mrs.
Whidden and her sister, Maria Longfellow, lie buried at Horton, N. S.,
in the very centre of the village of the historic Grand Pré, made forever
famous by the genius and soul of the great poet.

CHILDREN BORN IN HORTON, N. S.

1032. Sarah Allison,[5] b. in 1780, d. 1837. She m. Charles Rathbun, and res. in Falmouth and Newport, N. S. Children, all deceased:
I. Joseph Rathbun.[6]
II. Charles Rathbun.[6]
III. Sarah Rathbun.[6]
IV. Agnes Rathbun.[6]
V. John Rathbun.[6]
VI. Allison Rathbun.[6]
VII. Mary Rathbun.[6]
1033. John Allison[5] (1060), b. 1782, d. 1865; m. Hannah Smith.
1034. Joseph Allison[5] (1082), b. 1785, d. 1839; m. his cousin, Mrs. Anna (Prescott) O'Brien.
1035. Elizabeth Allison,[5] b. 1787, d. 1858. She m. John Elder, res. Falmouth, N. S. They are dead, and no descendants are living. Children:
I. Rebecca Elder,[6] d. in 1872.
II. William Elder,[6] d. when 19 years of age.
III. Bessie Elder,[6] d. of consumption in early life.
IV. Mary Elder,[6] d. of consumption in early life.
V. Margaret Elder,[6] m. J. Brown, of Falmouth, N. S., and d. without children at an early age.
VI. Nancy Elder,[6] d. of consumption when young.
VII. Sarah Elder,[6] d. of consumption when young.
1036. Ann Allison[5] (1088), b. in 1790, d. in 1866; m. Hon. Hugh Bell; res. Halifax, N. S.
1037. William Allison[5] (1092), b. in 1792 in Newport, N. S.; d. 1851, in Boston, Mass. He res. at Woodside, Newport, N. S.
1038. .James Whidden Allison[5] (1114), b. in 1795, d. in 1867; res. Newport, N. S.
1039. Mary Jane Allison[5] (1122), is deceased. She m. Winthrop Sargent, of Barrington, N. S.
1040. David Allison,[5] b. 1804, d. 1858. He m. Mary Fairbanks, who is still living at the age of 92 years. He was a leading merchant of Halifax, and a member of the firm of Fairbanks & Allison. He had six children; one, a daughter, is living. His only son died in early boyhood. Children:
1041. Fanny Allison,[6] m. Dr. S. Wells, of the English navy. She d. many years ago in Bermuda.
1042. Harriet F. Allison,[6] res. Morris St., Halifax, N. S.
1043. Joseph Allison,[6] d. in childhood.

1044. Joseph Allison[4] [1006] (Joseph,[3] William,[2] John[1]). He was born at Drumnaha, near Limavady, county of Londonderry, Ireland, sometime before the emigration of his parents to Nova Scotia in 1769; residence Horton, N. S. He married Alice, daughter of Israel Harding, a Loyalist. He represented Horton in the provincial legislature from 1808 to 1815; residence, Horton, N. S.

CHILDREN.

1045. Samuel Leonard Allison[5] (1134), res. Queens county, N. S.
1046. Joseph Allison,[5] m. Amelia Delancy, and had three daughters.

1047.   Rebecca Allison,[5] m. Caleb Huntley Rand; res. Kentville, N. S.
        Children:
I.   Elizabeth Rand,[6] m. Charles Allison, son of Jonathan C. Allison.
II. Jane Rand,[6] deceased.
III. William Henry Rand,[6] deceased.
IV. Edward Rand,[6] deceased.
V.   Ellen Rand,[6] deceased.
VI. Rebecca Rand,[6] m. Mather Boyle Almon, of Halifax, N. S.   Chil-
     dren: Ravenal Almon,[7] res. Boston, Mass., with her mother;
     Mather Almon,[7] res. St. John, Can.; Frank Almon,[7] res. Ottawa,
     Can.; John Almon,[7] res. Montreal, Can.; Percey Almon,[7] res.
     Halifax, N. S.; Eleanor Almon,[7] probably in England; Muriel
     Almon,[7] res. Halifax, N. S.; Louis Almon,[7] res. Halifax, N. S.
1048.   Israel Allison,[5] m. Abbie Dickson.   He was high sheriff of the
        county of Colchester.   Had three daughters:
I.   Kate Allison,[6] deceased.
II. Jane Allison,[6] deceased.
III. Anna Allison,[6] deceased.
1049.   Sarah Allison[5] (1163), m. Oliver Cogswell.   Seven children.   She
        res. in Kentville, N. S., and Sackville, N. B.
1050.   Jonathan Crane Allison[5] (1172), merchant in Halifax.
1051.   William Henry Allison,[5] m. Eleanor McHeffy.   He d. early, and
        left one child, a daughter:
I.   —— Allison,[6] m. Charles P. Tobin; res. Cornwallis, N. S.
1052.   Edward Allison[5] (1180), b. Cornwallis, N. S.; m. Catherine Henry;
        res. St. John, N. B.
1053.   Mary Allison,[5] m. Philip Augustus Knaut; res. Liverpool, N. S.
        Child: a dau., who d. in 1888.

1054.   James Allison[4] [1007] (Joseph,[3] William,[2] John[1]).
He was born in Limavady, county of Londonderry, Ireland,
in 1765; died in 1849.   He married Margaret Hutchinson.
He was a farmer and fruit-grower and merchant, and resided
at Cornwallis, N. S.   He was a magistrate.

CHILDREN.

1055.   James Thomas Allison,[5] b. Oct. 3, 1793.   He m. Ann McCalla, and
        left no children; lived on the homestead at Cornwallis, N. S.
1056.   Charles Frederick Allison[5] (1187), b. Jan. 25, 1795; d. Nov. 20,
        1858; m. Milcah Trueman, of Point de Bute, New Brunswick;
        res. Sackville, N. B.
1057.   John Hutchinson Allison,[5] b. Oct. 18, 1796; d. about 1845; m.
        Eliza Beggs, and had six children; res. Cornwallis, N. S.
1058.   Henry Burbridge Allison[5] (1189), b. Sept. 30, 1801; d. Dec. 1, 1890;
        m. Sarah Abrams, of Miramichi, N. B.; res. Miramichi, N. B.,
        and Sackville, N. B.
1059.   William Edward Allison,[5] b. July 23, 1806; d. 1846; m. Eliza
        McKenzie or Ann Wilkinson, and had six daughters—one sur-
        vives; res. Cornwallis, N. S.
1060.   Joseph Francis Allison[5] (1195), b. July 23, 1806; m. Mary Cogs-
        well; d. May 23, 1863; merchant; res. Sackville, N. B.
1061.   Margaret Ann Allison,[5] b. Aug. 29, 1808; m. Rev. More Campbell,
        an Episcopalian clergyman.
1062.   George Augustus Allison[5] (1202), b. April 27, 1811; m. Martha
        Prescott; m., second, Mrs. Rigby, of Sydney, Cape Breton; res.
        Halifax, N. S.

1063. Samuel Allison[4] [1010] (William,[3] William,[2] John[1]). He was born in Drumnaha, near Limavady, Ireland, in 1755; d. Dec. 3, 1818, in his sixty-fourth year. His "only brother," William Allison, lived at Bath, Eng. He married Miss Jane Flemming, and lived at Drumnaha, where he died. She died Sept. 2, 1848, aged 82 years.

CHILDREN BORN AT DRUMNAHA, COUNTY OF LONDONDERRY, IRELAND.

1064. Mary Allison,[5] b. July 26, 1790; d. single at Drumnaha, Ireland, June 19, 1871.
1065. Elizabeth Allison,[5] b. Jan. 22, 1792; d. young.
1066. —— Allison.[5] He was an apprentice, and lived in Coleraine, Ire., Oct. 2, 1819.
1067. William Allison,[5] b. Aug. 31, 1795. He emigrated to America with his uncle, Joseph Flemming, and settled in Petersburg, Va., where he lived a number of years. Trade being very much depressed, he went to New Orleans, La., and after his removal had not been heard from on Oct. 2, 1819.
1068. Samuel Allison[5] (1203), b. Nov. 21, 1797. He lived in Drumnaha, near Limavady, Ire., at a place called Magillegan, with the rest of his father's family, on Oct. 2, 1819. It was a place "our grandfather possessed" on the above date. He wrote a letter to his second cousin, Joseph Allison (son of John,[4] Joseph,[3] William,[2] John,[1] of Nova Scotia), which is now in the possession of Mrs. Elizabeth Whidden Doane, of Barrington, N. S.
1069. Robert Allison,[5] b. Nov. 11, 1799; single; merchant in Limavady, Ire.; d. June 9, 1862.
1070. John Allison,[5] b. Feb. 8, 1802; m. Mrs. Laura Sprott, and d. in Nova Scotia.
1071. Elizabeth Allison,[5] b. Feb. 8, 1802; m. Joseph Conn; res. in Magillegan, Ire., and d. about 1842.
1072. Anne Allison, b. Aug. 29, 1803; d. 1809.
1073. Jane Allison,[5] b. July 8, 1804; m. Clarke Stewart; res. Aghadowey, county of Londonderry, Ire., and d. about 1880.

1074. Nancy Allison[5] [1030] (William,[4] Joseph,[3] William,[2] John[1]). She was born in Nova Scotia, and married James Noble Shannon; res. Halifax, N. S. He was a prominent merchant.

CHILD.

1075. Samuel Leonard Shannon,[6] b. in Halifax, N. S., in 1816. For several years he was a member of the provincial government; at present (1891) he is judge of probate for the city and county of Halifax. He is owner of the historic silver spoons of his great grandfather, Joseph Allison, the emigrant; res. Halifax, N. S.
1076. Elizabeth Shannon,[6] d. of consumption in her youth.
1077. Mary Shannon,[6] d. of consumption when young.
1078. Nancy Shannon,[6] d. of consumption when approaching womanhood.
1079. Sophy Shannon,[6] d. of consumption before arriving at maturity.

1080.   John Allison [5] [1033] (John,[4] Joseph,[3] William,[2] John [1]).   He was born in 1782, and died in 1865.   He married Hannah Smith.   Mr. Allison was a gentleman of the old school, of courtly dignified manners.   He was the leading magistrate of his township, and his decisions as well as his character always commanded respect.   They had ten children, two of whom are now living.

CHILDREN.

1081.   Joseph Allison,[6] was a man of ability;   was high sheriff of the county of Hants, and was considered one of the best authorities on the early history of Nova Scotia.
1081a.   Robert Allison,[6] is a leading farmer. Res. Newport, Nova Scotia.
1081a.   D. Prescott Allison,[6] is a prominent business man. Res. Windsor, Nova Scotia.

1082.   Joseph Allison [5] [1034] (John,[4] Joseph,[3] William,[2] John [1]).   He was born 1785, and died in 1839.   He married his cousin on his mother's side, Mrs. Ann (Prescott) O'Brien. Mr. Allison was a member of the leading mercantile house of the province, " Collins & Allison," and for many years was a member of the legislative and executive councils of Nova Scotia.   Extensively did he travel, and was probably the only member of the Allison family in Nova Scotia who was on terms of personal intimacy with members of the branches of the Allison family remaining in Ireland.   He both visited and corresponded with his relative, Dr. Allison, of the East India Company, who died in Bath, Eng.   The subject of this sketch resided at Halifax, N. S.   He had six children. Neither of his two sons left any descendants.

CHILDREN.

1083.   Elizabeth Allison,[6] m. Dr. D. B. Fraser, of Windsor, N. S., and d. several years ago.
1084.   Mary Allison,[6] d. young.
1085.   Charles R. Allison,[6] graduated at King's college, N. S., and soon after died.
1086.   Frederick Allison,[6] b. 1835; d. 1879. He was a commission merchant at Halifax, N. S.
1087.   Anna Allison,[6] m. Rev. J. J. Hill, rector at Newport, N. S., and d. many years ago.

1088.   Ann Allison [5] [1036] (John,[4] Joseph,[3] William,[2] John [1]).   She was born in 1790; died in 1866.   She married in 1815, Hon. Hugh Bell, b. in county of Fermanagh, Ire , in 1780; came to Halifax with parents, 1781 or 1782; resided, Halifax, N. S.   He for a long period represented the

city of Halifax in the local parliament, and in his later years was a member of the legislative council.   He was an ardent philanthropist, and d. in Halifax, 1860, aged 80 years.   They had nine children.

CHILDREN.

1089.   Joseph Bell,[4] was high sheriff of the county and city of Halifax.
1090.   John Allison Bell,[4] is auditor for the city of Halifax, and is noted
    for his poetic gifts and fine literary taste; res. Halifax, N. S.
1091.   Sarah Bell,[4] m. Mr. Bennett. She is a widow, and is still living.

1092.   William Allison[5] [1037] (John,[4] Joseph,[3] William,[2] John[1]).   He was born 1792; died March 1, 1851, in Boston, Mass.   Married Martha Irish, of Falmouth, N. S., who died and left eight children.   He married, second, Lucy Rathbun, of Horton, N. S., who had five children, and died April, 1893. He resided at Woodside, Newport, N. S.

CHILDREN.

1093.   Margaret Anne Allison,[6] m. William Allison Bennett, of Willow
    Bank, Newport, N. S.   Children:
I.   Bessie Bennett,[7] is deceased.
II.   Martha Bennett.[7]
III.   William Bennett.[7]
1094.   Elizabeth Allison,[6] m. Rev. John McMurray, of Halifax, N. S., who
    d. Dec. 26, 1890, aged 78 years.   No children.
1095.   Mary Jane Allison,[6] m. Hugh McCallum, of Truro, N. S.   Chil-
    dren:
I.   William McCallum.[7]
II.   Annie McCallum.[7]
III.   John A. McCallum.[7]
IV.   Moreau McCallum.[7]
1096.   John Allison[6] (1215), b. Newport, Hants Co., N. S., May 16, 1821.
    Res. 2503 Stevens Ave., Minneapolis, Minn.
1079.   Martha Allison,[6] m. Hugh Chambers, of Newport, N. S.   She is
    deceased. Children:
I.   Helen Chambers.[7]
II.   Frederick Chambers.[7]
1098.   Maria Allison,[6] d. young.
1099,   William Allison,[6] d. young.
1100.   Henry Allison,[6] d. young.
1101.   Frederick Day Allison,[6] m. Emily Jost, of Halifax, N. S.   He d.
    May, 1886, aged 50 years.   No children.
1102.   Louisa DeWolfe Allison,[6] b. 1838, at Woodside, Newport, N.S.; m.
    Thomas I. Harris, of Hortón, N. S.; farmer.   No children.
1103.   Joseph Allison,[6] b. Woodside, Newport, N. S., July 1, 1840; m.,
    Aug. 3, 1861, Helen Matilda, dau. Joseph Scammell, of St. John,
    N. B.; b. Aug. 9, 1806, in Wiley, Wiltshire, England, and d.
    May, 1862, in St. John, N. B.   He m. Fanny Matilda Chute, b.
    Nov. 10, 1807, at Digby, N. S.   Mrs. Allison was b. March 25,
    1847, in St. John, N. B.   When nine years of age, he left his
    native place and went to live with his brother, Rev. John Alli-
    son,[6] at Woodstock, N. B., and three years later went to St.

John, N. B., where he has ever since resided. When thirteen years of age, he went into a store to learn the dry goods business, at which he has ever since been engaged. In 1866 he started on his own account, in partnership with James Manchester and James F. Robertson, under the firm name of Manchester, Robertson & Allison. They are still in trade, and have built up the largest wholesale and retail trade business ever reached in the maritime provinces. Children, b. St. John, N. B.:

1104. Walter Cushing Allison,[7] b. April 12, 1873.
1105. Helen Gertrude Allison,[7] b. July 15, 1875.
1106. William Scammell Allison,[7] b. Aug. 29, 1884.
1107. Winthrop Sargent Allison,[6] b. Newport, N. S.; m. Carrie Chambers, of that place. Children:
1108. Lucy Rathbone Allison.[7]
1109. Frank Allison,[7] dead.
1110. Louisa Allison.[7]
1111. Fannie Allison.[7]
1112. Harry Allison.[7]
1113. Francis Rathbone Allison,[6] d. young.

1114. James Whidden Allison [5] [1038] (John,[4] Joseph,[3] William,[2] John [1]). He was born in Horton, N. S., December 1, 1795; married, July, 1821, Margaret, daughter of Matthew and —— (Jenkins) Elder. She was born in Falmouth, N. S., June 12, 1799; died in Newport, N. S., March, 1872. Her father was a native of county of Donegal, Ireland, and lived in Falmouth, N. S. Mr. Allison was a farmer, and resided in Horton, N. S., from 1795 to 1804, and in Newport, N. S., from 1804 till his death in 1867. He was one of the leading magistrates of Newport, and for five years represented that township in the provincial parliament. He was Methodist in his religious affiliations.

CHILDREN.

1115. James Whidden Allison,[6] b. Newport, N. S., July 22, 1822; m. Margaret Master; merchant; res. Newport, N. S. No children.
1116. —— Allison,[6] a dau., d. in infancy.
1117. —— Allison,[6] a dau., d. in infancy.
1118. Sarah Jane Allison,[6] b. Newport, N. S., March, 1827; res. in Winnipeg, Manitoba.
1119. John Allison,[6] b. Newport, N. S., Jan. 1, 1834; m. first, Rachel Shaw; second, Mary Rathbun. He is a federal government homestead inspector; res. Winnipeg, Manitoba. Children:
I.   Leonard Allison, lawyer, Sussex, N. B.
II. Lewis Allison, civil engineer.
III. Mary Allison.
IV. Bessie Allison.
V.   Lily Allison.
VI. Edith Allison.
VII. Jennie Allison.
1120. David Allison [6] (1219), b. Newport, N. S., July 3, 1836. President of Mount Allison university; res. Sackville, N. B.

1121.   William Henry Allison,[6] b. Newport, N. S., June 14, 1838. He
represented the county of Hants, N. S., in the provincial parliament at Halifax, N. S.   Then for ten years he represented
the same constituency in the federal house of commons at
Ottawa, Can.   He is, in 1892, homestead inspector for the
southern district of Manitoba, under the federal government
of the dominion of Canada.   Res. Deloraine, Manitoba.

1122.   Mary Jane Allison [5] [1089]   (John,[4] Joseph,[3] William,[2] John [1]).   She was born at Long Island, Horton, N. S.,
October 13, 1798; married, July 17, 1819, Winthrop Sargent, son of John and Margaret (Barnard) Sargent, and a
grandson of Col. Epes and Catherine Winthrop, his wife, of
Salem, Mass.   John Sargent moved from Salem, Mass., and
settled in Barrington, N. S., during the American Revolution.   He was a Loyalist.   She died October 13, 1867.   Mr.
Sargent lived in Barrington, N. S., and was a prominent
merchant, legislator, and collector of customs.   He was born
at Barrington, N. S., June 6, 1794; died October 6, 1866.

CHILDREN BORN BARRINGTON, N. S.

1123.   Catherine Winthrop Sargent,[6] b. June 8, 1822; m. Joseph A. Doane,
July 23, 1851.   Removed to Australia in 1852.   She d. July 2,
1855, at Ballarat, Australia.   He is an architect, and res. at Melbourne, Australia.   The Doanes emigrated to Nova Scotia from
New England shortly before the Revolution.
1124.   Ann Sargent,[6] b. March 5, 1823; m., Feb., 1848, Joseph A. Doane;
res. Barrington, N. S.; d. Nov. 24, 1848, at Barrington, N. S.
Child:
I.   Ann Sargent Doane,[7] who died in infancy.
1125.   Epes Winthrop Sargent,[6] b. Sept. 17, 1824; d. at New York city,
May 14, 1869.   Commission merchant; res. at Halifax, at the
island of Cuba, and New York city.   Never married.
1126.   Mary Jane Sargent,[6] b. May 14, 1826; m., July 31, 1849, Capt. Seth
C. Doane, and accompanied her husband on some of his ocean
voyages.   She spent some years at Ballarat, Australia.   Her
health failing, she visited Sydney, N. S. W., and then left for
England, hoping to live to reach her old home in Nova Scotia.
When Cape Horn was reached, its cold and storms were too
severe for her delicate frame.   She sank rapidly, d. April 24,
1855, and was buried at sea.   She was accompanied by her sister, Elizabeth Whidden Doane, and her only daughter.   Child:
I.   Julia Doane,[7] b. at Barrington, N. S., Sept. 26, 1850; m. Warren W.
Atwood, collector of customs at Shelburne, N. S.   Child: Anne
Sargent Atwood.[8]
1127.   John Allison Sargent,[7] b. April 6, 1828; d. Oct. 26, 1851, at Saquala
Grande, Cuba.   He never married.
1128.   Elizabeth Whidden Sargent,[6] b. Feb. 20, 1830; m., June 28, 1852,
Arthur W. Doane, son of Josiah Payne Doane.   She, with her
husband, went to Melbourne, Australia, soon after their marriage, touched at the Cape of Good Hope on the voyage, and
were one hundred and six days at sea.   They spent some years
at Ballarat, Australia, and now (1892) reside at Barrington,
N. S.   Children:

I.   John Sargent Doane,' b. Australia, and d. there in infancy.
II. Ann Sargent Doane,' b. Barrington, N. S., and d. in infancy.
III. Elizabeth Mary Doane,' b. Barrington, N. S., where she still lives.
IV. John Allison Sargent Doane,' b. Barrington, N. S., and still lives
     there.
V.   Arthur Whidden Doane,' b. Barrington, N. S.; res. Boston, Mass.;
     P. O. Box, 2816, Boston, Mass.
VI. Emma Doane,' b. Barrington, N. S.; d. young.
VII. Robert Duncan Doane,' b. Barrington, N. S.; m. Florence Coffin;
     res. Oxford, N. S. Child; Dorothy Allison Doane.*
VIII. Catherine Sargent Doane,' b. Barrington, N. S.; d. in infancy.
IX. Mary Sargent Doane,' b. Barrington, N. S., and res. there in 1892.
X.   Joseph Doane,' b. Barrington, N. S., and res. there in 1892.
1129. Sarah Harding Sargent,* b. June 30, 1832; d. Barrington, N. S.,
     June 6, 1838.
1130. Margaret Sophia Sargent,* b. April 13, 1834; m. May 27, 1857, James
     H. Doane. He was a school teacher. They resided in Bar-
     rington, N. S., until his death, fifteen years after their marriage.
     She res., in 1892, in Truro, N. S. Children were b. in Barring-
     ton, N. S.:
I.   Charlotte Doane,' d. young.
II. Herbert Lander Doane,' m. Anna Ells; res. Truro, N. S.
III. Francis Augustus Doane,' res. Truro, N. S.
IV. Fanny Sargent Doane,' m. Jackson Ricker; res. Argyle, N. S.
V.   John Winthrop Doane,' res. Truro, N. S.
VI. William Avard Doane,' res. Truro, N. S., and d. there.
1131. Charles Rathbun Sargent,* b. June 17, 1836; m. Sarah Doane, of
     Halifax, N. S., May 27, 1861; d. Halifax, N. S., July 9, 1872.
     He was a book-keeper and bank clerk. Res. some years at
     Pierre Miquelon, but removed to Halifax, and d. there. His
     widow and children res. at Somerville, Mass. Children: Mary
     Esther Sargent', Charles William Sargent,' James Winthrop Sar-
     gent.' The latter m. Mabel E. Rich, of Boston.
1132. Frances Sargent,* b. Sept. 4, 1838; d. Barrington, N. S., March 21,
     1863. Always resided at Barrington, N. S. Single.
1133. William Sargent,* b. May 2, 1841; m. Frances Augusta Scott, of
     Windsor, N. S., Aug., 1875; d. Hillsborough, N. S., March 3,
     1877. He was a Methodist clergyman. She res. at Windsor,
     N. S. One child, d. young.

1134. Samuel Leonard Allison⁵ [1045] (Joseph,⁴ Joseph,³
William,² John¹). He was born at Horton, Kings county,
Nova Scotia, July 31, 1789, and died at Kempt, Queen's
county, Nova Scotia, in Feb., 1875. He married Sophia,
daughter of Joseph Barss, of Liverpool, Nova Scotia, Oct. 6,
1820. He first settled at Kentville, N. S., where he was
prothonotary of the supreme court for over twenty years.
In 1833 he removed to Liverpool, N. S., and from there to
Kempt, Queens county, N. S., in March, 1838, where he
died.

CHILDREN.

1135. Charles Allison* (1225), b. Sept. 22, 1821; res. Yarmouth, N. S.
1136. Samuel L. Allison,* b. August, 1823; died at sea.
1137. Joseph Allison,* b. April, 1825; d. in California.
1138. Caroline Allison,* b. Cornwallis, N. S., Oct. 26, 1828; m. Sept. 26,
     1853, Dr. Elias N. Payzant. He was b. at Wilmot, N. S., July 27,
     1830; res. Wolfville, N. S., in 1892. Five children.

1139. Julia Brown Payzant,[7] b. July 9, 1854; d. May 30, 1858.
1140. James Austin Payzant,[7] b. Feb. 8, 1856; m. Kate Mann, May 14,
       1886. He is a practising physician at Burlington, Hants Co.,
       N. S.   Child: Ellen Payzant,[8] b. Nov., 1889; d. Dec., 1889.
1141. Archibald Allison Payzant,[7] b. Dec. 19, 1857; d. Feb. 20, 1858.
1142. William Payzant,[7] dentist; res. Wolfville, N. S.
1143. Sarah Cathella Payzant,[7] b. March 10, 1859. She m. Capt. William
       J. Forbes; address, Zion's Herald Office, Boston, Mass.
1144. Charles Earnest Payzant,[7] b. Aug. 17, 1860; d. Sept. 18, 1883.
1145. Annie Lois Payzant,[7] b. Nov. 6, 1861. She m., Aug. 10, 1882, E.
       Sidney Crowley; res. Wolfville, N. S. Four children.
1146. Elias T. Payzant,[7] b. May 19, 1863; d. June 18, 1865.
1147. Carrie Sophia Payzant,[7] b. Sept. 20, 1864; m., Nov. 24, 1886, Hilton
       A. Pitt; res. Hamilton, Bermuda.
1148. William Aubrey Payzant,[7] b. Oct. 26, 1866; dentist; res. Wolfville,
       N. S.
1149. Bessie Allison Payzant,[7] b. Feb. 24, 1868; d. Jan. 15, 1888.
1150. Florence Rachel Payzant,[7] b. March 2, 1870; m. Oct., 1887, Clifford
       H. Fielding; res. Halifax, N. S., 57 South street.
1151. Elizabeth Allison,[6] b. Nov., 1830; m. Robert Brown, of Yarmouth,
       N. S., where they live. No family.
1152. Frances M. Allison,[6] b. Kentville, N. S., April 7, 1832; m., April 14,
       1881, Barnabas Miles, of Greenfield, N. S. They have no family.
1153. James B. Allison,[6] b. May, 1836; d. young.
1154. Tryphena Allison,[6] b. July 4, 1838; m. William E. Freeman, of
       Kempt, Queens Co., N. S. Five children.
1155. Archibald Allison Freeman,[7] b. Aug. 22, 1866.
1156. Maurice Urban Freeman,[7] b. March 29, 1868.
1157. Emma Freeman,[7] b. June 3, 1869.
1158. Mary Alice Freeman,[7] b. Dec. 13, 1875.
1159. Janet Freeman,[7] b. Dec. 5, 1880.
1160. Annie S. Allison,[6] b. May 17, 1842; m., Feb. 27, 1868, Edwin Kemp-
       ton, of Kempt, N. S. Two children.
1161. Laura Kempton,[7] b. Dec. 6, 1868; m., Jan. 15, 1890, Robert Atkins.
1162. Fred Kempton,[7] b. Dec. 21, 1871.

1163.   Sarah Allison [5] [1149] (Joseph,[4] Joseph,[3] William,[2]
John[1]).   She married Oliver Cogswell, of Kentville, N. S.,
and afterward resided at Dorchester and at Sackville, N. B.
She died at Dorchester, N. B., July 10, 1883.

CHILDREN.

1164. Mary Cogswell,[6] m., 1839, Joseph F. Allison of Sackville, who d.
       1863. She m., second, in 1864, Hon. Amos E. Botsford, senator
       in the Dominion parliament.
1165. Rebecca Cogswell,[6] m. Thomas B. Campbell, of Kentville, N. S.
1166. Edward Cogswell,[6] d. in infancy.
1167. Nancy Cogswell,[6] m. James B. Fitch, of Horton, N. S., and d. 1856.
1168. Maria Cogswell,[6] m. William C. Campbell, of Kentville, N. S., and
       d. 1869.
1169. Robert Cogswell,[6] m. Mary L. Graham, and d. 1864.
1170. Edward Cogswell,[6] b. 1823; m., 1850, Ruth, dau. of Hon. William
       Crane, of Sackville, N. B.; m., second, 1877, Sarah, dau. of
       Charles Dixon, of Sackville, N. B.
1171. Sarah Cogswell,[6] b. 1827; m., 1847, Blair Botsford, who was high
       sheriff of Westmoreland Co., N. B., for some years, and who is
       deceased.
       13

1172. Jonathan Crane Allison [5] [1150] (Joseph,[4] Joseph,[3] William,[2] John [1]). He was born April 3, 1798, at Grand Pré, N. S. He was a leading merchant in Halifax, and partner with David Allison in the firm of Fairbanks & Allisons, in their day the largest mercantile house in the maritime provinces. He married, October 9, 1824, Jane Boggs, daughter of Charles and Mary (Fraser) Boggs, of New Jersey, and had seven children. She died June, 1858. He died in Halifax, N. S., February, 1872.

CHILDREN BORN HALIFAX, N. S.

1173. Charles Allison,[6] b. Nov. 14, 1825; on June 30, 1854, he m. Elizabeth Rand of Kentville; merchant; res. in Halifax, N. S., and d. Oct., 1863.
1174. Alice Mary Allison,[6] b. June 14, 1827; m., Aug. 23, 1854, William Hare, of Halifax. P. O. address: Bedford, N. S.
1175. Louisa Allison,[6] b. Aug. 13, 1829; d. April 5, 1845.
1176. Harriet Allison,[6] b. Dec. 25, 1831; d. in spring of 1839.
1177. Jane Allison,[6] b. April, 1834; d. May, 1835.
1178. Augustus Allison,[6] b. April 19, 1837; m., April 28, 1868, Cevilla Hill, of Halifax, N. S. He is noted for his interest in literature and science; res. Halifax, N. S.
1179. Alfred Louis Allison,[6] b. Feb. 27, 1844; d. May, 1846.

1180. Edward Allison [5] [1152] (Joseph,[4] Joseph,[3] William,[2] John [1]). He was born in Cornwallis, N. S., November, 1803; married Catherine Henry; res. in Halifax, N. S., till about 1853, since then chiefly in St. John, N. B. They had twelve children: one survives. He died at Halifax, N. S., March 7, 1876.

CHILDREN.

1181. Lucius Carey Allison,[6] physician; res. St. John, N. B.
1182. Frank Octavius Allison,[6] b. St. John, N. B., Jan. 29, 1850; m., June 4, 1873, Mary Ansel Bonsard, b. December, 1852, in St. John. He is a deputy shipping-master at that place, and in April, 1878, was appointed consul there for Portugal, and still holds the position. He is an Episcopalian, and active in that denomination, and has filled several church offices. Children, b. St. John, N. B.:
1183. Ethel K. Allison,[7] b. May 19, 1874.
1184. Harold Ansel Allison,[7] b. Aug. 16, 1876.
1185. Edmund K. Allison,[7] b. Sept. 15, 1879.
1186. Frank Drummond Allison,[7] b. March 29, 1873.

1187. Charles Frederick Allison [5] [1056] (James,[4] Joseph,[3] William,[2] John [1]). He was born in 1795; died in 1858. He married Milcah Freeman. He resided in Sackville, N. B., where he carried on an extensive business in partnership with his cousin, William Crane. The name of no member of the Allison family is so widely known throughout Eastern

British America as his. He founded the Mount Allison educational institutions, consisting of a boys' school, ladies' college, and university. They are under the control of the Methodist church of Canada, of which Mr. Allison was an earnest member. In him the noblest character was associated with the most unassuming demeanor.

CHILD.

1188. Mary Allison, d. in 1871.

1189. Henry Burbridge Allison[5] [1058] (James,[4] Joseph,[3] William,[2] John[1]). He was born in Cornwallis, N. S., September 30, 1801; married in July, 1839, Sarah Abrams, a native of Scotland, and who is still living in 1892. Mr. Allison began his business life in Halifax, and after some years he went to Miramichi, N. B., and with his partner carried on an extensive business under the name of Crane & Allison. While there he lost heavily by a great fire. In 1854 he removed to Sackville, N. B., and engaged in business. That place ever after was his home. By his integrity and high sense of honor he won the respect and esteem of all. He possessed courtly manners of the old school. Till within a year of his death his health was perfect, with none of the infirmities of age. His sight and hearing and mental faculties were good to the last. He celebrated his golden wedding in July, 1889. He died at 11:30 a. m., on Sunday, December 1, 1890.

CHILDREN BORN NEWCASTLE, N. B.

1190. Jane Clark Allison,[6] b. June 10, 1840; m. Seward S. Paddings, of Bermuda, and d. in Bermuda, June 13, 1888. No children.
1191. Henry Burton Allison,[6] b. Oct. 16, 1841; m. Nettie Harrison, of Boston; no children; res. Sackville, N. B.
1192. Margaret Ann Campbell Allison,[6] b. Feb. 26, 1843; res. Sackville, N. B.
1193. Sarah Mary Allison,[6] b. Aug. 12, 1845; d. April 1, 1858.
1194. Howard Allan Allison,[6] b. Jan. 12, 1848; m. Lizzie Cheney, of Boston; res. 66 Inman St., Cambridgeport, Mass. Children:
I. Henrietta Beatrice Allison,[7] b. March 14, 1886; d. Sept. 23, 1886.
II. H. Burbridge Cheney Allison,[7] b. Aug. 30, 1890.
1194a. James Walter Allison[6] (1234 a), b. March 31, 1850; merchant; res. Halifax, N. S.
1194b. Chester Leonard Allison,[6] b. Sept. 26, 1852; d. Nov. 13, 1862.

1195. Joseph Francis Allison[5] [1060] (James,[4] Joseph,[3] William,[2] John[1]). He was born at Cornwallis, N. S., July 23, 1806, and died at Sackville, N. B., May 29, 1863. He married Mary A., daughter of Oliver and Sarah A. Cogswell, at Sackville, N. B., Dec. 17, 1839. She was born at

Cornwallis, N. S., Feb. 14, 1815.   Mr. Allison was a leading
merchant at Sackville, N. B., and member of the firm of
Crane & Allison.   He was an estimable man.   Mrs. Allison
married, second, in Sept., 1864, Amos Edwin Botsford.

CHILDREN.

1196.   Susan Alice Allison,* b. Oct. 22, 1840; m. Dr. William Johnston,
     July 1, 1863.   She married, second, Herbert Crosskill.   Her
     death occurred Sept. 7, 1889.
1197.   Francis Clifford Allison,* b. Feb. 27, 1846; d. Aug. 28, 1848,
1198.   Francis Allison,* b. July 16, 1848; m., Oct. 12, 1871, Sophia M.,
     daughter of Wilson Welden, of Bathurst, N. B.
1199.   James Frederick Allison,* b. Oct. 20, 1850; m., Sept. 8, 1881,
     Louisa M., daughter of the late Major William Beverly Robin-
     son, of St. John, N. B.   Postmaster at Sackville, N. B.
1200.   Cassie Allison,* b. May 10, 1853; m., Feb. 23, 1888, Alfred Temple-
     ton Parsons, 515 Clinton ave., Brooklyn, N. Y.   He is proprie-
     tor of extensive stone quarries at Sackville, N. B., where he
     resides in the summer months.
1201.   Grace Allison,* b. Feb. 3, 1856; d. Oct. 1, 1856.

1202.   George Augustus Allison [5] [1062] (James,[4] Joseph,[3] William,[2] John[1]).   He was born in 1811; married
Martha Prescott, by whom he had eight children.   He married, second, Mrs. Rigly, of Sydney, Cape Breton.   Mr. Allison dropped dead in his garden June 8th, 1893.   He resided
at Halifax, N. S.

1203.   Samuel Allison [5] [1068] (Samuel,[4] William,[3] William,[2] John[1]).   He was born in Drumnaha, Ireland, near
Limavady, Nov. 21, 1797; was a farmer, and resided in
that place, where he died Sept. 26, 1878.   He married, Oct.
18, 1832, Rachel, daughter of Samuel and Hetty (Steele)
Hazlett, of Liffock, Dunboe, county of Londonderry, Ireland,
where she was born April 27, 1813.   She was the granddaughter of Isaac and Margaret (Carr) Hazlett.   Mrs. Allison still lives (1892) in Drumnaha, Magillegan, Ireland.

CHILDREN BORN IN DRUMNAHA, IRELAND.

1204.   Samuel Allison,* b. Aug. 12, 1833; m., Nov. 14, 1872, Mary Moore.
     Farmer; res. Drumnaha, Ireland.   Three sons and three
     daughters.
1205.   William Allison,* b. March 19, 1835; m., Sept., 1863, Mary Brown.
     Physician; res. Claudy, county of Londonderry, Ireland.   He
     has four sons and four daughters.
1206.   John Allison,* b. Feb. 17, 1837; m., March, 1864, Eleanor Brew-
     ster; res. Brisbane, Australia.   One son and one daughter.
1207.   Hetty Ann Allison,* b. June 24, 1839; m. William Brewster: res.
     Drumnaha, Magillegan, Ireland.   Two sons and three daugh-
     ters.

1208.   Isaac Allison,[5] b. June 4, 1841; d. at Drumnaha, Ireland, April 11,
        1861.
1209.   Jane Allison,[5] b. June 24, 1843; m., May 9, 1865, James Binns;
        res. Kansas. Three sons and four daughters.
1210.   Robert Allison,[5] b. Oct. 28, 1845; farmer; res. Drumnaha, Ireland.
1211.   Joseph Allison,[5] b. March 28, 1848; d. June 17, 1848.
1212.   Hazlett Allison,[5] b. April 30, 1851; m., June 25, 1891, Mary Woods.
        Surgeon major; res. Madras, India.
1213.   Charles Warke Allison,[5].b. Oct. 7, 1853; m., Nov. 29, 1888, Eleanor
        Fleming. Medical doctor; res. Dungiven, county of London-
        derry, Ireland. Two sons and one daughter.
1214.   Hugh Allison,[5] b. Oct. 13, 1856; m., Oct. 4, 1889, Mabel Wads-
        worth.. Medical doctor; res. London, England. One son.

   1215. Rev. John Allison [5] [1096] (William,[4] John,[3] Joseph,[2]
John [1]). He was born on the Mantua Farm in Newport,
Hants county, Nova Scotia, May 16, 1821. He was educated
at Annapolis, N. S., and Dalhousie college in Halifax, N. S.
In September, 1849, he was ordained to the ministry in
Fredericton, New Brunswick. He afterward graduated as
A. B. and A. M. at Syracuse University, N. Y., was pastor of
the Methodist Episcopal church at Cornwallis, N. S., Wood-
stock, N. B., St. John, N. B., and was principal of the Mount
Allison Ladies' academy at Sackville, N. B., for eight years.
In 1863 he travelled in England, Scotland, Belgium, France,
Switzerland, and Germany. In 1864-'65 he was pastor of a
church in Buffalo, N. Y., and later was pastor four years in
Milwaukee, Wis. In 1872 he established the "Allison Clas-
sic" academy at Oconomowoc, Wis. Was pastor at Lanes-
boro', Minn., for three years; chaplain of the Minnesota state
senate in 1885; lectured for the Minnesota State Teachers'
Institute for three years. In 1891 he was writing for the
press and lecturing. He was, in Nova Scotia, considered one
of the first pulpit orators in the maritime provinces. He married in Fredericton, N. B., Nov. 24, 1847, Martha Louisa,
daughter of Richard and Mary Davis (Hosier) Knight. Her
father was of Exeter, England. She was born, Feb. 26,
1823, in Newfoundland. She was his excellent helper in his
life work, and was an A. B. and A. M. of Genesee college,
Lima, Livingston county, N. Y. She died in 1892. He resided at Minneapolis, Minn., and d. July 19, 1893.

CHILDREN.

1216.   Charles Edward Allison,[7] b. Woodstock, N. B., May 23, 1850; d.
        Dec. 25, 1852.
1217.   William Richard Allison,[7] b. Woodstock, N. B., Feb. 26, 1852; m.,
        April 22, 1874, Susie M. Curran. He is a physician; res. Minne-
        apolis, Minn. Child:
1218.   May Louise Allison,[8] b. March 10, 1878.

1219. David Allison[6] [1120] (James Whidden,[5] John[4], Joseph,[3] William,[2] John[1]). Prof. Allison was born at Newport, Hants county, Nova Scotia, July 3, 1836. He was educated at Halifax academy, and by a four years course at the academy at Sackville, N. B., where he took the highest stand as a student, at the Wesleyan university at Middletown, Conn., where he pursued his collegiate course and graduated in 1859 at the head of a large and brilliant class. For a short time he taught at Stanstead, Quebec, then he returned to Sackville, N. B., and was a teacher of the classics in the academy, and was made professor of the classics on the establishment of the college. In 1869 he succeeded Dr. Pickard in the presidency, which he resigned in 1878 to take the superintendency of education for the province of Nova Scotia. That position he held until Oct. 31, 1891. He was reappointed president of the university at Sackville in June, 1891, and entered upon the duties of the position in November, 1891. The eminent ability with which he filled these various positions furnishes an ample guaranty that there lies before him, as president of Mount Allison university for the second time, an administration of a most satisfactory nature. Among the accepted and cherished traditions of that college are his exceptional capacity as an instructor, and his power to impress himself for good on the heads and hearts of those under his charge and influence. As a classical scholar he has rare acquirements, and is noted for broad and tolerant views on matters of ecclesiastical and political dispute. His power as a preacher must not be omitted in enumerating the elements which go to make up his educational and life record. Students are unanimous in speaking with admiration of the manly, thoughtful, and weighty discourses which strongly impressed the hearts of his hearers, and often turned in the right direction forever some young career that might, but for those pregnant words, have ended in a lamentable failure. Many there are that for these sermons alone, can say to him, "It is better with me, it shall be better with me, because I have known you." In the history of this branch of the Allison family he has taken a deep and decided interest and furnished much information to the author which is gratefully acknowledged. He received the degree of A. B. and A. M. from Wesleyan university, Middletown, Conn., and of LL. D. from Victoria university, Coburg, Ontario, in 1871. He married, June 18, 1862, Elizabeth Powell of New Brunswick, a lady well qualified to grace the various circles in which her husband's various positions have called her to move. She

D. Allison

was born, March 26, 1889, at Richibucto, N. B., and is great-granddaughter of Solomon Powell, a Loyalist in the American Revolution, who emigrated from Poughkeepsie, N. Y., in 1784, to Nova Scotia.   Her parents were Edmund and Ann Powell.

CHILDREN.

1220.   James Whidden Allison,⁷ b. at Sackville, N. B., Sept. 16, 1864; d. March 21, 1870.
1221.   Edward Powell Allison, ⁷ b. at Richibucto, N. B., July 9, 1866; graduated at Dalhousie college, Halifax, N. S., in 1890; student at law, in the same institution, in 1891 and in 1892; is with the law firm of Powell & Bennett, Sackville, N. S.
1222.   Charles Frederick Allison,⁷ b. at Sackville, N. B., Aug. 22, 1868; d. March 29, 1885.
1223.   David Allison,⁷ b. at Sackville, N. B., July 22, 1871; student in 1892 at Mount Allison academy, Sackville, N. B.
1224.   Henry Augustus Allison,⁷ b. at Sackville, N. B., Aug. 6, 1877; student in 1892 at Mount Allison academy, Sackville, N. B.

  1225.   Charles Allison ⁶ [1135] (Samuel Leonard,⁵ Joseph,⁴ Joseph,³ William,² John ¹).   He was born in Kentville, N. S., Sept. 22, 1821.   In 1858 he was appointed justice of the peace for Queens county, N. S.; in 1864 was elected to the Nova Scotia parliament as representative of North Queens Co.; in 1865 was appointed lieutenant-colonel of the militia, and in 1867 was chosen a member of the provincial government with the office of commissioner of mines.   In September, 1867, he and all his colleagues were defeated at the election, with the exception of the attorney-general, Hiram Blanchard.   In 1879 he was appointed inspector of weights and measures for the Yarmouth division, a position he still holds.   He married, July 19, 1848, Lavinia, daughter of George and Kate (Kempton) Freeman, of Milton, Queens county, N. S.   She was born in the township of Caledonia, Nov. 30, 1828.   Resides Yarmouth, N. S.

CHILDREN BORN IN KEMPT, QUEENS COUNTY, N. S.

1226.   Alice Sophia Allison,⁷ b. Feb. 23, 1851; m. Feb. 12, 1879, J. Lewis Johnson, of Liverpool, N. S.; she is corresponding clerk in Youth's Companion office; res. Boston, Mass.   One child now deceased.
1227.   Charlotte Elizabeth Allison,⁷ b. July 8, 1852; m., June, 1870, to Richard Lewis, who died at Exploits river, Newfoundland, in June, 1890.   Res. Kempt, Queens county, N. S.   She died at New Germany, N. S., Oct., 1880.   Children:
I.   Leon Lewis,⁸ res. Boston, Mass.
II.   Letitia Lewis,⁸ res. Maitland, N. S.
III.   Kate Lewis,⁸ res. New Germany, N. S.

1228. Catharine Allison,[7] b. Aug. 18, 1854; m., Oct. 12, 1877, Frank H.
        McCoy, of Cambridgeport. Child:
I. Rosie McCoy.[8]
1229. Edith Allison,[7] b. Nov. 12, 1856; m., Sept. 3, 1883; Sylvester S. Mur-
        ray, of Liverpool, N. S., who d. leaving one child. She m.,
        second, George Johns of Maitland, N. S. They res. at Kempt,
        Queens Co., N. S. Children:
I. Helen M. Murray.[8]
II. —— Johns.[8]
1230. Mary Arabella Allison,[7] b. July 27, 1858; m., Oct. 26, 1877, Howard
        D. Kathrens, of Annapolis, N. S. They res. Somerville, Mass.
        Four children.
1231. Joseph Leonard Allison,[7] b. April 4, 1861. He was drowned in
        Henry Minard's lake, at Kempt, Queens Co., N. S., July 3,
        1874.
1232. Helen Maud Allison,[7] b. April 24, 1863; m., Sept. 1, 1890, Samuel
        F. Cohoon, of Beverly Farms, Mass. One child.
1233. Henry Allison,[7] b. June 28, 1865; d. at Halifax, N. S., Dec. 17,
        1888.
1234. Charles Edward Allison,[7] b. June 11, 1871.

1234a.   James Walter Allison[6] [1194 1194a] (Henry B.,[5]
James,[4] Joseph,[3] William,[2] John[1]). He was born in New Castle, N. B., March 31, 1850. His family removed to Sackville, N. B., when he was four years of age, and there he was
educated at Mount Allison academy and college, founded by
his uncle, Charles F. Allison. In 1871 he became a book-
keeper for Douall & Miller, a large business house in Halifax, N. S. There his business faculties unfolded rapidly, and
later he went into the commission business, and later still into
partnership with the late John P. Mott, and in 1876 his name
appeared as a member of the firm of John P. Mott & Co.,
where he has since been an active member. In its interest
he has travelled throughout the maritime provinces, through
Quebec and Ontario, and other parts of Canada. Since the
death of John P. Mott, in 1890, Mr. Allison has been the
manager and executor of the estate, which is above three
fourths of a million of dollars in value. He is a director in
the People's Bank of Halifax; a director in the Eastern Assurance Company (capital $1,000,000); a director in the New
Glasgow Iron, Coal and Railway Co. (capital $1,000,000); a
director in the Nova Scotia Permanent Benefit Building
Society and Savings Fund, one of the largest monetary institutions in the lower provinces; a director in the Ocean
Mutual Marine Insurance Co., and a director in the Nova
Scotia Steam Packet Co. His various monetary and commercial responsibilities tax his powers heavily, but not beyond their strength. He married, Oct. 10, 1876, Mary Prescott, of Bail Virte, N. B. No children. Resides at Halifax, N. S.

J. Watts Allison

ALLISONS OF EVISH HILL AND OF LIMAVADY, COUNTY OF
LONDONDERRY, IRELAND, AND LATER OF STILL-
WATER, MIRAMICHI COUNTY, NEW BRUNSWICK.

1235.   Thomas Morrison Allison lived in Limavady, county
of Londonderry, Ireland, in 1892, and his family of Allisons
came from Evish Hill in the immediate vicinity of Londonderry, Ireland. This Evish Hill is near Enoch Loch, somewhat off the road leading from Limavady to Londonderry.

1236.   Rev. James Allison, a great uncle of Mr. Allison,
preached for many years at Breckfield Presbyterian church
in the same district, but nearer Cumber Cloudy than to Londonderry.

The grandfather of T. M. Allison, born in 1768, sold his
farm at Evish Hill, and with his whole family, except one
son, the father of T. M. Allison, of Limavady, emigrated to
Stillwater, Miramichi, New Brunswick, in the early part of
this century, or about 1825. The names of his sons who
emigrated with him were,—

1237.   William Allison, who died about 1872.

1237a.   Samuel Allison.

1238.   David Allison.

1239.   Hugh Allison ; and two daughters emigrated.

This family is probably connected with the Allisons of
Drumnaha, Ireland, and of Nova Scotia.

THE MORRISONS, ALLISONS, HUNTERS, AND CROOKS.[1]

Claggan, county of Londonderry, Ireland, is about equidistant from Londonderry and Aghadowey, and on the road
between those places. There the Morrisons have lived from
long before the siege of Derry, 1688-'89, and live there
still. At one time they were in possession of the greater
portion of Bally Kilby Highlands. The deed to their farm,
granted by the Connally family, is dated in 1700. William
Morrison resided at Claggan in 1892. As early as 1644 it is
said that Hugh and Robert Morison came from Scotland and
settled in Dromore, and the Morrisons of Maghera, Claggan,
and vicinity are their descendants. It is claimed that James
Morison and Robert Morison, immortalized by Macauley as
among the brave defenders of Londonderry in 1688-'89,
were from Claggan. This is possible, but hardly probable.
The house in which one of the Morisons is said to have

[1] From a letter of Thomas Morrison Allison, Esq., dated Nov. 19, 1891.

lived was pointed out to me in Londonderry in 1884, and I met an inhabitant of that city of the same name who claimed to be a descendant.

My relatives, the Morrisons of Windham and Londonderry, N. H., together with the founders of the branch at Nottingham, N. H., endured the horrors of the "siege," and shared the honors of the final triumph.

At the time of the siege it is said,—"Lord Antrim's men, the Red Shanks, coming through Limavady, every one hurried for safety to Londonderry, among the rest, Rev. Mr. Crooks, the then Presbyterian minister of Bally Kilby, taking with him many of his people. Rev. Mr. Crooks was one of the Presbyterian clergymen who officiated alternately in the cathedral of Derry with their Episcopalian brethren. He is buried in Walworth (Bally Kilby) old burying-ground, beside the Hunters and Allisons of Claggan." The Allisons were old settlers in Claggan, and intermarried with the Morrisons.

Another branch of the Allisons lived at Evish Hill, as stated, in the immediate vicinity of Londonderry, Ireland. Some of them emigrated to Miramichi, New Brunswick, about 1825 to 1830, and are yet in that locality. Thomas Morrison Allison, of Limavady, Ireland, is as before stated, of this latter family.

CHAPTER XI.

THE ALLISONS OF HOLLAND, AND LATER OF ROCKLAND COUNTY, NEW YORK.

Godfrey McAlestor of Loupe, Scotland, adhered to the cause of James VII, and was at the Battle of Killiecrankie, Scotland; and also at Cromdale, May 1, 1690.' Later he went to Ireland, and was at the Battle of the Boyne. He had three sons: Hector McAlestor, or Alison, as the name is alternately called, of Loupe; Charles, who succeeded his brother, and Duncan McAlestor, or Alison, who settled in Holland (had a son, who was a general in the Dutch service and commanded the Scots brigade) and left many descendants. It is possible, and very probable, that this branch of the Allisons sprang from him.

1240.   Noah Allison [1] was born in Holland, migrated to the United States, and died in Rockland county, New York. His son

1241.   Thomas Allison [2] was born in New York, N. Y., Sept. 9, 1777. He was a sea captain and followed the seas for years. He married Catherine Hoffman, who was born May 26, 1789, and died June 4, 1828. They resided in New York, N. Y. One night the house of Mr. Allison was entered by an Irish sailor, who stabbed him eleven times on the head and breast, and escaped. Mr. Allison lingered for seven years, and died, Nov. 5, 1819, from the effects of the brutal assault. He had lived 42 years, 1 month, 27 days. At the time of the assault the fiend threw Mrs. Allison and one child down into the cellar. After the death of Mr. Allison his widow cared for her family for a few years, and died at Newburgh, N. Y., aged 39 years, 9 days.

CHILDREN BORN NEW YORK, N. Y.

1242. William Noah Allison [3] (1247), b. Oct. 30, 1808; m. Ann Eliza Colton, March 20, 1830, and died Sept. 25, 1872.

1243. Mary Ann Allison, [3] b. Aug. 18, 1811. She m. Charles Brown, of New York, N. Y. They are deceased, but left a large family. One son, William H. Brown, [4] was clerk in a drug store recently and lived in New York city.

1244. Caroline Allison,³ b. Nov. 27, 1813; m., May 31, 1828, David Sny-
daker. They are deceased, but left a large family. One
daughter, Mrs. E. S. Rhodes,⁴ lives in Adrian, Mich., and
another is Mrs. William Rhodes,⁴ Bath Beach, Long Island,
N. Y.
1245. Elizabeth Allison,³ b. June 13, 1816. She was several times married. Her last husband was William Downs, and she res.
recently in Summit, N. J.

1246.   Thomas Allison, Jr.,³ b. Aug. 28, 1819; d. March
26, 1820.   Mrs. Catherine (Hoffman) Allison m., second,
Elias Shipman, and had two children : Charles W. Shipman,
b. Dec. 5, 1822, Ayuba Shipman, b. Nov. 15, 1825.

1247.   William Noah Allison³ [1242] (Thomas,² Noah¹).
He was born Oct. 30, 1808, married, March 20, 1830, Ann
Eliza Colton.   He served an apprenticeship of seven years
with Dimond Chandler in the city of New York, as a maker
of spectacles.   This business he followed until his death,
Sept. 25, 1872, aged 63 years, 10 months, 26 days.   He lived
in Middletown, Conn., and moved to Newburgh, N. Y., about
1889.   Mrs. Allison died in Newburgh, N. Y., Oct. 17, 1841.
He died at Fruit Hill, R. I., of dropsy.   Soon after this the
home was broken up, and the children were separated and
went to live in different places.

CHILDREN.

1248. Ann Eliza Allison⁴ (1252), b. Albany, N. Y., Dec. 29, 1830; res. 206
8th Ave., New York, N. Y.   She m. William H. Bross, May 25,
1852.
1249. Louisa Amanda Allison⁴ (1265), b. Feb. 18, 1832.   She m., Nov. 21,
1852, Rev. Richard L. Shurter.   He was b. Sept. 17, 1832.   Res.
Sing-Sing-on-the-Hudson, N. Y.
1250. William Francis Allison⁴ (1277), b. New York city, Oct. 26, 1833;
res. Fruit Hill, R. I.; P. O., Centredale, R. I.
1251. Charles Henry Allison⁴ (1280), b. Oct. 20, 1826; res. 86 Oak St.,
Springfield, Mass.

1252.   Ann Eliza Allison⁴ [1248] (William Noah,³ Thomas,²
Noah¹).   She was born in Albany, N. Y., Dec. 29, 1830.
She married (the second wife), May 25, 1852, William H.
Bross, who is deceased.   She resides 206 8th avenue, New
York, N. Y.

CHILDREN BORN NEW YORK, N. Y.

1253. William H. Bross,⁵ b. April 15, 1854.
1254. Robert Bross,⁵ b. Jan. 17, 1855.
1255. Daniel Colton Bross,⁵ b. Jan. 11, 1857.
1256. Charles Allison Bross,⁵ b. March 4, 1858; d. July 8, 1858.
1257. John Edmund Bross,⁵ b. May 6, 1860; d. July 8, 1860.
1258. George Adrian Bross,⁵ b. July 23, 1861.
1259. John Lane Bross,⁵ b. Oct. 24, 1862.

1260.   Charles Allison Bross,[5] b. July 13, 1863; d. March 7, 1864.
1261.   Frank Bross,[5] b. July 30, 1866; d. Feb. 25, 1869.
1262.   Richard Shurter Bross,[5] b. March 11, 1868.
1263.   Sarah Louise Bross,[5] b. Jan. 2, 1870; d. Aug. 30, 1874.
1264.   Allison Bross,[5] b. Jan. 2, 1870; d. July 16, 1870.

1265.   Louisa Amanda Allison [4] [1249] (William Noah,[3] Thomas,[2] Noah [1]).   She was born in Albany, N. Y., Feb. 18, 1832; married, Nov. 21, 1852, Rev. Richard L. Shurter, born Sept. 17, 1832, in Dutchess county, N. Y.   They reside 52 North Malcolm street, Sing-Sing-on-the-Hudson, N. Y.   He joined the New York Methodist Episcopal conference in 1857, and is on his sixteenth pastorate, being now with the North Malcolm-street church in Sing Sing.   He is son of Felix and Mary E. (Carmen) Shurter, who resided at Fishkill, N. Y. His father was born Aug., 1784; died Aug., 1875; and was son of Frederick Shurter, born in Switzerland, and died in Poughkeepsie, N. Y.

CHILDREN.

1266.   Eliza Colton Shurter,[5] b. Newburgh, N. Y., Oct. 25, 1853; m., March 5, 1885, Rev. J. W. A. Dodge; res. Marlborough, N. Y.
1267.   Minnie Louisa Shurter,[5] b. Dec. 19, 1855; m., April 25, 1877, William G. Eades, b. Shiloh, Ky., Oct. 28, 1856.   He is a railroad clerk.   Res. 88 Broadway, Sing Sing, N. Y.   Child.
I.   Wilfred Eades,[6] b. Dec. 11, 1887.
1268.   Elijah Budd Shurter,[5] b. Highland Mills, N. Y., Oct. 7, 1858; m., Oct. 7, 1880, Elizabeth Katherine Lawson, b., 1860, West Hurley, N. Y.   Is private secretary to president of Northern & Wilmington R. R., and is secretary of the road.   Res. Ellsmere near Wilmington, Del., P. O. 100 Maryland ave., Wilmington, Del.   Children:
I.   Willie Bell Shurter,[6] b. Dec. 12, 1882.
II.   Frank Lawson Shurter,[6] b. Dec. 7, 1884.
III.   Robert Allison Shurter,[6] b. Sept. 11, 1887.
1269.   Frances Edith Shurter,[5] b. Gardentown, N. Y., July 8, 1860; d. Oct. 7, 1866, at Highland Mills, N. Y.
1270.   William Allison Shurter,[5] b. Gardentown, N. Y., March 27, 1862; d. Oct. 13, 1866.
1271.   Richard Wardworth Shurter,[5] b. March 10, 1864, at Warwick, N. Y.; m., 1890, Vinetta Stewart, b. New York, N. Y., Dec. 18, 1865.   Real estate agent.   Res. 151 E. 87th street, New York, N. Y.   Office in 42nd street.
1272.   Adele Shurter,[5] b. Highland Mills, N. Y., May 13, 1866; d. June 19, 1866.
1273.   Roberta Allison Shurter,[5] b. Highland Mills, N. Y., Sept. 8, 1867; m., Aug. 17, 1887, Frederick Buckley, a merchant; res. Liberty, N. Y.
1274.   Earnest Shurter,[5] b. Dec. 21, 1870; d. Dec. 31, 1870.
1275.   Willie Bell Shurter,[5] b. April 24, 1872; d. March 4, 1881.
1276.   Nedaline V. M. Shurter,[5] b. Aug. 14, 1874.   Student.   Res. Sing Sing, N. Y.

1277.   William Francis Allison [4] [1250] (William Noah,[3] Thomas,[2] Noah [1]).   He was born in New York city, Oct. 26,

1833; married, May 27, 1855, Mary Ann Sheldon Brown, daughter of Dexter and Ann Maria (Sheldon) Brown of Scituate, R. I. Her father died in North Providence, R. I., in 1861. He was son of Henry and Mary (Esten) Brown, of Scituate, and Henry died there Sept., 1854. Mrs. Allison was born in North Providence, R. I., Jan. 27, 1828. Her maternal grandfather was John Frazier Sheldon. He was an early and wealthy settler in Providence, R. I.; died there, aged 87 years. He was born in Providence, R. I. Mr. Allison served fifteen months in the Second regiment, Rhode Island volunteers, in "the late unpleasantness," and one year and nine months in the Second United States cavalry. Is a carpenter and mill-wright. Resides at Centredale, R. I.

CHILDREN.

1278. Frank H. Allison,⁵ b. North Providence, R. I., Sept. 3, 1860. He m. May Hutchinson. Farmer; res. Colby, Thomas Co., Kansas, for five years, and now (1892) res. The Oxford Club, Colorado City, Colorado.
1279. William Sheldon Allison,⁵ b. South Scituate, R. I., May 4, 1868; carpenter and builder; res. South Scituate, R. I.

1280. Charles Henry Allison⁴ [1251] (William Noah,³ Thomas,² Noah¹). He was born in Middletown, Conn., Oct. 20, 1836; married, Nov. 25, 1860, Louisa, daughter of Edmund and Mary Ann (Whitney) Smith, who died at West Granville, Mass., May 18, 1866. He married, second, Dec. 24, 1869, Lucy M., daughter of Otis and Ruth (Hopkins) Hawkes. She was born March 12, 1838, in Voluntown, Conn., and is still living. Her father was born at Smithfield, R. I., Sept. 14, 1798, and resided at Centreville, R. I. Her mother, Ruth Hopkins, died Oct., 1881, at Hopkins Hollow, R. I. She married, first, March 1, 1860, Charles Hyde Rice, born Norwich, Ct., Feb. 17, 1836, and died Jan. 20, 1868. He was a soldier in Third Rhode Island Light Artillery, from 1862 till close of the war. Residence, Providence, R. I. He died in Massachusetts General hospital at Boston, Mass. Mr. Allison, in early life, lived in Sparta and New York, N. Y., and at Centredale, R. I. The latter place was the first *home* of his life, and there he spent many years. He then went to Allendale, near Providence, R. I., later to Boston and Worcester, Mass., and to New York city, where he learned the trade of an optician. Later removed to Longmeadow, and then to Springfield, Mass., where he worked until the outbreak of the Rebellion. Then he enlisted as a private, Aug., 1862, in Company F, Twenty-seventh regiment Massachusetts volunteers, under Capt. John W. More, and shared the fortunes of the regiment; was in eighteen engagements. At Petersburg, Va., in a charge, June 18, 1864, he was shot through the right thigh, and a few minutes later a bullet ploughed its way through his left knee, which ended his fighting and made him a cripple for life. Weary months were passed in the hospital at Hampton, Va., but he finally was carried to his home in Springfield, Mass. He was discharged at Fort Monroe, Va., Nov. 3, 1864. He is past commander of the E. K. Wilcox Grand Army post of Springfield, is a Good Templar, and a member of the Masonic fraternity. He is employed in the United States armory. Resides at 86 Oak street, Springfield, Mass. No children.

MRS. ALLISON'S CHILD BY HER FIRST HUSBAND.

Janette Elnora Rice, b. Providence, R. I., Jan. 3, 1861; m., Oct. 6. 1878, Henri E. Jones of Springfield, Mass., who was b. in New Haven, Ct., Aug. 17, 1858. No children. He is a bookbinder. Res. New York, N. Y.

CHAPTER XII.

The name appears in the records both as Allison and Ellison. Three Allisons, Joseph Allison, John Allison, and Richard Allison, settled in Orange county, N. Y. The first mentioned appeared early at Southold, Long Island, N. Y. He and the others may have come directly from the old world, as Southold was a port of entry, and diligent search might fail to reveal his place of origin; or they may have landed in New England, and emigrated later to New York; or, possibly, they may have been offshoots of some Allison or Ellison family given in this book, but where the connecting lines have not been discovered. The similarity of Christian names would argue in favor of the latter proposition. On the other hand, there is a tradition in the family that Joseph Allison came from or near Edinburgh, Scotland. Diligent search has been made, in many offices, books, records, and places, for some clue to their earlier history and for their ancestry, but nothing has been found, and probably nothing more will ever be ascertained than what is given in this book. These Allisons were probably brothers.

1281. Joseph Allison,[1] about 1720, was at Southold, Long Island, N. Y., and was a resident there in 1721. He is called "yeoman" in various deeds. In 1725 or 1726 he went to the town of Goshen, Orange county, as one of the first settlers, having previously purchased a large tract of land. In the patent this purchase was called "the Allison tract," and has since been known by that name, is so designated in the Wawayanda patent, and is among the richest lands in the county. The home of Mr. Allison was in Goshen, where he lived till his death in 1755. He made his will in 1752, which is recorded in the surrogate's office in New York, N. Y. His daughters, Christian names not given, married as follows: one daughter married Mr. McNeal, and left a son, William Allison McNeal;[3] another married Mr. Edsall, and left a son, William Allison Edsall;[3] the third daughter married Mr. Jones, and left a son, Micah Allison Jones.[3] Mr. Allison left a money legacy to his granddaughter, Mary Horton,[3] with her mother's wearing apparel. Another legacy was to his grandson, Nathan Moore,[3] who was not of age. He left legacies to Ann Thompson and Margaret Bradner. The following are the known Christian names of his children:

CHILDREN.

1282. Elizabeth Allison,[2] not of age Oct. 17, 1752.
1283. Sarah Allison.[3] No record.
1284. William Allison[2] (1307), not of age Oct. 17, 1752. He resided in Goshen, Orange Co., N. Y., and d. in 1804.
1285. Phœbe Allison.[3] No record.
1286. Benjamin Allison.[3] No record.
1287. Cornelius Allison,[2] m. Rebecca ———.
1288. Richardson Allison[2] (1312), m. Anna ———; d. 1769; res. Goshen, Orange Co., N. Y.
1289. Joseph Allison.[3] He was the eldest son, and was living Nov. 8, 1757, and was appointed by his brother Thomas one of the executors of his will.
1290. Richard Allison.[3] He was living Nov. 8, 1757, and was appointed by his brother Thomas, one of the executors of his will.
1291. Thomas Allison[3] (1315), m. Margaret ———, and d. 1757; res. Goshen, N. Y.
1292. Isaac Allison[2] (1320), not of age Oct. 17, 1752; m. Anna ———, and d. 1793; res. Warwick, near Amity, Orange Co., N. Y.

1293. John Allison,[1] one of the three Allisons, and a probable brother of Joseph whose history has been given, lived near Florida, a precinct of Goshen, Orange county, N. Y. He died in the town of Walkill, Orange county, in 1764. His will was dated Sept. 12, 1763, proven June 11, 1764, and is recorded in the surrogate's office in the city of New York. His brother, Richard Allison, was named as executor.

CHILDREN.

1294. John Allison,[2] m. Abigail ———, and in 1776 lived in Orange Co., N. Y.
1295. Henry Allison,[2] res., in 1776, in Orange Co., N. Y.
1296. Richard Allison.[2]
1297. Keziah Allison.[2]
1298. Elizabeth Allison.[2]
1299. Bridget Allison.[2]

1300. Richard Allison,[1] another of the three Allisons. (The relationship to John Allison is shown by the latter's will.) He died in 1767. His wife was Martha ———. Resided in Warwick, Orange county, N. Y., where his death occurred. His will is recorded in Goshen, N. Y., and in it he mentions his brother-in-law, John Wells; will dated Oct. 23, 1766 or 1776.

14

CHILDREN.

1301. Joseph Allison.[3] He lived in Goshen, N. Y., made his will June
        6, 1762, proved June 16, 1762. He was a resident of Goshen,
        N. Y. He speaks of his lands bounded by those of John and
        William Allison. They must have been his brothers. He m.
        Abigail ——, and had children: Joseph Allison,[3] Richard
        Allison,[3] Deborah Allison,[3] and Mary Allison.[3] His brother-
        in-law, Nathaniel Roe, and cousin, James Sawyer, executors.
1302. John Allison,[3] m. —— ——. He was living Jan. 19, 1797.
        Children: Elizabeth Allison,[3] m. Mr. Smith. Child: Wis-
        ner Allison Smith.[4] John Wisner Allison,[3] m. Anne ——.
        He died in Warwick, N. Y., in 1802. No children.
1303. William Allison,[3] m. Martha ——, lived in New York city, and
        died in 1797. No children. He was a merchant. He was an
        inn-keeper in New York. Had a wife, Martha. He made his
        will Jan. 19, 1797, proven Feb. 5, 1797. His brother, John
        Allison, was then living. Among others mentioned was Wil-
        liam, son of Stephen Sears.
1304. Martha Allison,[3] m. Mr. Carpenter.   Child: Richard Allison
        Carpenter.[3]
1305. Margaret Allison,[3] m. Nathaniel Roe.   Child: William Allison
        Roe.[3]
1306. Elizabeth Allison,[3] m. Mr. Carpenter.   Child: Benjamin Car-
        penter.[3] She was living Jan. 19, 1797.

1307. Gen. William Allison[2] [1284] (Joseph[1]). He was,
for that period, a very wealthy farmer and land-owner, and
resided on the Drowned Lands, Goshen, Orange county,
N. Y. On April 20, 1777, he was a delegate from Orange
county, to a convention which met at Kingston to frame the
constitution of New York. He was patriotic, and during the
Revolutionary War did valiant service as an officer. He was
then colonel of the militia, and commanded an Orange
County regiment. Forts Clinton and Montgomery were
important strongholds on the Hudson river, and garrisoned
by the American troops. The British desired free passage
over the Hudson's waters. From early spring till late in the
fall the militia had been often summoned to the defence of
the forts. In September, 1777, Col. William Allison (with
other regimental commanders) was ordered to summon his
regiment to the defence of Fort Montgomery. The minute
men assembled, but not in sufficient numbers. Only a portion of his regiment was present. Thus matters stood on
Sunday, Oct. 5, 1777. Then the Sabbath's stillness was disturbed by excited people, who heralded the approach of the
enemy's ships on the Hudson for the attack upon the strongholds. On the day following (Oct. 6, 1777) the attack was
made by overpowering numbers, and after a stubborn resist-
ance the Americans were defeated with loss. Colonel Allison was taken prisoner, and his son, Micah Allison, was

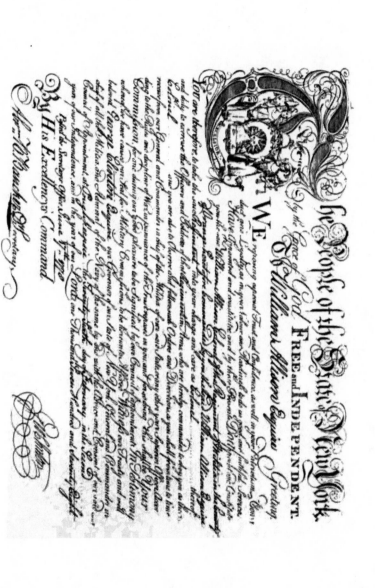

The People of the State of New York.

By the Grace of God FREE and INDEPENDENT.

To William Allison Esquire Greeting.

WE

killed.[1] For several months he was a prisoner on board a prison ship, and was exchanged during the following winter. On his return to his home he brought to Governor Clinton two thousand dollars in gold, in aid of the American cause, loaned by a patriotic citizen of Long Island. He commanded a division of the troops in the Battle of Long Island. In the early history of Orange county he was the most distinguished citizen and a prominent military leader. He was a member of the first provincial convention of New York from 1775 to 1777. On April 4, 1782, William Allison was brigadier general in the brigade formed by Allison's, Woodhull's, and Hathorne's regiments; state senator from 1783 to 1786; member of the assembly in 1795, and was judge of the court of common pleas. He married Mary Jackson, and died in 1804. He and his wife are buried opposite his old home on Drowned Lands, in Goshen, N. Y.

CHILDREN.

1308. Micah Allison.[3] He was a soldier, and was killed in the gallant defence of Fort Montgomery, N. Y., Oct. 6, 1777, aged 18 years.
1309. Stephen Allison,[3] m., June 15, 1786, Susanna Bronson, and d. in 1793. Children: Mary Allison.[4] Micah Allison.[4]
1310. Mary Allison[3] (1326), b. Nov. 16, 1762; m., June 29, 1779, Dr. William Elmer; res. Goshen. N. Y.
1311. Sarah Allison[3] (1331), m., Nov. 2, 1778, William W. Thompson, who was sheriff of Orange county in 1785.

1812. Richardson Allison[2] [1288] (Joseph[1]). He married Anne ————, and died in 1769. He was a housecarpenter, and res. at Goshen, Orange county, N. Y. His will is recorded in the city of New York; made Dec. 22, 1768; proven May 11, 1769.

CHILDREN.

1313. Pheby Allison.[3] She m. Abram Gale, of Sparta, N. Y. Children: I. Anna Gale.[4] II. David Gale.[4]
1314. James Allison[3] (1342). He was under twenty-one, Dec. 22, 1768; m. Amy Knapp, of Horseneck, or Norwalk, Conn. He lived at Ridgebury, Orange Co., N. Y., and d. about 1822. He received his father's dwelling-house and eighty acres of land.

1815. Thomas Allison[2] [1291] (Joseph[1]). He married Margaret ————, and died in 1757. Resided, apparently,

---

[1] Mrs. Mary Thompson Knight, of Monroe, Orange Co., N. Y., great-granddaughter of General Allison, has his commission as colonel, and an autograph letter of his written when he was in a prison-ship during the Revolutionary War.

in Goshen, N. Y. He made his will Nov. 8, 1757; proven
Dec. 5, 1757; recorded in surrogate's office, New York, N. Y.
The following children were mentioned in that document,
and all under the age of twenty-one years. His beloved brothers, Joseph and Richard, were appointed executors of the
will. John Allison was a witness; also Richard Westcott
and William Dunn, all of the precinct of Goshen.

CHILDREN.

1316. George Allison.⁸ No record.
1317. Richard Allison.⁸ No record.
1318. Mary Allison.⁸ No record.
1319. Thomas Allison,⁸ m. Fannie ————.

1820. Isaac Allison² [1292] (Joseph¹). He and his
brother, Richard Allison, coming, it is said, from Long Island,
N. Y., bought land some twenty miles from New York city
in Orange county, N. Y. The latter settled near Brookfield
(now called Slate Hill), town of Wawayanda, Orange
county. Isaac Allison settled about ten miles distant, near
Amity, in the town of Warwick. The latter was of medium
size, and with long black hair braided and tied up with a
ribbon in a cue, according to the fashion of the time. He
married Anna ————.

CHILDREN.

1321. Julia Allison,⁸ m. Capt. Nathaniel Ketchum, who was captain of
      a vessel.
1322. Isaac Allison⁸ (1383), m. Mary Davis; d. 1825.
1323. Nathaniel Allison.⁸ Single.
1324. Deborah Allison,⁸ m. Mr. Wood.
1325. Richard Allison⁸ (1391), m. Anna ————; d. 1810.

1826. Mary Allison³ [1310] (Gen. William,² Joseph¹).
She was born Nov. 16, 1762; married, June 29, 1779, Dr.
William Elmer,¹ of Goshen, N. Y. He was born in Florida,

---

¹ The Elmer family is a very ancient one. There are many of the name
in Switzerland, who claim to be able to trace their descent back to the
twelfth century, and theorize that before that date the Elmers came from
Italy or Greece. In 1006 Elmer, a person of great sanctity, was chosen
abbot of the monastery of St. Augustine, at Canterbury, England, and in
1022 was made bishop of Sherburne. After the Norman conquest, in 1016,
Elmer, one of the chiefs of William the Conqueror, was holder of several
pieces of land, one of which was at Braintree Hundred, county of Essex,
England, from thirty to forty miles east of London. John Elmer was a
bishop of London in the time of Queen Elizabeth. Representatives of
the family are in different countries. Alfred Elmere, a distinguished
artist, was a member of the Royal Academy, and died a few years since.

N. Y., Jan. 19, 1758, and died May 24, 1816, aged 58 years, 4 months, 5 days. She died April 20, 1821, aged 58 years, 5 months, 4 days. He was a physician; resided in or near Goshen, N. Y., where he and his wife lived and where they are buried. Dr. Elmer was the son of Dr. Nathaniel Elmer, Sr., and his wife, Ann Thompson. Dr. Nathaniel is said to have been "remarkably humorous." Dr. William Elmer was always a companionable man; was cheerful, and pleasant in his manners, and had a large vein of natural humor. Of Mrs. Elmer, his wife, her daughter, Sarah Maria, said,— "She was a kind, affectionate, self-denying mother, a woman of most correct principles and habits, a decided Christian as was also my father." He and his family were Presbyterians.

CHILDREN BORN IN GOSHEN, N. Y.

1327. Micah Allison Elmer⁴ (1399), b. May 13, 1781; m., Feb. 4, 1804, his second cousin, Elizabeth Allison. He d. Dec. 31, 1849.¹
1328. Horace Elmer⁴ (1406a), b. Sept. 23, 1783; d. at Morristown, N. J., June 1, 1850, and left a family.
1329. Stephen Allison Elmer,⁴ b. 1785; d. May, 1850; unmarried.
1330. Sarah Maria Elmer⁴ (1407), b. 1796; d. Dec. 12, 1874; m. Mahlon Ford.

1331. Sarah Allison³ [1311] (Gen. William,² Joseph¹). She married, Nov. 2, 1773, William W. Thompson, who was sheriff of Orange county, N. Y., in 1785.

He was born in 1815, at Clonakilty, county of Cork, Ireland. It is on the southeast coast.
  Edward Elmer, the emigrant ancestor of this American family, was a young man, probably not married, when he left England. He was a Puritan, and left England to escape the persecution to which that sect was subjected, as did those who came with him. It is probable that he came from the county of Essex, as did many of his fellow-passengers, and likely from Braintree, where Rev. Thomas Hooker preached before he came to New England. He with 123 passengers came in the ship *Lion*, which arrived in Boston, Mass., Sept. 16, 1632, having been twelve weeks on the ship and eight weeks from "Land's End." He settled first at Newton, now Cambridge, Mass., with Rev. Thomas Hooker and the others, and in June, 1635, he, with Mr. Hooker and his congregation, removed to Hartford, Conn., where he settled. Later he removed to Northampton, Mass., and returned to Hartford. He owned a farm at South Windsor, Conn., where he was killed by the Indians during King Philip's War, in 1676. A part of his farm is still owned by his descendant, Samuel E. Elmore, of Hartford, Conn. The emigrant, Edward Elmer, married Mary ———. Their son, Samuel Elmer,² married Elizabeth ———, and lived in Hartford, Conn. Their son, Dea. Jonathan Elmer,³ married Mary ———, and lived in Norwalk, Conn. Their youngest son, Dr. Nathaniel Elmer,⁴ married Anne Thompson. Their son, Dr. William Elmer.⁵ married Mary Allison, as mentioned above. (From MS. of Samuel E. Elmore, of Hartford, Conn.)

¹ In some records he is called *Michael*.

CHILDREN.

1332. William Allison Thompson,⁴ b. Aug. 8, 1775; baptized Sept. 17, 1775; m. Sarah Bucksbee, of Minisink, Orange Co., N. Y., clergyman; res. Northern New Jersey. Children: William Henry Thompson;⁵ res. Pennsylvania. Newton Thompson;⁵ res. Mount Pleasant, Iowa. Sarah Thompson,⁵ single.

1333. Julia D. Thompson,⁴ b. Feb. 17, 1778; baptized May 10, 1778; m., Mr. Gale; m., second, George Houston. Had nine children, and they lived in Orange Co., N. Y.

1334. Eleanor Thompson,⁴ b. Jan. 18, 1781; baptized June 17, 1781; m. James Morrison, whose father emigrated from Scotland or the north of Ireland. They had six children. Their son, Rev. John Hunter Morrison, D. D.,⁵ b. 1804 or 1805, was a missionary in North India, and died there, leaving three children who were missionaries. One son of Eleanor died young. Another son and three daughters went to Ohio and Northern Kentucky, where they died. Their old house was in Montgomery, now Wallkill, Orange Co., N. Y., in the neighborhood of "Honey Pot," two miles from the village of Scotchtown.

1335. Joseph Thompson,⁴ m. Patty Allison, daughter of James and Amy (Knapp) Allison. They had several children. Res. Steuben Co., N. Y.

1336. Anthony Dobbin Thompson,⁴ m. Nancy Helme. Child: Sarah Thompson,⁵ m. John Conklin, of New York, N. Y. Mr. Thompson died, and his widow married Meeker Miller, and died in the city of New York.

1337. Henry Thompson,⁴ m. Abigail Thompson and Nancy Bronson. Res. Owego, Tioga Co., N. Y. Six children. After his death his widow and some of the children went to Illinois.

1338. Mary Thompson,⁴ d. aged 4 years.

1339. Ann Thompson,⁴ m. James Howell. She lived and died in Huber Co., N. Y. Seven children.

1340. Sarah Thompson,⁴ m. John D. Vail, and died near New Windsor in 1850 or 1851. They had eight children; six died young. Their eldest, James Schuyler Vail,⁵ married Catherine Tompkins, had children, and they lived and died in New Windsor, Orange Co., N. Y. Sarah Jane Tompkins,⁵ m. James Potter; m., second, her cousin, William Thompson Howell, and d. in Michigan. Sidney Tompson,⁵ res. Northern Illinois.

1341. John Jay Thompson⁴ (1417), b. March 26, 1797; d. Jan. 12, 1849. His daughter, Mrs. Mary Thompson Knight, lives in Monroe, Orange Co., N. Y.

1342. James Allison ³ [1314] (Richardson,² Joseph ¹). He was born ————; and married Amy Keziah, daughter of ———— and Amy (Reynolds) Knapp. They first went to Long Island, and later settled at Slate Hill, Orange county, N. Y. He was in the military service during the Revolution. He lived at Slate Hill, Orange county, N. Y., where he owned a large tract of land. He also owned land near Turner's, Orange county, N. Y. His death occurred about 1822. Mrs. Allison was from New England, and after Mr. Allison's death married James Smith of Oxford, Orange county, N. Y., and had a daughter, Amy Smith, who married Mr. Reynolds.

CHILDREN.

1343. Jabez Allison.⁴ He went to Canada and settled there. Upon the declaration of war between the United States and Great Britain in 1812, he returned to the United States. After his death his wife lived in Canada.

1344. Caleb Allison.⁴ He probably settled in Canada.

1345. Lydia Allison.⁴ She m. Jason Howell and settled near Slate Hill, Orange Co., N. Y. He was a farmer. Walter,⁵ and James,⁵ are their only children now living. Children:

1346. Daniel Howell,⁵ d. unmarried.

1347. Walter Howell.⁵ He was a school teacher at Slate Hill, N. Y.; m., Eliza Pound, sister of Mrs. James Allison, and removed to the west.

1348. Gabriel Howell.⁵ Single. Res. Binghampton, N. Y.

1349. Milton Howell.⁵ He was drowned when a young man. He was unmarried.

1350. James Howell.⁵ He married and lived in Pennsylvania.

1351. Susan Howell.⁵ She d. when about fifteen years of age.

1352. Amizi Allison.⁴ He settled in Steuben Co., N. Y. Was twice married, and his second wife was Grace Davis. Their children:

1353. William Allison.⁵

1354. Almeda Allison,⁵ m. Mr. Marsh and had a son, George Marsh.

1355. Anson Allison.⁵

1356. Frances Allison,⁵ m. Mr. Van Gelder.

1357. Fanny Allison,⁴ m. Justus Brooks. After his death removed to Ohio, perhaps Norwalk. Children:

1358. Amy Ann Brooks,⁵ m. Richard Anderson. Res. Huron Co., Ohio.

1359. Emeline Brooks,⁵ m. Josiah Anderson, a brother of Richard Anderson. They res. in Ohio.

1360. Eliphalet Brooks.⁵ He m. ———. Res. in Ohio, probably in Newark or Norwalk, Ohio.

1361. Eldridge Brooks,⁵ m.; res. New York, N. Y.

1362. Phebe Brooks,⁵ m. George Sanger. Res. New York, N. Y.

1363. James Brooks,⁵ m. Martha Dallinson. Res. Ohio.

1364. Abby Brooks,⁴ m. Richard, son of Isaac Allison.

1365. William Allison,⁴ (Col. William) res. Slate Hill, Orange Co., N. Y. After his father's death he occupied the homestead. He m. Sarah Roe of Warwick, Orange Co., N. Y. His death occurred Aug. 30, 1830. Children:

1366. Elizabeth Allison,⁵ m. George Reeves. Res. Michigan.

1367. Timothy R. Allison,⁵ d. in Michigan.

1368. Amy Allison,⁵ m. DeWitt Hallock, son of Judge Hallock.

1369. Her child,

1370. Josephine Hallock,⁶ m. Mr. Denton; res. Greenville, Orange Co., N. Y.

1371. Susanna Allison,⁵ d. unmarried.

1372. James Allison.⁵ His descendants res. in Michigan.

1373. Gabriel Allison.⁵ His descendants are in Michigan.

1374. Henry B. Allison.⁵ His descendants are in Michigan.

1375. Sarah Allison,⁴ m. Isaac Allison, Jr., her second cousin. (See his record. No. 1425.)

1376. James Allison,⁴ m. Lottie Anna ———. His descendants are in Chemung Co., N. Y.

1377. Ambrose Allison,⁴ m. Annie E., daughter of Isaac and Mary Allison. He lived near the old homestead in Orange Co., N. Y. Descendants in Iowa.

1378. Richardson Allison.⁴

1379. Joshua Allison,⁴ m. Elizabeth ———; res. Sussex Co., N. J. Descendants in western New York and Iowa.

1380. Patty Allison,⁴ m. Joseph Thompson, son of Sarah (Allison) Thompson.

1881. Gabriel Allison, d. unmarried, it is said. (There was a Gabriel
          Ellison, m. Catherine Ellis, Sept. 4, 1772. Recorded in New
          York, N. Y.)
                    Perhaps there was a
1882. John Allison,[4] who m. and settled in Penn.

    1883. Isaac Allison [3] [1822] (Isaac,[2] Joseph [1]). He was
a soldier of the Revolution, and served at Fort Stanwix, now
Rome, N. Y. While there a messmate gave him his powder
horn, still most carefully preserved, and (in 1898) in the
possession of his great-granddaughter, Mrs. Sarah (Vail)
Divers, of Middletown, N. Y. It is an interesting and handsome relic of that war. Upon it is beautifully engraved a
picture of the fort with the surrounding houses and the church
steeple of a village. It bears this inscription (fac-simile):

PETER VANORDER

HIS HORN

MADE AT FORT STAN-

WIX NOVEMBER THE

17 1780.

    While Mr. Allison was in the army, his wife and family
were at home, in charge of the farm during his absence.
Often during that trying period the Indians came to the
home of Mrs. Allison. She treated them with kindness, gave
them food, won their good will, and their assurance, that to
her and hers, no harm should come from them.
    He married Mary Davis, whose brother, Benjamin Davis,
lived near the Allison homestead, near Amity, Orange county,
N. Y. Mount Adam and Mount Eve rear their summits near
this old home. Mr. Allison lived on the homestead. He
was of medium stature, of light complexion with blue eyes
and dark hair. Following rigidly the style of those early
years, he did not change with the changing fashion, but

wore his hair, which was at least two feet in length, braided, and tied up with a ribbon, into a *cue*. This style he followed till his death. The land he owned was extensive. He sold portions to Nathan Furman, Timothy Roe, Jed Sears, and John Gardner. He then gave his son Isaac a farm, and had enough land remaining for himself. In his time there was no church edifice in Amity, and he attended public worship in a school-house. He died in 1825, and is buried in the family burying ground, near the old farm-house. This cemetery, which forms part of a knoll, contains about three fourths of an acre, which, with the road leading to it, is still the property of the Allisons. Mrs. Allison was a very energetic woman. After the death of her husband, she removed to Ohio with her children, died there, and is buried in Newark, or Norwalk, Ohio.

CHILDREN.

1384. Isaac Allison [4] (1425), b. April 10, 1787; m. Sarah Allison. Res. Warwick, near Amity, Orange Co., N. Y. He d. Jan. 1, 1835.
1385. Sallie Allison,[4] m. Mr. Hopkins. She was a member of the Presbyterian church in Amity. Her descendants are in Ohio. She m., second, Mr. Mines.
1386. Nathaniel Allison.[4] Single. He was a young man and unmarried when the 1812–'15 war with Great Britain broke out. He took the place in the army of his brother Isaac, and while rendering military service contracted a fever of which he died, after his return home. He served till the close of the war. His nephew, Dr. Nathaniel Allison, of Mexico, Mo., was named for him.
1387. Samuel Allison [4] (1436), m. ———— Roe; settled in Ohio.
1388. Mary Allison,[4] m. Aaron Hatfield.
1389. Annie Allison [4] (1467), m. her second cousin, Ambrose Allison, son of James and Amy (Knapp) Allison. They removed to Ohio, and she d. in Licking Co., and their descendants are in Iowa.
1390. Richard Allison,[4] b. Jan. 29, 1799. (1479a.) He sold his farm in Orange Co., N. Y., and with his family removed to Ohio.
1391. Elizabeth Allison [4] m. Joseph Pound. Their descendants are in Ohio. Mr. Pound lived *perhaps* in Newark, Ohio.

1392. Richard Allison [3] [1825] (Isaac,[2] Joseph [1]). He married Anna ————, and died July 13, 1810. She died June 16, 1827, in Stewartstown, N. Y.

CHILDREN.

1393. Susan Allison,[4] m. Mr. Brown.
1394. Charlotte Allison,[4] m. Mr. Waring.
1395. Rebecca Allison,[4] m. Mr. Thompson.
1396. Elizabeth Allison,[4] b. Oct. 26, 1782; m. Micah Allison Elmer. (See his record, No. 1399.)
1397. William Allison [4] (1480), b. Oct. 28, 1797; m. Lavena Furgerson. He lived and d. in Canisteo, N. Y.
1398. Isaac Allison,[4] d., unmarried, Nov. 20, 1809.

1399. Micah Allison Elmer[4] [1827] (Mary Allison,[3] Gen. William,[2] Joseph[1]). He was born May 13, 1781, at Goshen, N. Y., and died at Unionville, Orange county, N. Y., Dec. 31, 1849. He married his second cousin, Elizabeth, daughter of Richard Allison, Feb. 4, 1804, who died in Unionville, and both are buried in Ridgebury, N. Y. He was named for his uncle, Micah Allison, who was killed, at the age of eighteen, in battle at the capture of Fort Montgomery. They were Presbyterians. Some of this family are buried in Slate Hill cemetery, Wawayanda, Orange county, N. Y.

CHILDREN.

1400. William Allison Elmer,[6] b. Jan. 1, 1805; d. April 8, 1805.
1401. Julia Ann Elmer,[6] b. April 13, 1806; d. Nov. 27, 1871, aged 65 years, 7 months, 14 days. She is buried in the Allison family plot in Chester, N. Y. Rev. C. E. Allison says of her,—" The memory of her unselfish life is sweet as the fragrance of flowers." She was unmarried.
1402. Richard Allison Elmer[5] (1491), b. Aug. 28, 1808; d. Aug. 8, 1867; res. Waverly, N. Y.
1403. Isaac Allison Elmer,[5] b. Nov. 24, 1810; d. young.
1404. Henry De Lancy Elmer[5] (1498), b. Feb. 18, 1812; d. Oct. 17, 1870; m. Julia Ann De Kay; res. at Unionville and Chester, N. Y.
1405. Nathaniel Elmer[5] (1514), b. at Wantage, N. Y., Jan. 31, 1816; d. July 11, 1884, in Middletown, N. Y.
1406. Teresa Amelia Elmer,[5] b. Nov. 6, 1819; d. Sept. 27, 1871. She m. Isaac W. Allison. (See his record, No. 1540.)

1406a. Horace Elmer[4] [1328] (Mary [Allison] Elmer,[3] Gen. William,[2] Joseph[1]). He was born in Goshen, N. Y., Sept. 23, 1783, and died June 1, 1850, at his home in Morristown, N. J. He married, at Goshen, N. Y., Nov. 14, 1807, Susan Stewart, who was born Dec. 30, 1788, and died April 6, 1842.

CHILDREN.

1406b. Catherine Maria Elmer,[5] b. July 22, 1808; m., Sept. 12, 1839, Silas H. Axtell, and d. March 15, 1866, without issue.
1406c. William Stewart Elmer,[5] b. March 29, 1810; d. single, Sept. 15, 1834; physician.
1406d. James Floyd Elmer,[5] b. May 11, 1812; m., March 29, 1837, Adaline Borland. She was b. in Orange Co., N. Y., Aug. 12, 1816; d. at Morristown, N. J., Sept. 10, 1878. He d. of typhoid fever March 16, 1863. He with his family were Presbyterians. He aided in church work, and was active in such matters as pertained to the general good. His children were well educated, and lovers of music and literature. Children b. in Morris Co., N. J.:
I. Frances Matilda Elmer,[6] b. Sept., 1838; d. Morristown, N. J., Dec. 29, 1865, of typhoid fever.
II. Sarah Elmer,[6] b. Feb. 22, 1841; res. Morristown, N. J.
III. James Horace Elmer,[6] b. Jan. 5, 1843; res. Morristown, N. J.

IV. Charles Lewis Elmer,⁶ b. Sept. 21, 1845; m., March 1, 1869, Mary
     Day; res. Baltimore, Md. Children: Lizzie Elmer,⁷ b. Jan. 25,
     1869. Carrie Ford Elmer,⁷ b. Oct. 18, 1871. Horace Brown
     Elmer,⁷ b. Nov. 11, 1873. Frank Elmer,⁷ b. Oct. 16, 1876. Will-
     iam Floyd Elmer,⁷ b. Dec. 8, 1885.
V.   Thomas Jefferson Elmer.⁶ b. Oct. 18, ——; m., in 1868, Mary Ella
     Wyman; res. Rockaway, N. J.; d. Nov. 21, 1889. Children:
     Rena Viola Elmer,⁷ b. Sept. 24, 1868; d. Jan. 6, 1886. Ella
     Eugenia Elmer,⁷ b. June 25, 1870. Julia Etta Elmer,⁷ b. Aug.
     29, 1872; d. June 6, 1889. Bertha Adaline Elmer,⁷ b. Aug. 5,
     1874. Effie May Elmer,⁷ b. March 10, 1877; d. Dec. 12, 1891.
     Maud Borland Elmer,⁷ b. Feb. 12, 1879. Ida Ames Elmer,⁷ b.
     Sept. 9, 1881. Floyd Lewis Elmer,⁷ b. April 18, 1884; d. Jan.
     24, 1886. Florence Lulu Elmer,⁷ b. April 18, 1884.
VI. Edwin Stewart Elmer,⁶ b. March 13, 1851; m., May 18, 1887, Flor-
     ence Doty; res. Morristown, N. J. Children: Marion Ade-
     laide Elmer,⁷ b. July 23, 1890. Harrold Elmer,⁷ b. April 29,
     1892.
VII. Emma Adaline Elmer,⁶ b. Sept. 19, 1853; m., May 11, 1881, Charles
     C. Bedell; res. Madison, N. J. Children: Mabel Adeline Be-
     dell,⁷ b. March 11, 1884. Ernest Elmer Bedell,⁷ b. Nov. 16,
     1886. Lester Raymond Bedell,⁷ b. Nov. 18, 1889. ——— Be-
     dell,⁷ b. Sept. 18, 1891; d. Oct., 1891.
VIII. Ella Maria Elmer,⁶ b. July 16, 1856; res. Newark, N. J.
IX. Mary Florence Elmer,⁶ b. Jan. 31, 1860. She graduated from the
     high school in Baltimore, Md.; was a teacher, and then for ten
     years was a copyist in the Patent Office, Washington, D. C.
     She m., Oct. 11, 1892, Basil Edgar Murray, and res. 1627 14th
     street, Washington, D. C.
1406e. Lewis Elmer,⁵ b. Goshen, N. Y., Sept. 28, 1814; m., Jan. 5, 1837,
     Mary Ann Wickersham. He resided in Morristown, N. J.,
     Petersburg, Va., and, after 1852, in Baltimore, Md., where for
     thirty years he was a manufacturer of vinegar, and where he
     died Jan. 19, 1892. Mrs. Elmer was b. in Pittsburg, Va., Jan.
     5, 1816, and d. in Baltimore, Nov. 9, 1871. She was daughter
     of Isaac and Susan (Stone) Wickersham, granddaughter of
     Thomas, of Reading, Penn. Children:
I.   Susan Marian Elmer,⁶ b. Morristown, N. J., Nov. 2, 1837; d. in Wood-
     stock, Va., Aug. 5, 1861.
II. William Stewart Elmer,⁶ b. Morristown, N. J., Nov. 2, 1840; m.,
     April 5, 1865, Mary Elizabeth Addison. He is a vinegar man-
     ufacturer; res. 818 W. North avenue, Baltimore, Md. Chil-
     dren: Minnia Florence Elmer,⁷ b. Feb. 8, 1867. William Addi-
     son Elmer,⁷ b. Sept. 11, 1868; d. Jan. 16, 1870. Mary Estella
     Elmer,⁷ b. Jan. 18, 1870; d. Nov. 6, 1870. Lewis Stewart El-
     mer,⁷ b. Aug. 1, 1872. ——— Elmer,⁷ b. and d. July 1, 1874.
     Ethel Addison Elmer,⁷ b. Aug. 27, 1881.
III. Walter Floyd Elmer,⁶ b. Pittsburg, Penn., Sept. 13, 1845; m., Dec.
     21, 1871, Eliza Edith Ruth, daughter of John and Mary (Ruth)
     Sturgis. He is a vinegar manufacturer; res. Baltimore, Md.
     Children: Mary Ella Elmer,⁷ b. Oct. 12, 1872. Frank Ruth
     Elmer,⁷ b. Jan. 26, 1879; d. July 4, 1879. Charles Wickersham
     Elmer,⁷ b. July 15, 1881.
IV. Lida Hizby Elmer,⁶ b. Pittsburg, Penn., June 12, 1847; unmarried;
     res. 1122 Mosher street, Baltimore, Md.
V.   George Hizby Elmer,⁶ b. Pittsburg, Penn., Dec. 2, 1849; m., Dec. 12,
     1872, Henrietta Langrall, b. Sept. 8, 1851. He is a vinegar
     manufacturer; res. Baltimore, Md. Children: Mary Etta
     Elmer,⁷ b. July 7, 1874. Florence Langrall Elmer,⁷ b. Aug. 1,
     1875. Lulu Grace Elmer,⁷ b. May 31, 1877. Percy Womble
     Elmer,⁷ b. March 17, 1879. Eva Stewart Elmer,⁷ b. Nov. 5,
     1880. Edna Earle Elmer,⁷ b. April 14, 1887.

VI. Emma Bartlett Elmer,⁶ b. Newark, N. J., May 22, 1843; m., Oct.
25, 1870, Joseph Martin Ashbury. He was a vinegar manufacturer; res. Baltimore, Md., where she died Oct. 25, 1891. Children: Marian Elmer Ashbury,⁷ b. July 31, 1871. Nellie Stewart Ashbury,⁷ b. July 3, 1873. Ida Virginia Ashbury,⁷ b. Dec.
13, 1876. Lillie Ruth Ashbury,⁷ b. Oct. 25, 1878. Howard
Elmer Ashbury,⁷ b. April 26, 1880.

VII. Mary Wickersham Elmer,⁶ b. Baltimore, Md., March 24, 1856, and
d. there June 25, 1858.

1406f. John Carpenter Elmer,⁵ b. April 7, 1817; m., Sept. 19, 1843, Jane
R. Stiles. He was a physician; and d. Oct. 17, 1863. His
daughter, Louise B. Elmer,⁶ res. Springfield, N. J. William
Stiles Elmer,⁶ d. Nov., 1863.

1406g. Luther Stewart Elmer,⁵ b. Goshen, N. Y., June 24, 1819; m.,
Sept. 22, 1845, Lavinia Grandon Smith, daughter of Major Cad-
walader and Ann (Wise) Smith, of Hackettstown, N. J. She
was b. in Hackettstown, June 10, 1824, and in 1892 resides in
Washington, D. C. Mr. Elmer was a lawyer; res. in Morristown and Newark, N. J., and in Jersey City, N. J., from 1856
to 1889. He died in Washington, D. C., July 10, 1889. He
was highly esteemed for his upright Christian life. Children:

I. Ida T. Elmer,⁶ b. Newark, N. J.; res. Washington, D. C.
II. Virginia Lavinia Elmer,⁶ b. Newark, N. J.; m., May 29, 1873, William Henry Ames, a graduate of Brown University. He was
formerly of Cincinnati, Ohio. Res. Jersey City, N. J., and is
deceased. He was b. at New Orleans, La. At the age of
twenty-three he entered the U. S. service as private in the 165th
Regt. N. Y. Vols.; March 15, 1864, made 2d lieut. of Co. B, 87
U. S. colored infantry stationed at New Orleans, La., and Aug.
31, 1865, was transferred to 84th Regt. U. S. colored infantry,
and was aid-de-camp to General Doolittle. Children: Elmer
Hampstead Ames,⁷ b. Jersey City, N. J., Jan. 23, 1876. Henry
Olcott Ames,⁷ b. Jersey City, N. J., Jan. 29, 1878. Adele
Ames,⁷ b. Feb. 1, 1882; d. March 13, 1885.
III. Lavinia Elmer,⁶ b. Dec. 15, 1855, in Jersey City, N. J.; d. there
July 20, 1857.
IV. Luther Stewart Elmer,⁶ b. Jersey City, N. J., Sept. 24, 1859; res.
1723 Corcoran street, Washington, D. C. He was a member of
the New York University class of 1881; studied law for three
years in Jersey City and one year in Washington, and in 1881
was appointed to a position in the post-office department in
Washington, D. C. He is now assistant chief clerk.

1406h. Thomas Evans Elmer,⁵ b. Dec. 9, 1821; d. Nov. 12, 1827; single.
1406i. Keziah Jane Elmer,⁵ b. June 12, 1824; d. April 18, 1842; single.
1406j. Sarah Elizabeth Elmer,⁵ b. Feb. 24, 1827; d. Dec. 7, 1848, at South
Hadley boarding school; single.

1407. Sarah Maria Elmer⁴ [1330] (Mary Allison,³ Gen.
William,² Joseph¹). She was born at Goshen, N. Y., in
1796; died in St. Louis, Mo., Dec. 12, 1874. She married
Mahlon Ford, who died March 23, 1888. She lived in Newark,
N. J., till 1870, and then removed to St. Louis, Mo.; is buried
in Newark, N. J. In a letter written in 1874 she says, " I,
an only daughter, was loved and indulged *all* I ought to be ;
had a very happy childhood, girlhood, and youth ; hardly
knew anything about care or sorrow ; had *all* the necessaries,
most of the comforts, and *many* of the luxuries of life. At

nineteen the first real sorrow of my life occurred in the death
of my dearly loved father.   I had then come into possession
of the property left me by my Grandfather Allison, who was
a very extensive, wealthy farmer.   Next, to fill my cup of
sorrow to the brim, my beloved mother, who was living with
us, died of apoplexy."

CHILDREN.

1408. Mary E. Ford,⁵ m. William Hulme.
1409. William Elmer Ford,⁵ d. young.
1410. John O. Ford,⁵ m. Jennie Mills. His son, William Elmer Ford,
        res. New Carthage, Mo.
1411. Julia F. Ford,⁵ m. Richard Terhune; d. in Montreal, Canada, Jan.
        25, 1882. Five children.
1412. Cornelia M. Ford,⁵ d. young.
1413. Emmeline C. Ford,⁵ m. H. O. Beach. She d. in St. Louis, Mo.,
        May 14, 1882. Four children.
1414. Newton H. Ford,⁵ m. Nettie Ackley. Res. San Antonio, Texas.
        Four children.
1415. Martha L. Ford,⁵ d. young.
1416. Silena M. Ford,⁵ m. Gabriel Long. Child:
I. Elmer Ford Long.⁶

1417.   John Jay Thompson ⁴ [1341] (Sarah Allison,³ Gen.
William,² Joseph ¹).   He was born in Goshen, Orange county,
N. Y., March 26, 1797 ; married, April 4, 1822, Sarah, daugh-
ter of Benjamin and Sarah (Vail) Webb of Middletown, N.
Y., and granddaughter of Jonathan Webb.   She was born in
Middletown, Orange county, N. Y., July 12, 1804 ; died
in Monroe, Orange county, N. Y., March 10, 1888.   Mr.
Thompson was a Presbyterian minister, and lived and
preached in different places in Orange and Green counties,
N. Y.   He died June 12, 1849, at Bloomingburgh, N. Y.

CHILDREN.

1418. Mary Thompson,⁵ b. Goshen, N. Y., Jan. 22, 1823; m., Sept. 3,
        1844, Chauncey B. Knight. He is a merchant; res. Monroe,
        Orange Co., N. Y.   Children:
I. Charles Thompson Knight,⁶ b. July 24, 1847; m., March 22, 1882,
        Maria R., daughter of James R. and Eliza Jenkins of Newburgh,
        N. Y. Merchant. Res. Monroe, N. Y.
II. Caroline Knight,⁶ b. June 18, 1850; m. Oscar Henry Elmer, a rela-
        tive and Presbyterian minister. Res. Crookston, Minn. (See
        Elmer record.)
III. Frederick Jay Knight,⁶ b. March 11, 1853; m., Aug. 11, 1891, Emma
        Irene Patterson. Civil engineer. Res. Phenix, Arizona. He
        is a graduate of Cornell university.
IV. Henry Brooks Knight,⁶ b. Dec. 25, 1854; m., June 20, 1888, Mary,
        daughter of John and Mary (Thompson) Wallace of Goshen,
        N. Y. Graduated at Cornell university. Res. Goshen, N. Y.
V. Mary Eugenia Knight,⁶ b. Feb. 9, 1857; m., Sept. 8, 1884, George
        Rensalaer Conklin of Monroe, Orange Co., N. Y.

1419. Howard Thompson,[5] b. Middletown, N. Y., Dec. 26, 1824; m., June
       1848, Sarah Jerusha Meigs. Civil engineer. Res. Port Byron,
       N. Y.; d. there Oct., 1862. Children:
I.   Mary Allison Thompson,[6] m. George I. Whipple of Malone, Franklin
     Co., N. Y. Res. Tonawanda, N. Y.
II. Frances Howard Thompson.[6] Single.
1420. Sarah Thompson,[5] b., Nov. 21, 1826, in Middletown, N. Y.; m.,
       March, 1854, Isaac Shultz Stickney. Merchant. Res. Wurts-
       boro', Sullivan Co., N. Y. She d. at Versailles, N. Y., April,
       1875. One child, d. young.
1421. Grace Thompson,[5] b. Goshen, N. Y., Nov. 21, 1830; m., June, 1855,
       David Felter. Res. Closter, Bergen Co., N. J. Child:
I.   Jessie Howard Felter.[6] m. Moses Webb Reed. Res. New York, N. Y.
1422. Benjamin Webb Thompson,[5] b. Middletown, N. Y., Nov. 5, 1833;
       m. Adeltha Twitchell, Sept., 1865; m., second, Clara Uptegraff,
       April, 1875. Real estate agent. Res. Minneapolis, Minn. He
       was a lieutenant colonel in the late war. Children:
I.   Howard Benjamin Thompson.[6]
II.   Adelbert Thompson.[6]
III. Katherine A. Thompson.[6]
IV.   Grace Webb Thompson.[6]
V.   Daniel U. Thompson.[6]
VI.   John Allison Thompson.[6]
1423. Julia Caroline Thompson,[5] b. Monroe, N. Y., Feb. 21, 1838.
       Teacher and editor. Res. Philadelphia, Penn., and d. there
       Feb. 22, 1883. She was editor of a magazine published by the
       Women's Board of the Presbyterian church.
1424. Margaret Boyd Thompson,[5] b. Monroe, N. Y., Nov. 5, 1843; m.,
       April 13, 1871, Rev. Charles Beattie Newton, D. D., a Presby-
       terian minister. They ⌐ missionaries. Res. North India.
       Children:
I.   John Charles Newton.[6]
II.   Frederick J. Newton.[6]
III. Edward F. Newton.[6]
IV.   Francis H. Newton.[6]
V.   Carrie L. Newton.[6]
VI.   George V. Newton.[6]

1425. Isaac Allison [4] [1384] (Isaac,[3] Isaac,[2] Joseph [1]).
He was born in Warwick, near Amity, Orange county, N. Y.,
April 10, 1787; died Jan. 1, 1835. He was of medium size,
with light complexion, blue eyes, and dark hair. His
heart was full of kindness, and he was fond of merriment
and wit. He loved children. In morals he was strict, was
the friend and helper of those less fortunate than himself,
and was industrious and frugal. About one mile from the
Allison homestead was built the first Presbyterian church in
Amity, which he aided in erecting. To this day the Allisons
own a pew in that church, although there is no one of the
family living there to occupy it. He, his wife, and his sister
Sarah were members of that church. All of his sons and
daughters were Presbyterians, except his daughter Mary, wife
of Egbert Mills, who was a member of the Calvary Baptist
church in New York, N. Y. The beloved pastors who ministered to the church in Amity during Mr. Allison's lifetime

Two lines

were Rev. Mr. Hopkins and his successor, Rev. William Timlow. The latter often held neighborhood prayer-meetings at
the Allison home. When the pastor came to make a pastoral
call at the Allison home, the dinner horn was blown, calling
the workmen from the fields, that they might be present with
the family at prayers. During the last war with Great Britain,
Mr. Allison was drafted into the service. He served for a
time, and then returned home on account of sickness in the
family, and his place in the army was supplied by his brother,
Nathaniel Allison. The work of his life was well executed.
In the strength of the years of his mature manhood (being in
his forty-eighth year) the summons for his departure came.
When he was dying he called his children to his bedside,
laid his hand lovingly on their foreheads, and upon them
invoked the blessings of God. He married his second cousin,
Sarah, daughter of James and Amy (Knapp) Allison of
Ridgbury, Orange county, N. Y. She was born May 18,
1794. Her father lived on a very large and beautiful
farm, about ten miles from Amity, town of Wawayanda,
Orange county, N. Y. Mrs. Allison was an attractive
woman, of medium stature, light complexioned, with rosy
cheeks, dark hair, and black eyes. She was a devout
Christian, generous in her nature and acts, and often ministered to the necessities of the sick and suffering. A great
bereavement came to her. Within a space of nine days her
husband and her sons, Gabriel and Andrew, were removed by
death. She bravely took up life's burden, looking for strength
to the God of the widow and the fatherless. So carefully
did she train her sons and daughters, that they in mature
years called her blessed. When their own locks were
"whitened with the snow that never melts," tenderly and
lovingly they spoke of her to their children and grandchil-
dren, gratefully acknowledging her solicitous care during
their childhood and youth.

CHILDREN BORN IN THE TOWN OF WARWICK, NEAR AMITY, ORANGE
COUNTY, N. Y.

1426. Amy K. Allison⁵ (1516), b. April 3, 1813; m. Asa Vail. Res. 28
Clifton Place, Jersey City, N. J.
1427. James Allison,⁵ b. Dec. 20, 1815; m. Eleanor Pound. He d. near
Amity, N. Y. No children.
1428. Nathaniel Allison⁵ (1529) b. June 30, 1818; m., 1844, Martha F.
Sullinger. Res. Mexico, Mo. Physician.
1429. Isaac William Allison⁵ (1540), b. Nov. 17, 1820; m. Teresa A. Elmer.
He d. at Chester, N. Y., Dec. 22, 1881.
1430. Lydia E. Allison,⁵ b. July 15, 1823; m., Jan. 14, 1886, David W.
Selleck. He was a farmer. He died June 27, 1893. Res. Fair
Oaks, N. Y. No children.

1431. Frances Jane Allison⁵ (1548), b. Aug. 15, 1825; m., Oct. 15, 1845,
     James H. Tooker. Res. Slate Hill, Wawayanda, N. Y.
1432. Mary Allison⁵ (1555), b. March 25, 1828; m., Nov. 1, 1848, Egbert
     Mills.
1433. William Lewis Allison⁵ (1568), b. March 22, 1830; m., March 7,
     1855, Ellen R. Lombard. Res. 76 Hancock street, Brooklyn,
     N. Y.
1434. Gabriel Allison,⁵ b. 1832; d. in Dec., 1834, or Jan., 1835.
1435. Andrew Jackson Allison,⁵ b. 1834; d. in Dec., 1834, or Jan., 1835.

    1486. Samuel Allison⁴ [1387] (Isaac,³ Isaac,² Joseph ¹).
He married —— Roe, and with his family and some twenty
other Orange county (N. Y.) families, removed to Ohio,
where he owned a large tract of land, near Newark. His
mother lived with him, and is buried in the family lot in the
cemetery near Newark. He died March 29, 1860.

CHILDREN.

1437. Harriet Allison,⁵ m. in Ohio, Albert Wilkins. Children:
1438. Ella Wilkins.⁶
1439. Edward Wilkins.⁶
1440. Frank Wilkins.⁶
1441. George Wilkins.⁶
1442. Rebecca Allison,⁵ m. in Ohio, George Harris. Children:
1443. Albert Harris.⁶
1444. Mary Ann Harris.⁶
1445. Allison Harris.⁶
1446. Ella Harris.⁶
1447. William Harris.⁶
1448. Isaac W. Allison,⁵ m. —— Wilkins; res. on homestead, near New-
     ark, Ohio. Children:
1449. Homer Allison,⁶ had child, F. Emmert Allison.⁷
1450. George Allison,⁶ had children, Lulu Allison,⁷ and John Allison.⁷
1451. Samuel Allison,⁶ had child, Mabel Allison.⁷
1452. Cline Allison.⁶
1453. Charles Allison.⁶
1454. Susan Allison,⁵ m. Elias Parker. Child:
1455. Hattie Parker.⁶
1456. Samuel Allison,⁵ b. 1827; d. Feb. 26, 1884; m. Rachel Bell, of
     Utica, Ohio. Rem. to Delhi, Delaware Co., Ia., in 1852;
     had 760 acres of land, and owned Pleasant Valley creamery.
     He was an honorable, upright man, and much respected. Chil-
     dren:
1457. Cora Arminda Allison,⁶ m. Frank Porter; res. Schaller, Ia. She
     d. Oct. 2, 1889.
1458. William Roe Allison,⁶ m. Elba Hancher. He is well educated;
     owns a large farm at De Soto, Ia. Children:
1459. Roy H. Allison.⁷
1460. Gladys Allison.⁷
1461. Mildred Allison.⁷
1462. John L. Allison,⁶ graduate of Drake university, Des Moines, Ia.;
     m. Laura Dewey, of Des Moines, Ia.; res. on homestead at
     Delhi, Ia. Child:
1463. Donald D. Allison.⁷
1464. Ella M. Allison,⁶ class of '89 in Drake university.
1465. Alice Allison,⁶ an "A. B." of Drake university, 1891.
1466. Samuel Emmert Allison,⁶ student.

1467. Annie Allison[4] [1389] (Isaac,[3] Isaac,[2] Joseph[1]). She married her second cousin, Ambrose Allison, son of James and Amy (Knapp) Allison, and removed to Ohio, and is buried near her brother, Samuel Allison. According to tradition Ambrose Allison migrated over the mountains into Pennsylvania and was never again heard from.

CHILDREN.

1468. Mary Ann Allison.[5]
1469. Isaac Allison.[5]
1470. Amy Allison.[5]
1471. Samuel Allison,[5] m. Joanna Harris, and owned 1,000 acres of land in Sac Co., Ia. Children:
1472. Oscar Allison,[6] res Sac Co., Ia.
1473. Annie Allison,[6] res. Sac Co., Ia.
1474. Mary Allison,[6] res. Sac Co., Ia.
1475. Minnie Allison,[6] res. Sac Co., Ia.
1476. Laura Allison,[6] res. Dakota.
1477. Frank Allison,[6] res. Sac Co., Ia.
1478. Eugene Allison,[6] res. Sac Co., Ia.
1479. Ida Allison,[6] res. Sac Co., Ia.

1479a. Richard Allison[4] [1390] (Isaac,[3] Isaac,[2] Joseph[1]). He was born in Warwick, Orange Co., N. Y., Jan. 29, 1799, and removed to Peru, Huron Co., Ohio, in 1832 or 1833, and removed to Leonidas, St. Joseph Co., Mich., in 1864, and died there Jan. 18, 1867. Mrs. Allison was born in Brookfield, Orange Co., N. Y., Nov. 6, 1801. They were married July 19, 1828. She died in Peru, Huron Co., Mich., May 24, 1842. Her maiden name was Abigail Brooks, and the maiden name of her mother was Allison. They had eight children : only three lived to be over two years of age.

CHILDREN.

1479b. Amanda Matilda Allison,[5] b. March 31, 1831; removed with her parents to Ohio from New York when a little more than two years of age, and later removed to Michigan. She m. John Murray Feb. 1, 1849; removed to Michigan in 1854, and lived on a farm two miles southwest of New Buffalo, Mich.; res. New Buffalo, Mich. Children:
I. Cecelia Murray,[6] b. Jan. 15, 1850; m. William Stites; res. New Carlisle, Ind. No children.
II. Viola Murray,[6] b. May 22, 1860; m. her second cousin, Hosea Slater. Four children.
1479c. Caroline Allison.[5] She d. Jan. 4, 1870.
1479d. Phebe Jane Allison,[5] b. Jan. 3, 1836, in Peru, Huron Co., Ohio; m., Sept. 26, 1861, Thomas Jefferson Downing, b: in Connecticut, Nov. 14, 1814. They lived in Norwalk, Ohio, until May, 1864, and then moved to Wakeshma, Kalamazoo Co., Mich., and purchased a farm. He d. Oct. 29, 1875. She m., second,

15

David Camp. She now lives at Wakeshma, Mich.; P. O.
Fulton, Mich. Child:
I.   Frank Allison Downing,⁶ b. April 28, 1867; res. with his mother.
1479e. Emeline Allison,⁵ b. Nov. 13, 1838; d. Jan. 4, 1870.

1480. William Allison⁴ [1397] (Richard,³ Isaac,² Joseph¹).
He was born Dec. 28, 1797. He lived and died in Canisteo,
N. Y. On Dec. 10, 1818, he married Levena Fergerson, who
was born April 22, 1797, and died March 2, 1851. He died
May 14, 1863.

CHILDREN.

1481. Phebe Ann Allison,⁵ b. Sept. 11, 1819; d. single.
1482. Charlotte L. Allison,⁵ b. Jan. 31, 1822; m. Wilson W. McHenery;
       res. Decorah, Iowa.
1483. Richard F. Allison⁵ (1585), b. Jan. 19, 1824; m. Hannah R. Cook,
       April 22, 1855; res. Hartsville, N. Y.
1484. Isaac Allison⁵ (1591), b. Nov. 1, 1825; m. Sarah R. Simons, May 23,
       1850; res. Canisteo, N. Y.
1485. Lawrence F. Allison,⁵ b. Nov. 19, 1828; single; res. Canisteo, N. Y.
1486. Mortimore Allison⁵ (1593), b. Oct. 15, 1829; m. Jane A. Davis; res.
       Canisteo, N. Y.
1487. Oscar Allison,⁵ b. Nov. 6, 1832; d. Jan. 11, 1889, single.
1488. Sally Ann Allison,⁵ b. Jan. 24, 1834; m. William C. Adsit; res.
       Cherokee, Iowa.
1489. Charles W. Allison⁵ (1602), b. Aug. 31, 1839; m. Ella Botheroe;
       res. Decorah, Ia.
1490. Adaline Allison,⁵ b. June 3, 1842.

1491. Richard Allison Elmer⁶ [1402] (Micah Allison
Elmer,⁵ Elizabeth Allison,⁴ Richard,³ Isaac,² Joseph¹). He
was born in Sussex Co., N. Y., Aug. 28, 1808. He was
grandson of Dr. William Elmer, of Goshen, N. Y., and
Richard Allison, of Wawayanda, N. Y., and a descendant of
Edward Elmer, who came to America in 1632, and settled in
Hartford, Conn., in 1636, and was one of the original proprietors of the site of the city. Thrown upon his own resources
at an early age, he also had the care and responsibility of the
education of his brothers and sisters. He was a farmer.
Under his guidance one brother entered college and became a
clergyman, and the other engaged in business. Through the
influence of his brother, Rev. Nathaniel Elmer, pastor of a Presbyterian church in Waverly, N. Y., he, in Nov., 1850, was induced to locate in that place. His business was insurance and
real estate. He became closely identified with the interests
and growth of that town. With its schools and churches, and
matters pertaining to the advancement of the morals of the community, he was always interestedly connected. He was quiet
and unobtrusive in his manners. He married, Sept. 11, 1832,
Charlotte, daughter of Col. Jonathan and Catherine (Stew-

art) Bailey, of Wawayanda, N. Y., who died Sept. 4, 1882. He d. Aug. 8, 1867. He and his wife and children were Presbyterians.

CHILDREN.

1492. Howard Elmer,[7] was b. in Wawayanda, Orange Co., N. Y., August 2, 1833. He prepared for college at the Ridgebury and Goshen academies, but delicate health prevented the taking of his course. In November, 1850, his parents moved to Waverly, N. Y., his father's brother, Nathaniel Elmer, being then the pastor of the Presbyterian church there. · Soon after removing to Waverly, then seventeen years of age, he entered the Waverly bank, after which he was employed in the Chemung Canal bank, and the First National bank of Elmira. In 1864 he organized the First National bank, of Waverly, and was its cashier until 1868, when he became its president, which position he held until the time of his death. In 1870 he associated with him C. L. Anthony, of New York, James Fritcher, and his brother Richard, of Waverly, and purchased about 1,000 acres of land, on which Sayre is now situated. On the death of Mr. Anthony, a few years later, he induced the Packer family, E. P. Wilbur, and Robert Lockhart of South Bethlehem to assume the Anthony interest, and this resulted in the location of the Lehigh shops at Sayre and the consequent growth and development of that village. Mr. Elmer was a potent factor in this development, and it was mainly to his faith in the future of the village, his planning, his encouragement, and his indefatigable efforts, that it owes its growth and prosperity. Through his encouragement the Cayuga Wheel foundry, the Sayre pipe foundry and Sayre steam forge was built. He also built the Sayre and Athens water-works. For several years past he has been president and active manager of the companies named, and also of the Sayre Land company. He was also the director of the Pennsylvania & New York Railroad company and the Geneva & Sayre Railroad company, treasurer of the Geneva & Buffalo railroad, and a trustee of the Robert Packer hospital at Sayre. He has been a member of the board of education of Waverly, but never held political office. He was an ardent Republican, but not active in politics, the work being distasteful to him.

Mr. Elmer was a man of cultured literary tastes, unostentatious, courteous, and honorable. On questions of general welfare he was broad-minded, public-spirited, and progressive; and in his death his locality lost one who labored most assiduously for its prosperity: one whose place in the community, church, and all good works will not readily be filled. He was one of the trustees of the Presbyterian church of this place, of which society he has been a member for upwards of twenty years. The pastor of the Presbyterian church at Binghamton, N. Y., writes,—"Howard Elmer impressed me as being a very pure, thoughtful, and lovable spirit. He spoke of the Saviour as One who walked with him, and of the church as an object of love and dear desire." He m., Oct. 10, 1865, Sarah P. Perkins, dau. of George A. and Julia A. Perkins, of Athens, Penn. No children; res. Waverly, N. Y. He d. Sept. 9, 1892.

1493. Mary Elmer,[7] b. March 17, 1835; unmarried; res. Waverly, Tioga Co., N. Y.

1494. Sarah Stewart Elmer,[7] b. April 3, 1838; d. June 10, 1841.

1495. Emma Antoinette Elmer,[7] b. June 28, 1840; d. May 29, 1841.

1496. Richard Allison Elmer[7] (1605), b. June 16, 1842; d. Oct. 1, 1888.

1497. Antoinette Elmer,[7] b. Feb. 25, 1845; unmarried; res. Waverly, Tioga Co., N. Y. She takes a large interest in her friends, and is the historian of her family.

1498. Henry DeLancy Elmer[5] [1404] (Micah Allison Elmer,[4] Mary Allison,[3] Gen. William,[2] Joseph[1]). He was born Feb. 18, 1812; d. Oct. 17, 1870; m. Julia Ann DeKay. He was a harness-maker and a merchant, and died at Chester, N. Y. He had resided at Unionville, N. Y., for many years.

CHILDREN.

1498a. John Elmer.[6] He graduated at Hamilton college, Clinton, N. Y., in 1870; studied law in the law school at Hamilton college, and was admitted to the bar. He was drowned in the Red river of North Minnesota; unmarried.
1499. William Wallace Elmer,[6] b. at Unionville, N. Y., July 15, 1842; m. Carrie, dau. of John Knapp, of Sugar Loaf, Orange Co., N. Y. He was engaged in mercantile business at that place. In 1882, on account of his ill health, they removed to Middletown, N. Y., and in 1887 to West Town, N. Y. There he died Nov. 15, 1887. His widow res. at West Town, N. Y. Children b. at Sugar Loaf, Orange Co., N. Y.
1500. Harry S. Elmer,[7] b. Oct. 14, 1871.
1501. Grace Elmer,[7] b. Jan. 27, 1880.
1502. Josephine Elmer.[6] She m. J. H. Sharp, and is deceased. He is a merchant; res. Morehead, Minn. Children:
1503. Julia A. Sharp.[7]
1504. James H. Sharp.[7]
1505. J. Edgar Sharp.[7]
1506. Emmett Elmer,[6] graduated at medical department of Michigan university. He was a physician in Cornwall, Monroe, and Walden, Orange Co., N. Y. He m. Sarah M., dau. of Morgan and Mary A. (Titus) Shuit. Child:
1507. Morgan Shuit Elmer.[7]
1508. Oscar Elmer.[6] He graduated at Hamilton college, Clinton, N. Y., in 1865, at Union Theological seminary in New York in 1868. He is a clergyman in the home missionary field. He is now pastor at Crookston, Minn., and is very favorably and widely known in that state. He m. Carrie Knight, a relative and a descendant of Sheriff W. W. Thompson, of Orange Co., N. Y. Children:
1509. Mary K. Elmer.[7]
1510. Julia A. Elmer.[7]
1511. Isabel Elmer.[7]
1512. Josephine Elmer.[7]
1513. Charles K. Elmer.[7]

1514. Rev. Nathaniel Elmer[5] [1405] (Elizabeth Allison,[4] Richard,[3] Isaac,[2] Joseph[1]). He was born at Wantage, N. J., Jan. 31, 1816; was graduated at Union college in 1840, and at Union Theological seminary in New York in 1843, and died at Middletown, N. Y., July 11, 1884. The following notice is prepared from an obituary of him by Rev. Charles

Elmer Allison, of Yonkers-on-the-Hudson : "Among the thirty-nine names on the roll of the Hudson, New York, Presbytery, the name of Rev. Nathaniel Elmer stood the first. His name, so long enrolled among God's ministers on earth, has been transferred to those pages which carry the names of victorious saints. After his life journey of sixty-eight years, the pilgrim's staff has dropped from his hand, and he is safe home. It is a privilege to lay a wreath on his grave, to pay a tribute to the memory of one whose words were 'like apples of gold in baskets of silver.' His nature was gentle ; meekness and kindness dwelt in his heart and spoke through his lips. The churches at Stanhope, Circleville, Waverly, Avon, Belmont, and Emporium, to which he ministered, bear grateful witness that his life was a sermon. He always spoke of the everlasting truths of the Bible with the accent of conviction. With the docility of a child, and with contrite heart he listened to the words of Scripture. The closing years of his life were spent in retirement in Middletown, N. Y., where he looked with thoughtful eyes upon the world's affairs, but with profound and loving interest upon his Redeemer's growing kingdom. His death was as peaceful as his faith was firm. His family, and God's church on earth, and the unforgotten friends and beloved Master above were the magnets of his loving thought. His life ended with the day, and for him 'at evening time it was light.' He married, in 1845, Caroline, daughter of Rev. John Ford, of Parsippary, Morris county, N. J. She lived but six months after marriage. He married second, in 1849, Mary A. Post, b. July 26, 1826. She was daughter of James Post, of Middletown, N. Y. His widow and daughter reside in Middletown, N. Y."

CHILD.

1515. Sarah Lizzie Elmer,[6] b. Jan. 27, 1850; res. Middletown, N. Y. She graduated at Ingham university, LeRoy, N. Y., in 1870; unmarried.

1516. Amy K. Allison[5] [1426] (Isaac,[4] Isaac,[3] Isaac,[2] Joseph[1]). She was born near Amity, Orange county, N. Y., April 3, 1813. She married, near Amity, by Rev. William Timlow, Asa, son of Absalom and Keziah (Kenner) Vail.

CHILDREN BORN IN TOWN OF WARWICK, NEAR AMITY, ORANGE
COUNTY, N. Y.

1517. Sarah K. Vail,[6] b.   ; m. Jonas E. Divers; res. Middletown, N. Y. He is a dealer in organs and pianos. Children:
1518. George E. Divers,[7] res. Newton, N. J.; m. Ida L. Courter, of
Newark, N. J., Oct. 19, 1881, by Rev. Charles. E. Allison, of
Yonkers, N. Y. They res. Freemont St., Jersey City, N. J.
1519. Emma Divers.[7]
1520. Floyd Divers.[7]
1521. Isaac Allison Vail.[6] He was of great promise; was connected
with the Orange Co. press, and had editorial life in view; but -
died in young manhood, in Jersey City, N. J.
1522. Lydia Jane Vail,[6] d. in childhood.
1523. Mary Elizabeth Vail,[6] m. William H. Vail. One child d. in
infancy; res. 61 Bright St., Jersey City, N. J.
1524. Floyd Vail,[6] son of Amy Knapp Allison (wife of Asa Vail[1]), was
b. Feb. 4, 1854, near Amity, town of Warwick, Orange Co.,
N. Y.; migrated with his parents to Pittsburgh, Penn., thence
to Jersey City, N. J., where he has since resided. He graduated from the public schools of that city; afterwards attended
for a short time one in Rockland county, New York; was then
instructed in private schools in New York city, and finally
studied with private tutors. He engaged for several years in
mercantile business, but left it to enter the office of "Wallace's
Monthly" in New York, as an editorial and general writer. He
has since contributed to *The Mail and Express* of New York
city, and to other periodicals under the nom de plume of
Flambeau.[2] He has translated from the French "The Two
Mottoes," "The Tattooed King," etc., and he is the author of
"Courted and Won in the Mountains," "His Choice," etc. In
1879 he became secretary to the banking house of R. P. Flower
& Co., in New York city, and private secretary to Hon. Ros-
well P. Flower (now governor of New York state), and in 1885
was appointed secretary and treasurer of the Kingston and Pembroke Railway Co., which position he at present holds. He m.,
Nov. 22, 1876, Sarah J. Crow. She was b. in Jersey City,
N. J., Oct. 19, 1856. She is dau. of David Johnson and Mary
(Jones) Crow, of Jersey City. His stately house is finely situated in Jersey City Heights, overlooking New York city and
harbor, and within easy distance of the city hall in New York.
Children b. Jersey City, N. J.:
1525. Floyd Eugene Vail,[7] b. Sept. 17, 1877.
1526. Lillian Vail,[7] b. Oct. 17, 1879.
1527. Roswell Flower Vail,[7] b. March 6, 1882.
1528. Eleanor Alberta Vail,[7] b. Oct. 1, 1883.

1529. Nathaniel Allison[5]. [1428] (Isaac,[4] Isaac,[3] Isaac,[2]
Joseph[1]). He was born in the town of Warwick, near
Amity, Orange county, N. Y., June 30, 1818; married, Jan. 18,
1844, Martha Frances, daughter of James Sullinger, a native
of Kentucky. She was born in Boone county, Mo., April 5,
1825; died in Mexico, Mo., Dec. 10, 1884, aged 59 years, 8
months. She was a faithful Christian, a loving and devoted
wife and mother. At her death the Audrain County Medi

[1] See "Papers of the Vail Family," by Alfred Vail, New York Historical Society Library, New York city.
[2] See "Pseudonyms—A Book of Literary Disguises."

JAMES W. ALLISON. GILES S. ALLISON.

MARTHA SULLENGER ALLISON.

LINNIE ALLISON. EMMA ALLISON EMMONS.

cal Society, of which her husband is a member, passed resolutions of respect and sympathy. Being then in session, they attended her funeral in a body, and the pall bearers were physicians appointed by the society. Mr. Allison is a physician. He resided in Orange county, N. Y., until Nov. 1, 1839, since then in Missouri. He travelled overland, and in May, 1841, located in Boone county and engaged in the practice of medicine. He married there, and Dec. 1, 1845, removed to Mexico, Mo., where he has lived and practised his profession, and where he now resides. This family are Presbyterians.

CHILDREN.

1529a. James William Allison,⁶ b. Boone Co., Mo., Oct. 11, 1844; m., Nov. 22, 1870, Addie Shultz. She was b. in Grantville, Md., Jan. 1, 1851. She was dau. of Hon. Chauncey Forward Shultz, b. May 29, 1824, in Somerset Co., Penn.; res. St. Louis, Mo. Her mother was Hadassah Chambers (Brown) Shultz. Her grandparents were Adam and Nancy (Shockey) Shultz. He was b. in 1789, in Somerset Co., and was son of Jacob Shultz, b. in 1742, in Paultz, Switzerland; emigrated to Somerset Co., in 1760, and d. there in 1808. His wife was Mary Howenstein, of Stuppensburg, Penn. Mr. Allison res. one year in St. Charles, Mo.; now res. No. 3,110 Eades Ave., St. Louis, Mo. He is in the glass business. Children:
1530. Chauncey Shultz Allison,⁷ b. Feb. 22, 1872; d. Oct. 13, 1872.
1531. Martha Frances Allison,⁷ b. Oct. 13, 1873.
1532. Nathaniel Allison,⁷ b. May 22, 1876.
1533. Chauncey Llewellyn Allison,⁷ b. Feb. 24, 1878; d. Aug. 1, 1878.
1534. Giles Sullinger Allison,⁶ b. Mexico, Mo., August, 1848; manufacturer; res. New York, N. Y.
1535. Sarah Malinda Allison,⁶ b. Mexico, Mo., Jan. 1, 1853; d. there April 18, 1857.
1536. Mortimer Allison,⁶ b. Mexico, Mo., Oct. 8, 1856; d. there March 24, 1859.
1537. Linnie Allison,⁶ b. Mexico, Mo., June 17, 1859; single; res. Mexico, Mo.
1538. Mary Emma Allison,⁶ b. Mexico, Mo., May 11, 1862; m., Nov. 17, 1886, James C. Emmons. She d. in Mexico, Mo., Feb. 4, 1888. Child:
1539. William Nathaniel Emmons,⁷ b. Sept. 10, 1887.

1540. Isaac William Allison⁵ [1429] (Isaac,⁴ Isaac,³ Isaac,² Joseph¹). He was born at the "old homestead," near Amity, in the town of Warwick, Orange county, N. Y., Nov. 17, 1820, and was an Orange county farmer and merchant, and lived at Slate Hill, and at the homestead near Amity and Edenville, also in Unionville and at Chester, Orange county, N. Y. He married, Feb. 6, 1845, Teresa Amelia, the youngest daughter of Micah Allison Elmer, a granddaughter of Dr. William Elmer, of Goshen, N. Y., and of Richard Allison, of Wawayanda, Orange county, N. Y. She was great-granddaughter of Dr. Nathaniel Elmer, of Florida, N. Y., and

of Gen. William Allison, of Goshen, N. Y. She was a descendant of Edward Elmer, a Puritan, who came to America in the
ship *Lion*, in 1632, settled in Hartford, Conn., in 1636, where
he was one of the early proprietors. She was born Nov. 6,
1819, and was educated at Chester academy, N. Y. She
was attractive in person, cheerful, and affectionate in her
disposition. Her mind was clear and strong and bright, and
she had a profound interest in all that was good. She was a
member of the Presbyterian church at Chester, where the
family lived many years. During the war she was secretary
of a society of ladies who furnished articles to the Sanitary
commission for the Union soldiers in hospital and field.
In her own village the poor knew her as their friend. In all
her relations as daughter, sister, wife, and mother, she was
true and faithful. She was a Christian, and her life was
sweet with tenderness and rich in counsel. Her children
rise up and call her blessed. She lived to see her two sons
graduated from Hamilton college, and Howard, the elder, a
practising lawyer. She died before her son Charles Elmer
had entered the Union Theological seminary, where he completed his preparation for the Christian ministry. She
entered into rest Sept. 27, 1870, and was buried in the family lot in the Chester cemetery.

> " Happy he
> With such a mother ! faith in womankind
> Beats with his blood, and trust in all things high
> Comes easy to him."

Mr. Allison was a person of great industry. He loved
learning, and by reading the best works supplemented his
slender early education. He and his wife made many sac-
rifices that they might give their surviving children a liberal education. They and their sons were members of the
Presbyterian church in Chester, N. Y. He was a Republican in politics, and clerk of his town.

Mr. Allison married, second, April 3, 1873, Elizabeth
Adelia, daughter of Samuel and Nancy (Parcel) Gardner,
who was born near Florida, Orange county, N. Y., and who
now lives at Oxford Depot, N. Y. Her grandparents were
Samuel and Hannah (Owen) Gardner, of Long Island, N. Y.
Mr. Allison died in Chester, N. Y., Dec. 22, 1881, and with
his first wife and deceased children is buried in the family
lot in Chester, N. Y. His father and grandfather are buried
in the family lot near Amity, N. Y., about eight miles from
Chester, Orange county, N. Y.

CHILDREN.

1541. Howard Allison⁶ (1609), b. at Slate Hill, town of Wawayanda,
N. Y., March 4, 1846; m., Jan. 2, 1872, Edith A. Thurber.
Lawyer; res. Hempstead, Long Island, N. Y.
1542. Charles Elmer Allison⁶ (1615), b. at Slate Hill, town of Wawayanda, N. Y., July 21, 1847; clergyman; res. Yonkers-on-the-Hudson, N. Y.; single.
1543. Egbert M. Allison,⁶ b. near Amity, town of Warwick, N. Y., March
15, 1850; d. Feb. 14, 1855.
1544. Willmot L. Allison,⁶ b. Feb. 16, 1852, near Amity, N. Y.; d. Dec.
25, 1852.
1545. Caroline E. Allison,⁶ b. Dec. 13, 1853, near Amity, N. Y.; d. March
22, 1857.
1546. Albert Allison,⁶ b. Chester, N. Y., Aug. 8, 1856; d. there Aug. 27,
1856.
1547. Lizzie Elmer Allison,⁶ b. June 19, 1862, at Chester, N. Y.; d. there
March 16, 1873.

1548. Frances Jane Allison⁵ [1481] (Isaac,⁴ Isaac,³ Isaac,²
Joseph¹). She was born near Amity, N. Y., Aug. 15, 1825;
married, Oct. 15, 1845, James H., son of Charles P. and
Hannah (Neely) Tooker, of Minisink, Orange county, N. Y.,
and grandson of Samuel and Catherine (Finch) Tooker, of
Patchogue, Long Island, N. Y. He was born near Slate
Hill, · Orange county, N. Y., Feb. 3, 1821, and has always
made his home in the place of his birth. Farmer, writer,
and lecturer; resides at Slate Hill, N. Y. Mrs. Tooker died
at Slate Hill, Nov. 18, 1881. He married, second, at Mount
Hope, N. Y., Arminda, daughter of Cyrus Skinner, of Otisville, N. Y. She was born April 20, 1822, and resided at
Mount Hope, N. Y.

CHILDREN, BORN NEAR SLATE HILL, ORANGE COUNTY, N. Y.

1549. Mary Eliza Tooker,⁶ b. Nov. 8, 1847; m., Nov., 1870, William H.
Green, and res. Slate Hill, N. Y. Six children.
1550. Charles W. Tooker,⁶ b. May 4, 1850; m. Carrie, daughter of Hon.
John H. Reeve, of Wawayanda, Orange Co., N. Y. Real estate,
res. Springfield, Mo. She d. April 10, ——. Six children.
1551. Samuel Tooker,⁶ b. Sept. 16, 1854; m. Minnie Welman. Res. Great
Bend, Penn. Farmer. One child, which is now deceased.
1552. Lewis Allison Tooker,⁶ b. May 16, 1858; m., Nov., 1881, Fannie
Reeve. Res. Springfield, Mo.; carpenter, doing business with
his two younger brothers. Three children.
1553. Egbert M. Tooker,⁶ b. April 16, 1861; m. Lillie Welman. Res.
Fentonville, N. Y. Farmer. Three children.
1554. Frank J. Tooker,⁶ b. Sept. 1, 1869; res. Carthage, Jasper Co., Mo.;
single.

1555. Mary Allison⁵ [1482] (Isaac,⁴ Isaac,³ Isaac,² Joseph¹). She was born near Amity, Orange county, N. Y.,
March 25, 1828; married, Nov. 1, 1848, Egbert Mills, who

was born Jan. 28, 1820, in Smithtown, L. I. He was a
builder and carpenter. Mr. and Mrs. Egbert Mills are deceased.

CHILDREN BORN IN NEW YORK, N. Y.

1556. Virginia Allison Mills,⁶ b. Oct. 23, 1849; d. March 12, 1852.
1557. Abbott Lawrence Mills,⁶ b. Sept. 19, 1851; m., Sept. 19, 1876, Mag-
       gie Rathbun. Res. Chicago, Ill. He was a student of the
       College of the City of New York. He is a broker, and member
       of the board of trade in Chicago. Children:
1558. Lottie Mills,⁷ b. Feb. 14, 1878.
1559. Abbot Lawrence Mills,⁷ b. April 28, 1880.
1560. Charles Hutchinson Mills,⁷ b. June 4, 1887.
1561. Sarah Edna Mills,⁶ b. May 25, 1853; res. 174 W. 64th street, New
       York, N. Y; single.
1562. George Phillips Mills,⁶ b. April 5, 1855; d. April 4, 1858.
1563. Frances Aurelia Mills,⁶ b. May 21, 1857; m., June 17, 1880, Gus-
       tavus Dallas Dickinson. He is a clerk; res. 174 West 64th
       street, New York, N. Y. No children.
1564. Egbert Mills,⁶ b. May 1, 1859; m., Feb. 10, 1886, Marietta Coffin.
       Clerk in banking house of Kountz Brothers, 120 Broadway,
       N. Y.; res. 334 West 145th street, New York, N. Y. Children:
I.   George Coffin Mills,⁷ b. June 1, 1889.
II.   Egbert Mills, Jr.,⁷ b. May 31, 1891.
1565. George S. P. Mills,⁶ b. June 21, 1865; d. April 8, 1868.
1566. Edmund S. Mills,⁶ b. July 1, 1868; d. Jan. 4, 1870.
1567. Willmot Allison Mills,⁶ b. Dec. 28, 1871; d. April 11, 1873.

1568. William Lewis Allison ⁵ [1433] (Isaac,⁴ Isaac,³
Isaac,² Joseph ¹). He was born near Amity, Orange county,
N. Y., March 22, 1830 ; married Ellen Russell, daughter of
Loring Livingston Lombard and Ellen Whitman (Russell)
Lombard of Boston, Mass., March 7, 1855. He was only five
years of age at his father's death. He was educated at Union-
ville and at the academy in Chester, N. Y. Before he was
fourteen he went into the printing office of *The True Whig*
at Goshen, N. Y. Later, this paper was united with *The
Goshen Democrat*, published by Mead and Webb, and was
the confidential organ of Hon. William H. Seward. In 1851
Mr. Allison went to the city of New York, and, with Charles
Mead of the Erie Railroad printing office, in 1852, he purchased the *Newburgh Gazette*, which he published till 1856.
In the latter year he became an editor of the *New York
Evening Mirror*, a daily. In 1862 he purchased *The
Working Farmer*, and later united with it *The National Agri-
culturist*. This paper he edited for fifteen years and then
disposed of it. In 1869 he purchased, of James O. Kane, the
book plant at the corner of Beekman and Nassau streets in
New York, since which time he has been in the book business
and has published about two hundred and fifty works. He is
the author of "Allison's Revision of Webster's Counting

House Dictionary," which in its several editions has attained
a circulation of half a million copies.   He revised Cushing's
Manual, "The Arctic Discovery in the Nineteenth Century,"
and edited Plutarch, Cooper, and other works.   The home of
Mr. Allison has been in New York city, Norwalk, Conn., and
other places.   Their residence is now 76 Hancock street,
Brooklyn, New York.   Mr. Allison died there March 4, 1893.

CHILDREN.

1569. Loring Lombard Allison,⁶ b. in New York, N. Y., Jan. 14, 1856; d.
        1856.
1570. Henry Leeds Allison,⁶ b. in South Norwalk, Conn., Nov. 5, 1857;
        m., Jan., 1887, Ellen Russell, daughter of George Platt, of Lon-
        don, England, and his wife, Mary Catherine (Russell) Platt of
        Boston, Mass.   He lives in Harlem, New York, N. Y.   Keeps
        a large bookstore and stationery store.   Child:
1571. Mary Catherine Allison,⁷ b. Feb., 1888; d. Oct., 1888.
1572. Ellen Russell Allison,⁶ wife of Henry L. Allison; d. April 27, 1888,
        at Yonkers, N. Y.
1573. George Platt Allison,⁶ b. in South Norwalk, Conn., May 8, 1859; d.
        Oct. 25, 1865.
1574. William Lewis Allison,⁶ b. in South Norwalk, Conn., April 14,
        1861; is in business with his father; m., June 19, 1883, Minnie,
        daughter of Garrett and Matilda (Van Drew) Ward of Paterson,
        N. J.   Res. Brooklyn, N. Y.   Children:
1575. Leroy Ward Allison,⁷ b. in Riverside, N. J., June 22, 1884.
1576. Ethel Allison,⁷ b. in Riverside, N. J., Dec. 23, 1886.   He res.
        763 Jefferson Ave., Brooklyn, N. Y.
1577. Grace Livingston Allison,⁶ b. in Yonkers, N. Y., July 20, 1864.
        Res. Brooklyn, N. Y.
1578. Sarah Ellen Allison,⁶ b. in River Edge, N. J., Dec. 14, 1865; d. April
        12, 1869.
1579. Emily Lombard Allison,⁶ b. in River Edge, N. J., Dec. 5, 1867; m.,
        July 22, 1891, Dr. Frank Parker Hudnut.   Res. Brooklyn, N. Y.
1580. Daisy Allison,⁶ b. in River Edge, N. J., Dec. 5, 1867; d. Dec. 5,
        1867.
1581. Nellie Russell Allison,⁶ b. in River Edge, N. J., March 21, 1869.
        Res. Brooklyn, N. Y.
1582. Phillip Livingston Allison,⁶ b. in River Edge, N. J., Nov. 20, 1871.
        Res. Brooklyn, N. Y.
1583. Percy Burchard Allison,⁶ b. in Paterson, N. J., March 2, 1875; d.
        Feb. 17, 1878.
1584. Edith Allison,⁶ b. in Paterson, N. J., May 20, 1879.   Res. Brooklyn,
        N. Y.

1585. Richard F. Allison ⁵ [1483] (William,⁴ Richard,³
Isaac,² Joseph ¹).   He was born Jan. 19, 1824 ; married
Hannah R. Cook, April 22, 1855, who was born Dec. 5,
1834.   Residence, Hartsville, N. Y.

CHILDREN.

1586. Addie Allison,⁶ b. Sept. 6, 1856; m. Ira W. Hall, Dec. 12, 1878.
        She d. Oct. 7, 1885.   Res. Canisteo, N. Y.

1587. Mary Allison,[6] b. May 21, 1859; m., Sept. 10, 1888, W. J. Darling. Res. Canisteo, N. Y.
1588. Hattie Allison,[6] b. July 6, 1861; d. Sept. 30, 1841.
1589. Kittie Allison,[6] b. July 31, 1863; m. Ira W. Hall, March 23, 1886. Res. Canisteo, N. Y.
1590. Phebe Ann Allison,[6] b. March 2, 1866; m., Sept. 28, 1885, F. D. Drake. Res. Canisteo, N. Y.

1591. Isaac Allison [5] [1484] (William,[4] Richard,[3] Isaac,[2] Joseph [1]). He was born Nov. 1, 1825 ; married, May 23, 1850, Sarah R. Simons. Residence, Canisteo, N. Y.

CHILD.

1592. William S. Allison,[6] b. Jan. 14, 1852; d. Sept. 6, 1853.

1593. Mortimore Allison [5] [1486] (William,[4] Richard,[3] Isaac,[2] Joseph [1]). He was born Oct. 15, 1829 ; married, May 10, 1859, Jane A. Davis of Greenwood, N. Y. Residence, Canisteo, N. Y.

CHILDREN.

1594. Lottie Allison,[6] b. June 10, 1860; m., Sept. 6, 1882, Jackson W. Bowdish. Res. Marion, Ia.
1595. Vinnie Allison,[6] b. May 11, 1863; m. Benjamin F. Ferris. Res. Canisteo, N. Y.
1596. Clarence Allison,[6] b. Oct. 10, 1865; d. May 29, 1868.
1597. Mira L. Allison,[6] b. May 7, 1868; m., Sept. 10, 1890, Hobert S. Lent. Res. Jasper, N. Y.
1598. William Allison,[6] b. July 24, 1870; d. April 20, 1871.
1599. Mortimore Allison, Jr.,[6] b. Feb. 6, 1872. Res. Canisteo, N. Y.
1600. Redmond D. Allison,[6] b. Jan. 24, 1874.
1601. Isaac Allison,[6] b. Aug. 1, 1876.

1602. Charles W. Allison [5] [1489] (William,[4] Richard,[3] Isaac,[2] Joseph [1]). He was born Aug. 31, 1839 ; married, Jan. 22, 1863, Ella Botheroe. Residence, Decorah, Iowa.

CHILDREN.

1603. Nellie Irene Allison,[6] b. Nov. 19, 1865.
1604. Georgianna Allison,[6] b. May 22, 1873.

1605. Richard Allison Elmer [7] [1496] (Richard Allison Elmer,[6] Micah Allison Elmer,[5] Elizabeth Allison,[4] Richard,[3] Isaac,[2] Joseph [1]). He was born at Wawayanda, Orange county, N. Y., June 16, 1842 ; d. Oct. 1, 1888. He graduated at Hamilton college in 1864 ; studied law, was admitted to the bar, then entered his brother's bank at Waverly, N. Y., where he was cashier for twelve years. There he resided till his removal to the city of New York. In 1870 he became interested in the organization of the Sayre Land company, under which was built up that thriving village. He was director of the First National Bank, the Sayre water company, the Cayuga wheel foundry, the Sayre pipe foundry, and the Sayre steam forge company. In 1881 he was appointed, by President Garfield, second assistant postmaster-general, and held this position for three years, where he was a most faithful and efficient officer. In 1884 he resigned, and organized the American Surety company at New York city, became its president, and remained such until his death at his home in New York, 54 West 20th street. He was a man of high character and greatly admired. As a banker and president of the American Surety company, he proved that he had "a genius for business." He married, June 16, 1870, Sarah France, of Middletown, N. Y. She was daughter of J. F. and Isabella France. She with her children live in the city of New York.

CHILDREN BORN WAVERLY, N. Y.

1606. Robert France Elmer,[8] b. July 3, 1871. He was a member of the scientific department of Yale college in 1888, and left college on account of his father's death.
1607. Richard Allison Elmer,[8] b. Nov. 10, 1875. He is a student preparing for Columbia college.
1608. Charles Howard Elmer,[8] b. Jan. 29, 1878. He is a student making preparations to enter Columbia college.

1609. Howard Allison[6] [1541] (Isaac W.,[5] Isaac,[4] Isaac,[3] Isaac,[2] Joseph[1]). He was born at Slate Hill, town of Wawayanda, Orange county, N. Y., March 4, 1846. On his maternal side he is the eighth generation in descent from Edward Elmer, a Puritan, who came from England to Boston, Mass., in 1632. His childhood and youth were spent on the homestead, and at Chester, N. Y., and early in life at the latter place he united with the Presbyterian church. He was educated at the public schools of Chester, prepared for college under Prof. Edward F. B. Orton at Chester academy, where he received first prize for superiority in declamation, and graduated at Hamilton college, Clinton, N. Y., in 1867, where he received the second prize in chemistry. He was principal of the academy and general superintendent of schools at Mount Morris, N. Y., following his graduation. His law studies were pursued with Judge David F. Gedney of Goshen, Orange county, N. Y. After he was admitted to the bar, he practised at Middletown, Orange county, N. Y., and for a brief time in Minnesota. Since 1887 he has been in the law department of the American Surety company at 160 Broadway, New York, N. Y., of which company his cousin, Richard Allison

Elmer, was founder and president. Mr. Allison has a wide knowledge of the department of law to which he has given his attention. He is a member of the college Greek letter society, Delta Kappa Epsilon, and is also a director in the Sydenham post-graduate course and hospital of the city of New York. He is a director of the New York, Boston, Albany, & Schenectady Railway company, and director and president of the " Allison Drug Company " of New York city, and of Orange, N. J., and director and vice-president of "The Chappaqua Mineral Spring Company." He married, Jan. 2, 1872, Edith A., daughter of George and Ellen (Douglass) Thurber, who was born, Nov. 14, 1849, at Patchogue, Long Island, New York. Residence, Hempstead, Queens county, Long Island, N. Y.

CHILDREN.

1610. Teresa Allison,⁷ b. Chester, N. Y., Nov. 1, 1872.
1611. Edna Allison,⁷ b. Middletown, N. Y., Nov. 14, 1874.
1612. Howard Allison,⁷ b. Middletown, N. Y., Sept. 25, 1879.
1613. Arthur Allison,⁷ b. Middletown, N. Y., April 10, 1881.
1614. Charles Herbert Allison,⁷ b. Middletown, N. Y., Feb. 3, 1884.

1615. Charles Elmer Allison⁶ [1542] (Isaac W.,⁵ Isaac,⁴ Isaac,³ Isaac,² Joseph¹). Rev. Charles E. Allison was born at Slate Hill, town of Wawayanda, Orange county, N. Y., July 21, 1847. On his maternal side he is the eighth generation in descent from Edward Elmer, a Puritan, who came from England to Boston, Mass., in 1632, and settled at Hartford, Conn., in 1636, as one of the original proprietors of the site of the city. His childhood was spent at the homestead, near Amity, and at Chester, N. Y. He united with the Presbyterian church in Chester, March 5, 1865. His preparatory course was received at the Chester academy, where he won the first prize for excellence of declamation. He entered Hamilton college, Clinton, N. Y., where he was graduated in 1870. During his junior year he was appointed one of the Clark prize orators of his class.

His theological studies were pursued at Union Theological seminary, New York, N. Y., where he graduated in May, 1874, and was licensed to preach by the Hudson, N. Y., Presbytery, April 21, 1875. During his senior year in the seminary he preached in Yonkers, N. Y., and also after his graduation. On April 21, 1879, he assisted in the organization of the Dayspring Presbyterian church in Yonkers, and was ordained and installed over that church by the Westchester presbytery April 30, 1879.

Mr. Allison is a member of the Greek letter college fraternity, Delta Kappa Epsilon, of the presbytery of West Chester,
N. Y., of which he was moderator in 1886, the Pastor's association of New York, N. Y., the Soldiers' and Sailors' Monument association of Yonkers, the Historical society of
Yonkers, the Westchester county Historical society, and
president of the Yonkers Clerical association in 1892. His
favorite studies have been belles-lettres, theology, and the
principles of persuasive public speech. The Yonkers *Daily
Herald*, Dec. 9th, 1891, has the following:

Rev. Dr. Cole said on Tuesday evening, in accepting the gift of a costly
oil portrait from the citizens of Yonkers, that they could not have selected a more acceptable presenter than the Rev. Charles E. Allison;
and we fully endorse the doctor's remarks. Unboundedly popular with
Yonkers audiences, both young and old, and wonderfully adapted to
the demands of public speech, he could not have been surpassed as the
orator of the occasion. His long companionship with the doctor in that
ministry of which both are such worthy examplars, gave him opportunities that a stranger could not have embraced, and the emblematic
eloquence of his oration was rendered doubly impressive by the tender
sentiment that characterized the speaker. It was a beautiful address,
and will be long remembered by those who were privileged to hear it.

For the press he is a frequent contributor, and is the
author of the "History of Hamilton College." In politics
Mr. Allison is a Prohibitionist, and is "a zealous and active
laborer in the temperance cause, and has given to it his time
and talents. He takes the high ground that the Bible and
the ballot are the two best weapons for the overthrow of
intemperance, and his published utterances indicate that he
is fixed in purpose and strong in faith in the prayers and
final triumph of temperance through moral and legal means."
(From the recent work, "Church and Sunday-School Work
in Yonkers, N. Y.," by Agnes E. Kirkwood.)
    Rev. David Cole, D. D., of Yonkers, N. Y., said, in a his-
torical sketch of that city,—"During his ministry in Yonkers Mr. Allison has been a most active, zealous, and popular
minister, and a most effective and successful worker. In the
pulpit he is clear, direct, and impressive. All his sermons
are warm and magnetic. He is a close student and a good
thinker. And above all, he is noted for a kind heart and for
a profound interest in all that belongs to the higher needs
of the people. Too much cannot be said for his devotion to
his work and its useful results to his own church and the
city. He is always ready to respond to the calls for service,
and is especially acceptable as a reader and speaker in every
social gathering that may be held." The flashes of wit and

glow of humor which brighten his addresses increase his popularity as a speaker. A specimen of his oratory is an oration, entitled, "The Monument's Message," which he delivered to a great audience in Music Hall, Yonkers-on-the-Hudson, on Memorial Day. It was published in full in the daily papers of that city, May 31, 1893.

In this "History of the Allison Family," Rev. Mr. Allison has taken a deep and active interest, from the moment that he knew the work was in progress to its consummation, and I am greatly indebted for facts of interest and for aid, especially in the preparation of the history of his own branch of the family. He is unmarried. Resides at Yonkers, N. Y.

GOSHEN, N. Y., RECORDS.

This information is taken from the oldest personal records of the First Presbyterian church of Goshen, Orange county, N. Y. The first entry is dated Dec., 1773. These records are in the possession of Charles G. Elliott, Esq., of Goshen, who is a descendant in the seventh generation from Elliott, the early missionary to the Indians.

The Goshen church was organized evidently as early as 1721, but the early records were probably burned, as well as the town records, as they are not to be found.

The following records of Allisons and others are not woven into the genealogies:

Joseph Allison, Sept. 4, 1775, was an elder in the Presbyterian church in Goshen, N. Y., when a petition for a charter was made.
Henry Allison, m. Hannah Jackson Nov. 18, 1776.
Richard Allison, m. Amy Case Sept. 15, 1777.
Mary Allison, daughter of Richard Allison and Mary Case his wife, b. Aug. 21, 1779.
Margaret Allison was wife of John McNeal. Children: William Allison McNeal, baptized Aug. 25, 1776. Thomas McNeal, baptized Aug. 25, 1776. Joseph McNeal, baptized Jan. 1, 1778.
Mary Allison, m. John McNeal Dec. 24, 1780.
Elizabeth Allison, daughter of John Allison, b. Oct. 21, 1775.
Michael Allison, son of John Johnes and Hannah Jackson his wife, b. April 4, 1779.
William Allison, m. Mary Graham Jan. 10, 1789.
Mary Allison, m. Nathaniel Harrison April 26, 1790.
Hamilton Morrison, m., Nov. 20, 1817, or May 23, 1818, Maria Miller.

OTHER RECORDS.

On Jan. 20, 1611, John Allison and Thomasin White were married at St. Mary, White Chapel, London, Eng.
In 1737, John Allison was an attorney in Orange Co., N. Y. In 1748, William Allison was a surgeon in New York, N. Y.

The following Allisons, Allistons, are found on the muster rolls of the state of New York. Vol. III:

1616. Van Ransaellaer Allison, 18 yrs. old, was in Co. G, 86th Reg't, N. Y. Vols.; enlisted at Canisteo, N. Y.
1617. William Allison, aged 29, was in Co. G, 86th Reg't, N. Y. Vols.; enlisted at Canisteo, N. Y.
1618. William I. Allison, aged 20, was in Co. F, 95th Reg't, N. Y. Vols.; enlisted at Haverstraw, Rockland Co., N. Y.
1619. Cornelius Allison, aged 20, was in Co. F, 95th Reg't, N. Y. Vols.; enlisted at Haverstraw, Rockland Co., N. Y.
1620. Joseph Allison was in Co. A, 70th Reg't, N. Y. Vols. This company was recruited at Paterson, N. J., and in the city of New York.
1621. Frank Alliston, 23 yrs. old, was a private in Co. K, 72d Reg't, N. Y. Vols. This company was recruited in New York, N. Y.

"The History of Monmouth and Ocean Counties, N. J.," has the following:

1622. John Ellison is named as a witness in court proceedings in 1705.
1623. Richard Ellison's will was dated March 5, 1719, proven Dec. 23, 1723.
1624. Daniel Ellison was taxed in Freehold, N. J., in 1776, for eighty-six acres of land and other property.
These parties all lived in Monmouth and Ocean counties, N. J.

REFERENCES FROM THE COLONIAL HISTORY OF NEW YORK.

From that interesting work published by the state of New York, entitled "Documents Relative to Colonial History of the State of New York," procured in Holland, England, and France by John Romeyer Broadhead, Esq., agent of the legislature to procure and transcribe documents in Europe relative to the colonial history of the state, and edited by E. B. O'Callaghan, M. D., LL. D., the following references are taken:

On Sept. 3, 1664, Sir Robert Carr, at Fort James in New York, was ordered to subdue the Dutch at Fort Delaware. The fort was stormed and captured Oct. 13, 1664. He reported to Colonel Nichols, and requested him to send him two men, whose services he needed, in these words,—"Lett mee begg ye favor of you to send Mr. Allison and Mr. Thompson, the one to ye reedifying of the fort, ye other to fix our arms."—*Vol. III, p. 74.*

The Christian name of Mr. Allison is not given.

A number of loyal citizens of New York city, adherents of King William (Prince of Orange) and his wife, Queen Mary (New York was then an English province), drew up a document declaring their abhorrence to illegal proceedings of certain men in the province. It was to have been

16

presented Jan. 25, 1689, to the mayor's court; but before that date persons of note were seized, houses broken open, so it was not thought safe to proceed in the matter. One of these usurpers was Jacob Leyster, a captain of a train band. On Aug. 16, 1689, he captured the fort, and by force of arms dragged thereto many persons of note. Among them was Mr. Robert Allison, a merchant and considerable trader in the city and province of New York.—*Vol. III, p. 678.* (Robert Allison is also indexed Robert Allinson.)

Leyster was arbitrary, and claimed the title of lieutenant-governor. Later on, Robert Allison and others assaulted Leyster. On June 6, 1690, Robert Allison and about forty others went to the city hall and said it was their day to get the prisoners out of the fort. They gave " two or three huzzas " (according to depositions taken June 8, 1690), and went toward the fort. On the way they met Captain Leyster, who claimed to be lieutenant-governor, and " there beset him close." Allison seized his sword to wrest it from him. During the scrimmage Leyster was roughly handled.

On Dec. 30, 1701, the Protestants of New York sent an address to King William III expressing their loyalty, and asking to be relieved of evils brought upon them by those who were divesting the king's subjects of their rights and possessions, and dividing the same among themselves and their confederates. This was signed by many citizens. Among the signatures were those of Robert Allison, John Ellison, and Thomas Ellisson.

Oct. 2, 1702. Among the chief inhabitants who signed an address to Lord Cornbury, governor of New York, were Robert Allison, Thomas Ellyseen, John Ellison. In a list of the freeholders and inhabitants of the county of Albany, N. Y., dated Dec. 30, 1701, is the name of Tennis Ellissen.

OCCURRENCE IN CANADA DURING THE YEAR 1747-'48.

In a letter dated " Cahos, Oct. 20, 1747," the French commander says,—" We have three Englishmen well treated and closely watched—John Hawkes, Matthew Ellison, and John Taylor." Hawkes commanded Fort Massachusetts in 1746.

Lt. Gov. James DeLancey wrote as follows:

New York, Jan. 31, 1755. Yesterday the Lieutenant-Colonels (Robert) Ellison and Mercer came to this town. I have ordered horses to be got for them to carry them to Connecticut in their way to Boston, for which place they will set out as soon as the weather permits.—*Vol. VI, p. 935.*

The 44th Reg't of Foot was commanded by Colonel Ellison, who was succeeded by James Abercromby March 13, 1756.

In 1687 complaint was entered by the Royal African Company of England against Robert Allison for infringement of the charter by importing negroes, elephants' teeth, etc., into New York from Africa. In the same year he was charged with making a threat that he would " take the *Ketch Adventure.*" In 1688 he petitioned to retain an Indian slave to be purchased in Honduras, which was rejected.

Robert Allison had license to marry Hannah Bray, Nov. 29, 1693.

On Sept. 15, 1704, he made his will; proved July 18, 1705. He was a resident of New York city, and had a wife, Hannah. He had a brother, Thomas Allison, apparently deceased, who had a son,

Robert Allison, to whom Robert Allison first named gave one third of his real estate when twenty-one years of age. In case Robert Allison, the younger, dies before that time, the property was to go to the "loving sister" of Robert, Sr., Sarah Holmes, living in Bridgewater in kingdom of England.

He also remembered Hannah Allison, daughter of his brother, Thomas Allison. This nephew and niece lived at his house in New York city.

Rip Van Dam and William Smith, executors.

Inventory of this estate taken March 28, 1706.

THE ELLISONS. UNASSIGNED RECORDS.

The following records were taken in Oct., 1891, by the author, from the surrogate's office in the city of New York, and from the records of the different counties of New Jersey, previous to 1804, which are kept in the office of the secretary of state, at Trenton, N. J., and from the records of Suffolk county, Mass., at Boston, Mass.

William Ellison, of Elizabeth, N. J., sold land Feb. 6, 1688. On Oct. 7, 1695, or Feb. 20, 1696, then of Woodbridge, N. J., he bought land of Capt. Samuel Walker, late of Boston, Mass., merchant, now of Piscataqua, N. J. On March 27, 1707, he made his will, proven Aug. 19, 1707. He had a wife, Mary Ellison, and children, Enoch Ellison and Emma Ellison.

John Ellison, merchant, of the city of New York, bought land of Hannah, widow of William Barton, in Perth Amboy, N. J., Nov. 22, 1699. He had, on Nov. 7, 1699, bought land in Middletown, N. J.

John Ellison, of New York, N. Y., made his will Oct. 12, 1718. He mentions his wife, Eleanor Ellison, his son, John Ellison, Jr., William Ellison, Thomas Ellison, Joseph Ellison, his sister, Elizabeth Finch, and his brother, William Ellison in England.

John Ellison, Jr., of New York, N. Y., was a merchant like his father. He made his will July 11, 1725. He mentions his wife, Mary Ellison, his eldest son, John Ellison, Jr., his daughter, Mary Ellison, and his brothers, William Ellison, Thomas Ellison, Joseph Ellison.

In the previous year, March 2, 1724, the three brothers of this John Ellison—William Ellison of New York, N. Y., a mariner, Thomas Ellison of the county of Ulster, merchant, and Joseph Ellison of the city of New York, mariner,—"three of the sons of John Ellison, late of the city of New York, merchant," relinquished all claim to some land in Perth Amboy, N. J. This brother John had relinquished to them various messuages in New York and elsewhere in that province.

William Ellison made his will Dec. 13, 1725. He mentions his wife, Mary Ellison, lands, slaves, etc., in Virginia and North Carolina, and property in the province of New York. He mentions his brother, Thomas Ellison, and gives this property to him at the death of his wife, including "two Indian boys named North and South."

Joseph Ellison made his will Dec. 15, 1732, and mentions his brother, John Ellison, his wife, Margaret Ellison, and his brother, Thomas Ellison.

Joseph Ellison, of Shrewsbury, N. J., bought land of Arthur Brown, March 1, 1731.

Joseph Ellison, of New Brunswick, county of Middlesex, N. J., apparently the same as above, made his will May 9, 1739; proven June 9, 1739. He had wife, Martha Ellison, and children, Anna Ellison, Mary Ellison, and daughter-in-law Ann ———. Thomas Allison was one of the executors.

Thomas Ellison, of Hempstead, N. Y., Queen's Co., "on Nassau Island," N. Y., bought land in New Jersey, called Havorsneck, of Walter and Mary Newman, one hundred and sixty-four acres, Sept. 4, 1708.

Thomas Ellison of Shrewsbury, county of Monmouth, N. J., yeoman, bought land in that town of John Lawrence, June 16, 1709.

Thomas Ellison, of Perth Amboy, N. J., husbandman, on March 20, 1728, and Seth Allison, carpenter, passed a legal document in relation to land.

Thomas Ellison, of Shrewsbury, N. J., bought land in that place, Jan. 21, 1739, of Beriah Goddard, of Dartmouth, Mass.

Thomas Ellison, of Shrewsbury, N. J., on April 13, 1762, bought land there of James Towney, of Buck's Co., Penn. He made his will Sept. 10, 1766; proven Dec. 1, 1770. He had a wife, Margaret Ellison. He had a daughter, Anna Ellison, who married Mr. Allen, and had a son, Samuel Allen. He had daughters,—Elizabeth Ellison, who married Mr. Morris, Rebecca Ellison, Hannah Ellison; sons,—Amos Ellison, Lewis Ellison, Thomas Ellison, and granddaughters,—Elizabeth and Mary Ellison.

FROM SUFFOLK COUNTY RECORDS, AT BOSTON, MASS.

Thomas Ellison, Jr., of the city of New York. Merchant. He married Mary Peck, Nov. 10, 1761. He and wife, Mary (Peck) Ellison, and Hannah Peck of the same place, spinster, two of the six daughters of and coheirs of Benjamin Peck, late of the city of New York, deceased, sold July 9, 1771, to Jeremiah Leaming, of Norwalk, Conn., their part of land and wharfs at Boston, Mass., which belonged to Benjamin Peck, which he got from his father, Thomas Peck.

William Ellison, of Boston, Mass., Oct. 28, 1773, sold land to Thomas Hill.

OTHER RECORDS.

Thomas Ellison, of New Windsor, Ulster Co., N. Y., made will Sept. 18, 1789, mention of his sons—Thomas Ellison, John Ellison, William Ellison, and daughters—Eleanor Ellison, Mary Ellison, and Margaret (Ellison) Crooke.

Thomas Ellison, of New York city; will dated Feb. 1, 1796. He mentions his wife, Mary Ellison, his brothers John and William Ellison, and his nephew Thomas Ellison, son of his brother William Ellison. He mentions Thomas Ellison Colden, his sister Elizabeth Colden, his sister Eleanor Ellison, his sister Mary Ellison, his niece Margaret Ellison, and John Inglis, Margaret Inglis, Ann Inglis, children of Charles Inglis, the bishop of Nova Scotia, by his niece Margaret Crooke. He mentions his sister Elizabeth Colden, his niece Alice Colden, wife of Lewis Antill.

Mary Ellison, of New York city, had a will dated Oct. 26, 1810. She mentions her sister, Elizabeth Colden, Alice Antill, granddaughter of Elizabeth Colden, her sister, Margaret Crooke, widow of John Crooke, John Inglis, son of Charles Inglis, bishop of Nova Scotia, and his daughter, Margaret Halliburton, his daughter Ann Pigeon. She speaks of her sister Eleanor Ellison, Margaret Miller's daughter, of her brother

William Ellison, her niece, Elizabeth Floyd. She appointed her brother, John Ellison, and nephew, Thomas Ellison, executors.

John Allison, of Oxford, county of Sussex, N. J.. Sarah Allison appointed administratrix of his estate, Sept. 1, 1759.

John Ellison of county of Burlington, N. J. Administration on his estate granted June 13, 1761.

John Ellison and wife, Rachel Ellison, of the city of New York, sold land at Perth Amboy, N. J., to John Griggs, Aug. 21, 1765. He was a sail maker.

John Ellison's will was proven Nov. 17, 1782, in Dutchess Co., N. Y.

John Ellison's will, dated Dec. 23, 1784, recorded in surrogate's office, New York, N. Y. He mentions his daughter, Martha Dorland, his brother, Richard Ellison, his father, Richard Ellison, his brother, Samuel Ellison, and his sister, Freelove Platt.

James Ellison of Hempstead, N. Y., will dated Feb. 19, 1780. He mentions his wife, Elizabeth Ellison, his son, William Ellison, and his surviving daughters, Freelove Ellison, Mary Ellison, Elizabeth Ellison, Hannah Ellison; one of the witnesses was Richard Ellison.

William Ellison, of New York, N. Y. Cabinet maker. Made a will, dated Sept. 3, 1788. He had a wife, Margaret Ellison, and a daughter, Mary Ellison. He married Margaret Brandt, April 19, 1779.

Seth Ellison, "of the southward of the city of Perth Amboy," N. J., made a will March 20, 1770, proven May 24, 1770. He mentions his eldest son, Thomas Ellison, daughter, Sarah Lumberson; to son Joseph Ellison one half the land the father lived upon was given. His daughter Martha Buckalew received land of him in Middletown, county of Monmouth, N. J. His son, Samuel Ellison, was deceased, but the sons of the latter, Seth Ellison and Samuel Ellison, were remembered in this will. (See previous notice of Thomas Ellison and Seth Ellison of Perth Amboy, N. J.

THE ELLISONS OF NEW WINDSOR AND NEWBURG, N. Y.

Cuthbert Ellison [1] was sheriff of Newcastle-on-Tyne, England, in 1544, and was mayor in 1549 and to 1554. He had a grandson, Cuthbert Ellison, of Newcastle-on-Tyne. The son of the latter, Christopher Ellison, also a resident of Newcastle, was born Jan. 26, 1612; died 1695. He had a son.

John Ellison, born 1688, emigrated to America and settled in New York, N. Y. The history of Orange county, N. Y., p. 214, says that he secured a claim to property in New Windsor, Webster county, N. Y., in 1718, by an investment of £160, and had an additional claim by a loan of £140, in 1721, and perfected the "title to the property in May, 1723." [2]

[1] In the August number, 1890, Magazine of American History, edited by Mrs. Martha J. Lamb, 743 Broadway, New York, N. Y., is a brief account of the Ellisons of New Windsor, N. Y.

[2] John Ellison made his will in 1718, but he may not have died till sometime later. He had a brother, William Ellison, in England, as appears from that document. See former quotations from probate records, which give his children. The preceding quotations from probate and other records relating to the Ellisons throw great light upon the Ellison family of New Windsor and Newburg, N. Y., and corroborate some of the information received from a distinct source. The author has not made a special *study* of the history and genealogy of the Ellisons, but

When his son Thomas Ellison took possession, he erected a stone mansion on the bluff overlooking the river, and a dock and storehouse, and founded the freighting business, which was continued a century by himself and his descendants. His house was occupied by General Washington in 1779 as his head-quarters.

JOHN ELLISON'S CHILDREN.

I.   John Ellison. No record.
II.   Thomas Ellison was a colonel in French and Indian war.
III.   William Ellison. No record.
IV.   Joseph Ellison. No record.

Col. Thomas Ellison, son of John, married Margaret Garrebrant in 1723. He built the homestead that year, the house afterwards occupied as Washington's headquarters. He died there.

CHILDREN.

I.   Thomas Ellison, d. young.
II.   Elizabeth Ellison, m. Cadwallader Colden.
III.   Margaret Ellison, m. John Crook, and had one daughter.
IV.   Eleanor Ellison, b. 1730.
V.   Thomas Ellison, b. 1732; m. Mary, daughter of Benjamin Peck. See notice of them and the Peck family from Suffolk Co., Mass., records, p. 244, and Mr. Ellison's will.
VI.   Mary Ellison. Single.
VII.   John Ellison, d. young.

VIII.   John Ellison, m. Catherine Jameson.
IX.   Francis Ellison, d. young.
X.   William Ellison, m. Mary Floyd and had three children.

If the foregoing account of the origin of this family is correct, these Ellisons of Newburgh and New Windsor, N. Y., are not related, on this side the ocean, to the Long Island Ellisons, who were, and are now, the Allisons of Rockland county, N. Y. But it is not improbable that upon the other side the sea they both sprang from a common source, and that, the Allisons of Scotland.

has incorporated what he has himself gleaned, and what has been furnished by others, so that the information would be preserved, and with the hope that it would aid and stimulate the future historian of the Ellison family.

CHAPTER XIII.

THE ALLISONS OF ROCKLAND COUNTY, N. Y.[1]

1625. Lawrence Ellison,[2] the progenitor of this branch of the Allisons, according to "Thompson's History of Long Island, N. Y.," was a Puritan, and came from Watertown, Mass., to Weathersfield, Conn.; removed from there to Stamford, thence to Hempstead, L. I., with other emigrants who accompanied Rev. Richard Denton in 1644. Most of the early families of Hempstead were under his leadership, and came from Hemel, Hempstead, England, about twenty miles from London. Some, however, came from Halifax, County of York, whence Rev. Richard Denton himself emigrated. The latter was for a time minister in Coley Chapel, Halifax. These emigrants are supposed to have been a part of the colony which came across seas with Robert Winthrop and Sir Richard Saltonstall in 1680.

In June, 1648, Lawrence Ellison obtained a verdict of £4 damages against Thomas Marshfield, in particular court, Connecticut. In 1657 he was taxed in Hempstead for twenty-nine acres. From the Hempstead, L. I., town records in 1658, Lawrence and John Ellison became sureties for the good behavior of Lawrence's son-in-law and John's brother-in-law, John Ellington. On Nov. 29, 1658, he had ten acres

[1] I am greatly indebted for information to the "History of Rockland County, New York," published in 1884 by J. B. Beers & Co., 36 Vesey St., New York, N. Y.; edited by Rev. David Cole, D. D. To the "Isaac Kool (Cool or Cole)" genealogy, by Rev. David Cole, D. D., of Yonkers, N. Y., and especially to the "Family Genealogy of Jonathan Barlow and Plain Rogers of Delaware County, New York;" compiled and edited by George Barlow, Esq,, of 405 Clermont Ave., Brooklyn, N. Y. From the latter work a great deal of my information has, with the permission of the author, been obtained and transcribed.

[2] From the fact that some of the Hempstead colonists came from Yorkshire, Eng., and from the custom of spelling the name Ellison and Allison interchangeably, and from knowledge that some of the Allisons in this book originated from Halifax, Yorkshire, Eng. (see No. 920), where Rev. Richard Denton officiated before coming to America, and his settlement at Hempstead, N. Y., it may not be amiss to state that that locality *may* have been the place from which came Lawrence Ellison, and the parish records in that place or locality might throw light upon his early history and that of his ancestry.

of land allotted him in Hempstead, L. I. Lawrence Ellison was chosen townsman in 1659. Not long did this early settler of Hempstead continue with the youthful settlement. He died in Hempstead, in the North Riding, Yorkshire, Long Island, N. Y., in 1664. At the court of sessions, held at Hempstead Jan. 2, 1665, letters of administration on his estate were granted to his three sons, Richard, Thomas, and John Ellison. This is the oldest record but one recorded in the surrogate's office in the city of New York. In legal documents he signed his name by " his mark."

CHILDREN.

1626. **Richard Ellison**[2] (1629), res. Hempstead, N. Y. He was b., presumably, about 1620.
1627. **Thomas Ellison**[2] (1638), res. Hempstead, N. Y. He was b., presumably, about 1622.
1628. **John Ellison**[2] (1645), res. Hempstead, N. Y. He was b., presumably, about 1624.
—— **Ellison** m. John Ellington; res. Hempstead, N. Y.

1629. **Richard Ellison**[2] [1626] (**Lawrence**[1]). He was born, presumably, about 1620. He was evidently at one time a resident of Braintree, Mass., and the peculiar and unusual name of his wife identifies the man. The record of the births of his children appears upon the Braintree records, showing that he was a resident there from 1645 to as late a date as 1660, and that he appears upon the Hempstead records in 1663. The name of his wife, " Thamasin," appears on the records of Braintree, and the same is mentioned in his will. In 1663 he was of Mad Nan's Neck, L. I., a strip of land which was granted that same year to his brothers, John and Thomas Ellison, and Thomas Hicks. In 1673 he was taxed in Hempstead on sixty acres of land. Land was allotted to him in 1677, and the same year more was allotted to him on Hempstead Plains; he was living there in 1682. He made his will Feb. 14, 1680, which is recorded in the surrogate's office in New York city. This was proven June 13, 1683, showing that he died between those dates. In that instrument he gave " unto my loving and well-beloved wife, Tamisen Elison, ten pounds," also the " bed with its furniture she now Lyeth on;" to his son John he gave one hundred and fifty acres of land and " one hors;" to his son Thomas he gave twenty-two acres; and he remembered his sons-in-law, Jonathan Smith and Joshua Jannock. In closing, he recommended his "Dearly beloved children and wife, aforesaid, to the merciful keeping and protection of our most

blessed Saviour, Jesus Christ our Lord." Residence, Hempstead, N. Y. The family of " Richard and Thomasin *Allison*
born Brantrey, Mass.," as found upon the records.

CHILDREN.

1630. Mary Ellison,³ b. June 15, 1646.
1631. Hanna Ellison,³ b. May 24, 1648.
1632. John Ellison,³ b. June 26, 1650; evidently not married. He left a
       will dated Nov. 8, 1684, proven in the city of New York, in
       which he gave his property to his brother, Thomas Allison;
       res. Hempstead, N. Y.
1633. Sarah Ellison,³ b. Oct. 4, 1652; perhaps m. Joshua Jannock.
1634. Thomas Ellison,³ b. Jan. 1, 1655. He was living Jan. 10, 1688, and
       received property by his brother's, John Ellison's, will.
1635. Experience Ellison,³ b. June 2, 1657.
1636. Richard Ellison,³ (1648), b. Feb. 7, 1660.
1637. Rachael Ellison,³ m. Jonathan Smith.

1638. Thomas Ellison² [1627] (Lawrence¹). He was
born, presumably, about 1622. He was a resident of Hempstead, N. Y., and signed his name by "his mark" to a legal
document in 1656. He had ten acres of land in Hempstead
allotted to him Nov. 27, 1658; in 1662 was chosen a townsman; in 1663 he became part owner of Mad Nan's Neck; in
1677, at a public meeting, land was allotted him in Hempstead; in same year land was given at Hempstead Plains;
in 1685 he was taxed on sixty acres of land and on two hundred and seventy acres; in December, 1696, he conveyed
lands in Hempstead to Richard Allison. Thomas Ellison,
Sr., died in summer of 1697. His will was dated April 7, 1697,
proved at Jamaica, L. I., Dec. 11, 1697. By that document
he had wife, Martha Ellison, and several

CHILDREN.

1639. Thomas Ellison.³ He was in East Jersey in 1702. A Thomas
       Allison and Cornelie Johnson had license of marriage granted
       them July 4, 1698.
1640. John Ellison.³
1641. Grace Ellison.³
1642. Mary Ellison.³
1643. Elizabeth Ellison.³
1644. Martha Ellison.³

1645. John Ellison² [1628] (Lawrence¹). He was born
presumably about 1624. John Ellison, then a young man,
in company with Rev. Richard Denton and his son, Robert
Coe, John Coe, John Karman, Jeremy Wood, Richard Gilder-
slieve, William Raynor, John Ogden, Jonas Wood, John
Fordham, Edmund Wood, Thomas Armitage, Simon Seiring,

Henry Pierson, Robert Jackson, Thomas Sherman, and Francis Yates, in 1644, composed a colony, which, according to the history of Stamford, Conn., were aggrieved at the limited franchises granted the town of Stamford by the New Haven colony, left the jurisdiction of England, and took up land under the Dutch government, on the south side of Long Island, N. Y. This was in 1644. In 1647 land was apportioned to him in Hempstead. In 1656 he signed legal documents by "his mark." In 1658 he became one of the sureties for the good behavior of his brother-in-law, John Ellington. On Nov. 29, 1658, ten acres of land were allotted to him in Hempstead. He was chosen townsman in 1662, and in 1668 land was granted to him and others at Mad Nan's Neck, and this same year he was taxed for thirty acres, and on ten acres, two oxen, and four cows. In 1676 he was chosen overseer. He was granted four acres of land, for which he was required to furnish the town with two gallons of rum to drink. At a public meeting in Hempstead, in 1677, land was given to him, and also land on Hempstead Plains. In 1678 he was chosen constable and real estate valuator. He made no will and his property went to relatives.

CHILD.

1646. John Ellison, Jr.³ (1656). Res. Hempstead, Long Island, N. Y. In 1677, at a public meeting in that town, land was allotted to him.
1647. Thomas Ellison,³ perhaps his son. (From Family Genealogy Jonathan Barlow and Plain Rogers of Delaware Co., N. Y., by George Barlow of Wall street, New York, N. Y. Page 347.)

1648. Richard Ellison ³ [1636] (Richard,² Lawrence ¹). He was born in Braintree, Mass., "7–2–1660," and went early in life to Hempstead with his parents. He was one of a committee to lay out Hempstead Plains in 1685. He then resided in Hempstead. On March 17, 1715, as appears from the records of Queen's county, Long Island, New York, he conveyed land in Hempstead, and signed his name Richard Ellison, but his name was written Richard Allison in the body of the deed. He was called Allison by the witnesses and was indexed Allison. He probably emigrated to Monmouth county, N. J., shortly afterward, as it appears from the records of that county previous to 1804, which are in the secretary of state's office in Trenton, N. J. (as are all other county records of that state previous to that date and after that date at the county seats); he emigrated to Freehold, Monmouth

county, N. Y., where he made his will March 5, 1719 ; pro-
bated Dec. 23, 1732.   He married Alice, or Elsie ——————,
who survived him.   His son, Daniel Ellison[4], was executor.
He gave to his three sons and daughter, Sarah, his land on
Long Island to be divided equally.

CHILDREN.

1649. Daniel Ellison,[4] who received plantation where he dwelt, and per-
          haps made legal document 1774-'76.   Recorded Liber L, secre-
          tary of state's office, Trenton, N. J.
1650. Richard Ellison.[4]
1651. Samuel Ellison,[4] perhaps made will 1766-'68.   Recorded page 154,
          Book I in secretary of state's office, Trenton, N. J.
1652. Ruth Ellison.[4]
1653. Mary Ellison.[4]
1654. Susannah Ellison.[4]
1655. Sarah Ellison.[4]

1656. John Allison, Jr.[3], [1646] (John[2], Lawrence [1]).
The subject of this sketch was the immediate founder of the
family of Allisons, which for a number of generations, and a
numerous race, have lived, acted life's part, and slept within
the soil of Haverstraw, Rockland county, New York.   Mr.
Allison was born in Hempstead, Long Island, N. Y., and was
one of the company that purchased the north part of the
Kakiat patent of land in Orange county, the portion which is
now in Rockland county, in the year 1719, on which they
founded the settlement of New Hempstead, now Ramapo.
He became owner of the greater part of De Hart's patent,
which included the present townships of Haverstraw and
Grassy Point in Orange county, now in Rockland county.
In the strength of his manhood and in the hey-day of life, he,
with his family, removed to New Hempstead and later to
Haverstraw, and founded his home, which remained such till
his death.   His house stood on the bank of the sparkling
Hudson river " on the west side of what is called Allison
street and about eight rods north of Main street " in Haverstraw. (History of Rockland county.) From the knowledge
we have of his business enterprises, he appears to have been a
man of push and executive ability.   In the history of Rockland county he is called of the English settlers, i. e., of English
descent.   He died in 1754, between June 6, when his will was
made, and Oct. 21, when it was proven in court.   He was
probably buried in the old cemetery on the "Neck " near the
Minisceongo creek, or in the old Allison burying-ground,
some sixty rods east of the former home of Benjamin
Allison.

1657. Benjamin Allison⁴ (1666). Date of birth unknown. Res. Haverstraw, N. Y.
1658. John Allison.⁴ On Oct. 1, 1773, was made a will by John Allison
of Haverstraw, N. Y., probably this man, proven Nov. 7, 1782,
wife Amy Allison executor. Children, John Allison,⁵ Elizabeth
Allison,⁵ Thomas Allison,⁵ Richard Allison,⁵ Margaret Allison,⁵
William Allison,⁵ Joseph Allison,⁵ Isaac Allison,⁵ Jeremiah
Allison,⁵ Benjamin Allison,⁵ each had one tenth of his estate.
1659. Joseph Allison⁴ (1673), b. Aug. 3, 1721, or Aug. 4, 1722; d. Jan. 2,
1796. Res. Haverstraw, N. Y.
1660. William Allison,⁴ d. about 1758. He was remembered in the will
of his father, as was his son, Edward Allison.⁵
1661. Elizabeth Allison,⁴ m. Mr. Cuyper.
1662. Deborah Allison,⁴ m. John Johnson.
1663. Mary Allison,⁴ m. Mr. De Grough.
1664. Hannah Allison,⁴ m. John Taylor.
1665. Richard Allison,⁴ was a physician and died before his father in
1749. He made a will Jan. 9, of that year, witnessed by his
brother, John Allison, and Cornelius C. Cuyper, probably his
brother-in-law and sister Elizabeth's husband. His father was
executor. He divided his estate between his brothers and sisters, who were then all living, and left legacies to his friend,
Phebe Hubs, and to her children, Richard Hubs and Hannah
Hubs. These Hubses seem to have been inmates of his father's
household, relationship, if any, not known. His father remembered her by his will in 1754, and mentions her daughter, Priscilla Hubs. Dr. Allison res. in Haverstraw, N. Y.

1666. Benjamin Allison⁴ [1657] (John,³ John,² Lawrence¹). He was born probably in New Hempstead, N. Y.,
as his father helped to found that place in 1720. The date
of his birth is unknown. He resided in Haverstraw, N. Y.,
in a house built in 1754, of brown stone blocks, located at the
meeting of two roads, the Grassy Point road and the old Benson road, and north of the First Presbyterian church about
half a mile. It was standing in 1890 in fair preservation, and
was an interesting old-time relic. He received this land from
his father, which originally belonged to Dick Crom and which
included all the land lying between the Minisceongo creek and
the Benson farm. His father left him besides, the south part
of lot No. 7 in Haverstraw, which he in turn left to Hannah
and Rebecca Allison, daughters of his son, Thomas Allison.
He was patriotic, and exemplified his love for American freedom, and hatred of British oppression, by furnishing, during
the Revolutionary struggle, a large amount of supplies to Colonel Hay and his men of the Continental forces, stationed at
Haverstraw. The Continental bills with which he was paid
proved, eventually, to be a total loss. He was twice married;
name of first wife is unknown. He married, second, Leah
Ackerman, marriage bond dated Nov. 1, 1769, who is mentioned in his will made March 19, 1796.

CHILDREN BORN IN HAVERSTRAW, ROCKLAND COUNTY, N. Y., PROBABLY.

1667. John Allison.[5] He was born probably between 1725 and 1730. He
was living at the time his father's will was made, March 19,
1796, and was then not married. There is no evidence that he
was ever married. He probably died single and was buried in
the family cemetery. The History of Rockland County is said
to be in error in giving his name in two marriages instead of
that of his brother, Thomas Allison.

1668. Robert Allison[5] (1691), b. Haverstraw, N. Y.; m. Elizabeth
————. Res. Haverstraw, N. Y.

1669. Peter Allison[5] (1695), res. Haverstraw, N. Y.

1670. Thomas Allison[5] (1703), res. Haverstraw, N. Y.

1671. Samuel Allison[5] (1709). He was living on March 19, 1796, when
his father made a will, and by it he received a consideration in
land and personal property. He m. Sarah Phillips.

1672. Joseph B. Allison[5] (1715), b. Dec. 13, 1761; m. Mary Storms. Res.
Haverstraw, N. Y.

1673. Capt. Joseph Allison[4] [1659] (John,[3] John,[2] Lawrence[1]). He was born probably in New Hampstead, N. Y.,
Aug. 3, 1721, or Aug. 4, 1722; died, Jan. 2, 1796, at the
age of 74 years, 4 months, 29 days. He married Elizabeth,
daughter of Matthew Benson, March 10, 1743. She died
Dec. 12, 1767, leaving ten children. He married, second,
May 4, 1769, Elsie Parcells, who died April 16, 1815, aged
64 years. Eight children. Resided at Haverstraw, N. Y.,
where he owned a large farm and much landed estate. The
headstone of Mr. Allison appears in the old Allison burying-
ground. His remains now rest in Mount Repose cemetery.

CHILDREN BORN IN HAVERSTRAW, ROCKLAND COUNTY, N. Y.

1674. Matthew Allison[5] (1727), b. July 18, 1743; d. before 1795, leaving
children: Joseph,[6] Peter,[6] Cornelius,[6] Hendrick,[6] Matthew,[6] and
Elizabeth Allison.[6] He res. in Haverstraw, N. Y.

1675. Elizabeth Allison,[5] b. Oct. 2, 1745; m. David Ten Eyck. Res.
Haverstraw, N. Y. She had a large family of children. Among
them were Thomas Ten Eyck,[6] res. Stony Point, N. Y.; James
Ten Eyck,[6] res. Peekskill, N. Y.; John Ten Eyck,[6] Samuel Ten
Eyck,[6] Richard Ten Eyck,[6] Harriet Ten Eyck,[6] and Hannah
Ten Eyck.[6]

1676. Mary Allison,[5] b. Oct. 17, 1747; m. Amos Hutchings. The marriage bond was filed at Albany, N. Y., Nov. 14, 1764.

1677. Hannah Allison,[5] b. Feb. 14, 1750; m. Adrian Waldron; res. Haverstraw, N. Y. She had a large family of children, the most of
whom lived in their native town. Among them were Abram
Waldron,[6] Jacob Waldron,[6] John Waldron,[6] Matthew Waldron,[6] and Calvin Waldron.[6]

1678. Joseph Allison,[5] b. May 29, 1752; res. Haverstraw, N. Y. He
received with his brothers a tract of land from his father; sold
April 9, 1793.

1679. John Allison,[5] b. May 12, 1754. He received with his brothers a
great tract of land from his father, which they sold April 9,
1793, situated in Haverstraw.

1680.   William Allison,⁵ b. March 11, 1756. With his brothers he was part owner of a large tract of land in Haverstraw, given by his father. Sold by them April 9, 1793.
1681.   Thomas Allison,⁵ b. Feb. 11, 1760; res. Haverstraw, N. Y. His son, Benjamin T. Allison,⁶ res. near Yorktown, N. Y.
1682.   Deborah Allison,⁵ b. June 29, 1762; m. William Willis.
1683.   Benjamin Allison,⁵ b. July 3, 1764; res. Haverstraw, N. Y. He left a family.

CHILDREN BY SECOND MARRIAGE.

1684.   Peter Allison⁵ (1734), b. Nov. 19, 1769; m. Margaret Suffern; res. Haverstraw, N. Y.
1685.   Amos Allison,⁵ b. May 29, 1771. He was a blacksmith, a man of great strength and of powerful physique; res. Haverstraw, N. Y. He m. ———— ————, and had several children. Among them were Leonard Allison,⁶ and Jacob Allison.⁶
1686.   Michael Allison,⁵ b. June 3, 1773; d. unmarried. He was a man of wealth, and res. in the city of New York, where he d. at his residence, 46 Vesey street, March 25, 1855, and is buried in Greenwood cemetery.
1687.   Parcells Allison,⁵ b. April 25, 1777; res. Haverstraw, N. Y. He m., Aug. 5, 1800, Nellie Parcells, his deceased brother's widow.
1688.   Richard Allison⁵ (1740), b. Oct. 23, 1780; m. Eliza Ruckel. He d. Nov. 26, 1825, in the city of New York.
1689.   Elsie Allison⁵ (1750), b. Nov. 9, 1783; m. Jacob Archer, in 1801; res. Haverstraw, N. Y.
1690.   Abraham Allison,⁵ b. Nov. 9, 1783; d. in infancy.

1691.   **Robert Allison⁵ [1668] (Benjamin,⁴ John,³ John,² Lawrence¹).** He was born in Haverstraw, N. Y., and by his father's will, made March 19, 1796, he received considerable land; res. Haverstraw, N. Y. He m. Elizabeth ———— ————, who became intemperate and depraved in morals. This preyed deeply on his mind. He became disheartened, lost ambition, and worked as a common laborer for his nephew, William Cosgrove. She survived her husband, and forty-five acres of land were given to Christopher Cosgrove for her support in her old age.

CHILDREN BORN IN HAVERSTRAW, N. Y.

1692.   Benjamin Allison.⁶ He is said to have lived and died a bachelor. He was named for his grandfather, who in his will left the use of a tract of land to his son, Robert, which should be inherited by this Benjamin, who was to pay his sisters £5 each, and to support his mother.
1693.   Hannah Allison.⁶ She m. Benjamin Youmans; res. in Haverstraw, N. Y., where he died. She m., second, James Kenney, of Sufferns, Rockland Co., N. Y. They had one child: Patty Kenney,⁷ m. Mr. Bostwick. He was employed by the Garner Print Works, Garnersville, Haverstraw, N. Y., and had a family of children.
1694.   Margaret Allison,⁶ m. John Devine. They res. on Long Island where he was a farmer, raising produce for the markets.

1695. Peter Allison[5] [1669] (Benjamin,[4] John,[3] John,[2] Lawrence[1]). He was born in Haverstraw, N. Y. He inherited the homestead from his father, and resided for many years in Haverstraw in the old stone house of Benjamin Allison, northeast of the First Presbyterian church, about one half mile distant, and at the junction of the old Benson and Grassy Point roads. He added to his possessions, and was a substantial and prosperous farmer. He ranked high among his fellow-citizens, and possessed abilities of no common order. He resided near the lime kilns, with his family, on the Byron place, in North Haverstraw, which he had purchased. He was twice married. The name of his first wife is not known. They had five children. He married, second, Mrs. Earl, of New York city. He died in 1815.

CHILDREN BORN IN HAVERSTRAW, N. Y.

1696. Margaret Allison.[6]
1697. Leah Allison.[6] After the death of her sister, Hannah, she married her brother-in-law, Baxter June. They res. in Haverstraw, N. Y., in a small frame dwelling, near the foot of the hill, on the opposite side of the highway from the old chemical works, and near the First Presbyterian church. No children.
1698. Hannah Allison.[6] She was a smart, enterprising, and fine looking woman, a tailoress by trade, and supported herself by her needle, working in different families. She m. Baxter June,[6] a man of indolent habits, but of strong build and large frame. Her sister, Leah, and brother, John Allison, lived with her in Haverstraw, where she died about ten years after her marriage. Children: Loretto June,[7] and a son.
1699. John Allison.[6] Res. in Haverstraw with his sisters, and d. unmarried. He was a farmer by occupation, and a prominent man in the town. In the militia he was a lieutenant, and held public positions. He was a person of fine appearance and high moral character.
1700. Peter P. Allison[6] (1759). Res. Haverstraw, N. Y.
1701. Sarah Allison.[6] She was a dressmaker; res. New York, N. Y.
1702. Elizabeth Allison.[6] She m. Lemuel June, who was a justice of the peace and held other town offices. He was a person of ability. He managed a freight sloop which carried brick and plied between Haverstraw and the city of New York. Children: Baxter June,[7] Charles June,[7] and others.

1703. Thomas Allison[5] [1670] (Benjamin,[4] John,[3] John,[2] Lawrence[1]). He was born in Haverstraw, N. Y., and by his father's will he received in that town a tract of land of about one hundred acres. He married Mary Kingsland.

CHILDREN BORN IN HAVERSTRAW, N. Y.

1704. Garret Allison[6] (1768), b. March 28, 1789; d. June 11, 1848; res. Haverstraw, N. Y.
1705. James Allison[6] (1780), b. Haverstraw; res. Haverstraw, N. Y.

1706. Catherine Allison.⁶ She probably d. unmarried.
1707. Rebecca Allison.⁶ She m. Lob. Lockwood; removed to Green-
       wich, Conn., and from there to the West. Children: George
       Lockwood,⁷ who m. ―――― ――――, and had two sons, now liv-
       ing, and a daughter who is deceased. ―――― Lockwood,⁷ a
       daughter, m., and lives in the West. Frederick Lockwood,⁷ a
       street car conductor, res. Providence, R. I.
1708. Hannah Allison.⁶ She m. James Guernsey. He was in the fur
       business in New York city.

1709. Samuel Allison⁵ [1671] (Benjamin,⁴ John,³ John,²
Lawrence¹). He resided for a time at Haverstraw, N. Y.,
and subsequently removed to the West. He married Sarah
Phillips, who was born Feb. 11, 1760; died Oct. 23, 1841.

CHILDREN.

1710. Hannah Allison,⁶ b. Oct. 16, 1792; d. March 8, 1885. She m. Seth
       Leonard. Children: Samuel Leonard,⁷ Joseph Leonard,⁷ Me-
       linda Leonard,⁷ Amasa Leonard,⁷ Betsey Leonard,⁷ Charles
       Leonard,⁷ Clarinda Leonard.⁷
1711. David Allison⁶ (1784), b. Sept. 21, 1794; d. at Pontiac, Mich., Oct.
       6, 1883.
1712. Polly Allison,⁶ b. June 19, 1796; d. April 15, 1839; m. Benjamin
       Collins. No children. She subsequently m. Mr. Wilkinson.
1713. Abigail Allison,⁶ b. 1798; m. Luther Sawtelle. Children: Henry
       Sawtelle,⁷ Emeline Sawtelle,⁷ Luther Sawtelle,⁷ Catherine Saw-
       telle.⁷
1714. Samuel Allison,⁶ b. 1800; m. Hettie Waterbury. Children: George
       W. Allison,⁷ Jane Allison,⁷ Hannah Allison,⁷ Charles Allison.⁷

1715. Joseph B. Allison⁵ [1672] (Benjamin,⁴ John,³
John,² Lawrence¹). He was born at Haverstraw, N. Y.,
Dec. 13, 1760 or 1761, in the old Benjamin Allison brown
stone house, situated at the junction of the Grassy Point and
old Benson farm roads, and one half mile northeast of the
First Presbyterian church. Here he lived, working at farm
work for his father till the age of manhood. When fifteen
years of age his father sent him on a perilous journey to
General Washington's encampment, back of Newburg, with
a bill for supplies furnished the Continental troops encamped
at Haverstraw. On reaching Washington's tent he was
overawed by the majestic bearing of the commander-in-chief.
The general invited him in, received his message, and, put-
ting his hand on the young man's head, commended his
bravery and fidelity. When seventeen years of age he was
enrolled as a "minute man," one liable to be called out for
military duty at a minute's notice. While acting as team-
ster, carrying supplies to the troops, he became well known
at head-quarters. He was a volunteer at the taking of Stony
Point. His portion of the trophies were a British cartridge-

box and a bayonet. These relics are now in the possession of the Demarest branch of his descendants. He was of medium size, wiry, and active. From his father he received a large farm, and he married, and settled down to the duties of a farmer and the quarrying of brown stone. His homestead, a large frame dwelling, with a kitchen extension on the end, was situated on the west side of Miniscongo creek, opposite to the spot where Peck's rolling mill now stands. This building was standing recently.

Some years after the death of his wife he sold eight thousand dollars' worth of land, and divided the proceeds among his children. His son, Abraham, and his daughters, Catherine and Margaret, received land from him and aid in erecting their buildings, and all were situated adjoining each other on the mountain side of the road to Ramapo, beginning about one eighth of a mile beyond the Mount Repose cemetery and running west. He gave to his son, Jonas Allison a place on the opposite side of this road and half a mile farther west, on the east side of the hill. The subject of this sketch spent the last years of his life in the homes of his children. He died Dec. 20, 1848, and the remains of himself and wife now repose in Mount Repose cemetery in Haverstraw, N. Y., and the place is marked by old brown headstones in good preservation.

Mr. Allison married, in 1781 or 1782, Mary Storms, who was born at Haverstraw, June 20, 1760, and who died there March 24, 1824. She was stout, had black hair and eyes and an amiable disposition, and was full of courage and patriotism. They resided at Haverstraw, N. Y.

CHILDREN BORN AT HAVERSTRAW, N. Y.

1716. Benjamin Allison,⁶ b. Sept. 13, 1782; d. Feb. 10, 1842; single. The later years of his life were spent in the home of his brother, Abraham Allison, where he died. He was buried in the Presbyterian churchyard on Calico hill, and included in 1889 in the grounds of Elisha Peck.

1717. Rebecca Allison,⁶ b. Feb. 17, 1784; d. June 7, 1863. She m. Christopher Cosgrove, April 19, 1801. He was a house carpenter. They res. in New York, N. Y., and then in Haverstraw, N. Y., where he died Nov. 12, 1842. Mrs. Cosgrove was five feet six inches in height, stout built, and good featured. Her complexion was dark, her hair and eyes were black. Her powers of endurance were great, and she had great perseverance and energy. Sixteen children were born to her in twenty-two years, fifteen of them maturing with sound bodies and pure morals, and all were well trained in habits of industry. They all became active, zealous Christians and highly esteemed citizens, and were members of the Presbyterian or Methodist Episcopal church. She d. June 7, 1863. Children except eldest b. in Haverstraw, N. Y.:

17

I. Mary Cosgrove,[7] b. April 9, 1802, in New York city; d. Oct. 20, 1865, in Grandville, Mich.; m. Luther D. Abbott.

II. William Cosgrove,[7] b. Aug. 18, 1803; d. Dec. 18, 1856; m. Rebecca Phillips; res. Haverstraw, N. Y.

III. Margaret Cosgrove,[7] b. Dec. 28, 1804; d. Oct. 16, 1828; m., Nov. 10, 1827, Daniel S. Kiles.

IV. Abraham Cosgrove,[7] b. May 27, 1806; d. April 16, 1849, in Haverstraw, N. Y. He m. Letitia, daughter of Garrett Allison. (See that family.)

V. Amelia Cosgrove,[7] b. Dec. 18, 1807; d. Dec. 28, 1828; m. Tunis Snedeker.

VI. Benjamin Cosgrove,[7] b. Aug. 31, 1809; d. in Haverstraw, Aug. 9, 1859.

VII. Wilhelmina Cosgrove,[7] b. Aug. 3, 1811; d. in Brooklyn, N. Y., March 8, 1881; m. William Barlow, Jr. One child: George Barlow,[8] b. Oct. 24, 1832, in the old Cosgrove homestead in Haverstraw, N. Y. He is a broker in New York; res. 405 Clermont avenue, Brooklyn, N. Y. He m., Oct. 20, 1858, Martha Ann Lockwood, b. Peekskill, N. Y., Dec. 9, 1835. He is the author of a very valuable work entitled "Family Genealogy of Jonathan Barlow and Plain Rogers, of Delaware Co., N. Y." Children: George Francis Barlow,[9] b. Oct. 4, 1860; lawyer. Caroline Lockwood Barlow,[9] b. May 29, 1862; m. William Cornell Hendrie. Nellie W. Barlow,[9] b. Feb. 8, 1868; m. Worden Dunham Loutrell. Elbert Spicer Barlow,[9] b. July 1, 1878.

VIII. Joseph Cosgrove,[7] b. Jan. 13, 1813; d. May 6, 1889, in Haverstraw, N. Y.; res. Haverstraw. He m. Sarah Ann Allison, daughter of Garrett and Sarah (Palmer) Allison. (See that family record.)

IX. Hannah Cosgrove,[7] b. March 16, 1815; m., April 11, 1833, John J. Peck. He d. July 26, 1884. She res. in 1889, in Haverstraw, N. Y. Children: Edward J. Peck,[8] b. March 30, 1834; d. Jan. 18, 1890. Jane Eliza Peck,[8] b. Aug. 28, 1837; d. May 19, 1842. John Newton Peck,[8] b. Dec. 15, 1842; res. Haverstraw, N. Y.

X. Jane Eliza Cosgrove,[7] b. Jan. 5, 1819. She m., Sept. 13, 1845, Michael Snedeker Allison, of Jersey City, N. J. (See his record.)

XI. Catherine Ann Cosgrove,[7] b. Jan. 5, 1819; m., June 21, 1837, Michael Snedeker Allison. She d. in Brooklyn, N. Y., Feb. 12, 1845. (See his record.)

XII. John Cosgrove,[7] b. Nov. 23, 1820; d. March 21, 1877, in Haverstraw, N. Y. He m. Catherine B. McLauren. She res. at Collinsville, near Morristown, N. J. Children: John Albert Cosgrove,[8] b. Sept. 6, 1848; d. April 2, 1886; clergyman. William McLauren Cosgrove,[8] b. May 15, 1858; d. July 19, 1858. Minnie Augusta Cosgrove,[8] b. April 28, 1862; m. Frost S. Green; res. Morristown, N. J.

XIII. Samuel Cosgrove,[7] b. Jan. 7, 1823; res. Jersey City, N. J.; m. Martha Matilda Benson, Feb. 2, 1848. She d. April 10, 1885. Children: George Benson Cosgrove,[8] b. Oct. 13, 1848; m. Rhomelia M. Myers. Is in business in the city of New York. Michael Allison Cosgrove,[8] b. March 4, 1832; d. unmarried April 6, 1877. Arthur Cosgrove,[8] b. July 15, 1856; m., April 10, 1883, Louise R. Kuhn; res. San Diego, Cal.

XIV. Harriet Cosgrove,[7] b. June 12, 1825; d. in Haverstraw, N. Y., March 28, 1826.

XV. Henrietta Cosgrove,[7] b. May 12, 1827; m., March 4, 1846, Charles Holmes, who d. Jan. 2, 1880. Children: William S. Holmes,[8] b. Nov. 2, 1846; unmarried. Emma Eliza Holmes,[8] b. Oct. 16, 1848; d. Jan. 31, 1883. Charlotte Holmes,[8] b. Aug. 3, 1850; m. Andrew Snedeker; res. Haverstraw, N. Y. Maria Frances Holmes,[8] b. Jan. 19, 1853; res. Haverstraw, N. Y. Ida M. Holmes.[8] Charles W. Holmes,[8] b. Dec. 17, 1857; res. New York

city. Albert E. Holmes.[8] Nettie Allison Holmes,[8] b. Oct. 12,
1865; res. Haverstraw, N. Y. Clara B. Holmes,[8] b. July 7,
1867; m., Jan. 22, 1891, Dr. Ira L. Nickerson; res. Haverstraw,
N. Y.

XVI. Charlotte Cosgrove,[7] b. Feb. 25, 1831; m. Jan. 11, 1855, William
H. King; res. Haverstraw, N. Y. Children: Elizabeth R.
King,[8] b. Jan. 25, 1856; d. July 26, 1876. Henrietta King,[8] b.
March 26, 1860. George Edgar King,[8] b. July 8, 1864; d. Sept.
2, 1865. Ella Charlotte King,[7] b. June 7, 1867; d. March 15,
1868. Emilie Amelia King,[8] b. June 20, 1869; d. Dec. 3, 1869.

1718. Abraham Allison[6] (1795), b. April 6, 1786; d. in Haverstraw,
N. Y.

1719. Margaret Allison,[6] b. Feb. 21, 1788; m. July 12, 1807, Joseph Dem-
arest, b. in Rockland Co., N. Y.; d. in Haverstraw, N. Y.,
Sept. 5, 1849, aged 64 years, 11 months, 5 days. He was a
house carpenter. She was handsome when young, was con-
scientious and upright, and faithful in all life's relations.
They lived in New York city, and later in Haverstraw. She
survived her husband. Children:
I. Walter Demarest,[7] b. May 13, 1809; d. unmarried Aug. 2, 1833.
II. Catherine Demarest,[7] b. April 7, 1811; d. March 2, 1830; unmarried.
III. Samuel Demarest,[7] b. Dec. 13, 1817; d. Jan. 29, 1850; unmarried.
IV. Mary Demarest,[7] m. Isaac Stevens; res. Haverstraw, N. Y., and
later removed to the West. Three children.
V. Willamena Demarest,[7] m. Moses Springsteed. She d. in the asylum
for the insane at Utica, N. Y.; res. West Chester Co., N. Y.
Two of the children married men by the name of Waldron.
VI. Matthias Demarest,[7] m. Hannah Pérry, of Clarkstown, Rockland
Co., N. Y. Children: Perry Demarest.[8] Emma Demarest.[8]
Walter Demarest,[8] b. at Haverstraw, N. Y.; house carpenter;
married, and has two children; res. Haverstraw, N. Y.

1720. Samuel Allison[6] (1803), b. Jan. 29, 1790; m. Ann Grey.
1721. Joseph Allison,[6] b. Jan. 15, 1792. Was drowned when a boy.
1722. Thomas Allison[6] (1810), b. March 10, 1794; d. at Ladentown, N. Y.
1723. Hannah Allison,[6] b. April 13, 1796; d. probably in or near Geneva, N. Y. She m. Matthias Coe, b. Oct. 28, 1792, who d. without children. She m., second, Jonas Dubois, a farmer, and
removed to the vicinity of Geneva, N. Y. They had several
children.

1724. Catherine Allison,[6] b. May 18, 1798; m. Benjamin Coe, b. Nov. 7,
1794; d. May 26, 1851, in Haverstraw, N. Y. They lived for
a while near Rochester, N. Y., but returned to Haverstraw and
spent their lives. She d. Aug. 15, 1878. Children:
I. Jonas Coe[7] was a wagon maker in New York, N. Y.; m. Emma ——
——. She d. in the city of New York, Jan. 28, 1889, and is
buried in Mount Repose cemetery, Haverstraw, N. Y. One
child.
II. Adelphi Coe,[8] b. July 26, 1819; d. Nov. 21, 1877, at Haverstraw,
N. Y.; single.
III. Halsted Coe,[7] mason; res. Yonkers, N. Y., and d. there. He m.
Sarah Perry, of Clarkstown, N. Y. One son.
IV. Marietta Coe,[7] m. David Romaine. She res. in 1890 in Haverstraw,
N. Y. Child: Laura Romaine,[8] m. Elmer Tremper, of Haver-
straw, and res. there.

1725. Jonas Allison[6] (1816), b. Oct. 2, 1800; d. 1861; res. Haverstraw,
N. Y.

1726. Christopher Allison,[6] d. single, in advanced life, at the home of
his sister, Mrs. Catherine Demarest, in Haverstraw, N. Y.

1727. Matthew Allison[5] [1674] (Joseph,[4] John,[3] John,[2]
Lawrence[1]). He was born in Haverstraw, N. Y., July 13,

1748; died before 1795 leaving a family. Residence, Haverstraw, N. Y.

CHILDREN.

1728. Joseph Allison.⁶
1729. Peter Allison.⁶
1730. Cornelius Allison.⁶
1731. Hendrick Allison⁶ (1822).   He m. Sarah Marks of Haverstraw, N. Y.
1732. Matthew Allison.⁶
1733. Elizabeth Allison.⁶

1734.   Peter Allison ⁵ [1684] (Joseph,⁴ John,³ John,² Lawrence ¹).   He was born in Haverstraw, N. Y., Nov. 19, 1769; married Margaret, daughter of John Suffern.   In early manhood he went to the city of New York and became a brass founder.   He carried on business in Maiden Lane, where he retained property till his death.   Later in life he disposed of his foundry business and engaged in the dry goods business in Greenwich street.   His home was on Vesey street, where he died of inflammatory rheumatism, Feb. 21, 1836, at 66 years, 6 months, 10 days.   In Oct., 1877, his body was removed to Mount Repose cemetery in Haverstraw, N. Y., and buried in the Allison plot on the west brink of the hill.

CHILDREN BORN NEW YORK, N. Y.

1735. George Suffern Allison⁶ (1829), b. Jan. 15, 1792; res. Haverstraw, N. Y.
1736. John Allison⁶ (1835), b. April 9, 1796; m. Mary Morgan. Res. New York, N. Y.
1737. Caroline Allison,⁶ m. Epenetus Wheeler. They res. in New York city and later in Haverstraw, N. Y.; then removed to Illinois, where he was a farmer. He d. in Ogle county, Ill., May 9, 18—, aged 76 years. Children.
I. Marguerette Wheeler,⁷ b. New York, N. Y.; m. Rev. Mr. Hopper. Res. New York, N. Y.
II. Caroline Wheeler,⁷ b. New York, N. Y.; m. Henry Garner. Res. Haverstraw, N. Y.
III. Alfred Wheeler.⁷ In 1849 he went to California and became a noted lawyer and judge in that state.
1738. Antoinette Allison,⁶ m. Henry J. Hopper. Res. New York, N. Y. He was a dry goods merchant in Greenwich street. She d. in the house of Preston Hickok, No. 10 Greenwich Ave., New York, N. Y., of a cancer, Jan. 24, 1851. No children.
1739. Peter Allison.⁶ He left no descendants. He followed the sea for many years and d. in young manhood.
1740. Joseph Allison.⁶ He left no descendants. He d. at Parnape, Rockland Co., N. Y., of brain disease, and is buried in Parnape cemetery.

1740.   Richard Allison ⁵ [1688] (Joseph,⁴ John,³ John,² Lawrence ¹).   He was born in Haverstraw, Rockland county, N. Y., Oct. 28, 1780; died Nov. 26, 1825.   He married Eliza

i

Ruckel at St. John, N. B., born Oct. 18, 1785; died May, 1870, in the city of New York. He died in the city of New York. His residence had been in Haverstraw and New York.

CHILDREN.

1741. Mary Caroline Allison,⁶ b. New York, N. Y., Feb. 5, 1808; d. in Newark, N. J., March 14, 1882. She m., in 1833, John Hegeman who d. 1851. Children:
I.   George Hegeman,⁷ who m. Jane Amelia Allison and had children: Elizabeth Hegeman,⁸ Georgia Hegeman,⁸ Jeanette Hegeman.⁸
II. Mary Hegeman,⁷ m. John Frederick Allen. Res. Newark, N. J. Children: Emma Allen,⁸ Ferdinand W. Allen,⁸ Sidney W. Allen,⁸ Louise Allen.⁸
1742. Michael Allison⁶ (1843), b. June 22, 1809; d. April 5, 1876, in Tappan, N. Y.
1743. Susan Elizabeth Allison,⁶ b. New York, N. Y., March 29, 1811; d. Glendale, Ohio, Oct. 18, 1883. Single.
1744. Richard Allison,⁶ b. in New York, N. Y., Aug. 7, 1813; d. Nov. 22, 1837. Single.
1745. Jasper H. Allison,⁶ b. New York, N. Y., July 12, 1815; d. Newark, N. J., Feb. 7, 1883. He m. Ellen Ward. Children:
I.   Edgar Allison.⁷ Single.
II. Anna Allison,⁷ m., in 1867, John Robb. She d. in 1868. Child, Anna Robb.⁸
1746. Edgar Allison,⁶ b. Nov. 22, 1817; d. Aug. 21, 1818.
1747. Amelia Southard Allison,⁶ b. New York, N. Y., May 13, 1820; d. at Glendale, Ohio, May 2, 1877. She m. Rev. David Pise, in 1846. He is rector of Christ church. Res. Glendale, Ohio. Children:
I.   Frederick David Pise,⁷ b. Manlius, N. Y., March 27, 1847; d. at Clarksville, Tenn., Feb. 16, 1851.
II. William Taylor Pise,⁷ b. Manlius, N. Y., July 19, 1850. Episcopal clergyman, d. at Glendale, Ohio, Sept. 15, 1882.
III. Josephine Amelia Pise,⁷ b. Clarksville, Tenn., Sept. 3, 1852.
IV. Francis Agnes Pise,⁷ b. Columbia, Tenn., June 23, 1856; d. Oct. 20, 1861.
V.   Charles T. Pise,⁷ b. Columbia, Tenn., Oct. 28, 1857. Episcopal clergyman. Res. Hamilton, near Cincinnati, Ohio.
VI. Elizabeth Ruapa Pise,⁷ b. Columbia, Tenn., Oct. 24, 1859.
1748. Abram Stagg Allison,⁶ b. Feb. 17, 1823; m. his second cousin, Henrietta, daughter of John Allison, Sept., 1851, and had children. He d. Jan. 29, 1872.
I.   Harry W. Allison,⁷ b. New York, N. Y., Aug., 1856; m. Ada, daughter of Watson Tomkins of Haverstraw, N. Y. (See that record.) He d. Nov., 1879.
II. Mary Morgan Allison,⁷ m., Feb. 6, 1887, Frank Nickerson.
1749. Sarah Jane Allison,⁶ b. Feb. 17, 1823; d., unmarried, in New Jersey, in 1873.

1750. Elsie Allison ⁵ [1689] (Joseph,⁴ John,³ John,² Lawrence ¹). She was born in Haverstraw, N. Y., Nov. 9, 1783; married Jacob Archer in 1801. Resided Haverstraw, N. Y.

CHILDREN.

1751. Harriet Matilda Archer,⁶ m. Samuel A. P. Snow. Children:
I.   Samuel Archer Snow.⁷
II. Elsie A. Snow,⁷ m. Samuel C. Blauvelt. They had three children: Samuel Augustus Blauvelt,⁸ Franklin Snow Blauvelt,⁸ Emma Snow Blauvelt.⁸

III. Charles Henry Snow,[7] m. Sarah W. Allison. Children: Harriet A.
      Snow,[8] Charles Dana Snow,[8] Richard Allison Snow,[8] Katie A.
      Snow,[8] Harriet Matilda Snow,[8] William Leigh Snow.[8]
IV.   Richard Allison Snow.[7]
1752. Maria Louise Archer.[6] She m. Levi Carman. Children:
I.   Elmira E. Carman,[7] m. Richard W. Coe. Child: Maria Louise Coe.[8]
II.   Martha Young Carman.[7]
III. George Lewis Carman,[7] m. Hattie Spraken. Children: John Car-
      man,[8] Maria Louise Carman,[8] George Lewis Carman.[8]
1753. Elsie Ann Archer,[6] m. Charles DuBois. Children:
I.   Maria Antoinette DuBois.[7]
II.   Eugenia DuBois.[7]
III. John Allison DuBois.[7]
IV.   Charles Archer DuBois,[7] m. Hattie Kendall. Children: Charles
      Archer DuBois,[8] Lillie DuBois,[8] Ettie DuBois,[8] Arthur DuBois.[8]
1754. Eliza Ann Archer,[6] m. Andrew Buckbee. Children:
I.   Rebecca Ann Buckbee.[7]
II.   Josephine Buckbee.[7]
III. Jacob William Buckbee,[7] m. Minerva Auston. Children: Charles
      Van Buren Buckbee,[8] Jacob William Buckbee.[8]
IV.   Harriet Matilda Buckbee.[7]
1755. Martha Young Archer.[6]
1756. Michael Allison Archer,[6] m. Sarah Cassida, and had one child. He
      m., second, Mary Watson. He m., third, Clarissa Amanda
      Trowbridge. Children:
I.   John Henry Archer.[7]
II.   Allison Michael Archer,[7] m. Margaret Lake. Children: Lillian
      Amanda Archer,[8] William Watson Archer.[8]
III. Charles DuBois Archer.[7]
IV.   George B. Archer.[7]
1757. Margaret Amanda Archer.[6]
1758. John Jacob Archer.[6]

1759. Peter P. Allison[6] [1700] (Peter,[5] Benjamin,[4] John,[3]
John,[2] Lawrence[1]). He was born in Haverstraw, N. Y.,
and was a wheelwright and blacksmith, his shop standing
near the First Presbyterian church and at the corner of the
Garnersville and Grassy Point roads. He resided after marriage near his shop, in the old Briggs house. In 1808 or
1809 he married, in Haverstraw, Catherine Allison,[7] a relative; daughter of James (and Mary) Allison.

CHILDREN BORN IN HAVERSTRAW, N. Y.

1760. Mary Allison,[7] b. Jan. 26, 1810; m. John Odell; res. in Haver-
      straw, N. Y. He d., leaving two children. She m., 2d, ——.
      She d. in Haverstraw, N. Y.
1761. Thomas Allison,[7] b. Nov. 3, 1811; m. Mary Jane ——, and d. in
      Haverstraw, N. Y.
1762. Hannah Allison,[7] b. Nov. 2, 1814; m. James Conover. He was a
      brick manufacturer; res. Haverstraw, N. Y. They were excel-
      lent people, and were highly esteemed. They left children.
1763. John P. Allison,[7] b. April 15, 1817; m., in Haverstraw, Oct. 3,
      1844, Eliza, dau. of James and Ann (Douglas) Onderdonk.
      She was b. in Haverstraw, N. Y., June 1, 1822; res. East Sagi-
      naw, Mich. No children.
1764. Benjamin Allison,[7] b. Oct. 15, 1819; d. unmarried about 1869.

1765. Margaret Allison,[7] b. Feb. 14, 1820; m. George Fulmer. He was a
        brick manufacturer in Haverstraw, N. Y., and removed to
        Greenport, L. I., N. Y. They were people of excellent repu-
        tation. She is deceased. No children.
1766. Adelia Allison,[7] b. Nov. 13, 1821; m. Peter Post. They resided in
        Jersey City, N. J. She is deceased.
1767. Collins Allison,[7] b. Dec. 3, 1823. He is deceased.

1768. Garrett Allison [6] [1704] (Thomas,[5] Benjamin,[4]
John,[3] John,[2] Lawrence [1]). He was born in Haverstraw,
N. Y., March 28, 1789 ; m., Oct. 4, 1812, Sarah, daughter of
Jonathan and Elizabeth (Wood) Palmer. She was born in
New York, N. Y., July 1, 1791; died May 4, 1863. He died
at Haverstraw, June 11, 1848.

CHILDREN.

1769. Letitia Allison,[7] b. Sing Sing, N. Y.. Aug. 28, 1813; m., May 29,
        1830, Abraham, son of Christopher and Rebecca Allison Cos-
        grove; b. at Haverstraw, N. Y., May 27, 1806; d. April 26,
        1849. P. O. address of the wife, Haverstraw, N. Y. Children
        and descendants b. at Haverstraw, N. Y.
I.   Charles E. Cosgrove,[8] b. April 3, 1831; d. Sept. 4, 1875; m., July 31,
        1853, Cornelia H. Vanderwerken, dau. of Tunis and Harriet
        Vanderwerken. She d. 1853. He m., second, May 14, 1855,
        Henrietta Spear.
II. Mary Elizabeth Cosgrove,[8] b. Feb. 10, 1833; d. Oct. 10, 1852.
III. Joseph Cosgrove,[8] b. May 19, 1835; d. March 7, 1839.
IV. Catherine A. Cosgrove,[8] b. April 7, 1837; d. Feb. 26, 1839.
V.   Sophie G. Cosgrove,[8] b. June 21, 1840; m., Oct. 30, 1861, Edward J.,
        son of John J. and Hannah (Cosgrove) Peck; res. Haverstraw,
        N. Y. Children b. there: Louisa A. Peck,[9] b. Aug. 18, 1862;
        d. March 6, 1872. Letitia May Peck,[9] b. April 9, 1873; d. Sept. 5,
        1873. Everett Peck,[9] b. July 26, 1874.
VI. Joseph A. Cosgrove,[8] b. Nov. 6, 1842; d. Dec. 17, 1866.
VII. Abraham Cosgrove, Jr.,[8] b. May 29, 1846; d. Jan. 23, 1859.
1770. Michael Snedeker Allison[7] (1856) b. Tarrytown, N. Y., July 10,
        1815; res. Jersey City, N. J.
1771. Mary Elizabeth Allison,[7] b. at Tarrytown, N. Y., March 28, 1817;
        m., Nov. 4, 1839, Edward, son of Michael and Mary Palmer
        Snedeker. He was b. at Clarktown, Rockland county, N. Y.
        He was a ship carpenter and draughtsman, with a genius for
        modelling swift-going vessels, and his skill contributed much
        to the reputation of his brother-in-law, Michael S. Allison, by
        whom he was employed for many years. He d. Aug. 4, 1868.
        His wife possessed a fine physique and a lovable disposition,
        and was faithful in all relations of life. At an early age she
        united with the Methodist Episcopal church, of which she has
        since been a faithful member and a living witness of the power
        of divine grace in sustaining the human soul under severe trials
        and afflictions; res. Halliday St., Jersey City, N. J. Children:
I.   Lawrence DeNoyelles Snedeker,[8] b. Brooklyn, N. Y., Oct. 18, 1840; d.
        Feb. 9, 1845.
II. Edward Lawrence Snedeker,[8] b. April 23, 1846; m., Oct. 29, 1867,
        Addie Ham. She res. Haverstraw, N. Y. He d. April 23, 1868.
        Child: Edward Lawrence Snedeker,[9] b. Sept. 19, 1868.
III. Mary Elizabeth Snedeker,[8] b. at Hoboken, N. J., March 19, 1855;
        res. Halliday St., Jersey City, N. J.

IV. Garretta A. Snedeker,* b. in Hoboken, N. J., Nov. 9, 1859; res.
Halliday St., Jersey City, N. J.
1772. Sarah Ann Allison,⁷ b. Tarrytown, N. Y., June 10, 1818; d. Sep-
tember, 1819.
1773. Sarah Ann Allison,⁷ b. at Haverstraw, N. Y., April 18, 1820; m.,
Nov. 21, 1838, Joseph Cosgrove, son of Christopher and Rebecca
(Allison) Cosgrove; b. Haverstraw, N. Y., Jan. 13, 1813. P. O.
address, Haverstraw, N. Y. Children:
I. Edward Snedeker Cosgrove,* b. Oct. 7, 1839; m., Dec. 20, 1866, Nellie
Zeluff, widow of Samuel Breeze, and dau. of William and
Catherine Miller Zeluff. P. O. address, Haverstraw, N. Y.
Children: Edward Cosgrove,* b. Nov. 11, 1869. Melville Cos-
grove,* b. Jan. 7, 1873.
II. Caroline A. Cosgrove,* b. Jan. 31, 1843; res. Haverstraw, N. Y.
III. Lawrence D. Cosgrove,* b. Jan. 15, 1845; d. 1846.
IV. Sarah Elizabeth Cosgrove,* b. Aug. 8, 1846; d. Sept. 26, 1847.
V. Mary Elizabeth Cosgrove,* b. Aug. 8, 1846; d. in 1849.
VI. Anna Cosgrove,* b. Dec. 20, 1854; res. Haverstraw, N. Y.
VII. Harriet A. Cosgrove,* b. August, 1856; d. 1862.
VIII. Lillian Cosgrove,* b. Nov. 11, 1861; P. O. address, Haverstraw,
N. Y.
1774. Garrett G. Allison⁷ (1865), b. at Haverstraw, N. Y., March 17,
1822; m. Harriet Stokum; res. Haverstraw, N. Y.
1775. Caroline Smith Allison,⁷ b. at Haverstraw, N. Y., March 30, 1824;
m., Aug. 1, 1843, Henry, son of Henry C. and Phebe (Gardiner)
Mather, b. in Suffolk Co., N. Y., Aug. 1, 1818; res. Hoboken,
N. J. Caroline Smith Allison developed into womanhood
with those delicate graces of mind and heart which make the
true woman. Her gentleness of spirit drew her in early life to
"the meek and lowly Jesus," whom she accepted as her
Saviour and has found to be a friend above all others. She is
a member of the Methodist Episcopal church. Mr. Mather is
a member of the Methodist Episcopal church. He is a ship
carpenter by trade and occupation. They res. in Brooklyn,
N. Y., until about 1848-'49, and then removed to Hoboken,
N. J., their present home. Children:
I. Mary Elizabeth Mather,* b. Brooklyn, N. Y., Sept. 19, 1844; d. Aug.
14, 1845.
II. William Henry Mather,* b. Brooklyn, N. Y., Dec. 23, 1845; m.,
June 24, 1868, Lena S., dau. of Ebenezer and Mary (Wiest)
Flint, b. at Esopus, Ulster Co., N. Y. P. O. address, Hoboken,
N. J. Children: Eudora Livingstone Mather,* b. May 23,
1869. Sarah Eva Mather,* b. July 14, 1875. Henrietta Mather.*
III. Allison Gardiner Mather,* b. Brooklyn, N. Y., April 18, 1847; d.
Oct. 24, 1849.
IV. Sarah Elizabeth Mather,* b. in Hoboken, N. J., Sept. 20, 1850; d.
July 14, 1851.
V. Catherine Amelia Mather,* b. in Hoboken, N. J., Sept. 20, 1850; d.
Aug. 20, 1851.
VI. Edwin Titus Mather,* b. in Hoboken, N. J., Aug. 2, 1857; d. Dec. 6,
1859.
VII. Michael S. Allison Mather,* b. in Hoboken, N. J., March 1, 1867.
1776. Willamena Byron Allison,⁷ b. at Haverstraw, N. Y., March 29,
1827, and possesses a fine womanly character. She is a mem-
ber of the Methodist Episcopal church. She m., Nov. 21,
1849, James H., son of David B. and Sarah (Lockwood) Gardner. He was b. in 1824; d. Jan. 19, 1868. For many years he
was engaged in the commission produce business at West
Washington market. P. O. address of Mrs. Gardner and her
children, Hoboken, N. J. Children b. Hoboken, N. J.:
I. Charles Edward Gardner,* b. Jan. 1, 1852; d. Aug. 28, 1852.
II. Caroline A. Gardner,* b. Sept. 15, 1854; d. June 5, 1857.

DAVID ALLISON.

III. Sarah L. Gardner,⁸ b. Feb. 1, 1856; d. March 5, 1857.
IV. Willamena A. Gardner,⁸ b. Dec. 13, 1858.
V. Carrie C. Gardner,⁸ b. April 24, 1859.
VI. Cassie A. Gardner,⁸ b. Oct. 4, 1863.
VII. Hattie A. Gardner,⁸ b. Oct. 26, 1867; d. Dec. 4, 1868.
1777. Walter Smith Allison⁷ (1869), b. at Haverstraw, N. Y., March 15, 1829; res. Brooklyn, N. Y.
1778. Catherine Amelia Allison,⁷ b. at Haverstraw, N. Y., March 14, 1832. She was a member of the Methodist Episcopal church. She m., July 27, 1853, Daniel, son of Lyman and Juliana Toles. He was b. Jan. 29, 1830, and res. Jersey City, N. J. Children b. Hoboken, N. J.:
I. Emory L. Toles,⁸ b. Jan. 6, 1855.
II. Daniel Allison Toles,⁸ b. Nov. 1, 1856.
III. Clarence Toles,⁸ b. Sept. 27, 1858; d. July 28, 1860.
IV. Florence Amelia Toles,⁸ b. Jan. 24, 1867; d. Jan. 29, 1870.
1779. Emily Allison,⁷ b. at Haverstraw, N. Y., Feb. 12, 1834; d. Feb. 14, 1834.

1780. James Allison⁶ [1705] (Thomas,⁵ Benjamin,⁴ John,³ John,² Lawrence¹). He was born in Haverstraw, N. Y. Ship carpenter. Resides Haverstraw, N. Y. He was in stature short and stout, with auburn hair and blue eyes. He married Mary ————, who was born in England.

CHILDREN.

1781. Garrett T. Allison⁷ (1877) b. Haverstraw, N. Y., and res. there.
1782. William Allison,⁷ b. Haverstraw, N. Y.
1783. Catherine Allison,⁷ b. Haverstraw, N. Y.; m. Peter P. Allison. (See his record.)

1784. David Allison⁶ [1711] (Samuel,⁵ Benjamin,⁴ John,³ John,² Lawrence¹). He was born Sept. 21, 1794; died at Pontiac, Mich., Oct. 6, 1883. Farmer. He married Susan Hamer, who was born March 14, 1798, and died Sept. 16, 1865. Residence, Pontiac, Mich.

CHILDREN.

1785. Sarah Allison,⁷ b. Aug. 3, 1819, and d. Aug. 14, 1887, at Pontiac, Mich. She m. Thomas Flinn, a farmer, b. April 26, 1817; d. at Birmingham, Mich., July 6, 1883. Children:
I. William Flinn.⁸
II. Wesley Flinn.⁸
III. Eugenia Flinn.⁸
IV. Thomas Wesley Flinn,⁸ b. May 2, 1845; d. Nov. 20, 1873.
V. Ellen S. Flinn,⁸ b. Oct. 10, 1846; d. March 14, 1878.
VI. Elizabeth E. Flinn,⁸ b. Feb. 17, 1850; d. Feb. 3, 1885.
VII. Charles W. Flinn.⁸
VIII. Bertha Flinn.⁸
1786. Almira Allison,⁷ b. Dec. 28, 1820; d. Aug. 13, 1870. She m. Rev. Lorenzo N. Denison. Children:
I. David Avery Denison.⁸
II. Susan Denison.⁸
III. Cylinda Denison.⁸
IV. William Denison.⁸

V.   Sarah Adelaide Denison,[5] d. Aug., 1874.
1787.   Vincent Allison,[7] b. April 15, 1823; m. Martha M. Bickford. Jeweller. Res. Pontiac, Mich. No children.
1788.   John H. Allison,[7] b. Jan. 11, 1825. Jeweller. Res. Elkhart, Indiana. He m. Eunice Herrick. Children:
I.   Eliza Allison,[8] b. June 2, 1851; d. Aug. 20, 1851.
II.   Frank Allison,[8] b. ———
1789.   Charles Allison[7] (1879), Binghamton, Browne Co., N. Y., Feb. 21, 1827; d. at Brooklyn, N. Y., July 7, 1892.
1790.   William Allison,[7] b. May 13, 1829; d. Aug. 30, 1830.
1791.   Henry Allison,[7] b. July 19, 1831. Jeweller. Res. at Pontiac, Mich. He m. Lorena Rhodes. Children:
I.   Henri David Allison.[8] He graduated at Michigan university in 1886. Lawyer.
II.   Edwin Vincent Allison.[8] Jeweller. Res. Pontiac, Mich. He m. Georgie Bowlby.
III.   Bertha Allison.[8] Res. Los Angeles, Cal.
IV.   John Allison.[8] Res. Pontiac, Mich.
V.   Mary Allison.[8] Res. Pontiac, Mich.
VI.   Frank Allison.[8] Res. Pontiac, Mich.
1792.   William Allison,[7] b. April 6, 1834. Jeweller. Res. San José, Cal.
1793.   Franklin James Allison,[7] b. Oct. 4, 1836. Unmarried. Jeweller. Res. San Francisco, Cal.
1794.   George Wesley Allison,[7] b. Dec. 28, 1842; d. at Troy, Mich., Sept. 3, 1863.

1795.   Abraham Allison[6] [1718] (Joseph B.,[5] Benjamin,[4] John,[3] John,[2] Lawrence[1]). He was born in Haverstraw, N. Y., April 6, 1786; died there and is buried in Mount Repose cemetery. He was a farmer and carpenter. His father gave him the land for his farm and homestead and aided him in erecting his buildings. He owned another farm at Mead's corner, about a mile beyond his home on the Ramapo road. He was very industrious and frugal in his habits, a devout Christian, upright in all his dealings, and was highly esteemed as a man, citizen, and friend. He married Jane De Pew, born Jan. 18, 1787; died in Haverstraw. He resided in Haverstraw, N. Y.

CHILDREN BORN IN HAVERSTRAW, N. Y.

1796.   Charlotte Allison,[7] b. Feb. 26, 1810; m. Garrett T. Allison. (See his record.)
1797.   Joseph A. Allison[7] (1887), b. Nov. 26, 1812. Res. Haverstraw, N. Y., and Jersey City, N. J.
1798.   Mary Allison,[7] b. May 2, 1815; d. at Newton, Penn., May 27, 1824, and is buried in Mount Repose cemetery, Haverstraw, N. Y. She m., Nov. 27, 1837, Harvey W. Gurnee of Rockland Co., N. Y. He became professor in Pennington seminary, N. J., and then at Newton, Penn. He was a man of superior mental abilities and high character.
1799.   Matthias Coe Allison,[7] b. Feb. 13, 1818; d. Oct. 29, 1819.
1800.   Margaret Allison,[7] b. Nov. 10, 1820, and d. in middle life. She m. Spencer Springsteed. They had a daughter who grew to womanhood. He m. a second wife.

MRS. SUSAN (HAMER) ALLISON.

1801. Edmund D. Allison,[7] b. Oct. 6, 1826. He received a good education
          and was brought up to a farmer's life, now a carpenter. He m.
          Sarah, daughter of Peter Coe. Res. Haverstraw, N. Y. No
          children.
1802. Christopher Allison,[7] b. Feb. 12, 1824; d. in Haverstraw, N. Y.,
          Feb. 5, 1843.

1803. Samuel Allison[6] [1720] (Joseph B.,[5] Benjamin,[4]
John,[3] John,[2] Lawrence[1]). He was born in Haverstraw, N.
Y., Jan. 29, 1790. He was a brass founder and foreman in
a bell foundry in New York city for a long period. The last
years of his life he lived with his son Thomas, and is said to
have died in Texas with an unmarried son. He married, in
the city of New York, Ann Grey, daughter of a sea captain.
She was accomplished and high spirited, and considered
handsome. She died previous to the death of her husband,
at the home of her daughter, Mrs. Sarah Ann Totten.

CHILDREN BORN IN NEW YORK, N. Y.

1804. James Augustus Allison.[7] He owned and occupied a residence at
          Tottenville, Staten Island, N. Y. He m. ———. Children:
I. Sarah Allison,[8] m. ———.
II. Alida Allison,[8] m. ———.
III. Andro Vert Allison,[8] merchant at New Brunswick, N. J.
IV. Wesley Allison.[8]
1805. Thomas Allison.[7] He was an able, energetic man, and conducted
          an extensive grocery and poultry business at the corner of
          Grand and Columbia streets in New York city. He was twice
          married and in late years lived with his daughter in Brooklyn,
          N. Y.
1806. Samuel George Allison.[7] He settled in the South, probably in
          Texas, became wealthy; d. in the South unmarried.
1807. Jonas Allison.[7] He went to Texas, bought a cattle ranch, had it
          well stocked when marauders came down upon him and stole
          all his stock and movable property.
1808. Amelia Gertrude Allison.[7] She m. Mr. ——— of Connecticut and
          had three daughters.
1809. Sarah Ann Allison,[7] m. John Totten of Staten Island, N. Y., where
          he was born and where he died. They had two children.

1810. Thomas Allison[6] [1722] (Joseph B.,[5] Benjamin,[4]
John,[3] John,[2] Lawrence[1]). He was born in Haverstraw,
N. Y., March 10, 1794, and died at Ladentown, N. Y. His
remains were probably buried in the Quaker burying-ground
at Ramapo, N. Y. He was a house carpenter, and lived in
Ladentown, Rockland Co., N. Y., on a farm given to his
wife by her father. It is said that they would go to Haverstraw village and return by ox-team, being afraid that horses
might run away with them. The journey occupied from
early dawn to nearly midnight. They were all members of
the Society of Friends. He married Theodosia Seacor.
Some of the children died young.

1811. Mary Allison.⁷ She m. Benjamin Seacor. He was a farmer, and resided at West Haverstraw. Had one son.

1812. Elizabeth Allison.⁷ She m. Lyman Pitman Jones. No children. Res. Haverstraw, N. Y. He m., second, Cordelia Kiles.

1813. Benjamin F. Allison.⁷ Farmer; res. near Peekskill, N. Y. He m. ———. Child:
I. Mary Allison.⁸

1814. Amelia Allison.⁷ She m. Edward Swaithout, a widower. He is a farmer. They reside at Clarkstown, Rockland Co., N. Y. No children.

1815. Whitefield Allison,⁷ d. when sixteen or eighteen years of age.

1816. Jonas Allison⁶ [1725] (Joseph B.,⁵ Benjamin,⁴ John,³ John,² Lawrence¹). He was born at Haverstraw, N. Y., Oct. 2, 1800. He received a good education, and became a carpenter. For many years he was employed at Peck's rolling-mills in Haverstraw. He built his dwelling on a few acres of land which had been given him by his father, situated on the road to Ramapo, and about one mile from Mount Repose cemetery. There he and his family lived until he was far advanced in life, when he removed to the village of Haverstraw and established a bakery business which he carried on for several years. He and his wife and children were all members of the Methodist Episcopal church, and were sincere and devoted Christians. He died Aug. 1, 1861, and is buried in Mount Repose cemetery.

He married, Feb. 7, 1829, Emeline Felter, who was born at Haverstraw, N. Y., Sept. 9, 1809. Hers was a truly Christ-like character. Her gentleness of spirit was an inspiration of goodness to all with whom she came in contact. Her life was devoted to her home and family. She died in Haverstraw, March 8, 1866.

1817. Whitefield Allison,⁷ b. Aug. 29, 1829; d. Nov. 18, 1844.

1818. Mary Elmira Allison,⁷ b. Jan. 20, 1833. She is a member of the Methodist Episcopal church. Unmarried.

1818. Edward Allison,⁷ b. Aug. 24, 1835; d. Jan. 19, 1837.

1819. Emily Adelaide Allison,⁷ b. Aug. 24, 1838; d. Aug. 20, 1865, and is buried in Mount Repose cemetery, in Haverstraw, N. Y.

1820. Erastus T. Allison,⁷ b. May 12, 1843. He enlisted in the 17th Regt. N. Y. Vols. during the late war. He was taken ill in the service, returned home, and died of typhoid fever Oct. 16, 1865. Buried in Mount Repose cemetery in Haverstraw.

1821. Ann Sophia Allison,⁷ b. Feb. 13, 1848; m. Isaac W. Abrams, of Haverstraw. They are members of the Methodist Episcopal church.

1822. Hendrick Allison⁶ [1731] (Matthew,⁵ Joseph,⁴ John,³ John,² Lawrence¹). He was born in Haverstraw,

N. Y., and married Sarah Marks of that place. She was the daughter of George Marks. Mr. Allison lived on Manhattan island, later at the New Dock, N. J., and subsequently removed to Hackensack Township, N. J., and located beneath the Palisades, near Englewood.

CHILDREN.

1823.   Evander Allison,⁷ res. Ft. Lee, N. J.
1824.   Harriet Allison.⁷
1825.   James Allison.⁷
1826.   William Henry Allison⁷ (1892), res. Englewood, N. J.
1827.   Edward Allison.⁷
1828.   Rachel Allison.⁷

1829.   George Suffern Allison,⁶ [1735] (Peter,⁵ Joseph,⁴ John,³ John,² Lawrence¹). He was born in New York, N. Y., Jan. 15, 1792. He married, Oct. 28, 1818, Hannah, daughter of Jonas and Mary (Burns) Brewster, of Haverstraw, Rockland Co., N. Y. She was born July 13, 1794, and died in Haverstraw, Sept. 2, 1867. He died there Aug. 27, 1884.

Mr. Allison passed his early life in the city of New York. In the last war with Great Britain he took an active part, and in 1812 was an officer in Colonel Washburn's regiment, and was stationed at Sandy Hook. When hostilities had ceased he removed to Haverstraw upon the invitation of his grandmother, who was occupying the old Allison homestead, which had been left to her by her husband. Soon afterward she purchased land in North Haverstraw, now Stony Point, where his residence stood, occupied by his, son Brewster J. Allison, in 1892. This land was owned by Wandell Mace, who was anxious to sell and move to what was then the "West," now the central part of the state of New York, "where 100 acres of good land could be bought for fifty dollars."

The first business of Mr. Allison was to keep a small store and furnishing goods needed in a country neighborhood. By marriage and by purchase he became the owner of a large tract of timber land, and he connected with his mercantile business that of wood and lumber. He afterward purchased a tract of farm land adjoining his homestead, and carried on quite an extensive farm in connection with his other enterprises. The brick-making business soon gave him a wider field for the exercise of his powers, and this, with the rapid advance in the value of real estate, increased his wealth to such an extent that he became one of the wealthiest men of the county. In 1829 he was elected a member of the assembly of New York, and reëlected in 1880. He took a deep and active interest in the military profession, and was a colonel and afterward a brigadier-general of the militia of Rockland county, N. J. He also became judge of the court of common pleas.

CHILDREN BORN IN HAVERSTRAW, IN THAT PORTION WHICH IS NOW (1893) STONY POINT, ROCKLAND CO., N. Y.

1830. Eugenia Allison,[7] b. Sept. 19, 1819; m., at her father's home, Aug. 13, 1844, William McArdle, a lawyer by profession. He was a captain of a military company in the city of New York, and died while serving as an officer during the Seminole war. He left no children. She m., second, at her father's home at Stony Point (by Rev. James J. McMahon, of the Presbyterian church, late of Marion, Southwestern Virginia), Sept. 5, 1865, William Knight, a resident of Stony Point, Rockland Co., N. Y. He was a merchant, and d. in the summer of 1891. She d. June 15, 1890, aged 70 years, 9 months, 6 days. No children.

1831. Brewster Jonas Allison[7] (1897), b. July 5, 1821; res. Stony Point, Rockland Co., N. Y.

1832. Mary Margaret Allison,[7] b. May 3, 1823; m., at her father's home, March 1, 1859, Rev. James J. McMahon, who was b. in Amahilla, County of Tyrone, Ireland, who is now pastor of the First Presbyterian church in Haverstraw, N. Y. She d. in Stony Point, N. Y., May 20, 1868. Children:

I. George Allison McMahon,[8] baptized July 8, 1860; single; res. New York, N. Y.

II. Ellen Montague McMahon,[8] baptized April 6, 1862; res. at Stony Point and New York, N. Y.

III. Arthur Brewster McMahon,[8] baptized Jan. 3, 1865; deceased.

IV. Hannah McMahon,[8] baptized April 7, 1867; m. Thomas Lee, a graduate of Hamilton college, N. Y. He is a lawyer, and res. at Stony Point, N. Y.

V. Mary Allison McMahon,[8] b. Feb. 18, 1868, baptized Sept. 17, 1871. Her mother dying gave her to her sister, Mrs. Eugenia Knight, by whom she was brought up. She res. at Stony Point and New York, N. Y.

1833. George Allison,[7] b. July 7, 1825; d. in Haverstraw, N. Y., Sept 21, 1827.

1834. Amanda Allison,[7] b. Aug. 6, 1827; m., Sept. 3, 1851, Watson, son of Daniel Tomkins. He was b. in Newark, N. J., May 5, 1829, and removed from Orange, N. J., to Haverstraw, N. Y., and lives in that portion which is now Stony Point, with other heirs of his father; he is part owner of the battle-ground of Stony Point. From that high projecting eminence in the Hudson river, surmounted by a United States light-house, there is a most lovely view of the river, plain, and hills for many miles. The beautifully situated and attractive home of Mr. Tomkins, built in 1872, overlooks the Hudson and Stony Point, where "Mad Anthony" Wayne won his famous victory. He is a practical man, of sound sense, of advanced ideas, a Republican in politics, and in religion a Presbyterian. Mrs. Tomkins d. Aug. 14, 1887, aged 60 years and 8 days.

CHILDREN.

I. Helen Amanda Tomkins,[8] b. at Tomkins's Cove, Stony Point, N. Y., Jan. 26, 1853; d. Oct. 14, 1890.

II. Ada Frederika Tomkins,⁵ b. at Stony Point, N. Y., Feb. 19, 1856;
     m., Dec. 11, 1878, Harvey W. Allison, son of Abram S. and
     Henrietta Allison, of New York city. They were second
     cousins. He was cashier in F. P. Freeman & Co's. banking
     house, 53 Exchange Place, New York, N. Y. He d. at Stony
     Point, N. Y., Nov. 17, 1879. Mrs. Allison resides at her
     father's home.
III. Mary Allison Tomkins,⁵ b. Stony Point, N. Y., Nov. 3, 1859; res. at
     her father's home, Stony Point, N. Y.

1835. John Allison⁶ [1736] (Peter,⁵ Joseph,⁴ John,³
John,² Lawrence¹). He was born in New York city April
9, 1796. He married Mary Morgan, born Sept. 15, 1803;
resides in New York city. He was in the mercantile business
in Greenwich St., then later was in grocery business, corner
of 6th Ave., 15th St. He died at his home, 239 West 50th
St., New York city, Oct. 2, 1865, as did his wife. Mr.
Allison was buried in Greenwood cemetery, lot No. 14–357,
section, 162–169 between Grape and Vine avenues.

· CHILDREN BORN IN NEW YORK CITY.

1836. Henrietta Allison,⁷ b. Jan. 16, 1825; m. Abram S. Allison. They
       res. 82d St., New York city. He d. and she now lives there.
       They were cousins. He was a stationer. Children:
I. Henry Weed Allison,⁸ m. Miss Ada Tomkins, of Haverstraw. (See
    that record. No. 1834, II.)
II. May Allison,⁸ m. Frank Nickerson; res. 82d St., New York city.
    Children: Margaret Nickerson.⁹ Helen Nickerson.⁹
1837. Edward Allison,⁷ b. Jan. 24, 1828; single; res. New York, N. Y.,
       and d. there.
1838. Peter John Allison,⁷ b. Feb. 5, 1830; d. March 23, 1832.
1839. Ann Augusta Allison,⁷ b. Jan. 30, 1832; res. New York city, 82d
       St.
1840. George Henry Allison,⁷ b. Dec. 7, 1834; res. Morrisania, N. Y.;
       m. and has a family.
1841. Emily Josephine Allison,⁷ b. March 31, 1837; m. —— Griggs; res.
       in New York, N. Y., and d. some years ago.
1842. Alfred Morgan Allison,⁷ b. Sept. 28, 1841; d., when a young man,
       Dec. 2, 1862; res. New York, N. Y.; single; bookkeeper.

1843. Michael Allison⁶ [1742] (Richard,⁵ Joseph,⁴ John,³
John,² Lawrence¹). He was born in the city of New York,
June 22, 1809; died in Tappan, N. Y., April 5, 1876. His
home was in New York city till 1868, when he moved to
Tappan, where he lived till his death, April 5, 1876. He
married Susan Gentil, who died in New York city, April 5,
1846, leaving children. He married, second, Harriet M.
Calhoun. She was daughter of Henry and Eliza Melvina
(Conkling) Calhoun, and granddaughter of Andrew Cal-
houn, who was born in the Parish of Ray, near the towns of
Raphoe and Labadish, in the County of Donegal, Ireland,

and who was son of William Calhoun of Scotch blood. The church he attended was at Manor Cunningham. He was born in 1764; came to America in 1790; lived in Boston, Mass., and is buried in Concord, N. H. The Calhouns are said to be descended from the ancient family of Colquhouns and Lairds of Luss, whose original home was at Luss, on the west side of Loch Lomand in Scotland.

Mrs. Allison was born in Canajoharie, N. Y., May 5, 1827, and in 1880 removed to Nebraska, and now resides in Beatrice, Neb. Her eight children were born in Bleeker St., New York, N. Y.

CHILDREN BORN IN NEW YORK, N. Y.

1844. Jane Amelia Allison,⁷ b. June 20, 1833; m. her cousin, George Hegeman, an engraver; res. Newark, N. J. Children:
I. Elizabeth Hegeman.⁸
II. Georgia Hegeman.⁸
III. Jennette Hegeman.⁸
1845. William Gentil Allison,⁷ b. August, 1835; m. Hester J. Meserole. He res. New York, N. Y., and d. there April 5, 1869. Children:
I. Ida Allison.⁸
II. William Allison.⁸
1846. Richard Allison⁷ (1912), b. 44 Vesey St., New York, N. Y., July 7, 1838; m. Mary A. Love; res. Rutherford, N. J.
1847. Thomas Allison⁷ (1917), b. Sept. 19, 1840; m. Mary E. Millett, attorney; office 59 Liberty St., New York, N. Y. Children by 2d marriage:
1848. Howard Calhoun Allison,⁷ b. April 4, 1852; d. Feb. 19, 1853.
1849. Harriet Allison,⁷ b. May 29, 1853; teacher; res. Beatrice, Neb.
1850. Michael Calhoun Allison,⁷ b. April 1, 1856; m., Feb. 4, 1885, Helen Blake Johnston, b. Gloucester, Mass., May 10, 1859; farmer; res. Beatrice, Neb. Children b. Beatrice, Neb.:
I. John Johnston Allison,⁸ b. Oct. 20, 1886.
II. Richard Saville Allison,⁸ b. May 19, 1888.
III. Frances Field Allison,⁸ b. April 20, 1892.
1851. Lelia Calhoun Allison,⁷ b. July 19, 1857; m., Sept. 16, 1885, Charles Rudolph Lawson, b. Halifax, N. S., June 16, 1859; res. New York, N. Y. Child b. New York, N. Y.:
I. Gertrude Pringle Lawson,⁸ b. Dec. 10, 1886.
1852. Irving Allison,⁷ b. Dec. 18, 1859; m., July 24, 1881, Emma Clara Battey, b. Roseville, N. J., Nov. 10, 1861; manufacturer; res. Omaha, Neb. Children b. Omaha, Neb.:
I. Mabel Calhoun Allison,⁸ b. Oct. 18, 1883.
II. Grace Elliot Allison,⁸ b. Aug. 6, 1885.
III. Mildred Allison,⁸ b. Dec. 12, 1889.
IV. Irving Allison,⁸ b. March 21, 1891.
1853. Winthrop Allison,⁷ b. Aug. 26, 1861; res. St. Paul, Minn.
1854. Elliot Condich Allison,⁷ b. July 1, 1866; farmer; res. Beatrice, Neb.
1855. Mabel Hitchcock Allison,⁷ b. Sept. 12, 1867; res. Beatrice, Neb.

1856. Michael Snedeker Allison⁷ [1770] (Garrett,⁶ Thomas,⁵ Benjamin,⁴ John,³ John,² Lawrence¹). He was born at Tarrytown, N. Y., July 10, 1815. Before he was

Michael S. Allison

five years of age his parents removed to Haverstraw, Rockland county, N. Y., where he received a good academic education, and learned the trade of ship carpentry with his father. He worked at his trade as a journeyman in Brooklyn, N. Y., for several years. Then he leased a ship-yard in Hoboken, N. J., and removed his family to that city. Here he did a very large business, repairing vessels and building new ones, chiefly three-masted schooners, for the Virginia trade, stanch sea-going vessels with very fast sailing qualities, and steamboats, all of which were remarkable for their speed, notably the steamboats J. W. Baldwin and Mary Powell. From Hoboken he moved with his family to 178 Pacific avenue, Lafayette, now a part of Jersey City, N. J. This dwelling and grounds he purchased, and it became his permanent home. He also became the owner of an extensive ship-yard at Jersey City, where he continued the business during the remainder of his life.

Love and veneration for his mother and her memory were distinguishing traits in his character. He inherited from his father a sound, vigorous constitution. He was about five feet and nine inches in height, thick set, with a powerful frame, very muscular; he had double teeth all around in both jaws; brown hair, becoming partly bald on the top of his head, and blue eyes. From his mother he derived deep reverence for God and his revealed truth. Early in life he became identified with religious work as a member of the Methodist Episcopal church, of which he continued a useful and honored member, holding the office of steward or trustee during life. He contributed largely of his means to church and benevolent causes. His hospitable home was always open to the ministers of the Methodist Episcopal church, and was the headquarters of its bishops when their duties called them in that vicinity. He was a member of the order of Odd Fellows and of the Masonic fraternity, and a director in several banking and other institutions. He died at his home in Jersey City on May 22, 1881. On May 24 impressive funeral services were held at the residence, thirty clergymen being present, besides the relatives and friends in that vicinity. Rev. Mr. Lowrie, a former pastor, referred to him as a model man in every phase of life. Other clergymen followed in the same strain, some of whom, having been very near to him in religious and social life, spoke with great tenderness, even with tears. The following day his remains were conveyed to Haverstraw on the steamboat John Sylvester, which he had built and always owned in part. Accompanying the remains were del-

18

egations from the Amity lodge, No. 108, F. and A. M., Amity chapter, No. 31, R. A. M., Columbia lodge, No. 68, I. O. O. F., all of Jersey City, six clergymen, and the workmen in his employ, members of his family, and a large number of friends. They were met by the Stony Point lodge of F. and A. M., and the procession, including over fifty carriages, slowly proceeded to the Methodist Episcopal church. The day was serene and lovely. Five clergymen participated in the services, four of whom, Messrs. Lowrie, Coit, Ellison, and Monroe, had been pastors of the deceased. His remains were interred in the family plot in Mount Repose cemetery. He had accumulated a large property and left his family in good circumstances, with a wise provision for the continuance of the business by his sons. ·

He married, at the home of her parents in Haverstraw, Catherine, daughter of Christopher and Rebecca (Allison) Cosgrove. She was born in Haverstraw, N. Y., Jan. 15, 1819; died in Brooklyn, N. Y., Feb. 12, 1845, and her remains are interred in Mount Repose cemetery. She was reared to a life of useful industry, and in the love and fear of God. Possessing an amiable disposition, with a bright, cheerful expression of countenance, she became the sunshine of her home, and greatly endeared to her husband and family. Her early death was partly due to her rather delicate physical organization. She possessed a fine mind, with deep religious convictions. She died as she had lived, in the full consciousness of her Saviour's love. She was a member of the Methodist Episcopal church.

Mr. Allison married, second, Sept. 17, 1845, at the home of her parents in Haverstraw, Jane Eliza Cosgrove, a sister of his first wife. She was born in that place Feb. 9, 1817. Brought up on the old homestead, under the guidance of her remarkable mother, she acquired habits of useful industry in doing her full share in the varied duties of farm life, which included assisting in garden work, gathering fruits in season, husking corn, milking, churning, baking, cooking, spinning, and sewing, thus fitting her to become a model housewife. She was converted early in life and joined the Methodist Episcopal church. Since then she has found the comforts and consolations of religion her highest joy and support in the many afflictions she has been called to endure. She is about five feet, seven inches in height, and large framed. She has dark hair (now gray), regular features, and black expressive eyes, a mild and forbearing disposition; is domestic in her tastes and habits, and cherishes a loving devotion to all her friends. Since her husband's decease she has continued to reside with her three unmarried daughters in their home on Pacific avenue, Jersey City.

CHILDREN.

1857. Catherine Delemater Allison,* b. in Haverstraw, N. Y., March 12, 1838; m., Oct. 20, 1870, Oscar A. Jobes. She died in Jersey City, N. J., May 9, 1885, and is interred in Mount Repose cemetery in Haverstraw. Her religious training early induced her to give her heart to God. Her adult life was largely devoted to the Sunday-school work of the Methodist Episcopal church, of which she was a member. She excelled as a teacher of infant classes, her sweet spirit winning the hearts of the little ones, inducing many to become lambs of the Good Shepherd's flock. Her life was not without its sorrows or trials, all of which she bore with meekness and Christian fortitude. She died a triumphant death. The funeral services were held at the residence of her mother, from which she had passed into eternal rest. Several of her former pastors were present and officiated. She had one child, Michael Allison Jobes,* b. in Jersey City, N. J., Aug. 8, 1871.

1858. Edward Snedeker Allison,* b. Brooklyn, N. Y., July 12, 1844; m., Dec. 20, 1866, Sarah Frances, daughter of William and Catherine (Miller) Zeluff. He received a superior education, and was taken into business by his father, and, since his father's death, has in company, with his brother, Samuel Allison, and a competent ship-builder as foreman, successfully carried on the business. He is a member of the Methodist Episcopal church, and has been for many years. Res. in Newark, N. J. Children:

I. Marian Zeluff Allison,* b. in Jersey City, N. J., Dec. 16, 1868.
II. Catherine Cosgrove Allison,* b. in Jersey City, N. J., Sept. 27, 1870.

CHILDREN BY SECOND WIFE.

1859. Samuel Cosgrove Allison,* b. in Brooklyn, N. Y., July 26, 1846. He was well educated, and was then taken into his father's office, where were developed his abilities as an accountant and book-keeper. This has since been his special branch of the business, continuing with his father till his death. Since then he has continued the business with his brother, Edward Allison, their energies being devoted to the more profitable branch of this business, the repairing of vessels. Early in life he gave his heart to God, when he joined the Methodist Episcopal church, and he has continued to live an upright, unblemished life. He m., Oct. 1, 1873, Henrietta W. Olliphant, daughter of Selah H. and Eliza Pertine (Remsen) Olliphant. She is a member of the Methodist Episcopal church. No children.

1860. Jane Elizabeth Allison,* b. Brooklyn, N. Y., Jan. 15, 1848; educated at the Packer institute in the city of Brooklyn, N. Y., and is accomplished as a pianist. She is an active member of the Methodist Episcopal church, especially in Sunday-school work. She has always resided in the parental home, and is unmarried; res. Jersey City, N. J.

1861. Letitia Cosgrove Allison,* b. in Hoboken, N. J., Nov. 23, 1849. She was educated at the Packer institute, Brooklyn, N. Y. She paints in oil and water-colors, and is a fine pianist. Early in life she united with the Methodist Episcopal church, and became actively identified with its Sunday-school work. She is short in stature, has black hair and eyes, with dark complexion and regular features. She has enjoyed the benefits of American and European travel. She m., May 23, 1872, Jerome Delmar Gillett, son of Morilla and Maria (Hendrickson) Gillett. He was b. in Mifflin, Wyandotte Co., Ohio, educated at Oberlin college, and became associated with his father in business. He has an office in Wall street, New York, N. Y., where he is engaged in the banking and brokerage business with Mr. Griswold, under the firm name of Griswold & Gillett. He is a member of the St. Andrew's Methodist Episcopal church in New York city. Children:

I. Morilla Gillett,⁹ b. in Jersey City, N. J., June 12, 1873.
II. Jerome Delmar Gillett,⁹ b. in Jersey City, N. J., Jan. 7, 1875.
III. Samuel Allison Gillett,⁹ b. in Jersey City, N. J., Dec. 26, 1876.

1862. Sarah Allison,⁸ b. in Hoboken, N. J., July 15, 1851. She was educated at Pennington seminary, N. J.; has a fine soprano voice; is a member of the Methodist Episcopal church, and deeply interested in church work. She has always resided in the parental home, and is unmarried.

1863. Josephine Cosgrove Allison,⁸ b. in Hoboken, N. J., March 18, 1853. She was educated at the Packer institute, Brooklyn, N. Y. She united many years ago with the Methodist Episcopal church, and is thoroughly identified with church and Sunday-school work. She res. in the parental home in Jersey City, N. J., and is unmarried.

1864. Sophie Cosgrove Allison,⁸ b. in Hoboken, N. J., Nov. 12, 1854; d. Aug. 13, 1855.

1865.   Garrett G. Allison ⁷ [1774] (Garrett,⁶ Thomas,⁵ Benjamin,⁴ John,³ John,² Lawrence ¹).   He was born at Haverstraw, N. Y., March 17, 1822; married Harriet Stokum in 1845.   He was a ship carpenter for many years.   He then became a brick manufacturer, by which he became wealthy. He purchased the Miller place, opposite the Leonard Gurnee homestead in Haverstraw, N. Y., where he and his family have resided for many years.   He and his family are members of the Methodist Episcopal church.   Of the village church he has been a trustee for many years.

CHILDREN.

1866. Wilbur Earl Allison,⁸ b. in Hoboken, N. J., or Haverstraw, N. Y.; m. Mary Conklin. Child:
I. Susan D. Allison.⁹
1867. Eugene C. Allison,⁸ b. Haverstraw, N. Y., Nov. 13, 1856. He was engaged for some years in the coal business; res. Haverstraw, N. Y.
1868. Frank S. Allison,⁸ b. Haverstraw, N. Y.

1869.   Walter Smith Allison ⁷ [1777] (Garrett,⁶ Thomas,⁵ Benjamin,⁴ John,³ John,² Lawrence ¹).   He was born at Haverstraw, N. Y., March 15, 1829; ship carpenter; resided in Brooklyn, N. Y., in 1889.   He married, April 15, 1852, Ann Eliza Rowan, daughter of Seth and Emmaretta (Booth) Rowan.   She was born in Brooklyn, N. Y., Feb. 5, 1834.

CHILDREN.

1870. Charles Edmund Allison,[8] b. in Hoboken, N. J., Nov. 18, 1853; m.,
        Dec. 4, 1874, Ella Mullery, b. in England, Nov. 4, 1854. Child:
I. Florence Angeline Allison,[9] b. in Jersey City, N. J., Oct. 17, 1875.
1871. Augustus Allison,[8] b. in Hoboken, N. J., Nov. 5, 1856.
1872. Harriet Allison,[8] b. in Hoboken, N. J., Jan. 5, 1860.
1873. Carrie Cadmus Allison,[8] b. in Hoboken, N. J., April 29, 1862.
1874. Henry Booth Allison,[8] b. Jersey City, N. J., May 30, 1864.
1875. William Allison,[8] b. Jersey City, N. J., Nov. 1, 1866.
1876. Frederick Johnson Allison,[8] b. Jersey City, N. J., July 1, 1869; d.
        Jan. 9, 1870.

1877. Garrett T. Allison[7] [1781] (James,[6] Thomas,[5] Benjamin,[4] John,[3] John,[2] Lawrence[1]). He was born in Haverstraw, N. Y., and was a house carpenter by trade and occupation. He was upright and industrious, quiet and retiring
in his manners, a sincere Christian, and a member of the
Methodist Episcopal church. Residence in Haverstraw,
where he owned a few acres of land, on which was a comfortable frame dwelling with barn, situated on the mountain
side of the Ramapo road, just beyond the Mount Repose
cemetery. There he lived with his family till advanced in
life, when with his companion he located in the village
where he died. He and his wife are buried in Mount Repose
cemetery in Haverstraw, N. Y.

He married, in Haverstraw, May 25, 1833, Charlotte,
daughter of Abraham and Jane (De Pew) Allison. She
possessed a sensitive, nervous temperament. Her delicate
constitution was easily overcome by any undue excitement.
She was very devout. Her Bible and the church of God
were her chief sources of enjoyment. She was never so
happy as when attending the revival services of the Methodist Episcopal church, of which she was a member and a
shining light, and would sometimes be overcome by her
emotions amid the spiritual excitement of those meetings.
She died at Haverstraw, N. Y.

CHILD.

1878. Martha Allison,[8] b. Haverstraw, N. Y., April 4, 1834. She received
        a superior education. It may truthfully be said of her, "She
        was always a Christian." Taught to avoid all appearance of
        evil from her earliest years, and inheriting the pious, devo-
        tional spirit of her mother, her life was truly "hid with Christ
        in God." Her sweetness of spirit inspired the purest thoughts
        and purposes of all who came in contact with her. She died
        at Princeton, N. J., and is buried in Mount Repose cemetery,
        Haverstraw, N. Y. She married Mr. Jamison, a professor in
        the Mountain institute at Haverstraw village. After marriage
        they removed to Princeton, N. J., where he practised med-
        icine. He married a second wife.

1879. Charles Allison [7] [1789] (David,[6] Samuel,[5] Benjamin,[4] John,[3] John,[2] Lawrence [1]). He was born in Union township, Broome county, N. Y., three miles from Binghamton, Feb. 21, 1827. When nine years of age he went to Troy, Oakland county, Mich., with his parents. He was educated in the common schools and at the academy at Romeo, Macon county, Mich. He soon became very prominent in business circles. For twenty-six years prior to 1880 he was extensively engaged at Oswego, N. Y., in the canal and lake transportation business between New York, Oswego, Cleveland, and Chicago. He had been agent, general manager, and vice-president of the Northern Transit Co., of Cleveland, Ohio, which had a fleet of twenty-five steamers plying between the lake ports. He was president of the Oswego and Bay of Quinte Navigation Co., and agent of the Royal Mail line and several other steamboat companies. He was largely interested in canal property, and was the principal owner of the Northern Transit Co. canal line, which did the chief part of the canal freight business between New York and Oswego. At the time of his decease he was the head of the firm of Allison, Stroup & Co., of New York, N. Y., dealers in fertilizers. He died in Brooklyn, N. Y., July 7, 1892. He married, in 1857, Catherine E., daughter of Thomas Macfarlane. She was born in Cleveland, Ohio, May 16, 1834, and resides at Brooklyn, N. Y.

CHILDREN.

1880. Charles Rollo Allison,[8] b. New York, N. Y., Nov. 15, 1858. Graduated at Cornell university in 1880; lawyer. He m., Brooklyn, N. Y., Ella Tichenor. Child:
I. Edna Louise Allison,[9] b. 1892.
1881. Eugene Ellsworth Allison,[8] b. at Birmingham, Mich., April 19, 1861. He was a student at Harvard, and graduated at Bellevue Medical college in 1882. He m. Elinor J. Stott; res. New York, N. Y. No children.
1882. George Franklin Allison,[8] b. Birmingham, Mich., June 10, 1863. He graduated at Union college, Schenectady, N. Y., in 1884, and has received the degrees of A. B., of C. E., and M. A.; he was admitted to the bar of the state of New York in 1888; lawyer; office, 203 Broadway, N. Y. He m., 1885, Charlotte Louise De Witt, b. at Sterling, N. Y.; res. Brooklyn, N. Y. Children:
I. Catherine De Witt Allison,[9] b. June 7, 1886; d. May 25, 1887.
II. Charlotte De Witt Allison,[9] b. Nov. 9, 1888.
III. Marion Maud Allison,[9] b. Oct. 19, 1892.
1883. Mary Maud Allison,[8] b. Oswego, N. Y., April 10, 1865; res. Brooklyn, N. Y.; m. Samuel Richardson Bickford. Children:
I. Samuel Allison Bickford,[9] b. May 15, 1889.
II. Marie Blanche Bickford,[9] b. Jan. 20, 1891.
1884. Kate Augusta Allison,[8] b. Oswego, N. Y., Aug. 2, 1867; res. Brooklyn, N. Y.
1885. Jennie Blanche Allison,[8] b. and d. at Oswego, N. Y.

CHARLES ALLISON.

1886. Victor Barrow Allison,⁸ b. and d. at Oswego, N. Y.
1886a. Franklin Philo Allison,⁸ b. Feb. 14, 1877; living at Brooklyn, N. Y.

1887. Joseph A. Allison ⁷ [1797] (Abraham,⁶ Joseph B.,⁵
Benjamin,⁴ John,³ John,² Lawrence ¹). He was born in
Haverstraw, N. Y., Nov. 26, 1812. He received a good education, and then became a house carpenter. He and his
family resided in Haverstraw until advanced in life, and later
have lived with their daughter, Mrs. Michael Snedeker, in
Jersey City, N. J. Mr. Allison had a strong, well-knit
frame, and an excellent constitution. He had black hair and
eyes; quiet and unassuming in manners, genial and sunshiny
in disposition, his home has always been peaceful and happy.
Honest and upright, he commanded the respect of his fellow-
citizens. He married, Feb. 21, 1838, Mary Ann Titus, born
June 17, 1817. She was mild, and had a sweet and loving
spirit. She filled well her mission as a devoted Christian
wife and mother. She, with her husband and family, were
consistent members of the Methodist Episcopal church. She
died Jan. 21, 1888, and is buried in Mount Repose cemetery,
Haverstraw, N. Y. Children born Haverstraw, N. Y.:

1888. Antoinette Allison,⁸ b. Jan. 11, 1839; m., May 5, 1869, Peter F.,
son of Peter and Christiana Campbell, who were born in Argyleshire, Scotland. Mr. Campbell is a carpenter; res. Jersey
City, N. J. No children.
1889. Margaret Allison,⁸ b. June 21, 1843; m., Dec. 19, 1866, Michael
Snedeker, son. of Tunis and Amelia (Cosgrove) Snedeker;
ship carpenter and farmer; res. in Haverstraw, N. Y., now
430 Fairmount Ave., Jersey City, N. J. Children: Mabel
Snedeker,⁹ b. Aug. 3, 1872. Clarence Snedeker,⁹ b. February,
1877; d. Oct. 31, 1877.
1890. George Wilmer Allison,⁸ b. May 27, 1851; carpenter. He m., at
Tallman, N. Y., Jan. 14, 1877, Elmira, dau. of Joseph and
Fanny Young of that place. They res. Jersey City, N. J. No
children.
1891. Charles Armstrong Allison,⁸ b. Aug. 22, 1854. He received a superior academic education, and became a book-keeper in the
employ of Messrs. DeMott and Durant, of New York, N. Y.
His fidelity, ability, and industry commanded their confidence
and esteem. He was secretary of Highland Council No. 398,
Legion of Honor, in Jersey City. He died suddenly, March 19,
1888, in the city of New York, and was buried in Mount Repose
cemetery, Haverstraw, N. Y. He was unmarried.

1892. William Henry Allison ⁷ [1826] (Hendrick,⁶ Matthew,⁵ Joseph,⁴ John,³ John,² Lawrence ¹). He was born in
Hackensack township, N. J., Sept. 10, 1820; married, in the
city of New York, in 1840, Catherine, daughter of David¹ and

¹ David Jordan was son of Joseph Jordan, a French soldier, who came
to America with Lafayette and fought for American independence.
After the war he remarried and settled at Closter, N. J., on the top of
Palisades, where he died. He m. Elsie Parsells.

Elizabeth (Blauvelt) Jordan. Mr. Allison lived at Closter, N. J., and since 1845 in Hackensack township, now Englewood township, N. J.

CHILDREN.

1893. John Washington Allison.[8]
1894. David Jordan Allison.[8]
1895. William Outis Allison[8] (1923), b. March 30, 1849; res. Englewood, N. J.
1896. Mary Jane Allison,[8] res. Jersey City, N. J.

1897. Brewster Jonas Allison[7] [1831] (George Suffern,[6] Peter,[5] Joseph,[4] John,[3] John,[2] Lawrence[1]). He was born in Haverstraw (in the portion now Stony Point), Rockland county, N. Y., July 5, 1821. After attending the district school of his neighborhood, he was sent to an institution at Peekskill, N. Y., where he obtained a more extended education. The first part of his business life was spent in a store with his father, and he afterward engaged with him in brickmaking, which he continued two years. The yards were then leased to other parties, and he engaged in land surveying. He held the office of town superintendent of schools from 1848 to 1853, when the office was abolished. He was a member of the assembly in 1850, and served on the committee on roads and bridges and towns and cities. The rival candidate for the position was Edward Pye. Mr. Allison was elected on a " free soil " ticket and naturally drifted into the Republican party, at its formation, to which he is still attached. In 1853 he again entered into the manufacture of brick, in which he is still engaged.

Mr. Allison was connected with the First Presbyterian church of Haverstraw, with which he united in 1854, and was one of its elders until August, 1892, when he united with the Presbyterian church of Stony Point, and was elected to the same position. He is a pronounced temperance man, and has been a zealous worker in that cause. He lives at the village of Stony Point, N. Y., in the house where lived his father, Hon. George S. Allison. He married, Nov. 19, 1856, Anna Elizabeth, daughter of William C. Housman, of Haverstraw. She died in Haverstraw, April 27, 1862. He married, second, May 2, 1868, Anna Given, daughter of Nelson and Mary C. (Denniston) Andrus, of Haverstraw. She was born Dec. 3, 1848; died Aug. 2, 1889, and is buried in the Allison plot in Mount Repose cemetery, in Haverstraw. He resides in Stony Point, Rockland county, N. Y.

CHILDREN.

1898. Cornelia Houseman Allison,' b. at North Haverstraw, N. Y.,
Oct. 28, 1857; m. Daniel Morrison Coffin. They res. in the
city of New York, 19 West 69th St. Children: Daniel Morrison Coffin, Jr.' Catherine Morrison Coffin.'
1899. George Suffern Allison,' b. Brooklyn, N. Y., Jan. 22, 1860. He was
educated at the military academy at Peekskill, N. Y. He is a
brick manufacturer with his father, and lives at Stony Point,
N. Y. His home, overlooking the shimmering waters of the
Hudson, is romantically situated, and commands a view of
that river for many miles. He m., Feb. 22, 1881, Sarah, dau.
of Denton Fowler, of Haverstraw, N. Y. Children b. Stony
Point, N. Y.: George Suffern Allison,' b. Sept. 2, 1883. Horatio Wood Allison,' b. Feb. 11, 1885. Catherine Fowler Allison,'
b. Jan. 31, 1887. Lucretia Allison,' b. Aug. 20, 1889.
1900. William Brewster Allison,' b. Stony Point, N. Y., Feb. 5, 1862;
d. April 6, 1862.

CHILDREN BY SECOND MARRIAGE.

1901. Brewster Jonas Allison,' b. Stony Point, N. Y., July 15, 1869. He
is a book-keeper in his father's office; res. Stony Point, N. Y.
He was educated at Phillips academy, Exeter, N. H., and other
similar schools.
1902. Samuel Sears Allison,' b. Stony Point, N. Y., July 8, 1870; d.
there March 9, 1873.
1903. Amanda Tomkins Allison,' b. Stony Point, N. Y., Feb. 23, 1872.
She was graduated at Houghton seminary, Clinton, N. Y., in
June, 1889; home at Stony Point, N. Y.
1904. Sarah Andrus Allison,' b. at Stony Point, N. Y., Feb. 16, 1874.
She was graduated at Houghton seminary, Clinton, N. Y., in
June, 1892. At home.
1905. Calvin Tomkins Allison,' b. at Stony Point, N. Y., June 3, 1876.
He graduated at Lawrenceville, N. J., in 1893, and intends to
enter Princeton college in September, 1893.
1906. Anna Mary Allison,' b. Stony Point, N. Y., Feb. 11, 1878; at
school at Houghton seminary, Clinton, N. Y.
1907. Hannah Brewster Allison,' b. Stony Point, N. Y., March 31, 1880.
student at Houghton seminary at Clinton, N. Y.
1908. Eugenia Knight Allison,' b. Stony Point, N. Y., July 11, 1881; d.
Oct. 5, 1887.
1909. Fanny Gertrude Allison,' b. Stony Point, N. Y., July 27, 1883.
1910. Ralph Denniston Allison,' b. Stony Point, N. Y., Feb. 24, 1885.
1911. Edward Lane Allison,' b. Stony Point, N. Y., Feb. 14, 1887.

1912. Richard Allison[7] [1846] (Michael,[6] Richard,[5]
Joseph,[4] John,[3] John,[2] Lawrence[1]). Major Allison was
born in the city of New York, July 7, 1838; married,
June 16, 1870, Mary A., daughter of Thomas and Sarah M.
Love. She was born in New York, N. Y., April 25, 1840.
Her father was a native of Salisbury, England, and son of
Thomas Love. Her mother was of Edinburgh, Scotland.
Mr. Allison was educated in the public schools of the city of
New York. He enlisted in 1861 in the 7th Reg't of New
York Vols., and served in the defence of Washington. In

May, 1862, he was promoted to be first sergeant. He again enlisted in September, 1862, and was commissioned as captain in the 127th Reg't, New York Vols., and served till the close of the war. He was provost marshal of Charleston, S. C., from its capture till he was mustered out of the service in 1865. After the war he rejoined the 7th Reg't; was elected captain in 1878, and soon after was elected major. He retired after twenty-five years' connection with the organization. Major Allison holds a government position in the custom house in New York, N. Y., and resides in Rutherford, N. J,

CHILDREN.

1913. Theodore Taylor Allison,[8] b. New York, N. Y., March 31, 1872; d. Feb. 28, 1875.
1914. Edith Allison,[8] b. Rutherford, N. J., and d. there.
1915. Adele Allison,[8] b. Rutherford, N. J., March 3, 1876.
1916. Helen Allison,[8] b. Rutherford, N. J., Feb. 25, 1878.

1917. **Thomas Allison**[7] [1847] (Michael,[6] Richard,[5] Joseph,[4] John,[3] John,[2] Lawrence[1]). He is son of Michael and Susan Gentil Allison. He was born in New York, N. Y., Sept. 19, 1840, and was educated in the public schools of that city. He entered the Free academy, now college, of the city of New York, from Ward School No. 85, in West 13th St., and was graduated in 1860. He was admitted to the bar in November, 1861, having studied law in the office of Hon. John W. Edmonds, and has ever since been in the active practice of his profession, and ranks high as a lawyer. He was nominated for judge of the court of common pleas for the city and county of New York, in 1889; endorsed by the Republicans, and polled some 92,000 votes, but was defeated by the Tammany Hall Democratic candidate. He was offered by Mayor Edson, in 1884, the appointment as corporation counsel of New York city, which was declined. The degrees of Bachelor of Arts and Master of Arts have been conferred upon him. He married, Aug. 30, 1871, Mary E. Millett, born in New York, N. Y., Oct. 28, 1842. She is daughter of William E. and Mary (Conershover) Millett, of New York, N. Y.; law office 59 and 61 Liberty St., New York; res. New York, N. Y.

CHILDREN.

1918. Mary Allison,[8] b. Brooklyn, N. Y., April 27, 1873; student in college; res. New York, N. Y.
1919. Florence Allison,[8] b. Brooklyn, N. Y., Oct. 15, 1874; student in college; res. New York, N. Y.
1919a. —— Allison,[8] b. June 21, 1875; d. June 21, 1875, in Brooklyn, N. Y.

1920. Albert Allison,⁹ b. Brooklyn, N. Y., Jan. 17, 1876; d. at New
York, N. Y., June 18, 1876.
1921. Olive Allison,⁹ b. New York, N. Y., Oct. 16, 1877; at school; res.
New York, N. Y.
1922. Thomas Allison,⁹ b. New York, N. Y., Sept. 23, 1879; d. in New
York, N. Y., May 26, 1882.

1923. William Outis Allison⁸ [1895] (William Henry,⁷
Hendrick,⁶ Matthew,⁵ Joseph,⁴ John,³ John,² Lawrence¹).

The following sketch of Mr. Allison was written by his
friend, J. M. Peters, Esq.:

Lawrence, the first Allison of this branch of the family
known in America, who was one of the early settlers in the
New Haven colony, left the place to join his son John whom
the records show was one of the founders of the town of
Hempstead on Long Island about 1644. Whether John was
born in this country is unknown to us, but he appears to
have engaged in this enterprise before attaining his majority.
In 1719 his grandson John, who was evidently a man of
some wealth for the time, went with a number of others
from the Hempstead settlement to the west of the Hudson,
and bought a large tract of land known as the Kakiat Patent, in Orange, now Rockland county. He subsequently
became the owner of a large part of the land lying between
what is now known as Rockland Lake and Stony Point on
the Hudson river. He had a numerous family, among them
a son Joseph, who added largely by purchase to his inherited possessions in land, and was one of the most extensive
landholders in that section. Joseph's oldest son, Matthew
Allison, died before his father, and left a number of children,
among them Hendrick, who married Sarah Marks, a Haverstraw maiden, with whom, about 1810, he settled on the
bank of the Hudson at a point considerably south of his
native place. Here William H. Allison was born in 1820,
and after marriage settled in old Hackensack, now Palisades
township, in Bergen county, N. J., where William O. Allison, the subject of this sketch, was born on March 30, 1849.
The maternal ancestry of William O. Allison had resided
for more than two hundred years within a few miles of
this spot. His maternal great-grandfather [Jordan] was
French, having come to this country with Lafayette and
become a Revolutionary soldier. He subsequently married
a Jersey Dutch wife and settled upon the Palisades, a few
miles north of the present home of his great-grandson, whose
other ancestors on his mother's side were among the original
Dutch settlers at old Tappan, one of the earliest settlements
in New Jersey.

The student of heredity and the defender of the law of entail will each find something of interest in tracing the history of the ancestry of the subject of this sketch. From the earliest records of Lawrence Allison, or, more directly, from those of his son John, we find the evidences of foresight and thrift which, developing in the third iu descent from the resident of the New Haven colony, led to the foundation of a great fortune in land on the west banks of the Hudson. With succeeding generations ownership of this vast estate became divided and subdivided, but no generation of the family down to the present has been wholly without an inheritance from the estate acquired more than a century and a half ago. This possession proved enough to afford the means of a livelihood, growing more meagre, however, with successive generations, but yet enough to dispel want, and so, perhaps, to curb ambitions; for circumstances more affluent or less comfortable might have developed in a larger number of the descendants of John Allison the traits which the records of his operations as a pioneer showed him to possess. But the assurance of enough land from which to earn a livelihood by working, or to acquire a living by sale, is not a favorable culture-medium for those qualities which make pioneers, or develop conspicuous successes in any walk of life; and for several generations many of the strongest qualities of the Allison family lay dormant in this branch of its descent, for the need of the actual necessities for their development, or for some other incitement to their employment.

From his early boyhood the subject of this sketch lived much of the time in the family of William B. Dana, a prominent resident of the Palisades, a man of forceful and exemplary character, and a journalist of culture. The intelligent observer of his own life cannot deny the important part which the accident of his environment has had in his successes quite as much as in his failures, and it has been alike creditable to his intelligence and his loyalty to so good a friend as she was, that William O. Allison has never failed to give full measure of acknowledgment, no less by deed than by word, of the benign influence which Mrs. (Katharine Floyd) Dana exerted upon his life. This good woman, herself childless, took a deep interest in the boy, and his intellectual development was guided by her in a manner born of the superior intelligence and the inbred refinement, and wielded by the great strength of character which she possessed. That she found in him the inherent traits for development, was as satisfactory to her as was her training grateful to him, and I doubt if such a befriending was ever more liberally rewarded, than was hers by the character which she saw develop into manhood, no less than by the devotion which he accorded to her. His middle name, Outis, was adopted by him to gratify a fancy of Mrs. Dana's that his initials should correspond to those of her *nom de plume*, "Olive A. Wadsworth."

In 1868 young Allison entered the office of the *Financial Chronicle* and the *Daily Bulletin*, which was owned by Mr. Dana, and the brother of Mrs. Dana, Mr. John G. Floyd, and he there gained a general and thorough knowledge of the publishing business. With this knowledge, and possessing keen business instincts, he developed in a few years into the best reporter of commercial markets that has ever been on the New York press, and instituted a system of thoroughness in reports which had previously been unknown and which few reporters have been able to successfully copy. From a salary of $7 per week, which he received when he entered Mr. Dana's employ, he reached inside of three years a salary of $40 per week as a reporter; but this rapid progress did not satisfy his ambition even for the time, and on October 21, 1871, as a result of the confidence which he felt in his system of making a specialty of a few markets and doing them thoroughly, he issued the first number of the *Oil, Paint and Drug Reporter*. The early issues of the *Reporter* were in the form of a small four-page paper of extremely modest appearance as compared with other papers already prominent in the industries to which it was devoted, but contained more of real value to the subscribers than the conductors of any other sheets had possessed sufficient comprehension of the possibilities of market reporting to furnish. The growth of the paper in circulation was remarkable, and its advertising patronage, in connection with added departments of valuable reading matter, was sufficient to force numerous successive enlargements. But it was only after a hard struggle of several years that the plucky young publisher saw the fulfilment of the hope he entertained at the beginning of his career, that he should some day make five thousand dollars per year. From this point, however, the successful growth of the paper is, I believe, without any parallel in commercial journalism, and the *Reporter* soon became one of the most profitable class publications in the country, and exerted an influence in the trades to which it was allied such as no other commercial publication has ever wielded. This influence was the direct result of the policy of obtaining and furnishing accurate, comprehensive, and, therefore, valuable information concerning all the markets which the paper reported ; and upon all these markets the proprietor of the *Reporter*, so long as he was actually engaged in the conduct of the paper, was admitted to be the best informed man in New York. This fact brought Mr. Allison closely into personal contact with a large clientage, and made his judgment and opinions much sought after. It also led him into enterprises outside of the publishing business, and proved a source of profit to him in many ways. In addition to these interests, a perhaps inherited tendency to operate in real estate has led him to acquire from time to time tracts of land, chiefly on or in the vicinity of the Palisades, until he has become one of the largest land-owners in that section.

As a publisher, financier, and real estate operator, William O. Allison has achieved successes which have won for him the admiration and respect that legitimate successes, born of industry and good judgment and gained by no sacrifice of integrity, gain for any man. He had enjoyed the confidence of merchants and financiers, for the most part many years his senior, to the extent that is rarely accorded a young man, long before he attained to that mile-post in life which the lexicographers define as the beginning of middle age. And even before that period had been reached, he had gained a prominent place as a factor in very extensive commercial and financial enterprises. But his most attractive qualities are best known to those who have come into the closer social contact with him, and are not measured by financial successes, nor influenced by them except as they have afforded him the opportunities for extending unostentatious and ofttimes unappreciated benefactions. When a man has made a good use of every opportunity that has presented itself to him, and has lived a thoroughly exemplary life amid surroundings shorn of none of the temptations which beset every man, it affords me much satisfaction to be permitted to record the facts to his praise, and I take it that in a sketch intended for the purpose to which this is to be put, I may be permitted to indulge this inclination without being guilty of that ostentation which is as far from my wishes, as it would be unjust and distasteful to him of whom I write.

He married, Oct. 22, 1884, Caroline Longstreet Hovey, daughter of Alfred Howard Hovey and Frances (Noxon) Hovey, of Syracuse, N. Y. Her parents died when she was very young. She was adopted by Hon. George F. Comstock and his wife, and took the name of Comstock. Mr. Com-

Residence of Wm. O. Allison on the Palisades at Englewood, New Jersey.

stock was one time attorney-general of the United States and chief judge of the N. Y. Court of Appeals.

Mrs. Comstock was a sister to Mrs. Allison's mother. Mrs. Allison was born June 12, 1862, in Syracuse, N. Y. In that city was her home till her marriage. She was educated in the Keble school of Syracuse, and at a French school at Neuilly, near Paris, France.

CHILDREN BORN AT ENGLEWOOD, N. J.

1924.   Katharine Floyd Allison,⁸ b. July 13, 1885.
1925.   Frances Cornelia Allison,⁹ b. Nov. 23, 1887.
1926.   Allis Allison,⁸ b. Sept. 30, 1888; d. April 14, 1889.
1927.   William Dana Allison,⁹ b. Sept. 8, 1890.
1927a. John Blauvelt Allison,⁹ b. Jan. 13, 1893.

ALLISONS OF COUNTY DONEGAL, IRELAND, AND NORTH CAROLINA AND TENNESSEE.[1]

1928.   Archibald Allison, of the county of Donegal, Ireland, born in 1786, came with a colony from that place and settled in Mecklenburg county, N. C., where he died. He had

CHILDREN.

1928a. Margaret Allison, who m. William Clark.
1928b. Nancy Allison, who m. Reuben Freeman.
1928c. Elizabeth Allison, who m. Samuel Beryhill.
1928d. Sarah Allison, never married.
1928e. William Allison, never married.
1929.   Andrew Allison (1930), res. Mecklenburg Co., N. C.

1930.   Andrew Allison[2] [1929] (Archibald[1]). He was born in 1770, and lived in North Carolina and Tennessee, and died in Gibson county, Tenn. He married Margaret Varner or Verner. He and his descendants were Presbyterians, with many elders and clergymen among them.

CHILDREN.

1930a. Rebecca Allison, m. William Erwin, both of Gibson Co., Tenn., where she d. Her descendants are in southern Illinois.
1931.   Joseph Allison (1948), b. Feb. 11, 1796; d. Aug. 20, 1862; descendants in Coles Co., Ill., and Indianapolis, Ind.
1931a. Henry Allison,⁸ m. Margaret Erwin; m., second, Elizabeth Clark, both of Tenn. They d. in Tennessee, where his descendants live.

[1] Many of these Allisons lived near Trenton, Tenn., and later lived near Humboldt, Tenn.

1932. William Allison,² m. Mary Ann Erwin; m., second, Eleanor Wilson; m., third, Elizabeth Dove; removed to Cumberland, Coles Co., Ill. He left a family.
1933. John Allison³ (1939), clergyman, b. Dec. 8, 1801; d. March 7, 1845.
1934. Elizabeth Allison,² m. Mr. Killough, both of Gibson Co., Tenn. : removed to Cumberland, Coles Co., Ill. They are deceased, but left a family.
1935. Robert Allison.² He was a bachelor, and d. in Tennessee.
1936. Andrew Allison.² He was a clergyman, and d. soon after being licensed to preach. His death occurred in Gibson Co., Tenn.
1937. Jane Allison,² m. Rev. Charles Hodge, both of Gibson Co., Tenn.; she d. in Tenn.
1938. Nancy Freeman Allison,² m. Jonathan Dryden, both of Gibson Co., Tenn. Removed to Cumberland, Coles Co., Ill. They are deceased, but left a family.

1939. John Allison³ [1933] (Andrew,² Archibald¹). Rev. John Allison was born on Sugar Creek, Mecklenburg Co., North Carolina, Dec. 8, 1801; was reared and worked upon a farm until he was married. He then studied for the ministry, and was pastor, or acting pastor, in Murfreesborough, Shelbyville, Clarksville, Nashville, and Symrna, Tenn. He went to Princeton, Ken., and had charge of a female seminary and was pastor of the First Presbyterian church. He went to Kentucky in 1844, and died March 7, 1845. He was a Presbyterian of the old school. Mr. Allison married, Feb. 7, 1822, Nancy, daughter of Robert and Jane (McCullough) Lemmond. She was born in Charlotte, N. C., March 2, 1798; died in Windsor, Mo., Feb. 17, 1864.

CHILDREN.

1940. Robert Cyrus Allison,⁴ b. Dec. 7, 1822, in Mecklenburg Co., N. C.; raised to manhood in Tennessee; physician. He received his medical education in Louisville, Ky. He m. Catherine Weiss, of Louisville, April 16, 1844; m., second, Elvira McCarthy. Dr. Allison died near Princeton, Ky., December, 1866. Children:
I.   John Edmund Allison,⁵ b. Princeton, Ky., May 5, 1845.
II. Elijah Edward Allison,⁵ b. near Princeton. Ky., November, 1845; res. Star Line Works, Lyon Co., Ky.
III. Robert Henry Allison,⁵ b. near Princeton, Ky.; res. Kuttawa, Ky.
IV. Sarah Ann Allison,⁵ b. near Princeton, Ky., July, 1854; m. Robert Holloway, of near Princeton, Ky., and d. November, 1889.
1941. Margaret Rebecca Allison,⁴ b. Oct. 22, 1824; m., in Princeton, Ky., April 16, 1846, George Washington Cone, of Painesville, Ohio; res. Princeton, Ky. She d. in Nashville, Tenn., April 23, 1885. Children:
I.   Marietta Ellen Cone,⁵ b. Jan. 27, 1847; m. Judge Goodner, of Nashville, Ill.; res. Chicago, Ill.
II. Ida Cone,⁵ b. April 28, 1856; m. Charles Rose, of Nashville, Ill.; res. Chicago, Ill.
1942. Jane Ann Elizabeth Allison,⁴ b. in Gibson Co., Tenn., Feb. 17, 1827; m. Oct. 22, 1850, Alexander Brame; res. Princeton, Ky. She d. in Windsor, Mo., April 21, 1888. Children:

I. William Alexander Brame,[5] b. Aug. 8, 1851; m., Nov. 6, 1872, Ora
     Waddell, of Windsor, Mo.; res. Nevada, Mo.
II. Robert Allison Brame,[5] b. Jan. 1, 1864; d. in Washington, March 12,
     1891.
III. Lelia Brame,[5] b. June 27, 1867; m., Sept. 24, 1885, Mason Fewell;
     res. Windsor, Mo.
1943. Nancy Adeline Allison,[4] b. in Gibson Co., Tenn., March 28, 1829;
     m., January, 1853, William Pitt Withers; res. Princeton, Ky.;
     she m., second, October, 1866, James D. Baker; res. Windsor,
     Mo. Children:
I. John Thomas Withers,[5] b. Sept. 7, 1854; m., Sept. 19, 1877, Elizabeth
     Durall, of Windsor, Mo.; res. Deepwater, Henry Co., Mo.
II. William Allison Withers,[5] b. May 19, 1877; unmarried.

1944. Mary Elvira Allison,[4] born Murfreesborough, Tenn.,
Jan. 14, 1834; married, in Livonia, Ind., Feb. 9, 1853, Cor-
nelius Hine Pering. He was born in Chard, Somersetshire,
England, March 19, 1831. He was living at the time of his
marriage in Bloomington, Ind. He enlisted in Company E,
Seventy-first regiment Indiana volunteers, served nearly three
years, and was killed in 1864 near Cartersville, Ga. Mrs.
Pering resides Windsor, Mo.

CHILDREN.

1945. John Allison Pering,[5] b. Livonia, Ind.; m., Aug. 23, 1874, Mary
     Lavina Chowing. Res. Diona, Coles Co., Ill.
1946. Emma Susan Pering,[5] b. Jan. 27, 1856, in Livonia, Ind., m., Nov.
     18, 1877, Whitney Williams Barrows. Res. Windsor, Mo.
1947. William Edwin Pering,[5] b. in Terre Haute, Ind., Aug. 29, 1858; m.,
     Dec. 17, 1879, Louisa Sheridan. Res. Dexter, Kansas.

1948. Joseph Allison [3] [1931] (Andrew,[2] Archibald [1]).
He was born in Mecklenburg county, North Carolina, Feb.
11, 1796. Res. in Cumberland, Coles county, Illinois; m.,
Margaret Ann Cathey of Gibson county, Tenn., where he
had previously lived. He died Aug. 20, 1862.

CHILDREN.

1949. Sarah Caroline Allison,[4] b. in North Carolina, Dec. 3, 1822; m.,
     Aug. 10, 1841, James H. Morrison, a farmer in Coles county,
     Ill. She d. Jan. 16, 1865.
1950. Andrew Henry Allison,[4] b. in North Carolina, Nov. 20, 1823; m.,
     Dec. 21, 1843, Harriet E. Dryden. He d. Nov. 15, 1864.
1951. Margaret Frances Allison,[4] b. in Tenn., June 6, 1829; m., Jan.
     1, 1851, Rufus Allison. Res. Lerman, Ill.
1952. Rebecca Elizabeth Allison,[4] b. in Tenn., Dec. 2, 1831; m., Dec. 15,
     1835, James A. Balch. She d. March 15, 1857.
1953. Nancy Prudence Allison,[4] b. Feb. 11, 1833, in Tenn.; m., Jan. 15,
     1866, Joseph B. Nicholson.
1954. John William Allison,[4] b. in Coles Co., Ill., Oct. 20, 1837; m., Sept.
     20, 1867, Isabella Ewing. He d. Nov. 15, 1886.
1955. Mary Jane Allison,[4] b. Coles Co., Ill., June 18, 1841; m. Feb. 21,
     1861, Thomas W. Grimes. Res. Campbell, Coles Co., Ill.
     19

ROBERT ALLISON AND HIS DESCENDANTS.

1956. Robert Allison.[1] He was a resident of Pennsylvania, Fayette county, where he lived till 1789, when he with his family removed to Marietta, Ohio, where he lived until 1795, when he removed to the Alexander farm, nearly opposite Lowell, Ohio, on the Muskingum river. While at Marietta the family lived in the Campus Martius stockade, as a protection from the Indians. When he went onto his farm he and his associates built their four log houses so that their corners touched, thus making a square of ground enclosed, known as " Kinney's Garrison." This was done as a protection from the wild sons of the forest.

CHILDREN.

1957. Nancy Allison,[2] b. in Fayette Co., Penn., Oct. 22, 1784. She went with her father to Marietta, Ohio, and she shared all the vicissitudes of the new settlement. On the 18th of December, 1800, she m. Stephen Frost. She was a great reader of the Bible and was deeply religious. She lived to be considerably over 100 years old.

1958. Charles Allison,[2] b. in Fayette Co., Penn.; removed to Ohio and m. Miss Stull. Child:
I. Robert Allison,[3] removed to California in 1855, and d. in San Diego in 1891.

1959. Josiah Allison,[2] removed to California and resides at Vaca Station, Solano Co.

1960. Napoleon Allison,[2] removed to California and res. at Pajarito, Santa Cruz Co.

1961. George Allison,[2] (1966) removed to California in 1855.

1962. Mary Ann Allison,[2] d. in Iowa.

1963. Lucretia Allison,[2] d. in California.

1964. Joseph Allison.[2]

1965. William Allison.[2]

1966. George Allison [3] [1961] (Charles,[2] Robert [1]). He removed to California in 1855. He married ———. He married, second, Mary Jane Owen, of Marion county, Ia., where she was born. Mr. Allison was engaged in farming, fruit growing, stock raising, and merchandising. In 1875 he removed his family to Arizona, and was engaged in the same line of business. He died at Tucson, Arizona, June 13, 1891, aged 66 years. Mrs. Allison still lives at Tucson.

CHILDREN.

1967. George Irving Allison,[4] res. Sacramento, Cal.

1968. Francis Marion Allison,[4] aged 36. He has been several times elected a member of the board of supervisors of Pima Co., Arizona, and member of the common council of Tucson, Arizona, where he resides.

1969. Henry Warner Allison,[4] aged 35. He with his brother formed the firm of Allison Bros., and are engaged in mining, farming, and are the owners of a large irrigating canal or ditch. Res. Tucson, Arizona.

1970. Laura Kate Allison,[4] aged 27. She m. C. C. Wheeler, a member of the firm of Wheeler & Perry. Res. Tucson, Arizona.

EX-GOVERNOR ALLISON, OF FLORIDA.

1971. Abraham K. Allison, who was at one time governor of Florida, died about July 8, 1898, aged 88 years.

INDEX I.

Alisons and Associated Names in Scotland and Australia.

The number set against each name indicates the page where the name will be found.

INDEX II.

Alisons and Allisons, with Associated Names, in Canada and the United States.

The number set against each name indicates the page where the name will be found.

CPSIA information can be obtained at www.ICGtesting.com
Printed in the USA
LVOW041803120212

267885LV00004BD/133/P